THE ARCHIPELAGO

Milan since the Miracle: City, Culture and Identity
Calcio: A History of Italian Football
Italy's Divided Memory
Pedalare! Pedalare!: A History of Italian Cycling
Modern Italy
The Man Who Closed the Asylums: Franco Basaglia and
the Revolution in Mental Health Care

THE ARCHIPELAGO

Italy Since 1945

John Foot

BLOOMSBURY PUBLISHING

LONDON · OXFORD · NEW YORK · NEW DELHI · SYDNEY

BLOOMSBURY PUBLISHING
Bloomsbury Publishing Plc
50 Bedford Square, London, WC1B 3DP, UK

BLOOMSBURY, BLOOMSBURY PUBLISHING and the Diana logo are
trademarks of Bloomsbury Publishing Plc

First published in Great Britain 2018

Copyright © John Foot, 2018

John Foot has asserted his right under the Copyright, Designs and Patents Act,
1988, to be identified as Author of this work

For legal purposes the Acknowledgements on p. 415
constitute an extension of this copyright page

A catalogue record for this book is available from the British Library

Library of Congress Cataloguing-in-Publication data has been applied for

ISBN: HB: 978-1-4088-2724-6; eBook: 978-1-4088-4351-2

2 4 6 8 10 9 7 5 3 1

Typeset by Newgen KnowledgeWorks Pvt. Ltd., Chennai, India
Printed and bound in Great Britain by CPI Group (UK) Ltd, Croydon CR0 4YY

To find out more about our authors and books visit www.bloomsbury.com
and sign up for our newsletters

To Corinna

Contents

Preface

My great-grandmother, Aurelia Lanzoni, was Italian. She met her husband, a Scotsman called Arthur Tod, in Mesopotamia (now Iraq) in 1907. She spent much of her early life in the Ottoman Empire. There is a family photograph of her holding me as a tiny baby in her arms. She died in Edinburgh in 1965. In 1987 I decided to do a PhD at Cambridge. The subject was to be twentieth-century Italy, although I wasn't sure exactly what I was going to study. My supervisor advised me to go to Milan. My first trip there was to stay with old friends of his in the former industrial neighbourhood of Sesto San Giovanni, on the northern edge of the city. This was my first experience of the great generosity of Italians and their willingness to talk about their own history (or even just to talk!). I also made the mistake of drinking an espresso after dinner, and spent a sleepless night as a consequence. It was as if I had imbibed pure electricity.

I returned in 1988 to start work on my thesis – on the First World War and its aftermath in Milan. I quickly began to learn Italian, mainly through listening to people talk, and reading. My stamping grounds were the beautiful libraries and archives of Milan, with their frescoes and comfortable wooden chairs. As I read about the Great War and fascism, I took in the city I was living in: its flatness, its mass of concrete, its hidden beauty. This was a place that was full of factories, but many of them were closed. It was also exotic, and glamorous. Another natural home was the stunning San Siro stadium, and its fervent fans. I would stay in Milan for more than twenty years, regularly commuting back to London to teach. During that time I grew to love Milan, and Italy. I had been seduced by what the journalist Luigi Barzini called Italy's 'fatal charm'.

It was an extraordinary time to live there, with political upheavals, World Cup victories (and defeats), mass immigration, and epochal transformations in society, politics and the cultural world. This book is the product of that double-decade, and of twenty years of teaching, reading and writing about Italy; it is the work of both an insider and outsider. I look at Italy both with the worldview of a non-Italian and also as someone with deep connections to Italian culture through residence, family, new and old friends, and twenty years of trying to understand the vicissitudes of *il bel paese*. My son Lorenzo was born in Milan in 1993. I also saw Italy through him, the schools he attended and his way of seeing things.

When historians attempt to write about this country, they often employ a master-theme or connecting thread to make sense of things. This could be the role of the family, or the relationship between citizens and the state, or the attempt to create 'Italians'. This book has no such master-theme running through it. Thus, *The Archipelago*, a title that conjures up an image of a group of islands, uses stories, court cases, sporting events and biographies to paint a picture of a country. I see these fragments as a virtue, as the only way I could construct a history of modern Italy and communicate this to my readers.

Nonetheless, certain ideas and tropes do recur throughout this book. One is the idea of a *divided country*, fractured over its past and its present (as well as over a vision of its future). These divisions were both long term and short term, some reaching back to the very formation of the nation itself in the nineteenth century, others to fascism and the world wars fought in the twentieth century. There were also deep fractures between the north and the south, and the city and the countryside. Italians were divided over how to modernise Italy, or even whether it needed modernising at all.

Italy matters, and not just for Italians. Far from being at the margins of Europe, as is often claimed, it has always been at the centre of political innovation and change. Fascism originated in

Italy after the First World War, and the country produced one of the most powerful and effective resistance movements *against* fascism in the 1940s. It drew up a post-war constitution that some see as one of the most elegant and carefully constructed in the world. Its post-war system has seen stunning and innovative developments in the political, economic and social spheres. This is a country from which we have much to learn, *nel bene e nel male*, as Italians say. Writing this book has been a journey into Italy's past, but also into, perhaps, our own futures. Some lessons are there, I hope, in the pages that follow.

Italian history has often been thought about as a series of things that *aren't there* – as a kind of wish list of what Italy doesn't have. As John Agnew has argued, 'The image of a backward Italy struggling (somehow) with modernity is a dominant representation of the country in the eyes of both Italian and foreign commentators.'[1] Entire studies have argued that the nation should never have been born, that it is an 'historical mistake'. *The Archipelago* rejects this way of seeing Italy. This is a history of real Italy: of what is *actually there*.

The Archipelago is an eclectic history, linked to my own preferences, experiences and passions. It is aimed at those who want to find out more, not at experts. It has been said that Italian history has been marked by short revolutions, and long counter-revolutions. At times since 1945 Italy has appeared to be on fast-forward, rushing towards the future, and at others it has almost seemed to stop altogether, or go backwards. It is also true that it is often individuals who change the course of history. Ordinary Italians changed their own country: a woman refusing to marry despite the pressures of convention and society, a psychiatrist saying 'no' to practices of repression and dehumanisation, a magistrate not bowing to political pressure, a priest determined to give even the poorest of children a decent education, a film-maker trying to create beauty from the chaos of war. These stories help us understand Italy, and its struggles over how to shape the lives of its people since 1945.

Introduction: 1945 – Year Zero

'How much of ourselves had been eroded, extinguished?'

Primo Levi[1]

'The night must pass.'

Eduardo De Filippo[2]

'Nobody can deny the fact that ... in this world torn apart by war there is trepidation now, more than ever before, about the life that will be born from so much death.'

Concetto Marchesi, April 1945[3]

April 1945: much of Italy lay in ruins. The Nazi occupiers had been driven out, but the legacy of five years of war was everywhere. Other foreign powers, the Allies, who many viewed as *liberators*, were still around, despite the fact that the war was over. Some cities had been flattened, others were reduced to a primitive state. People lived off scraps in the street. Across the world, Italians were struggling to return home. Some had been part of defeated fascist forces, others had been deported on racial or political grounds, or for refusing to carry on fighting. Many failed to make it. A good few took months or even years to return, emaciated and unrecognisable, often presumed dead. On arrival, they found a country on its knees, lacerated by violence and an unprecedented crime wave. Basic institutions were on the verge of collapse. Prisons were not just lacking in locks: they had no doors. It wasn't even clear where authority lay. Who was in charge, after all? King Vittorio Emanuele III, the Allies, the anti-fascist partisans?

Less than two years earlier, on 24 July 1943 at 5.20 p.m., five military policemen (*carabinieri*) had arrested Benito Mussolini in Rome. The *carabinieri* were loyal to the King (who had given the orders). It was the end of a regime – the last act of the double-decade dictatorship (*il ventennio*), as it would come to be known – but not the end of fascism. Mussolini's fateful decision to enter the war in 1940 had been his undoing. Swift victories on the back of Nazi gains were soon undone by a series of humiliating defeats. The Allied bombing of Rome and invasion of Sicily in July 1943 forced the King into the drastic decision to bring down the dictator with whom he had governed Italy for so long.

Nazi troops took control of much of the country. The King fled south and formed a Kingdom of the South in liberated Italy. Mussolini was set up in a puppet government in the north. Over the next twenty months the country descended into a vicious civil war, alongside the conflict between the Allies and the German Army, and the anti-fascist Resistance. Italians fought Italians across the peninsula as anti-fascists and fascists divided along political and ideological lines. It was lacerating, as with all civil wars, and it left a bitter legacy of division and hatred. Meanwhile, thousands of Jews and political opponents were deported to camps in Germany and elsewhere, while aerial bombing struck most of the country. Invaded and humiliated, Italy struggled to maintain any kind of autonomy, with various figures claiming to be in power. When liberation from Nazi occupation and from fascism finally came for the whole of the country in April 1945, some argued that Italy had ceased to exist – that it had 'died' at some point during the war. Others, on the contrary, talked of rebirth, of a 'new Italy'. Divisions emerged over the country's history, even as it was being made.

When and how did the war finally end? Officially, villages, cities and regions were 'liberated' as the Allied armies moved their way up through Italy, from July 1943 in Sicily to April 1945 in the north. This 'ending', however, was messy and ambiguous. Official liberation did not signify that the war in Italy was over, and the interplay between the Allies, the Kingdom of the South (ruled over by the King and the anti-fascist parties), the Nazis and the Italian Fascists meant that it was unclear who was really in power until well after April 1945. The country was faced with an existential crisis. Meanwhile, the Catholic Church, which had remained neutral during the war, looked on with trepidation. A fragile government made up of the anti-fascist parties that had fought in the Resistance took power, but no elections had yet been held.

Violence against the defeated exploded after an official end to hostilities. In late April 1945 Benito Mussolini and his mistress were caught and executed by partisans in the small village of Giulino di Mezzegra near Lake Como. His body was then taken to Milan to be hung by the feet from a petrol station in a suburban square, the Piazzale Loreto, so that the people could see that he really was dead. Thousands of fascists and others were killed in this period of the so-called *resa dei conti* – 'the settling of accounts'. Some (the luckier ones) merely had their heads shaved, or were marched through the streets. In a few more radical areas violence continued at a lower level throughout the 1940s and even into the early 1950s. It was then that the 'class war' aspect of the Resistance was at its most powerful. Guns were buried and kept ready for the 'right moment'. Some were used in the meantime against priests, former fascists, factory owners or landlords. The idea that the revolution had merely been postponed was a strong one in certain sectors of the working class and peasantry.

The Return

Una mattina mi son svegliato / O bella ciao, bella ciao, bella ciao ciao ciao
(One morning I woke up / O bella ciao, bella ciao, bella ciao ciao ciao) (partisan song)

It took Primo Levi nine months to make it back from Auschwitz in Poland to his home town of Turin. He would later recount this odyssey in *The Truce*. In September 1943 Levi had been captured by Italian fascists soon after joining a tiny partisan group in the Valle d'Aosta on the border with France. He was twenty-four years old and had worked as a chemist briefly after completing his studies. Levi was held in a transit camp in Italy before being transported by train to Auschwitz. On his return, after recovering from his ordeal (at least physically) and finding work, Levi sat down in the evenings and began to write, or used time on his commute and during his lunch breaks. *If This Is a Man*, which first appeared in book form in 1947, is one of the great works of world literature. Its 'preface' begins with the extraordinary lines:

> It was my good fortune to be deported to Auschwitz only in 1944, that is, after the German Government had decided, owing to the growing scarcity of labour, to lengthen the average life-span of the prisoners destined for elimination; it conceded noticeable improvements in the camp routine and temporarily suspended killings at the whim of individuals.[4]

But Levi's dark story of his 'good fortune' struggled to find an audience in post-war Italy. Notoriously, the manuscript was turned down by the prestigious Turinese publisher Einaudi (controversy still rages on as to why and how this rejection took place) and first appeared in an edition of just two thousand or so copies with a minor publisher. Many of the unsold copies of this first edition found their way to Florence where they would be destroyed by a devastating flood in 1966. Einaudi would later change its mind, but the debate over their refusal to publish *If This Is a Man* in 1946–7 burst into the open again after Levi's death in 1987. Fingers were pointed and denials were made. Whatever the individual responsibility, this affair was a powerful indicator of the minor role played by the Holocaust in post-war Italy, and the strong desire to forget (or not talk about) what had happened, even on the left, and even amongst intellectuals on the left from within the Jewish community. The novelist Giorgio Bassani captured some of these issues in his short story, 'A Plaque in Via Mazzini', in which a Holocaust survivor returns to Ferrara to find that he has been included on a plaque of victims. Soon there are whispers that he is 'too fat' to be a real deportee. It took decades for the true extent of the Italian Holocaust, and the role of different groups of Italians as perpetrators, bystanders or victims, to emerge with any force.

Cycling Back to Normality

Fausto Coppi won the Giro d'Italia, Italy's equivalent of the Tour de France, on 9 June 1940 at the age of just twenty (the first of his five victories). The day after his unexpected triumph, Mussolini declared war on France and Great Britain. A conscript, Coppi fought briefly in the doomed African campaign before being taken prisoner by the British. He finally returned to Italy in 1945, arriving in Naples. A public appeal was made by a local newspaper to get him a bicycle. He then proceeded to try and get back to his home in the village of Castellania in northern Italy, hundreds of miles away. His journey was made in the way he knew best, cycling, on his own. When he walked in the door, after an adventurous journey, his mother was amazed to see him alive.

Coppi lost no time in building up his fitness and in March 1946 he entered the Milan-San Remo, one of Italy's most celebrated one-day classic races and the event that kicks off the cycling season. Huge crowds lined the route. Coppi broke from the field just outside Milan and rode most of the race on his own. He later emerged, dusty and alone, from the tunnel that marks the pass above San Remo. At that point, victory was assured. Pierre Chany, the celebrated French cycling journalist, later wrote these words in a book called *Les Rendez-vous du cyclisme, ou Arriva Coppi*:

> The tunnel was of modest dimensions, just 7-metres long, but on 19 March 1946 it assumed exceptional proportions in the eyes of the world. That day it was six years in length and lost in the gloom of the war ... A rumbling was heard from the depths of those six years and suddenly there appeared in the light of day an olive-greenish car stirring up a cloud of dust. 'Arriva

Coppi' the messenger announced, a revelation only the initiated had foreseen.[5]

Coppi won the race by *fourteen* minutes and Italian radio played music in the interval while the commentators waited for the other cyclists to turn up. It was an almost superhuman sporting achievement. Six years had passed since his previous victory. Coppi's war, and that of most Italians, was finally over.

Gino Bartali had also had an interesting war. A great cyclist in the 1930s, the Tuscan rider had won the Tour de France in 1938 and the Giro d'Italia in 1939. During the conflict Bartali smuggled forged documents across central Italy hidden in his bike frame. The documents were then used to save hundreds of Jews from capture and deportation. Bartali rarely spoke about this activity. A Catholic and anti-fascist (he refused to wear the black shirt, despite pressure from the regime), Bartali was known as 'the pious one' as well as 'the man of iron'. He was also on the starting line in that 1946 Milan-San Remo race – but way behind Coppi at the finish. Soon, a great rivalry would divide Italians into *Coppiani* and *Bartaliani*. The 1946 Giro d'Italia – renamed the 'Giro of Rebirth' – took place against the background of the war, with tiny crosses marking the dead by roadsides, temporary bridges and bomb damage. Bartali won, by just 46 seconds, Coppi was second, and Italy was transfixed.

One rider who could not compete in the 1946 Giro was Fiorenzo Magni, who hailed from a small town called Vaiano near Prato in Tuscany. Magni was due to go on trial for his alleged role during the war on the fascist side, and was temporarily banned from professional cycling. He was accused of taking part in a fascist round-up of partisans, three of whom were killed. Cleared by the courts, he would return to the sport and achieve great success. Magni's murky wartime record was another reminder of the way in which politics and history were deeply intertwined with sport and other forms of popular culture. This story would continue to haunt Magni for the whole post-war period. He never referred to the war again in any public statement.

Big stars rarely won on their own – they needed faithful *gre-gari*, or support-riders. Andrea Carrea had survived the hell of Buchenwald after being deported there during the war, and he was also forced to undergo a horrific 'march of death' across the snow. He returned to Italy weighing a mere 40 kilos. After that, cycling up a few mountains seemed almost pleasurable. Carrea took up professional cycling and became Coppi's most faithful *gregario*. The life and sporting stories of Coppi, Bartali, Magni and Carrea exemplify how the war impacted on people's lives in a variety of ways, even within one restricted realm of professional sport, and how any return to normality was heavily patterned by experiences during the conflict.

1946: Viva Toscanini!

By the time the war ended, much of Italy had been destroyed – both physically and psychologically. Reconstruction was needed at every level – from buildings wiped out by bombing across the peninsula, to the moral and political legacy of more than twenty years of dictatorship that included five years of total war. On 15 August 1943 an Allied bomb had smashed through the roof of the world's most famous opera house – La Scala – in the centre of Milan. The ruins were untouched during the war itself – with a large hole in the ceiling of the famous auditorium. But as soon as the conflict was over, the authorities set about rebuilding this magnificent space. Plans were put in place for the return of Italy's most celebrated musical exile – the great conductor Arturo Toscanini.

Toscanini accepted La Scala's invitation with great enthusiasm. 'I am proud to return,' he wrote, 'as a citizen of free Italy and not as a subject of the Kings and Princes of the House of Savoy.'[6] Toscanini was a dedicated Republican, and his return coincided with the campaign around the abolition of the monarchy. It is said that the royal symbols were stripped from the royal box in the opera house and retired musicians were given the best seats in the house. Toscanini was seventy-nine years old, but still at the height of his powers. His return was also a political one. In 1931 he had been physically attacked by fascists for his refusal to play the Fascist hymn, *Giovinezza*, during a concert in Bologna, and had been forced into exile in the United States. Thereafter he became a beacon for anti-fascists across the world. When the fascist regime fell in the summer of 1943, people had openly called for Toscanini to return. His homecoming was therefore pregnant with powerful symbolism. As one commentator, Giulio Confalonieri, wrote at the end of the war, 'some people were surprised not to see Toscanini, or his head, emerge from an American tank'.[7] It was clear that this would be no ordinary concert.

On 11 May 1946 the so-called 'Concert of Reconstruction' took place in Milan. This was a moment of reconstruction in a literal sense – La Scala now had a new roof, and could host a concert – but also one of moral and political rebirth. Toscanini played a key role in both these forms of reconstruction. It is said that funds raised by benefit concerts conducted by Toscanini were used to fund part of the building costs. He also gave a million lire from his own pocket. There were still doubts as to whether the theatre's famed acoustics had been maintained intact, but Toscanini clapped his hands on entering the auditorium and allegedly exclaimed 'it's still my La Scala'. The highlight of the concert was a magisterial and moving performance of the 'Chorus of the Hebrew Slaves' from Verdi's *Nabucco* – a nod back to Italy's unification in the nineteenth century and the political role of opera in that period. Later in the concert a twenty-four-year-old debutante soprano, Renata Tebaldi, caused a sensation. She had been selected by Toscanini himself for the occasion. A star was born.

As the journalist Filippo Sacchi wrote:

It was a popular concert in the Italian sense of the word. Toscanini intended it to appeal to the people, the humble people of the streets. That evening the concert-hall had been connected up with loudspeakers placed outside about the Piazza della Scala and in the great Piazza del Duomo. Seated on the steps, on the pavement, perched on railings and on refuse bins, a dense crowd listened rapturously: humble folk from the overcrowded dwellings nearby ... the bombed suburbs. They were workmen, artisans, small shop-keepers; whole families with their children, young mothers with their babies asleep in their arms.[8]

This event became world news. A paper in Broken Hill in the Australian outback reported that 'weeping women attempted to kiss the conductor's hands while armed Italian military police tried to clear the street'.[9] The concert was also transmitted live on the radio and recorded (in crackly quality) for posterity.[10] Toscanini had left Italy under fascism. He returned to a nation where people were able to choose their own destiny.

Paisà

'We were surrounded by a whole new race of people, who seemed to be drawing hope from the very hopelessness of their situation. There were ruins, trees, scenes of disaster and loss and everywhere a wild spirit of reconstruction.'

Federico Fellini[11]

Italians tried to make sense of the experience of war and liberation through culture and art. In January 1946 the director Roberto Rossellini began to shoot a film that would be called *Paisà* or *Paisan*.[12] It was to be a film in six episodes, the follow-up to his path-breaking *Rome, Open City* (1945), which had depicted the capital city under Nazi occupation and had made waves across the world, winning the Cannes Film Festival and running for nearly two years in New York. Filming on *Paisà* was difficult, with blackouts and numerous supply difficulties. A power generator left by the retreating Germans was a life-saver. The film moved up Italy from south to north, mirroring the way the Allies themselves had fought their way up through the country between 1943 and 1945. Real experiences on location interacted with what Italy had become in part thanks to the war, while the film that was made was a set of stories set in the immediate past. These two periods (the making of the film, and the film itself) were often juxtaposed: ex-partisans played partisans, and friars represented friars. Memories were so fresh you could touch them. Rossellini was telling history as it was happening.

He plucked his cast from the streets. A fifteen-year-old fisherman's daughter – Carmela Sazio – was recruited for the first episode, set in Sicily. Rossellini later described Sazio as 'a little animal ... not understanding anything, moving only by impulsions'.[13] She never made another film. German POWs were also used as characters in the film. Some of the story was invented during the filming itself. Federico Fellini, who was working on the film as an assistant director (and would go on to become one of the most celebrated of all film directors between the 1950s and 1980s), came across a local monastery in the same location as where the first episode was shot, a small town near Amalfi. It was a place that seemed to be out of time. Fellini duly wrote the script for a new episode, set in a monastery.

The next stage was Naples, which had experienced heavy bombing, occupation and hardship during the war. Rossellini shot scenes in caves that were being used by those displaced by the conflict. Fellini remembered how 'Rossellini pursued his film in the middle of the streets, with allied tanks passing one metre from us ... with people crying and screaming from the windows, with hundreds of people around us trying to sell us something or steal something from us.'[14] Shooting went right on into June, then the money ran out. The production was kept going through loans and handouts. Like Italy itself, these film-makers were struggling to make ends meet.

Editing continued during the making of the film, which was also a 'moral ascent through the peninsula'.[15] One night Fellini found Rossellini staring at a tiny editing screen. 'The images were silent,' he wrote, 'you heard only the buzz of the film rolls. Enchanted, I stayed there watching. What I saw seemed to me to have that lightness, mystery, grace, and simplicity that cinema so rarely manages to attain.'[16] Fellini continued:

The troupe of people working on *Paisà* travelled through an Italy they scarcely knew, because for twenty years we'd been in the grip of a political regime which had literally blindfolded us. But at the same time as this moving discovery of my own country, I realised that the cinema miraculously made a big, double game possible: to recount a story and, while telling it, personally to live another, an adventure, in the company of characters as extraordinary as those of the film being made – often even more fascinating – and which would be evoked in another film, in a spiral of invention and life, observation and creativity, simultaneously spectator and actor, puppeteer and puppet.[17]

Making *Paisà* was a form of rebirth. Its raw material was found in the ruins.

Next up was Florence, which had lost all but one of its bridges during the war. This episode was set during the time of the Resistance, in the final days of the conflict, and told a story that was in part about a British woman looking for a partisan leader in a divided city. Rossellini and Fellini discussed their ideas for the film with the former partisans in Florence. This episode depicted events that were fresh in the minds of many Italians, including the summary shooting of fascists and the deaths of so many young men and women on both sides of the conflict.

The final episode was shot in the vast expanses of water of the Po Delta, in the north of the country. Former partisans were employed as 'actors'. The episode begins with dead partisans floating down the river, held up by signs around their necks saying '*partigiano*'. This had happened during the war when it was a tactic used by the Nazis as a warning to others. The French critic André Bazin wrote that the Po Delta in Rossellini's film 'resembles oral rather than written literature, a sketch rather than a painting. Even the roughness of the camera movements contributes to the effect … they make us feel that everything we see is from a human point of view'.[18] *Paisà* ends with the splashes of partisans pushed into the water with their hands tied behind their back. It was not a heroic vision of the war, or the Resistance. The critics were less than enthusiastic about *Paisà*. But in Paris, Rossellini's film caused a sensation. Out of tragedy, and death and destruction, Rossellini and Fellini had created poetry; they had also reinvented cinema itself. It was not by any means a heroic view of the past. Italy's future would be built around these stories of suffering, martyrdom and ordinary heroism.

Republic of the Dead

Italians had lived through total war, at home and abroad. The dead were everywhere, and bodies would re-emerge literally and symbolically in the post-war period. Italy's wartime experiences had left the country with millions of widows and hundreds of thousands of orphans. The trauma was widespread and enduring, and on a national scale. Some saw the dead and their memory as the very basis upon which the Republic had been founded. Piero Calamandrei, legal expert and anti-fascist, wrote of 'those who fell at our sides, or in prison and on the gallows, in the mountains and down on the plains, in the Russian steppes and on African sand, in the seas and the deserts'.[19] They could not be ignored.

Wounds remained open, and physical ruins remained untouched for years. People scrawled 'This is due to the war' on bombed ruins in Rome. Cities and streets were marked by gaps and holes. Moreover, selective and politicised forms of memory politics meant that many ordinary victims of war were ignored. Some victims were always more important than others. The million or so Italian soldiers who refused to fight for Hitler after September 1943 and who were interned in Germany and elsewhere for their collective 'no' were largely ignored. Victims of Allied bombing didn't fit coherent narratives, so they were also excised from official histories. Official memories struggled to reflect the often contradictory realities of the war experience. Complicated memorial landscapes emerged across Italy (endless plaques, memorials, anniversaries, gravestones) that were subject to constant discussion and revision. Italy was at peace, but by no means at peace with its past. 'Memory wars' – ongoing battles over Italy's understanding and interpretation of its own past – would break out during the post-war period. Not all the dead were the same, nor were they remembered in the same way. And some of the dead were very problematic indeed.

The Duce's Body

No cadaver had as much power as that of Mussolini himself. Fascism was officially over, but it was still ever-present – carved into the very fabric of Italian cities and through the propaganda of the small but not insignificant Movimento Sociale Italiano (MSI), a neo-fascist party created in 1946 by politicians who had worked under the former regime. On 22 April 1946, as a revolt raged in Milan's vast San Vittore prison (used previously by the regime to imprison oppositionists and by the Nazis to hold Jews and others before deportation), Il Duce's body vanished from its unmarked grave in a vast municipal cemetery to the north of the city. Persons unknown had taken Mussolini's corpse from its supposedly secret resting place less than a year after his death. Soon, it became clear that the body snatchers were themselves fascists, and their ghoulish act was a political one. It was a propaganda coup on the eve of the first anniversary of the liberation. The group, led by a young fascist called Domenico Leccisi, called themselves the *Partito Fascista Democratico* and had published a journal, *Lotta fascista* ('Fascist Struggle'). A bizarre message had been left in the empty grave: 'Finally, Oh Duce, you are with us. We will cover you with roses, but the smell of your virtue will overpower those roses.' The theft had a profound effect on public opinion and made worldwide news. 'Mussolini Has Been Stolen', screamed the headlines of local and national papers.

The symbolic and shocking nature of the grave robbery, along with a series of other demonstrations of fascist 'faith' (for example, on 1 May 1946 a fascist group occupied a Rome radio station and broadcast the fascist hymn *Giovinezza*), was clear. The fascists had not gone away. Rumours circulated about the whereabouts of the former dictator's body. Was it being taken to Rome? Was it already abroad? Had it reached his birthplace, Predappio, in Emilia? For the fascists the invincibility myths built up during

Mussolini's twenty-year rule had to be preserved and respected. For the anti-fascists these myths were at the basis of the desire to treat fascist corpses (particularly Mussolini's) with intense disrespect.

Alternative martyrs had quickly emerged as examples of heroism and sacrifice for a new democratic nation. In June 1924 the Socialist parliamentary deputy Giacomo Matteotti had been murdered by a fascist gang in the centre of Rome. His body was dumped in a wood. Anti-fascists succeeded in keeping Matteotti's memory alive during the period of the dictatorship through pilgrimages to the places where he was abducted and killed and where his body was hidden, and by the (illegal) celebration of key dates associated with the martyred politician. Not surprisingly, Piazza Matteotti or Via Matteotti were the most common denominations for new squares and streets across the country after liberation. The Socialist martyr was a powerful patron for a new anti-fascist state.

The dead also came home, as Italy's anti-fascists were brought back from abroad for reburial. Filippo Turati had been a towering figure on the left, a reformist Socialist forced into exile in 1926. He died in Paris in 1932 and was buried in Père Lachaise cemetery. In 1948 his ashes and the remains of another lofty Socialist from the pre-fascist era, Claudio Treves, were handed over by French Socialists in Paris to an Italian delegation. There was then a further ceremony at the Italian-Swiss border. Turati's and Treves's remains travelled to Milan by train and were then driven slowly to the City Hall, Palazzo Marino, where their ashes were put on display, alongside two large photographs of the men, surrounded by red flags. The next day the ashes were taken through the city again, and plaques were unveiled at their former homes. Michael Foot from the British Labour Party was among those attending the ceremony. Various high-level politicians and family members, as well as many socialists from the pre-fascist era, were also present. Prime Minister Alcide De Gasperi (decidedly not a Socialist) made a speech that attracted boos and whistles but also applause. The coffin bearers included Sandro Pertini, a future President of Italy. Finally, the remains of Turati and Treves were reburied in the city's beautiful Cimitero Monumentale, accompanied by a vast crowd of supporters and mourners. Later, the remains of the Rosselli brothers, Carlo and Nello, murdered in France on Mussolini's orders in 1937, were returned for reburial in 1951. Others forced into exile came back to play a part in democratic Italy, such as the anti-fascist historian Gaetano Salvemini and many Communist and Socialist politicians, as well as a number of future Christian Democrats.

Italy's dead were part of contemporary political struggles and battles over memory – on both sides of the divide. The search for viable martyrs was a constant one – as was the battle over who should become a martyr. In August 1946 what remained of Mussolini's illustrious corpse was finally tracked down to a church outside Milan. Two Franciscan monks (one the brother of the city's fascist former prefect) were charged with hiding the body. During the intervening sixteen weeks Mussolini's corpse had been kept on the move, variously hidden in a villa, a monastery and a convent. The difficulties faced by Italy's fragile new democracy in dealing with the power of Mussolini's legacy, even in the guise of his corpse, summed up its weakness in constructing a new state, its lack of legitimacy in the eyes of many Italians, and the continuing fear of a return to fascism.[20]

I

Rebuilding and Remaking Italy

Democracy

'The first time I voted, the first time that women voted, was
in 1946. I was thirty years old and with a high fever, a terrible
flu, and I was trembling with emotion ... it was emotional to
vote and I have always felt the same way ... I also felt a sense of
responsibility, a sense of belonging to a collectivity, a sense that
I was finally a citizen.'

Elvira Baldaracco[1]

Italian democracy was born in 1945–6. After twenty years without elections of any kind (apart from Mussolini's propagandist
'plebiscites'), suddenly all Italians were called to the ballot box
for the first time. Elections before the emergence of fascism had
been severely limited – to certain categories of men. Now, finally,
women were also given the right to vote. It was a democratic
revolution. There was no gradual shift towards voting rights –
they were awarded to all, immediately.

On 10 March 1946 Italian men and women went to the polls in
local elections to elect mayors and councillors, freely and without
the context of fascist intimidation that had marked limited elections in the 1920s, for the first time in the country's history. In
the heady atmosphere of post-war Italy, parties and movements
flourished and multiplied (and many disappeared with equal
speed). Some of the older parties, which had disappeared underground during the Fascist era, were reborn in the open, such as

the Socialist, Communist and Republican parties. Others were new, or had given themselves new names. Some faded quickly from view. The anti-fascist Action Party was extremely influential before, during and after the Resistance period. But it soon disappeared, although its intellectual legacy was long-lasting.[2] The local elections in March were followed in June by national elections to a Constituent Assembly. At the same time, Italians were asked to make a further, momentous decision.

Republic or Monarchy?

Fascism had collapsed, and Italy was now a democracy. Yet the head of state was an unelected King. In June 1946 Italy's transitional government called a referendum to decide on the future of the monarchy. Italians were being asked not merely to decide who was to govern them, but the future shape and architecture of Italy. They had to choose between two very different kinds of nation – a republic or a monarchy. Italy had been a monarchy from its birth in the nineteenth century, and there were imposing statues of various kings across the country. King Vittorio Emanuele II (1820–78) was one of the official 'heroes' of the Risorgimento – the process by which Italy was eventually unified in 1861 – one of the fathers of the Italian nation itself. Yet, his successors (above all his grandson Vittorio Emanuele III who became King in 1900 after Emanuele II's son Umberto was assassinated by an anarchist) had so undermined the legitimacy of the institution of the monarchy that many thought its days were numbered. Vittorio Emanuele III had aided Mussolini's ascent to power in 1922 and then governed alongside Il Duce for the next two decades. He, and the monarchy itself, was intertwined with and thereby compromised by the Fascist regime.

The King was deeply aware of the precariousness of his position. He had effectively been pushed out of his role by the anti-fascist parties in June 1944, and forced to appoint his son Umberto as 'Lieutenant General of the Realm'. Umberto was a kind of 'not-quite King' – and this was an abdication in all but name.

A commitment was made at the same time to elect a Constituent Assembly after the war to draw up a new constitution. According to the great British historian of modern Italy, Denis Mack Smith, the King argued that 'in a republic every Italian would insist upon being president and the result would be chaos. The only people who would profit would be the communists.'³

Umberto – the 'not-quite King' – was well aware of the legacy left by his father, who remained in Italy for now, in a villa in Posillipo near Naples. As Umberto told the *New York Times* in October 1944, 'the weight of the past is the monarchy's greatest handicap'. The Resistance leader Sandro Pertini, who would later become head of state himself in the 1970s and 1980s, warned Umberto against visiting Milan at the time. It was too dangerous, he said. The monarchy was fighting for its life. The arbiters of its future would be the Italian people.

The question over the final institutional shape of Italy had thus been postponed to the post-war period. Umberto didn't become a proper King (Umberto II) until 9 May 1946, in a desperate attempt to renew a dying institution. The former King Vittorio Emanuele III and his wife Elena left, by boat, for Alexandria in Egypt, just four hours after their son, the new monarch, had been privately 'crowned' (another bad sign – they couldn't risk a public declaration) on 9 May. The left did not spare the old King from criticism. For example, the Action Party newspaper *Italia Libera* wrote that 'The Fascist King abdicates and escapes to avoid the judgement of the people.'⁴ Notoriously, that same King had abandoned Rome in 1943 as the Nazis arrived. This 'escape from Rome' earned Vittorio Emanuele III a marvellously hostile plaque in Ortona (from where the royals took flight by boat for a safe haven in the liberated South), pronouncing an 'eternal curse, in the name of the Republic, on the heads of the traitorous Royal Family ... who had left Italy in ruins'.⁵

Republicanism remained a dream for many democrats. The two Giuseppes – Garibaldi and Mazzini, two of the other original 'fathers of the Italian nation' – had both been convinced Republicans. Garibaldi was forced to accept the monarchy as a compromise in order for Italy to unify in the nineteenth century.

Mazzini, who was more hard-line, went to his grave refusing to recognise the legitimacy of the Italian state he had done so much to create, a reaction mainly due to the continuing power of the monarchy. A King as head of state was, for many, an open wound.

There had been a long-running debate about whether to hold a referendum at all. Could an elected Constituent Assembly simply establish the Republic by law, or would it be necessary to go to the Italian people for such a decision? But in the end a date (or rather two days) for the referendum was set: 2–3 June 1946. All Italians would be eligible to vote, but high levels of illiteracy meant that symbols would count as much as words on the ballot paper. Italians were given a straight choice – Monarchy or Republic? That same day would see Italians choose the members of the Constituent Assembly, a parallel body that would prepare an Italian constitution from scratch. These were momentous decisions. This was not a vote about who would govern Italy, but about *what* Italy was to be – what kind of country did Italians want?

The Referendum Campaign

Apocalyptic statements abounded. Palmiro Togliatti, the formidable leader of the Communist Party, who had spent much of the period of fascism in exile in Moscow, was clear in an editorial in the party's daily newspaper, *L'Unità*. 'You must vote for the Republic', he told his readers, 'and against the Monarchy, if you want the nation to be unified … a vote for the monarchy is a vote for division, discord … it will leave Italy in ruins.'[6] The Communists also called the monarchy 'an accomplice of fascism and the fascist war'.[7] Meanwhile, the centrist parties – above all the Christian Democrats – played a waiting game.

The monarchy itself made its presence felt in the campaign. Umberto II, a fresh-faced, more modern figure than his archaic and traditional father, issued a message to the Italian people on the eve of the referendum on 1 June 1946. He claimed that he would accept the verdict of the people. But the new King also underlined that the questions asked in the referendum would have to be asked again, once the constitution had been set down. He also complained that some Italians (such as prisoners of war still abroad) were not able to vote at all. It was clear that he was not going to go quietly, whatever the result.

Italy's young democracy was fragile. Umberto II appeared to provide a more liberal future for the monarchy: one less compromised with the Fascist regime. The new, young King even spoke of 'social justice'. It had been the monarchists themselves who had pushed for a referendum, in the hope that a broader decision would favour the more conservative forces in the country. The choice of a referendum 'had the additional advantage of relieving the parties of the necessity to adopt a clear-cut line about this institutional problem'.[8] Amongst the parties themselves there was an overwhelming Republican majority. But amongst the Italian people this majority was not nearly so strong, as the referendum results would soon reveal. There were long discussions over the symbols to be used on the ballot paper. In the end, the Republic was represented by a symbolic woman's head with a tower-like crown (an ancient symbol of Italy with roots in the Roman Empire) superimposed on two branches with oak and bay leaves respectively, and the Monarchy by the House of Savoy symbol and a crown. Both symbols were printed over an identical outline of Italy. The ballot paper was simple: the two symbols and two small boxes by the side of each for an **X**.

To the Polls

At 6 a.m. on 2 June 1946 the voting began. Most shops were closed. Many of the women at the polls were dressed in black, in mourning for those who had died, or had not yet returned from the war.[9] Some of those who voted were old enough to remember the pre-fascist era. Francesco Saverio Nitti (who was seventy-seven at the time and had been Prime Minister in 1919–20) and Ivanoe Bonomi (who was seventy-two and had been Prime Minister in 1921–2 and 1944–5) – remnants of liberal Italy – both cast their votes in Rome. They had memories of when some Italians had last cast their vote. But millions had never voted before. There were very few incidents or acts of violence. An incredible 89.2 per cent of those who had the right to vote made their mark on the ballot papers. For many women it was an emotional moment. One remembered 'on that 2 June I was scared to make a mistake and choose the wrong symbol in the ballot box'.[10] Another said, 'In a simple wooden cabin I found myself faced with a pencil in my hand and two symbols in front of me – and I was also faced with myself – a citizen.'[11]

Counting the Votes

It certainly wasn't a landslide. Nearly 25 million Italians turned out to vote, and just over half of those opted for the Republic (12.7 million). Some 10.7 million backed the Monarchy while an astonishing 1.5 million ballot papers were annulled (a fact that remains something of a mystery). It was this latter figure that caused the greatest controversy and led to uncertainty as to who had won at all. Italy in 1946 was a divided country – politically, socially and culturally – and these deep fissures could be seen with great clarity in the referendum results.

History and geography played a key role. Generally, the 'red' traditionally left-wing regions of Italy voted heavily for the Republic: 77 per cent rejected the King in Emilia, 71.5 per cent in Tuscany and 69 per cent in Liguria. Some cities were almost entirely Republican, such as Ravenna and Cesena where over 90 per cent voted for the Republic. Piedmont, on the other hand, with its historic links to the royal family, was less solidly Republican (60 per cent). The South, meanwhile, remained monarchist, and sometimes spectacularly so. As the British political scientist Percy Allum pointed out, 'The vote for the monarchy ... in the South was almost double that of the North.'[12] The explanations for this were generally historical and political, both long term and short term. The South had been much less involved in the Resistance, and it also had far deeper attachments to forms of monarchical rule than many other parts of the country. Some 80 per cent of Neapolitans, 81 per cent of Catania voters and 84 per cent of Palermo voters backed the monarchy. The deep South thus opted heavily for the monarchy, but even in Rome 54 per cent chose to keep the King in place. So Italy was split between North and South, as it always had been, but in new and complicated ways. There had been a strong vote for the Republic, but not an overwhelming one. Italy was, as Aldo Ricci wrote, 'both deeply divided and confused about the future of its institutions'.[13]

The wily leader of the Christian Democrats (DC) and Prime Minister, the bespectacled and diminutive Alcide De Gasperi, who had spent much of the war cataloguing in the Vatican Library, played a careful waiting game, despite the strong Republican majority within his own party. He took a pragmatic approach, allowing for a 'free vote', and thus effectively hedged his bets and took a 'non-decision'. As Ricci has written, 'the members of the party were not the same as its electorate, and De Gasperi was well aware of this fact'.[14] The vote itself proved that he was right. The winds of radical change had come from the North, as the Socialist Pietro Nenni had predicted, but they had not penetrated the South.[15] At this point in its history, Italy's political class was more progressive, anti-fascist and radical than many of its people.

And there were many who were afraid of what they saw as too much change. The celebrated philosopher and historian (and symbol of anti-fascism) Benedetto Croce, for example, voted to keep the monarchy in place. Croce was sceptical about the signs of renewal in 1946. He wrote in his diaries that 'the referendum has divided Italy into two parts, which are almost the same'. On 11 June, just over a week after the referendum, he added that 'A National Day of Celebration for the Republic? But what are we celebrating? A very difficult period has been opened up by the vote of the 2 June, with lots of problems. There isn't much to celebrate.' Nonetheless, there were those who tried (unsuccessfully) to persuade Croce to become President of Italy in the same year.[16]

Another King Departs

Nothing was straightforward, given what was at stake, and after the votes were cast a tense standoff ensued. The new King contested the results, and described the referendum as 'arbitrary, untimely and generally badly organised'. His last statement as monarch was bitter and accusatory: 'Last night … with flagrant disregard for law and for the independent power of the judiciary, the government performed a revolutionary act in assuming, uni-laterally and arbitrarily, powers not its own, and this has left only two roads open to me; either to cause blood to be shed or to sub-mit to an outrage.'[17] There was great uncertainty. As Stuart Woolf later wrote, 'the survival of the monarchy, which had seemed impossible in 1945, now seemed an open question'.[18] On 2 June it 'showed that it still had great power'.[19]

The first results from the referendum were not released until 5 June. A fiery debate then ensued as to whether what mattered was a majority of votes cast, or of the *valid* votes cast, which called attention to the large numbers of disputed ballot papers. The outcome now became a legal question, with heavy political and historic overtones, and the final result was not confirmed legally until 10 June. Given this uncertainty the King stayed in place, and waited. Tensions rose. Negotiations continued and intermediaries scuttled between the two symbolic sites (ten minutes' walk apart) of the new and the old Italy in the capital city – the Viminale (Interior Ministry) represented the anti-fascist and democratic state, and the Quirinale (Royal Palace) the old Italy. Groups of monarchists 'stood guard' in the Piazza outside the Royal Palace, calling on the King to remain in charge.

Meanwhile, Italy was in ferment. Demonstrations for and against the monarchy took place across the country. The King piled the pressure on, writing to the Prime Minister to say that he would only accept a verdict if it related to votes *cast*. In the meantime, De Gasperi took on some of the powers of the head of state (Italy did not yet have a President, or a constitution). There were also fears over the loyalty of the armed forces and in par-ticular the *carabinieri* (a semi-militarised police force), who had all sworn an oath of allegiance to the King.

On 11 June a monarchist demonstration in Naples turned nasty. Reports came in of at least seven deaths. A Communist Party office was wrecked.[20] It was a warning and a very serious one. Italy had, after all, only just emerged from civil war. Memories of the violence of that time were still fresh. De Gasperi and the Council of Ministers decided to assume the role of head of state. At this point, the fate of the monarchy was sealed. Finally, on 13 June, Umberto II left Italy. He was driven to Ciampino Airport outside Rome and gave a last wave as he boarded a plane at around 4 p.m. He would never return to Italian soil (not even in death) and settled in Cascais, a sleepy seaside town in fascist Portugal close to Lisbon (where he took the title of the Conte di Sarre). He continued to complain bitterly about the process that had led to his removal, but only a small minority took much notice.

The Republican dream held by so many and for so long had been realised – at last. Celebratory parties were held in some parts of Italy, and plaques put up that recorded overwhelming votes in favour of abolishing the monarchy. In Radicondoli, for example, a small hill town in the Province of Siena, a memorial was unveiled which noted the fact that 1,958 voters there had opted for the Republic, while a mere 227 citizens had chosen to keep the monarchy in place. Meanwhile, in Pisa, nearly 31,000 voted for the Republic, as opposed to 12,000 or so for the monarchy, and this result was also recorded, for posterity, in marble. In Castelfidardo in the Marche region it is etched on a plaque that 4,098 out of 4,893 voters were Republicans.

On 18 June, with the King already gone, the High Court announced its final decision. The Republic had won on both counts, it said – including in terms of the majority of votes cast. Legally, the country *had* voted for a Republic. Not everyone was convinced, least of all the monarchists, but it was too late to change things. Italy was now a Republic. Umberto II had been the monarch for less than a month – and thus earned his (disparaging) nickname of 'the May King'.

Italy wanted to make sure that the monarchy would never be restored. The 1948 Constitution later stated that 'members and descendants of the House of Savoy shall not be voters and they shall not hold public office or elected offices. To the ex-kings of the House of Savoy, to their consorts and their male descendants shall be forbidden access and sojourn in the national territory.

The assets, existing on national territory, of the former kings of the House of Savoy, of their consorts and of their male descendants shall revert to the State. Transfers and the establishment of royal rights on said patrimony which took place after 2 June 1946 shall be null and void.' Article 139 made it clear that 'The form of Republic shall not be a matter for constitutional amendment.'

Alcide De Gasperi's statement in the wake of the 1946 referendum was realistic: 'this final act of the thousand-year-old House of Savoy must be seen as part of our national catastrophe; it is an expiation, an expiation forced upon all of us, even those who have not shared directly in the guilt of the dynasty.' This was a statement that neatly avoided extremist positions on either side of the vote.[21] The end of the monarchy was a historic moment, but it was not all bad news for conservative forces in Italy. As one commentator has argued, 'The disappearance of the monarchy made the Vatican the major institutional support of the status quo inside the country.'[22] Italy had changed, but the forces of conservatism and tradition were still powerful, and in some cases more so than before.

United Italy had been ruled by a monarch for less than a hundred years. Statues of heroic kings and roads dedicated to monarchs remained in place all over the country, but royal palaces were abandoned (and long legal battles ensued). An oath of loyalty (by politicians and others) was now taken to an institution – the Republic – and no longer to a person – the King. Royal photos came down (but not all of them). The Quirinale in Rome was taken over (again, it had been a Papal Palace until 1870) and eventually became the official residence of the new head of state – the President of Italy.

Meanwhile, in Genoa, back in 1946, something very odd was happening. In the wake of the referendum results, it was decided that the body of one of the 'fathers of the nation' should be displayed to the people. Giuseppe Mazzini – a great proponent of Republicanism and one of the fathers of the Italian nation – had been (badly) embalmed (against his own previously stated wishes) after his death in 1872 and buried in that city's cemetery (famous, later, for the image on the cover of Joy Division's *Closer* album).

On 23 June 1946 a macabre event took place. Mazzini's body was dug up and put on show. It didn't look good. Nonetheless, many ordinary citizens and democrats made the pilgrimage to the city to pay homage. There was a lot of interest in a small tube and document inside the coffin. Was this a last message to the Italian people from Mazzini himself? But in the end the letter was simply a statement that this really was Mazzini's body. The great Republican was reburied.[23]

The farcical story of Mazzini's exhumed body and the letter was a sideshow, but it tells us something about the power of that moment. Mazzini's Republican dream was becoming a reality eighty years on. Italy's monarchy, which had presided over the country's fortunes since unification, was gone. With the monarchy went the Albertine Statute of 1848, Italy's first semi-constitution, which had remained in place (despite everything) throughout the period of fascism. Italy now needed new rules, new laws and different ways of doing things. The First Republic was about to be born, but rebirth and change were always accompanied by continuities.

Resistance, Anti-Fascism and Post-War Italy

Between 1943 and 1945 thousands of Italian men and women took part in what became known as 'The Resistance'. Men and women took to the mountains to carry out guerrilla warfare against the occupying German army and Mussolini's faithful followers. Others fought their battles in the cities, as part of an urban partisan movement. They did so out of ideological conviction (as Communists, Socialists, Catholic anti-fascists or even monarchists loyal to the King) or simply to rid Italy of its foreign invaders. This was a brutal war of attrition, where prisoners were rarely taken. The Resistance worked in a sea of support that included political parties, anti-fascist networks and sections of the peasantry. Many of the participants were extremely young, and as a result most of those who died at the hands of the Italian Fascists and the Nazis – the so-called 'martyrs for freedom' – were in their teens or early twenties. Not everyone took up arms, and there were forms of 'civil resistance' that opposed fascism by other means. Survival itself was also a form of resistance, in the face of the extreme pressures imposed by the conflict.

The Italian Resistance has been at the centre of historical and political debates ever since 1945, both inside and outside of Italy. Novels, films, artworks, poems, museums and historical work were all dedicated to its legacy and memory. Many former partisans moved into positions of political power, whereas others found it difficult to adapt to post-war peace. The Resistance was a potent source of political legitimation and power but was also highly malleable to manipulation and falsification. The divisions that were briefly overcome during the 1943–5 period (although there were often violent diatribes between the various forces involved at the time) came back with a vengeance after the war.

Many of those who had taken part in the guerrilla war against fascists and Nazis felt betrayed by the post-war settlement. Some kept their guns oiled and ready in case of a revolution or the rebirth of fascism. There were occasional 'returns to the mountains' by angry ex-partisans, but these events were more symbolic than a real attempt to revive the armed resistance. The Resistance had won in the short term, but many of its more radical aims were not to be realised. Above all, the presence of former fascists in positions of power, or just on the streets, was hard to take for those who had seen their comrades give their lives to defeat Nazifascism. Many were shocked by the formation of an explicitly neo-fascist party in 1946.

What was to happen to all those who had faithfully and zealously served the regime – judges, policemen, architects, generals? Despite rapid democratic renewal, there seemed little desire in Italy for a thorough purge of former fascists from public life. The worst and most dangerous time to be a fascist was during the immediate post-war period – when at least 15,000 people were summarily shot in the days that followed liberation, and a few fascists were given the death penalty or long prison sentences after quick trials. Soon, a series of amnesties led to the release of thousands of ex-fascists – some of whom had held posts of prestige and power. Many went on to lead perfectly normal lives in Republican Italy.

The most important of these amnesties was passed by the Communist Party leader, Palmiro Togliatti, when he was Justice Minister in 1946. Togliatti's decision to forgive was driven by a desire to avoid a new civil war, and by a crisis in the prison system in 1946, which had been hit by a series of bloody riots. The amnesty saw thousands of fascists and ex-fascists freed, and large-scale reductions in their prison sentences. Perhaps the most grotesque case in this sense was that of the high-level military officer Rodolfo Graziani, who had been involved in numerous massacres during Italy's colonial period and the Second World War. Despite being given a nineteen-year sentence in 1948, he served a mere four months. He then went on to become honorary president of the neo-fascist party, Movimento Sociale Italiano, before his death in 1955.

The effect of this process was one of reassurance for many who had felt threatened by the violent settling of accounts and mild purges of the post-war period. But for others it led to anger and outrage. Togliatti's amnesty did not go down well with the Communist base, nor with many others who had fought in the Resistance. Former fascists had not just made it through to the post-war period without suffering much punishment, but many appeared to still hold authority. Others felt confident enough to try to spread fascist views and organise politically. Partisans even began to be arrested across Italy for political and other crimes. What had it all been for? There was a strong sense of betrayal. Some took the law into their own hands. Many felt that although Mussolini was gone, fascism was still very much around. A battle was now on course for Italy's soul.

Democratic Italy was at a crossroads. Should all laws and legal codes simply be swept away and reconstructed from zero, or would change be piecemeal? Would there be a full-scale de-fascistisation of institutions governed by fascist rules and regulations, such as prisons, asylums and even schools? Italy took an ambiguous position in the face of these dilemmas. Some of the more objectionable fascist measures were immediately struck from the law books, such as the odious anti-Semitic laws from 1938. However, most laws and overarching legal codes passed under fascism remained. This meant that the explicitly anti-fascist constitution of 1948 (discussed in detail below) was, from the outset, in conflict with many ordinary laws, applied as they were by judges and policemen across the land, many of whom had moved seamlessly from their positions under fascism to employment in the anti-fascist Republican state. It was not until 1968, for example, that it became illegal to interrogate a suspect without a defence lawyer being present. These clear conflicts took considerable time to work in favour of legal reform. And what about the people themselves? Would they be sacked if they had enthusiastically propped up fascism and profited from it?

Let us look at one key area: the judiciary. Powerful judges who had operated under fascism were not purged (in most cases) and continued to hold positions of great power in the new Republic. Gaetano Azzariti had been much more than an ordinary judge under the Fascist regime. In 1939 he had served as president of the notorious fascist body the Tribunal for the Defence of the Race, which adjudicated on matters relating to the racist discriminations introduced by 1938's anti-Semitic laws. Azzariti remained in that post until the collapse of fascism in 1943.

In 1944, with Rome liberated from fascism and from the Nazis, Azzariti was asked officially about his past. An investigation into his role under fascism was begun. Part of the process consisted of a kind of questionnaire (which might seem a rather odd way to run a purge). Question 16 was as follows: 'Did you ever take part in Racial commissions or other bodies?' This was Azzariti's answer: 'No. I was part of a technical-judicial commission, made up mainly of magistrates who could declare people to be Aryan even if on civil registers they were designated as Jewish. *In this way a number of Israelite families were able to escape from the effects of the racial laws* [my emphasis].' As the researcher Massimiliano Boni, one of the few people to look in detail at what happened to people like Azzariti, has written, 'In a few lines everything was turned on its head ... He claims that his job was to save Jews.'[24] Luckily for Azzariti, most of the documents relating to the Tribunal for the Defence of the Race had 'disappeared'. The judge used this opportunity to lie, tell half-truths and reinvent his past.

It was also clear that Azzariti had made a vast amount of money under fascism (there were rumours of payoffs from families to 'save themselves'). He was deeply involved with all levels of the regime, and over a considerable period. Yet Azzariti managed to present his activities as president of a Racial Commission under the guise of those of a classic 'good Italian'. The myth that Italians had behaved well and were above all victims of the aggression of others was pervasive in post-war Italy. It seemed that everyone had really been an anti-fascist all along, and that nobody was responsible for anything that had happened under the regime, even if they had held positions of power. Azzariti also changed a few dates, to manipulate his past and downplay any possible punishment he might receive. Who then decided to help Azzariti? The documents don't tell us. They only show that somebody intervened, from on high, to block the purging process. Boni concludes that 'the network of friends and support that Azzariti relied on during his long career helped him escape from any danger'. Many other people who had supported the Fascist regime adopted similar tactics. And for thousands of them, it worked.

With the end of the purging process, Azzariti worked with the Communist Minister of Justice, Palmiro Togliatti. He then retired officially in 1951, after service at a high level, for the entire post-war period – his pension and reputation intact. But his career was not in fact over. Worse was to follow (but not for him). In 1955 the President of Italy appointed him as a judge on the newly formed Constitutional Court. This was one of the most influential positions within the judiciary. Azzariti then rose again, almost incredibly, to become President of the Constitutional Court in 1957 – a post he held until his death in 1961.

The Constitutional Court was required to apply the anti-fascist constitution. It had taken so long to set this body up that the ruling Christian Democrats were accused of blocking the very constitution they had helped to write. Moreover, the procedures for the election of its members were and still are particularly byzantine. After 1955, laws could finally be brought before this court and wiped off the statute book as 'unconstitutional'. This court quickly became one of the most important bodies in the Republic, a guarantor of democracy and the constitution itself. Its first act was to declare itself able to judge past laws. But the court was also called upon to adjudicate on new laws. It would ensure – in theory – that contemporary politics was in line with the anti-fascist principles of the constitution.

Not everything the Constitutional Court decided was progressive, and in many ways it was a deeply conservative body. This was not surprising, if we remember that many of its members (like Azzariti) came straight from the fascist establishment. The Constitutional Court rarely acted on its own initiative, and often it was only thanks to social and political change in the real world that the court felt it was time to change things legally. It was reactive, not proactive. This conservatism often led to baffling decisions. For example, in 1961 the court decided that the law on adultery (which largely punished only women for this 'crime') was *not* unconstitutional.

In his public speeches and pronouncements Azzariti scrupulously avoided any reference to fascism. 'The past,' writes Boni, 'was completely forgotten.' This 'forgetting' continued after Azzariti's death, where he received universal praise that made – once again – no reference to the regime. His bust still stands (despite tepid protests) in the Constitutional Court building in Rome.[25] Occasionally, there were some small signs of change – that this state of affairs could not be allowed to continue. In 2015, for example, it was decided that a street named after him in Naples (in 1970) would be renamed in honour of the city's youngest victim of the Shoah.

Azzariti's was one of the more extreme and grotesque cases of 'recycling', but it nonetheless helps to explain the slow process by which fascist laws were removed from the statute books. Castes and professional classes protected their own, despite the supposed effects of the 'wind from the North'.[26] The people who had written and applied fascist laws were still in positions of influence in a democratic, republican state. And they were still writing and applying the law. The curious case of Azzariti was not the only such example of 'continuity' in the judiciary. Antonio Manca was also a judge on the Constitutional Court, from 1956 to 1968. He, like Azzariti, had served on the Tribunal for the Defence of the Race. At least three other long-serving Constitutional Court judges (including another president) had worked under fascism and two of these had written in racist newspapers under the regime.

Beyond the judiciary there were other glaring examples of continuity with fascism. Marcello Piacentini had been one of the most prolific architects under the regime, designing landmark fascist monuments and buildings across Italy. His oeuvre included the highly controversial and extremely fascist Monument to Victory in Bolzano – a massive marble arch covered with symbols of the regime. His buildings can still be seen all over the country. Banks, universities and law courts all bear his name – and many are still in use as public buildings.

After the war Piacentini continued to work as an architect in the Department of Architecture in Rome's imposing and prestigious La Sapienza university (which he had earlier helped to build, in fascist style). Initially, Piacentini had been condemned for his links to the regime and sacked from his university post, but he was later cleared with this justification: 'Active participation in the political life of fascism can only be deduced for those who took direct part in the political system of the past regime, and not for those who merely carried out technical duties or had some sort of relationship with the regime.' Piacentini, whose buildings were adorned with fascist symbols, was able to argue that his extensive work had been made up of 'technical activities'.[27]

Later, Piacentini asked a little-known painter called Marco Siviero to 'de-fascistise' a large mural inside Rome University – a mural he himself had helped commission from the original artist Mario Sironi in the 1930s.[28] From a potential purgee, Piacentini became a purger (at least of artworks). It was an astonishing about-turn, symptomatic of many others at that time. Piacentini was, in an almost literal sense, covering his tracks. Later, a different project 'restored' the fascist parts of the mural, in the name of artistic freedom. There are currently roads named after Piacentini in Rome, Ravenna, Taranto, Bergamo and other places in Italy. He also played a role in the preparations for the 1960 Olympics in Rome before his death, just before the games themselves, in that same year.

Some former fascists simply pretended that nothing had happened – that they had never been fascists at all, or had gone along with the regime's demands to avoid censure and make a living. Occasionally, these people would be exposed in the press in post-war Italy. In many other cases, nothing at all was said. It was almost as if it was bad taste even to bring up the issue. Many people had, of course, formally adhered to the regime because they had little choice. Others, quite legitimately, changed their minds before, during or after the war. There were also cases of celebrated intellectuals later 'outed' as supporters of fascism – either by documents or former colleagues, or thanks to the work of investigative journalists. The archives held damaging material, which might 'emerge' at any time.

Italy thus had no serious purging process, and many fascists and former fascists remained at large. There was no 'Italian Nuremberg'.[29] The country's war crimes were never punished, either within or outside of Italy. The wartime Fascist invasions and occupations of Greece, Albania, Yugoslavia, France, the USSR, the colonial wars in Ethiopia, Somalia and Libya, and the intervention in Spain during the civil war were all forgotten – at home. Not one single Italian soldier or politician was ever held responsible for war crimes connected to the fascist wars of the 1930s or the events of the world war. Only in a few high-level cases were Nazis prosecuted in the post-war period on Italian soil. Herbert Kappler was a key figure in the Nazi occupation of wartime Italy, responsible for the deportation of many Jews from Rome (mainly to Auschwitz) and the horrific Fosse Ardeatine reprisal-massacre in the capital in March 1944. In 1947 he was handed a life sentence (by a military court) for his activities during the war in Italy.

A further kind of tacit amnesty was extended to most of the Nazis who were involved in massacres in Italy during the occupation. The great majority were released back to Germany, and most investigations were dropped before trial. After the war, the 'ratlines' through Genoa or Bolzano in collusion with the Vatican had led to dozens of high-ranking Nazis finding sanctuary in Argentina and other places in the aftermath of the war – including Adolf Eichmann. A decision was quickly taken not to continue with judicial inquiries into numerous outrages and a filing cabinet containing detailed information was turned with its doors to the wall in an archive in Rome. It was not 'rediscovered' until 1994, when it was quickly dubbed the 'Cupboard of Shame'.

The years 1945–6 were also a period when the old powers reasserted themselves in other areas. Women were almost immediately expelled from the labour force. Often it was those men who had taken part in the Resistance itself who pushed for this process. The politician Paola Gaiotti De Biase argued that 'unfortunately, it was the partisan commanders or entire Liberation Committees who asked for women to be sacked in the summer of 1945 to make way for the men'.[30] Much had changed in Italy with the war and the Resistance; but much had also remained the same. Family structures seemed little affected by a democratic revolution in parts of the country. For historian Maria Linda Odorosio 'The old-style patriarchal family which had been the bedrock of the Fascist state was not subjected to any kind of analysis. Family relationships appeared as something that was given and immutable.'[31]

This lack of a critique of the family and the power structures within it also existed on the left. The Communist Party women's organisation, Unione Donne Italiane or UDI (formed in 1944), was conservative on family issues. There was very little sense that the family was a problem in itself or needed reform. For many, it was a solution and a source of comfort, especially given the fractures, splits and horrors of the war years, when families had been destroyed or separated for years. Not surprisingly, perhaps, there were also many who rejected the political system in its entirety.

Qualunquismo and Anti-Politics

'OUR DESIRE IS THAT NOBODY BREAKS OUR BALLS
ANY MORE.'

Guglielmo Giannini [his capitals][32]

Guglielmo Giannini wrote jokes and songs, worked as a journalist, and was an aspiring playwright and film director. An imposing figure, he grew up in Naples (his mother was English and his father an Italian anarchist) and fought during the First World War. In his youth he was attracted to communist ideals. He clearly had a way with words and in the immediate post-war period, quite unexpectedly, he found himself at the head of a rapidly growing political movement, which briefly threatened the established party system, before fading quickly from view.

In the end Giannini's main legacy was probably the phrase '*qualunquismo*' (used to describe his movement, but derived from the name he gave his 'party'), which Sandro Setta has defined as 'a generalised dislike of politics and politicians, who are seen as greedy and corrupt without distinction between those who are in power and the opposition ... ideological indifference, a tendency to ignore society and interest oneself in one's own particular space and interests'.[33]

Giannini set up a newspaper in December 1944 called *L'Uomo qualunque* (*The Ordinary Man*). The whole thrust of this publication, and the resulting movement, was against the 'class' of 'professional politicians'. Politics itself was seen as essentially useless. The economy, for Giannini, was to be run by a 'good accountant'. Using blunt political language (which would later be picked up and copied by other populist and anti-political movements), Giannini railed against parties and state institutions. He dubbed 'the wind from the north' (the phrase given to the radical changes proposed by the Resistance generation) 'the burp from the north' and rebaptised the RAI state media organisation as *Restituirla Agli Italiani* (Give it Back to the Italians). Giannini was not a fascist, and he was extremely rude about Mussolini, but many of his targets were anti-fascists.

In the elections of 1946 Giannini's new movement won a very surprising 5.3 per cent of the national vote, and much more was to come in the local elections of November 1946. *L'Uomo qualunque* swept the board in many Southern cities – becoming the biggest party in places as important as Catania (34.6 per cent), Palermo (24.5 per cent) and Bari (46 per cent), and winning over 20 per cent of the vote in Rome itself, while also making an impact in a city like Florence (13.7 per cent). Giannini was triumphant. 'We are the only ones to have won,' he wrote. But Giannini was no political strategist, and he proceeded to make a series of errors that would lead to the swift decline of his movement, including an ill-fated series of talks with Communist leader Palmiro Togliatti. Clearly, Giannini's supporters were not interested in working with that part of the left.

There were further attempts to do deals with other parties, all of which failed. Giannini was unable to command his own party, and his deputies rebelled against his orders. 1948 saw a decline in his support and the movement was effectively wound up soon afterwards. *Qualunquismo* has since become part of the Italian language, and is used almost exclusively in a negative sense – as an insult. *L'Uomo qualunque* had quickly faded from view, but the forces behind it, and which inspired its rise, remained. Anti-political rhetoric, language and tactics continued to play a part in Italian political and public life.

Figureheads and Symbols in Republican Italy

Enrico De Nicola was a Neapolitan legal expert and a liberal anti-fascist who had held office before fascism took full control. He had even served as President of the Lower House in the early 1920s. De Nicola was not particularly well known, charismatic or ambitious, but these were 'attributes' that fitted the bill for the post of President after the cults of personality linked to Mussolini and the King. De Nicola was always well dressed and sported a splendid moustache. He was elected by a large majority within Parliament and took power on 1 July 1946 as Italy's first President. His investiture ceremony was delayed because he was late, having driven to Parliament in his own car, carrying a leather suitcase. De Nicola was also fairly old (sixty-six), another 'attribute' guaranteed by the Constitution. Presidents still must be at least fifty years old on election. Italians didn't want anyone to hold power for too long. De Nicola was a reluctant head of state, in stark contrast with the style and substance of Mussolini's time in power. He turned down any pay for his role and refused to live in the Quirinale Palace. Having overseen the transition to a constitution, he resigned in May 1948 after the election of a new President, Luigi Einaudi.

Italy also required a new national anthem. The old one – the Royal March – was clearly no longer appropriate. Its opening lines, after all, were *Long live the King! Long live the King! Long live the King!* The Royal March had been temporarily replaced in 1943 with a song from the First World War, and the search for a new, Republican anthem only took place after 1945. In the end Italy chose a new song that was in fact very old – dating as it did from the Risorgimento. Goffredo Mameli's song was selected by the Italian cabinet in October 1946 as the national anthem.[34] This 'inno' or 'Song of the Italians', as it was sometimes called, struggled to inspire much affection for much of the post-war period and was, for a long time, associated with the far right. It is now usually referred to as *Fratelli d'Italia*. The lyrics themselves did not help, with their references to 'Scipio's helmet' and 'Slave of Rome':

> Brothers of Italy,
> Italy has awakened,
> She has girded her head
> With the helmet of Scipio.

With time, more Italians accepted the anthem and it is now more widely sung, at least the first verse. There was also a new flag – without the royal symbol in its centre. Some simply tore out that symbol, leaving a gaping hole that emphasised in a physical sense how change had come to Italy. Portraits of the King and

Mussolini had already been consigned to rubbish bins across Italy, as had numerous statues. Street names were altered, as were the names of stadiums and football teams that had been forced to 'Italianise' themselves under fascism, such as *Football Club Internazionale*, which had become *A. S. Ambrosiana-Inter*, or *Associazione Calcio Milan* (which had added an 'o'). Both teams returned to their original names after the war. Italy had begun to look and sound like a democracy.

Building a New State: Italy's Constitution

'The sky was empty.'

Giuseppe G. Floridia[35]

By June 1946, despite political, social and cultural upheaval, Italy no longer had a dictator, or a King. Democracy was blossoming, while parties were flourishing and gaining members by the day. It was now time to attempt to construct a new state. The next twenty-two months would see a crucial series of events for the Italian nation: the beginning of the Cold War, the launch of a new constitution in January 1948, and landmark elections in April of that year. These three linked moments fixed Italy's political and cultural make-up for much of the post-war period.

On 2 June 1946 – the same day as the historic referendum on the monarchy – 556 individuals were elected to a Constituent Assembly. A period of mass politics had begun, dominated by parties with big memberships and linked organisations: unions, newspapers, cultural policies. Nearly 75 per cent of voters opted for the Christian Democrats (35.1 per cent), the Socialist Party (20.6 per cent) or the Communist Party (18.9 per cent). All the other forces were in single figures. The Assembly's task was to write a new constitution. Recurring debates were held in the main chamber and in commissions from 25 June 1946 to the end of 1947. There were long and sophisticated discussions about every comma, word and clause. Members of the Assembly were aware of the importance of all their decisions. They were trying to create a new nation – a democratic republic. The spectre of the last twenty years hung over everything. Mussolini was dead but, as we have seen, his ghost lingered.

Every phrase was worked over until a consensus could be found. The famous opening article of the constitution saw numerous amendments and versions before agreement was finally reached. One early version, for example, read 'The Italian State has a republican, democratic, parliamentary and anti-totalitarian system.' In the end everyone settled for this elegant compromise: 'Italy is a democratic Republic based on labour.' It was a clear beginning: anti-fascist, almost socialist, and its message was a powerful one. It was a revolutionary and foundational moment. It was an extraordinary time. Almost everything was up for grabs.

Who were the members of this Constituent Assembly? Many had been active anti-fascists, who had spent years in prison, in exile, or in internal confinement under the regime in remote jails or camps. A number had taken up arms for the Resistance, while others had played a more passive role. There were some heavyweight partisan leaders involved in the discussions – such as Arrigo Boldrini (battle name 'Bulow'), Vincenzo Moscatelli ('Cino'), Teresa Mattei (Partigiana Chicci), Giuliano Pajetta (who had been in Mauthausen concentration camp) and Giuseppe Dossetti. Constituent members included experts on law, on politics, on education. Amongst the Christian Democrats were the names of those who would go on to construct the political history of the Republic – Aldo Moro, Giulio Andreotti, Alcide De Gasperi, Amintore Fanfani. These four men alone would hold the office of Prime Minister twenty-six times between 1946 and 1992.

Celebrated names from liberal, pre-fascist Italy participated in the debates – Ivanoe Bonomi, Francesco Saverio Nitti, Benedetto Croce and Vittorio Emanuele Orlando – as well as trade unionists who had been active way back in the Giolittian period such as Ludovico d'Aragona and Giuseppe di Vittorio. The writer, socialist and former communist, Ignazio Silone, was part of the Assembly, while the so-called autonomists included the Sardinian soldier and writer Emilio Lussu, who had escaped from fascist confinement to exile in France. Other constituent members included Giacomo Matteotti's two sons, Giancarlo and Mario. Some had been in Moscow under fascism, others in France or Switzerland. Seven of the so-called 'constituents' would go on to become presidents of the Republic in an arc of time ranging from the 1950s to the 1990s – Luigi Einaudi, Giovanni Gronchi, Antonio Segni, Giuseppe Saragat, Giuseppe Leone, Sandro Pertini and Oscar Luigi Scalfaro.

Only twenty-one of the constituent members were women. As we have already seen, Italian women were able to vote for the first time – at last – in 1946. They could also be elected to various bodies, although this right was not conceded without a struggle, and was not yet universal.[36] Public (and private) institutions and the political system itself remained deeply biased towards men. Of those twenty-one women in the Constituent Assembly (a mere 3.7 per cent of the total), two were Socialists, nine Christian Democrats and nine Communists.

Who were these pioneering women, the first to enter the Italian Parliament? All were anti-fascists, and some had been active in the Resistance. Teresa Noce, for example, had been a founding member of the Italian Communist Party, taken part in the Spanish Civil War, and spent time in the notorious camps of Ravensbruck and Flossenburg after she was deported from France. Her autobiography, published in the 1970s, would be entitled *Professional Revolutionary*. She was also (along with another four women) part of the more select Special Commission of seventy-five members who prepared texts for discussion in the general chamber. It was a struggle at times to be taken seriously. Newspapers commented in detail on the appearance of these first female deputies, and their outfits. Yet these women managed to bring the issue of equality and women's rights into the heart of the Assembly.

Almost all the constituent members were agreed on at least one aspect of their work. Fascism (and the monarchy) must never be allowed to return. This was the overriding, minimalist position around which fragile alliances had been formed within the Resistance. The President of the Assembly – the moderate Socialist Giuseppe Saragat – was elected in 1946 and for 1947 this role was taken by Umberto Terracini, a Communist. None of the constituent members are still alive. The last member to die was Emilio Colombo in 2013.

The overwhelming desire to avoid another Mussolini (or King) led to the laying down of complicated systems of power, whereby no one person could ever dominate the system again (or so it was hoped). But every state needs a head. So the constitution came up with a compromise. Italy's President was given a seven-year term, and important powers – the dissolution of Parliament and the calling of elections, the appointment of ministers and prime ministers, the signing of all laws, the appointment of senators for life. But the President of Italy was elected by Parliament, not the people, and the position was usually assigned to those from within the system – with a correspondingly statesmanlike approach and mindset.

Mussolini's 1929 agreements between Church and State (the Lateran Pacts) had resolved the so-called 'Roman Question', which had divided the official Catholic world from Italy and its rulers since the creation of Italy itself in the 1860s and 1870s. Article Seven of the constitution was waved through on the orders of Communist Party leader Palmiro Togliatti, who was anxious not to alienate Catholics. The Article stated that: 'The State and the Catholic Church are independent and sovereign, each within its own sphere. Their relations are regulated by the Lateran pacts. Amendments to such Pacts which are accepted by both parties shall not require the procedure of constitutional amendments.' This was a major victory for the Church, and a compromise that essentially left Church-State relations as they had been under fascism. Nobody would touch this relationship, which was extremely advantageous to the Church, until the 1980s.

Parliament was designed to be strong and all laws were subject to extensive scrutiny. Most legislation had to pass both elected houses unchanged if it was to make it to the statute books. This made reform difficult, but it also made counter-reform extremely problematic. And this was the point. Reform – it was hoped – would only be achieved with wide consensus. Never again would one party or individual be able to transform the country on a whim and suppress others. Above all this, the principles of the constitution would guarantee that the laws themselves did not become instruments for repression. Checks and balances were everywhere. Power was dispersed and kept within strict limits. The constitution was built to last. Once agreed upon, it was very difficult to change.

Meanwhile, the Prime Minister (who was called the President of the Council of Ministers) was also limited in what he or she could do. They could not even appoint their own ministers, or call elections. Prime Ministers were often – as a result – prisoners of their cabinet, their party and Parliament itself. A system of continual negotiation was put in place, with different actors and institutions sharing power.

Italy's political system was both stable and unstable. True to its anti-fascist ideals, the Republican Constitution provided for a particularly 'pure' form of proportional representation. This meant that almost everyone was represented in Parliament, from the neo-fascists and monarchists on the right to parties on the far left. Small parties flourished under this system, and they usually exercised much more power than their level of support seemed to deserve. After coalition governments became almost obligatory, Rome was associated with political rituals such as consultations between the President of Italy (who formally appointed prime ministers and ministers) and party leaders. All the party leaders would troop in and out of the President's office (there were a lot of parties to consult) as agreement was sought over the next Prime Minister. It could last for weeks, or even months.

Governments came and went with great regularity (outside of elections) and often fell over what seemed to be relatively minor issues, but those in power remained there. The same party – the Christian Democrats – would go on to rule the country until 1992, but they rarely governed alone. Alliances were built with the left, the centre and sometimes the right, but the Christian Democratic Party was always at the centre. Some said it couldn't lose, given the delicate political balance imposed by the Cold War. In any case, the Christian Democrats never did lose an election. As such, its leading members were never out of power, with all the ramifications of near-permanence in the structures of influence and within the institutions. The constitution and the social and political climate of post-war Italy meant that the real players in the First Republic were political parties. In the era of mass parties (roughly from 1945 to the early 1990s) Italy was frequently described as a 'partytocracy': a place where the parties ruled. Parties decided on candidates and leaders, and could make or break governments. They operated both inside and outside of Parliament. The party system was also structured and fed by a rigid international climate of division. Italy's parties were soon lining up on either side of the Cold War.

Cold War

'The Cold War is wrongly perceived as a kind of ice age. The world didn't freeze: all sorts of things happened.'

Rossana Rossanda[37]

The Second World War was officially over, but another conflict had already begun: the Cold War. In January 1947 Alcide De Gasperi visited the United States. Italy badly needed money. It was a difficult journey – it took him two days to get to Washington. Hard negotiations followed. The trip ended on 15 January with promises of a big American loan. But the visit was also presented as a 'public relations triumph' that included a trip to New York where the city 'treated De Gasperi as a conquering hero'.[38] Money later flowed through the Marshall Aid programme, and this was not just a question of hard cash. American money came with propaganda attached, including 'friendship [or Freedom] trains' that criss-crossed Italy in 1947 replete with flags and packed with supplies for the population.[39]

Words were not the only weapon in the struggle against communism. On May Day 1947, a festive trade union demonstration in Portella della Ginestra in Sicily was fired upon from above. Machine guns were used to mow down the crowd. Eleven people died, including two seven-year-old children. Ten days earlier an alliance of Communists and Socialists had come out on top in regional elections in the island. This infamous massacre was carried out by a self-styled Sicilian 'bandit' called Salvatore Giuliano with his gang. But the motives for the killings have always been the subject of debate. Interior Minister Mario Scelba later concluded that there was 'no political motive' for the slaughter, whereas others have always claimed that the attack was closely linked to the fear of a left-wing takeover of the island's political institutions. The Mafia was almost certainly involved. Many other communists, socialists and trade unionists would pay for their militancy with their lives in the post-war period, in Sicily and elsewhere. The battle between the left and right in post-war Italy was not merely verbal or symbolic: it also led to death and suffering.

Soon afterwards, Italy's Cold War officially began, while the Constituent Assembly was still deep in discussions about the new constitution. In a surprise move, on 13 May 1947, De Gasperi resigned as Prime Minister. He then formed a government at the end of May without Italy's Communist and Socialist parties, who were thus effectively thrown out of power by the Christian Democrats. Some would later argue that this was the political price De Gasperi had to pay for the dollars he was promised during his trip to the United States. The same process also took place in France, around the same time. A split within the Socialist Party along Cold War lines – when a number of members and parliamentarians left to form a small moderate and pro-Western party – had helped De Gasperi and the Christian Democrats to form a solid alliance. Italy's fragile anti-fascist political unity was broken. Politics was – from that moment onwards, and right up to the 1990s – divided in line with international blocs.

Italy was on the front line of this new war-in-peacetime. Italy's Cold War was often at its hottest on the edges of the country – and above all on the eastern border, which also marked part of Europe's Iron Curtain. Here, the effects of the world war itself continued for years. Gorizia, a small town on the Italian Yugoslav border that had been razed to the ground during the First World War, was cut apart by the provisions of the 1947 peace treaty, which drew up new borders. Yugoslavia soon built a fresh city across the border, called Nova Gorica. But the real prize was Trieste, a former great port and still a highly symbolic city for both Italy and Yugoslavia.

Trieste was liberated by Tito's Yugoslav partisans in 1945, but soon retaken by the Italians. This was a city where divided memories were strongly held and felt – and where the very word 'liberation' is still debated today. As a contested zone Trieste and its environs was divided into national occupied zones, like Berlin and Vienna. Not surprisingly, very different versions of the past were carried forward throughout the post-war period in Trieste. In that city the legacy of the Second World War and the Cold War were fused – and it was a place where both conflicts overlapped.

When the Giro d'Italia tried to reach Trieste in 1946, the cyclists were attacked by pro-Yugoslavian communists in open country-side. Stones were thrown and there were reports of shots being fired. Trieste was under Allied control at the time, and disputed territory. Most of the riders refused to go on, but seventeen 'volunteers' were bundled into an American army truck and dropped off at the edge of town. The local Triestan rider Giordano Cottur then 'won' the truncated stage. His victory led to an orgy of patriotic rhetoric in the press, and a burst of bloodletting in town. One senior journalist wrote that 'the Giro d'Italia has done its duty. It has gone, once again, to seek out the Italians. It has gone out to say to the Italians that they should be united and love each other.' The reality was more brutal. In riots following the end of the race, people were killed. Italy's control over her own destiny was uncertain. Trieste's cycling fracas also sent out a clear message. One war was over, but another one had begun.

April and July 1948: Election and Revolution – Counting Votes, Weighing Votes

'God can see you in the secrecy of the election booth, but not Stalin.'

Election Slogan, Christian Democrats, 1948[40]

April 1948 marked the central battle of Italy's cold war. In December 1947 the Constituent Assembly was dissolved. Its job was done. The first proper general election after the creation of the constitution was then called. A date was set: 18 April 1948. It was a day that would see Italy's political system set in stone for the next forty-four years. The choice facing the Italian people was stark. On the one side stood the Christian Democrats, and the Vatican, on the other the 'Popular Front for Freedom, Peace and Work' – comprising the Communists and Socialists – who had formed a political and electoral alliance.

It was a tumultuous campaign. Appeals to the voters pitched the choice facing them in terms of life or death. The Christian Democrats told Italians that 'on the 18 April you can save or destroy your freedom ... the freedom to think and express your own ideas ... the freedom to profess the faith of your fathers'.[41] 'The choice,' they continued, 'is between Bolshevik totalitarianism, which is hidden under the mask of the so-called Popular "Front" and the range of sincerely democratic parties.' Christian Democratic propaganda also underlined its connections to the United States. Each side in this titanic electoral struggle was 'financed and armed clandestinely by its respective superpower sponsor'.[42]

Communist appeals also contained dire warnings. 'There is the threat,' wrote Communist Party leader Palmiro Togliatti, 'of a return to a reactionary regime and even the danger, recognised by everyone, of the rebirth of fascism.' Togliatti added that Italy would lose control over its own affairs if the Christian Democrats were to win, and would be involved in future wars. There were dark hints of a return to the (recent) past.[43] Scaremongering took the form of massive posters that were plastered on walls or paraded as banners through the streets. As the historian Rosario Forlenza recounts, 'Catholic visual propaganda depicted communists as skeletons, the personification of death, or as monstrous beasts – devils, bears, serpents and dragons – trampling on Italy's cenotaph or devouring (a metaphor for raping) young women.'[44]

The Cold War reached deep into the lives of every citizen and its ramifications were soon almost apocalyptic. Even the afterlife was affected. In December 1946 Pope Pio XII had warned that the choice facing Italians was 'with Christ or against Christ'. As the historian Robert Ventresca has put it, 'For Italian voters,

then, unlike voters in traditional democracies, the choice was not
between political parties or philosophies, but between heaven and
hell.'[45] More drastic measures and announcements were to follow.
A series of rulings was issued by the Church that 'excommunicated'
card-carrying Communists, and even those who simply voted for
the Communist Party. This was how one such edict began:

> The leaders of the Communists, although they sometimes pro-
> fess in words that they do not oppose religion, do in fact show
> themselves, both in their teaching and in their actions, to be
> the enemies of God, of the true religion and of the Church of
> Christ.[46]

Excommunication was not purely a symbolic matter. It precluded
christenings, confessions, religious marriages and religious funerals. These measures were not always applied to the letter by local
priests, but the threat remained. Communists and communist
sympathisers were destined for hell, not heaven. At a popular
level, there were dozens of reports of visions of the Madonna in
the weeks leading up to the election across Italy. Everywhere,
it seemed, there were 'weeping Madonnas, bleeding Madonnas,
luminous Madonnas who appeared to children, adults, old people. Only after the victorious election result did this Marian fever
diminish.'[47]

In the run-up to that decisive general election of 1948, the
Church went into overdrive. Three weeks before the vote, on
28 March 1948, the Pope made his traditional Easter address from
the balcony of the Vatican. He told the faithful that 'the great hour
of Christian conscience has sounded'. Italians had to choose.[48] It
was *us or them* – and the election was presented as a matter of
life or death, for those individuals who risked excommunication
by voting for the left, but also for the Church, religion itself, and
Western capitalism. 'Catholic propaganda treated the election
as nothing less than a battle between God or Satan, Christ or
Antichrist, civilisation or barbarism, liberty or slavery.'[49] In every
parish, priests railed against the Communists during mass. Local
Catholic organisations mobilised house by house.

Sport was also a weapon in the machinations of the Cold War. The great rivalry between cyclists Fausto Coppi and Gino Bartali took on powerful political and cultural overtones. Bartali's Catholicism was part of his public image. Pope Pius XII even mentioned Bartali by name from the balcony of St Peter's as the Tuscan rider became a (willing) participant in the battle against communism, campaigning for the Christian Democrats in 1948. Fausto Coppi was no communist, but he was often associated with the 'other side' in the Cold War. Italians were divided in every sphere of their public and private lives. The Popular Front had adopted a new symbol on the ballot paper. It was Garibaldi's head on a green star (representing work) with a red hat. Garibaldi signified Italy – the left was attempting to claim patriotism for itself – but also harked back to the Resistance, where communist partisans had often fought in 'Garibaldi brigades'.

The Church's extensive national networks of youth organisations and civic committees worked tirelessly to get the Christian Democratic vote out. The organiser of a network of Civic Committees, Luigi Gedda, issued a statement that underlined the importance of voting. 'Everyone must go to the ballot box ... Remember what I am going to tell you. The 18 April is the last chance for Catholicism in Italy.'[50] Election day was an astounding moment of political mobilisation. Over 92 per cent of Italians turned out to vote, a record for a Western democracy at the time. There were tales of elderly people being carried to the polls on the shoulders of others. People brought weapons in fear of the consequences of the results.[51] In Rome 'the sick from ... religious hospitals were taken to the polls by ambulance and compelled to vote "with the help of a nun"'.[52] Very few Italians failed to make it to the ballot box. Some, it was said, had voted at least twice.

It was a rout. A total of 12.7 million Italians opted for the Christian Democrats, who came close to an overall majority of the votes with 48.5 per cent. Meanwhile, the two left-wing parties received less support in their alliance than they had, separately, in 1946. Some 8.1 million voters backed the Popular Front (31 per cent), while 1.8 million (7 per cent) chose a Socialist Unity list that offered a left alternative while backing the West. The gap between first and second was impressive, some 3.6 million votes. It hadn't even been close. In some places there were high votes for the Popular Front – traditional left-wing areas and cities such as Ferrara, Bologna and Perugia. Central Italy remained largely 'red'. But right across Italy the real story was domination by the Christian Democrats. Some 73 per cent of voters chose the Christian Democrats in the Province of Bergamo, as did 61 per cent in the city of Brescia. Just 2 per cent of Italians made an explicit neo-fascist choice, while a mere 2.8 per cent opted for the Monarchist Party. Many in the Popular Front had been convinced that they would win. As the Communist Rossana Rossanda recalled, 'We were completely floored, bewildered.'[53] Lucio Magri later argued that 'Defeat was inevitable, but the Communists experienced it as a bitter surprise.'[54]

Translated into seats, this wave of votes made the Christian Democrats into the dominant force in post-war Italy. As the historian David Ellwood has written, '18 April inaugurated the era of perpetual Christian Democrat rule in Italy'.[55] The crushing defeat of the Popular Front led to the virtual exclusion of the 'reds' from the central echelons of power for the foreseeable future. Alcide De Gasperi and his party had a majority in Parliament, on their own. No allies were required, although this would never happen again; the national Christian Democratic vote peaked in 1948.

April 1948 also set in motion Italy's international alliances. Italy officially joined the North Atlantic Treaty Organisation (NATO) a year later, in April 1949. But these allegiances divided the country. The Communist position was one of immediate and trenchant opposition to NATO membership. In March 1949 party leader Palmiro Togliatti made this clear:

We say 'no' to the Atlantic Pact, 'no' because it is a pact of preparation for war. We say 'no' to ... a policy of hostility and aggression against the Soviet Union ... we say 'no' to the imperialist intrigues which you are plotting to the harm of the Italian people, their independence and their liberty; and we shall do everything in our power to unmask this policy of yours and make it a failure.[56]

In reality such a position was purely symbolic. As the histor-ian Silvio Pons has written, 'After the establishment of NATO and the final division of Germany in 1949, the task of the West European Communist parties was clearly limited to propaganda and domestic issues.'[57] The Cold War would be mainly fought out in the domestic realm.

1948 set up what has been called a 'blocked' system. A vast part of the Italian population was effectively excluded from gov-ernment, if not from all power, until the Cold War was over. But 1948 was also central for another reason, which had nothing to do with elections, or with normal political processes. The votes had been counted. But now power would be weighed up in a different way – on the streets.

July 1948: Italy at the Barricades[58]

Antonio Pallante was just twenty-four years old when he pur-chased a 'Hopkins' gun and five bullets and embarked on the long journey from Sicily to Rome in July 1948. He put on a dark pinstripe suit for the occasion. His mission was dangerous, and deadly. He had one thing in mind. He was going to Rome to assassinate Palmiro Togliatti, 'il migliore' (the best one), the formidable Communist Party leader who had spent most of the fascist period in exile in Moscow. Pallante would always claim that he had acted alone, and that he was convinced the Soviets were about to invade Italy. Yet, many others would become con-vinced that a plot had been hatched by neo-fascists to eliminate the Communist leader. A copy of Hitler's *Mein Kampf* was later found in Pallante's bag. His precise political views, however, were never particularly clear.

In Rome, Pallante merged with the crowds outside one of the side entrances to Parliament. Togliatti was on his way to the city's famous *Giolitti* ice-cream parlour, with his partner Nilde Iotti (he had left his wife, a 'scandal' that was an open secret in Italy at the time). Pallante walked up to them, and appeared to hesitate. But then he started firing. Togliatti was hit. Iotti cried out – 'murderer' – and Pallante was arrested. Togliatti was taken away to hospital covered in a blanket. One of the bullets had struck him in the head, but stopped against a bone, while another penetrated part of Togliatti's lung, and it was this that threatened his life. Iotti was told to distance herself from Togliatti, so as not to create a scandal, but she went to the hospital anyway. The judicial case against Pallante was quickly closed (he called Togliatti 'an enemy of Italy') and he spent a mere five years and five months in jail, thanks to yet another amnesty. Togliatti would recover and was later given the actual bullets as a strange memento, and they were then passed on to Iotti.

Revolution?

Almost immediately after the shooting, strikes and demonstrations exploded across Italy. As Mario Isenghi has written, 'proletarian Italy rose up angrily. The workers took control of the big factories, occupied squares and distributed guns from the partisan war'.[59] Workers downed tools and drivers abandoned their trams. Guns appeared on the streets. It felt like a revolution, and in some places local Communist leaders appeared to be egging on the crowds. Meanwhile, the government criticised the strikes as 'political' and 'ideological' and talked of the defence of democracy and the institutions of the state. Some blamed the assassination attempt on the climate of hatred that had been created in 1948 during the election campaign. As the Communist politician and intellectual, Concetto Marchesi, stated: 'behind that gun there were many written and spoken phrases, many whispered or silent desires, all the poison created by that journalism which was financed by our fascist democracy'.[60]

Italy's press agency, ANSA, had made the dramatic announcement at 12 p.m. on 14 July. Togliatti had been shot on the steps of Parliament, in broad daylight. National radio waited until the news at 1 p.m. the next day to repeat the story, but it quickly spread across the country. There were rumours that Togliatti was dead. The government met to discuss its tactics. Yet Mario Scelba, the formidable and much-feared Interior Minister, had already announced his decision – all demonstrations 'of any kind' were to be repressed. That same afternoon Italy's biggest trade union federation called a general strike (although strikes had started spontaneously in many areas). Workers were asked by unions to 'defend democracy'. *L'Unità* called for the removal of what they called a 'government of civil war' and published two special editions.

Two building workers were killed in Rome the same day, as the authorities followed Scelba's orders. In Turin the offices of the *La Stampa* newspaper were occupied and the paper failed to appear for the next two days. Meanwhile, in FIAT's huge Mirafiori factory in the same city Vittorio Valletta – the leading manager at the company – was held hostage by armed workers. It was later said that he was given permission to leave, but decided to stay in his office. Two further demonstrators were killed after a police charge in Naples, and another in Taranto. Barricades went up in Genoa, where two more demonstrators died. Genoa was briefly 'liberated' and a state of siege was declared. The army were sent in to quell the revolt.

On the ground it felt like a revolution. In the Tuscan port-factory-town of Piombino roadblocks were set up by armed workers and a 'citizens committee' took control of the town for a time as well as seizing the telephone system. Angry workers wrecked the party offices of the Christian Democrats, the Republican Party and the Liberal Party. Reinforcements were called in from surrounding areas to quash the uprising. In another and bigger Tuscan port-town – Livorno – which had deep-rooted subversive traditions – events were even more incendiary. Shots were fired on 14 July, and workers moved en masse to the centre of the city. A policeman was stabbed to death. He turned out to be a Communist Party member and a former partisan.[61] Close to Genoa, in Sestri Ponente, 'barricades went up in the night and the trams were soldered to their lines'.[62]

In Ferrara in northern Italy, another city with a strong left-wing and anti-fascist tradition (14 per cent of the entire population were Communist Party members), which had seen violent forms of fascism in the 1920s and 1930s, the response to the news was immediate. For Giancarlo Ziotti, an ex-partisan and Communist Party member who was in his early twenties in 1948, 'the attempt on Togliatti's life had an explosive impact'. Soon after noon there were spontaneous strikes in the countryside. Crowds gathered in the centre of the city. A series of connected demands came together – from frustration with the results of the 18 April general election, to a desire to remove fascist elements in the police force and the judiciary. Some called openly for revolution. Roadblocks were set up and then dismantled by the police, and armed workers arrested. Former partisans turned up in their uniforms and scarves – often with guns in their hands.

At 5 p.m. on 14 July, Togliatti woke up in Rome. He had been operated on by one of the top surgeons in Italy. Meanwhile, in Ferrara, the forces of law and order fired on the crowd, and in the air. Machines guns also appeared. There were numerous gunshot wounds amongst the demonstrators and bystanders. An electrician was shot in the eye. It was a miracle that nobody was killed. Bullet holes could be seen on the windows of the city hall.

In Siena, when the news came through of the assassination attempt, all factories closed and some fascists were beaten up. Only the employees of the ancient city bank, the Monte dei Paschi, refused to join in. After a demonstration outside the bank they too stopped work. The offices of the Christian Democrats were attacked. A big crowd formed on 15 July, and 'everyone waited for the speakers to give us the go ahead, or some more precise directions about the continuation of the struggle'.[63] But, instead, the speakers called on the demonstrators to disperse.

In the small mining town of Abbadia San Salvatore, in southern Tuscany, things went even further. At about 1 p.m. on 14 July a group of protestors forced the telegraph office to stop transmitting.[64] Ex-partisans met and decided that 'the comrades want to go all the way'. At 5 p.m. the telephone lines were also blocked. This effectively led to a breakdown of communications between northern and southern Italy. Shoot-outs took place with police and some were disarmed. Later, a policeman was shot dead and a carabinieri officer stabbed to death. Eventually, the revolt was put down. Some four hundred arrests were made and many of those arrested were beaten up. Numerous trials followed and hundreds of years of sentences were passed down.

Conservative opinion was alarmed. The Christian Democratic newspaper *L'Avvenire d'Italia* described the events in Ferrara as 'fifteen minutes of revolution' and added that 'provocations, destruction, injuries have just one name: Red Communism.' Once the revolt was over, as in Abbadia San Salvatore, mass arrests took place followed by quick trials. Over two hundred people were arrested or held in Ferrara and its province. Some of the revolts had also had a social edge to them. One of the places attacked in Ferrara was the hated local employment exchange. Around fifteen people were killed across Italy.

At the same time as many Italians were building barricades or occupying factories in 1948, another Italian was beating all-comers in France. Gino Bartali had won the Tour de France in 1938 and he rode magnificently in the mountains to destroy his rivals and win again in July 1948. His heroic sporting feats took place almost in parallel with the attempt on Togliatti's life and the uprisings that followed, back in Italy. In the popular imagination, and in many history books since, these two separate and unconnected events have since become intimately linked. Bartali was said to have 'saved Italy by pedalling'. He had 'distracted' the striking workers. There were even stories that the Prime Minister, De Gasperi, had phoned Bartali on 14 July and asked him for help. This whole tale is, of course, a myth, an invention, a piece of historical fiction. But its power as a story suited many of those connected to the events of 14 July. The Christian Democrats could point to the supposed role of their own Catholic hero – Bartali the 'pious one' – who had also campaigned for them in the April election. Meanwhile, the Communist leadership, who wanted to play down and forget the revolt of July, were happy to allow the Bartali story to take root. Bartali did not save Italy. The truth was much more uncomfortable.

Once the dust had settled, two versions of the events in Italy in July 1948 began to take shape. For the Christian Democrats (and the Church), there had been a pre-prepared revolutionary plan that had swung into action. This was the so-called 'plan K', which was ready and waiting for its 'hour x'. The cutting of the strategic telephone lines in Abbadia was cited as evidence for this 'plan'. Communists-strikers-demonstrators were depicted as anti-democratic and subversive. Meanwhile, the Communist Party itself tried to minimise what had happened (and rarely mentioned it afterwards). They denied there was any revolutionary plan, although many accused the party and its leaders of duplicity – or *Doppiezza*. The party, it was said, had an official line for public consumption and another set of tactics or dreams to be spread amongst the more radical members. Perhaps, more accurately, radical communists had been allowed to think that revolution was not off the agenda. This was a hard sell to the communist base after July 1948.

On the ground, the role of communist activists and others was ambiguous. Guns were everywhere. Often, Christian Democratic or *Uomo Qualunque* offices were attacked, as well as those of the neo-fascist Movimento Sociale Italiano. There were cases of police joining the demonstrators. In Rome the communist movement mobilised with great rapidity. The secretary of the Rome federation of the Communist Party was supposedly asked by the crowd to 'give us the sign'. Many were ready to carry out what they saw as being held over from April 1945: a social revolution. For some local leaders there was a temptation to wait and see how far the movement would spread. *L'Unità*, meanwhile, in an initial phase, had used incendiary language, calling for the government 'of civil war, disunity and hunger' to resign. The hard-line Communist politician Pietro Secchia later wrote that:

> the extensive nature of the general strike has shown us – more than hundreds of parliamentary speeches or inquests – that the elections of the 18 April were due to ballot irregularities, corruption and religious and political terrorism, and foreign intervention ... the general strike is the ultimate proof that the DC's majority which it snatched on the 18 April does not represent either the will of the Country, nor the vital forces of this nation.[65]

Not surprisingly, this kind of analysis was later used to argue that the Communists had simply not accepted their defeat at the ballot box in April. They weren't democrats at all, it was said. Secchia's was a class reading of the situation, linked to the power of the workers over the uncomfortable numbers that had emerged from the election. In Milan, at the height of the strikes, the Communist Party leader Giuseppe Alberganti spoke to a big crowd in the Piazza del Duomo and said something that was very similar: 'On the 18 April we counted the votes numerically. Now we will weigh things up: politically. This strike won't finish today, or tomorrow.'[66] When the strike did end, angry workers besieged Alberganti's house.

But the Communist leadership was divided. Togliatti himself was appalled when he woke up from his surgery to find out what was happening. He was always extremely sceptical about the possibility of revolution in Italy – either tactically or ideologically. The South, as the 1946 referendum had shown, would never come on board were such an event to take place. As a result, the order was given to bring things quickly to a close. It is also claimed that Togliatti whispered 'be calm, don't lose your heads' after being shot and before he lost consciousness (although this may well be a myth). The main trade union federation called off the general strike on 15 July, in the evening, but this order was largely ignored. For Isnenghi, it was the union leader Giuseppe di Vittorio – who had initially ordered a general strike on 14 July – who finally brought the situation under control.[67] But this was neither easy nor popular with many militants. On 16 July many factories remained closed.

Most workers drifted back. The state, meanwhile, acted with great speed to 'restore order'. By the end of August there had been around 7,000 arrests linked to the events of 14–16 July. Heavy prison sentences were handed down. The legacy of July 1948 was a bitter one. The trade unions split and these divisions survive to this day, with a Catholic federation (CISL) breaking away from the more left-influenced and Communist-led grouping of unions (CGIL). Defeat and disillusionment set in. It was a 'third' defeat (1945, April 1948 and now July 1948) and a hard one to bear. Never again would such insurrectionary activities cover such wide parts of the peninsula. That form of revolution was gone – forever.

Parishes, Priests and Catholic Culture

'Those imposing walls across the Tiber, the six-hundred-odd churches in Rome, the thousands of clergymen and nuns, and the millions of front-line militants in Catholic Action organisations are daily reminders that Rome is not one capital, but two. Joseph Stalin, who once derisively asked how many divisions the Pope commanded, never saw Saint Peter's Square on almost any Sunday morning.'

Joseph LaPalombara[68]

The Catholic Church was, and is, everywhere in Italy. Its range of institutions create a galaxy of networks that cover most areas of public and private life. There are more than 900 churches in Rome alone, and in the 1950s there was 'a clerical population of a quarter of a million' with '65,000 bishops and parish priests'.[69] But there are also thousands of 'oratories' across Italy, a mixture of Sunday and summer schools, playgrounds and youth clubs, which were usually physically attached to churches. There were also high-circulation newspapers and magazines, radio stations, sports clubs, bars, cultural bodies, publishing houses, banks, insurance and credit outlets.

The key in terms of local operations was the parish. Locally, parishes were the 'basis for Catholic hegemony' and (for years) the 'rural priest' was 'a kind of "organic" intellectual in an inter-class community which was linked to the local church'.[70] Parish priests were religious leaders (locally) but they were also much, much more than that. They acted as middlemen for work and marriage negotiations, and they often managed Church lands directly or indirectly.

Christian Democracy tapped into this extended local network to cement its power. Politics, as Mario Isnenghi argued, never acted 'autonomously, in itself' in rural Italy, 'but always through the mediation of the holy, the institution, the codes, the figures, the outlooks of traditional religion'.[71] Religious terms and concepts – salvation, triumph – were applied to concrete political events – elections – in post-war Italy. These were communities that, in some ways, attempted to remain immune to history. But there were times, such as with the Second World War, the Resistance and the Cold War, when history forced its way in. The post-war period was also one of intense social conflict – the last great strikes took place in the countryside – and they evoked bitter memories of the violent social conflict that had divided Italians in the period before fascism.

Catholic culture and its institutions were set up – as they had been for hundreds of years – in opposition to forces that it saw as undermining its values and a possible threat to its very existence. It is also important to see Catholic culture as mass culture.[72] 'Cultural production' was never simply handed down from above, but also produced and modified from below. The key values at the heart of this culture or cultures were 'the value of private property, the family and the subordinate position of women, the myth of the land, the acceptance of one's social station and the virtue of obedience, and the castigation of atheists, sinners and revolutionaries'.[73] For the historian Giovanni Levi, 'Catholicism is ... pervasive, part of our [Italian] character: it is intrinsic for us, in the air that we breathe; it is everywhere, but invisible.' Levi argues that this 'cohabitation' with Catholicism has led to a situation where 'the state is widely seen as extraneous, an institution which almost everyone has the right (almost a duty) to defraud'.[74] Politicians come and go, but the Church is always there: it takes a (very) long view.

After 1945, for the first time in the history of unified Italy, the Church was right at the centre of daily politics. Its men (and a few women) were in charge. This was a far cry from the early days of unification in the nineteenth century, when the Pope 'hid' in the Vatican and Italy's kings were excommunicated. It was also a happier time than under fascism, when the regime tried to create a new political religion that challenged the Church at a series of levels. Through the Christian Democrats, the Church now had a direct transmission belt into the mechanisms and resources of political power. The Italian state and nation was no longer an enemy, but an ally.

The decline (and demise) of the monarchy and the end of fascism left Italians with few leaders they could identify with. The Pope often filled this gap. As the historian John Pollard has written, 'The Roman Catholic Church with its network of 24,000 parishes throughout the peninsula was now the major surviving *national* Italian institution.'[75]

The White Whale: Christian Democrats

In post-war Italy, Christian Democratic leaders and functionaries became near-permanent fixtures in what became known as *il palazzo* – the structures of authority within the Italian state. After 1948, the 'white whale' – as the Christian Democratic Party was known – developed into a gargantuan organisation with powerful factions, alongside numerous local bases and party bosses. 'White' because the Catholic movements were associated with the colour white as opposed to red, 'whale' because it was such an enormous structure. Given its firm grip on power, especially after April 1948, political disputes at a national level were often fought out within the Christian Democratic Party itself, which became a state within a state.

Christian Democratic politics covered an extensive range of strategic positions and power bases. Much of the hold of the party on power was based around the distribution of resources in exchange – explicitly or otherwise – for votes. This was a particularly strong connection in the south of Italy. To cite the historian John Pollard, 'From 1953 onwards, and possibly earlier, the Christian Democratic Party in the south began to metamorphose into a largely clientelistic party, and one also increasingly penetrated by organised crime: the Mafia in Sicily, the 'Ndrangheta in Calabria and the Camorra in Naples.'[76]

The Christian Democrats quickly extended their tentacles into all areas of the state – such as the media and the judicial system – and across large parts of the private sector. The party was backed and part-funded by the United States (through the Marshall Plan and other channels), it had an inter-class appeal beyond that strictly linked to religion, and it used the state and the Church to build networks linked to resources (jobs, welfare, housing) and their distribution, which reinforced its own networks of control. Christian Democratic ideology preached social peace and 'order'.[77] This was a national party in the true sense of the word, but with strong local roots. It was not tied to any specific ideology (beyond anti-communism) and moved with the times. The party was willing and able to pass reforms, build houses and roads, and create a welfare state for its voters.

Catholic umbrella organisations also had success amongst the working class – from the Christian Workers' Association (ACLI) to the extensive 'white' (and therefore non-communist) union federation, which split from the CGIL (a large federation formed in 1944) in 1948 and took the name CISL in 1950. The Christian Democratic base ranged from landowners (big and small) in the South to small businessmen in the North, and from the working class to the peasantry to the middle classes employed by the state as clerks, postal workers and teachers, right up to big business leaders and the rich.

There were 'white' trade unions, cooperatives, pressure groups and then the party itself. It was a social, cultural and political galaxy, a world of organisations and influence that moved up and down the scale. Gatekeepers and mediators oversaw the distribution of funds, jobs and contracts – in exchange for votes and support. Without political intervention it was often impossible to make progress in any sphere. Politicians exercised their power in all walks of life, not just in Parliament or in town halls.

This was also a party that could absorb variations in policy and outlook – acting as a kind of open house to those from the left and the right of the spectrum. The Christian Democrats never experienced a major split during the Cold War, containing within its boundaries many factions and complicated party structures, personal and policy-based positions. With a divided left, the party was guaranteed electoral victory. The Christian Democrats were never, or never simply, the 'party of the Italian ruling class'. The party was much more than that, and this 'much more' explains its power and longevity. Alcide De Gasperi saw it as a hegemonic party that would bring together all Catholics, and when the party grew alongside its numerous sub-organisations it connected politics, people and power.

The Christian Democrats would have liked to govern forever, and without the need for allies, but the crushing victory in the 1948 election was not repeated. After the next election in 1953, coalition government became the norm. In the run-up to that campaign, the Christian Democrats tried to further solidify their power. They introduced a proposal for electoral reform that was quickly attacked as a 'swindle law' (*legge truffa*). The plan was to award extra seats to parties with the most votes in order to – it was argued – create political 'stability'. For many this seemed a little too reminiscent of fascism (which had passed a similar law in 1923) and appeared to be a way of entrenching Christian Democratic control. A powerful campaign grew against the reform inside and outside Parliament, and the speed with which it was passed in the upper house caused consternation. Yet in 1953 the votes for the Christian Democrats narrowly failed to activate the extra seats' clause. In July 1954 the 'swindle law' was struck off the statute books. The party's attempt to govern alone had been defeated. A new phase of coalition politics began.

Corridors of Power

Politics in democratic Italy was governed by a set of written rules – the constitution, ordinary laws, political structures – but often marked by forms of behaviour that had far deeper anthropological roots. Sometimes unwritten rules were even written down. This was true, for example, of the infamous *Cencelli Manual*. Coalition governments were a challenge to put together. Smaller parties all wanted a little bit of power, which unlocked access to significant quantities of resources – jobs, money, public projects. They would often complain about fairness and proportions. An extra Junior Minister was a glittering prize worth fighting over, so a formula was needed to resolve ongoing conflicts. This led to the creation of the so-called *Cencelli Manual* in the 1950s, a mathematical formula that distributed ministerial posts between parties depending on votes and seats. This formula was named after the person who had drawn it up – Massimiliano Cencelli – a minor Christian Democratic functionary and mediator from the 1950s onwards.

The formula was not perfect, but it worked. Somebody would do the calculations once agreements had been made, and jobs would be handed out accordingly. Of course, this was never an exact science. Some ministries were more important than others – not simply because of resources but due to political weight. The Christian Democrats kept a tight grip on the Defence Ministry and the Interior Ministry. Under-secretary numbers rose and fell with the political times. In periods of tension and instability they tended to increase.

Clientelism, the use of patronage and nepotism, were not always against the law. Rules were often applied to serve systems of exchange, or favour relatives, friends, associates and party supporters. It was difficult to prove that somebody had been 'recommended' for a post. Documentation was scrupulously collected and compiled, and interviews were held as outlined in the rules and regulations. But the system was usually fixed. Miraculously, the 'right' candidate would always win, and everyone knew that this would happen. Moreover, given that the entire system worked in this way, there was no real outrage over many decisions. This was how things were, and how they had always been. A collective shrugging of shoulders was often the only real response.

There were, of course, also straightforward cases of corruption within and outside of the political system. Bribes were paid to parties and politicians by businesses, the Mafia and others. These bribes were often imposed upon the payees, but this was not always the case. Sometimes this money – these 'little envelopes' as Italians call them – simply oiled the wheels, but on other occasions they altered structures and even the system itself. Kickbacks led to personal wealth, but also reinforced party organisations and power. Politics was expensive. Campaigns required resources, and in a system of exchange the voters had to be 'paid back' for their support.

Frequent corruption scandals marked political and public life during the Republic, and most of these scandals were linked to payments made to politicians to procure political favours or contracts. But not every act of corruption was the same. Nor was everyone corrupt. Some took bribes for their parties, others merely enriched themselves. Some did both. A few took nothing. Several did deals with the Mafia, and a brave minority actively took on organised crime. Some died at the Mafia's hands, although some of those had done deals with them in the past. Certain politicians built up a reputation for honesty, so much so that they were called 'honest', as with Benigno Zaccagnini, a leading Christian Democratic figure from the 1950s onwards, who was often referred to as 'honest Zac'. As the Christian Democrats put down deep roots across Italy, their rival political force, the Communist Party, was also preparing for the long haul. These two great mass parties would face off against each other for most of the post-war period. It was a titanic struggle, which covered not just the political sphere, but also culture, society and influence, and moulded local and national identities.

Reds: Communists and the Communist Party in Italy after 1948

April and July 1948 were a terrible double defeat for the Communist Party and its members. Both the revolution and hopes of national power had been quashed. Nationally, the Partito Comunista Italiano or PCI settled into its role as a powerful opposition and cultural force. Locally, a reformist model imposed itself, with innovative programmes of institutional change and popular participation. Revolution was rarely mentioned again. The Communist Party, slowly, became part of the system.

At local government level, however, Communists were allowed to govern. In some areas – above all in the 'red' zones of central

Italy, where the Popular Front had sometimes won a majority of the votes – they imposed their own policies built on radical reformism. The so-called 'Emilian model' of radical reform – experimented with in cities like Bologna and Reggio Emilia – was later adopted by the party as a whole. These council administrations provided examples of real, practical and creative change. Communists could point to the world-famous nursery schools of Reggio Emilia, the innovative housing projects of Bologna, and the cultural networks of the 'Houses of the People', as well as annual cultural festivals run by volunteers, as examples of the building of socialist places within a capitalist society. These model institutions attracted attention around the world. The 'Italian road to socialism' had followers in the United Kingdom and many other countries, and 'Eurocommunism' was, for a time, extremely fashionable. It envisaged a kind of long march through the institutions – a practical and realisable collection of structural changes that could be achieved without a violent revolution. Technical and political knowledge and commitment were placed at the service of the community. In some parts of Italy, it seemed, there was a kind of 'really existing socialism'. A new generation of Communists, elected in the post-war period, took to their task with gusto and a sense of sacrifice.

Cult of Personality

Palmiro Togliatti's first public appearance after the July 1948 assassination attempt was at the Foro Italico (a place dominated by fascist architecture) in Rome in September of that year. According to his biographer, Aldo Agosti, some 500,000 people were there to hear his speech that day.[78] Carlo Lizzani, a film director close to the party, made a hagiographic documentary about the event called *Togliatti is Back*. Togliatti was not just a strong, popular leader, he was also, now, a kind of living martyr. For Agosti, this was a key episode in the history of the PCI and a moment when 'a naive and spontaneous "cult" of Togliatti would emerge'.[79] Others have argued, however, that this cult was carefully constructed. The journalist Giorgio Bocca noted the way in which the party later organised the celebrations for Togliatti's 60th birthday (in 1953) with 'a special commission for the festivities, which brought out a volume of his speeches, an illustrated biography with 134 pages of photos, as well as collections of essays and writings'.[80] Much of Togliatti's life was normal, ordinary, boring even, such as his mundane summers in the mountains of the Aosta Valley, which he much preferred to the Soviet Union. But there were also aspects, such as the aftermath of the 1948 shooting, which raised him to heroic status.

The 'Big Moustache' is Coming: Stalin, the Soviet Union and Italian Communism

In 1949 Togliatti held a meeting with Stalin for the first time in over five years. There was little doubt as to which side Italian Communists were on in the Cold War, despite the devastating result in April 1948. Stalinism in Italy was both popular and imposed from above. The bond with the Soviet Union was particularly strong after 1945, when memories of war were at their height. It wasn't just the Communists who were affected by the immense sacrifice of the conflict in the USSR. There was widespread admiration for the role played by the Soviet people – and Stalin 'the big moustache' as their leader – in the Second World War. Stalin himself was often revered by party members and the 'Soviet Model' of real socialism was an inspiration to many. The Italian Communist Party's relationship with the USSR and the Eastern Bloc, and 'actually existing communism' more generally, was organic and constant. Money (often referred to as 'Moscow Gold') flowed from the Soviet Union into the Italian Communist Party's coffers, illegally, throughout the Cold War.

After Stalin's death in March 1953, *L'Unità* (the PCI's daily newspaper) echoed this powerful attachment to his cult of personality with a banner headline: 'The Man who has Done the Most for the Liberation of the Human Race is Dead'. The rhetoric continued in official statements, which linked Togliatti and Stalin:

The Italian Communists gather together, with their party, their central committee and with comrade Palmiro Togliatti, the man who, in following Stalin, has done more than anyone else for the national and social liberation of our country. We call on all Italians to unite themselves around their flag, symbol of humanity's highest ideals, to which Stalin has dedicated all of his prodigious and legendary existence. Eternal Glory to Giuseppe Stalin![81]

There was more to come. As the anthropologist David Kertzer has written: 'The PCI sent its entire leadership to the funeral ceremonies in Moscow: at the insistence of the PCI, the Italian parliament adjourned for a day in deference to the death.'[82] Little 'saint-cards' were printed for party members to carry, with a semi-religious inscription: 'Eternal Glory to Stalin – friend, teacher, a guide for all peoples'. The PCI magazine *Rinascita* described Stalin as a 'genius'. But this cult was not simply imposed from above. There was genuine grief. The historian Paolo Spriano remembered that the 'workers [were] crying'.[83] The journalist Giorgio Bocca – never a communist – later wrote that on hearing the news of the death of Stalin 'the pain felt by the Italian proletariat was deep and sincere'.[84]

This Stalinist hyperbole did not just come from the Communists. Sandro Pertini, Socialist and future President of Italy, made a speech in Parliament in 1953 that was full of praise for Stalin:

He is a giant of history and there will be no end to his memory. We are overwhelmed by this death and the emptiness it creates for his people and the whole of humanity. Gentlemen, if you can see beyond your own political hostility, as I am doing in this moment, you will have to admit that the life of this man has coincided for the last thirty years with that of all humanity.[85]

PCI leaders and many militants were frequent visitors to the Soviet Union and other Eastern Bloc countries. They also holidayed there. Togliatti, for example, stayed for two months in Moscow in 1951. He would later die in Yalta on the Black Sea (again, on holiday, in 1964). Enrico Berlinguer, PCI leader from 1972 to 1984, also visited often.

Channels between the PCI and the Communist bloc helped the party to 'spirit away' those who were in danger of being convicted of crimes in Italy. In this way, Communist exiles sometimes ended up in Czechoslovakia where they often worked for a propagandist radio station transmitting to Italy. The most famous personality amongst this community was a man called Franco Moranino, who had been a partisan leader, a member of the Constituent Assembly, a minor minister in government and a PCI deputy. In 1956 Moranino was convicted of ordering the executions of five presumed spies and two of their partners/wives during the war, and given a life sentence. His sentence was reduced in 1958, but he did not return to Italy until 1965, when he was given a presidential pardon. In 1968 he was re-elected to the Senate. Others from this exiled community lived out their lives abroad, becoming what one writer called 'ex-men'.[86]

In cultural and political terms, Italian communism borrowed frequently from the Soviet model and Soviet or Socialist Realist style. Soviet art, sport, culture and politics were all praised in PCI publications and by its leaders. For example, in September 1959, L'Unità carried a banner headline, 'A Soviet Rocket has Reached the Moon', and in April 1961 the headline was 'A Soviet Man has Conquered Space'.

The PCI was not above using Stalinist 'methods', domestically. Censorship and character assassination were often employed to ignore or lambast its supposed enemies. Togliatti would intervene personally if the subject matter was important to him and the party, as with the anti-communist collection of essays The God that Failed, which Togliatti reviewed with the disparaging title 'The Six who Failed'. He accused the six authors of falling into 'a corrupt and degenerate abyss, which has the cheek to present itself with a refined mask of intellectualism'.[87] The absorbing magazine Il Politecnico (1945–7) was effectively closed by the party because of its creative and open approach to culture. Nonetheless, the PCI was also a semi-democratic party in terms of its outlook and those who worked within its orbit. Openings were made towards a changing world. The party grappled with modernity and Americanisation, but it did not reject these trends altogether.

There were occasional signs of dissent over the Stalinist line in the party. In January 1951 two Communist deputies, Aldo Cucchi and Valdo Magnani, left the PCI and attempted to set up a new movement. They supported an alternative to Stalin, along the lines of that supposedly experimented with in Tito's Yugoslavia. Magnani had also fought as a partisan with Tito during the war, and was a powerful figure in one of the party's heartlands: Reggio Emilia. The deputies' resignation was given wide coverage in the press, but the Communist Party leadership was dismissive. Togliatti wrote that 'even a pedigree race horse has two or three fleas in its mane'. The party also described them as 'traitors'. This reaction seemed to prove Cucchi's point about the lack of internal party democracy and discussion. As he wrote in 1951, 'the Party leadership has shown that it is opposed to freedom and democracy within the party ... it believes social change will be brought about through foreign bayonets'.[88]

Powerful personality cults were built up around certain leaders and martyrs – most notably Togliatti himself (especially, as we have seen, after the failed assassination attempt in 1948), but also the Marxist theorist and founder of *L'Unità*, Antonio Gramsci (despite his own troubled relationship with Stalin and Stalinism, which was largely covered up or censored by the party). Gramsci's imprisonment under fascism and premature death in 1937 made him into a central martyr figure. Big black and white photos of the two men would often appear behind speakers at mass rallies, and numerous streets and piazzas were named after Togliatti or Gramsci. Togliatti kept tight control over the way in which Gramsci and his work was published and interpreted in Italy. A cult of personality around Togliatti was also developed in the USSR itself. After his death, a town in the Soviet Union was renamed as *Togliattigrad* and Togliatti's face also appeared on a Soviet stamp.[89]

Following Orders?

Could the PCI leadership make its own decisions on policy? Or was it simply 'following orders' from the Soviet Union? Was there an 'Italian road to socialism' – with the implication that Italian Communists enjoyed considerable independence from Moscow? The celebrated British historian and communist Eric Hobsbawm published a small (but influential) interview-book in 1977 with that very title.[90] In this vision of the PCI, the party elaborated its own democratic tactics – using Gramsci and others – which were reformist, not revolutionary, and very much part of the European social democratic tradition. Some have argued that 'inside Italy ... they [the Communists] had always determined their own strategy and tactics'.[91]

But others have painted a more repressive picture, with orders being handed down that had to be followed. This version of history sees the PCI as a puppet of Moscow. PCI foreign policy was strongly conditioned by Soviet needs in the 1940s and 1950s. Domestic policy was more flexible. In any case the USSR was not interested in a communist revolution in Italy. Moderation served its own ends. Togliatti made it clear, many times, that he didn't believe a Bolshevik model of revolutionary change was possible (or desirable) in Italy. As he wrote in *Rinascita*, a party magazine, using his pseudonym 'Roderigo di Castiglia', in 1950: 'Who really believes that by taking power like the Russian workers did in 1917 we will create paradise?'[92]

Communist identification with the Soviet Union effectively excluded the party from a role in Italian national government from 1947 right up to the 1990s. As Silvio Pons has argued, 'Despite the mass character and social base of the PCI, it gained only a peripheral role in Italian politics during the early Cold War and after ... the policies of Stalin and Togliatti from 1944 to 1948 defined the limits of Communist activity for decades to come.'[93]

Yet PCI policy remained theoretically in favour of an entirely new kind of society for much of the post-war period. For example, the party statutes in the late 1960s read as follows:

The Italian Communist Party is the vanguard political organisation of the working class and of all workers, which – within
the spirit of the Resistance and of proletarian internationalism
and the reality of the class struggle – fights for the independence and freedom of the Country, for the construction of a
democratic and progressive regime, for the abolition of man's
exploitation of man, for the freedom and appreciation of human
personality, for peace among peoples: for socialism.[94]

In practice, especially after 1948, the PCI was a reformist party,
which worked within the system. The revolution – any idea of an
eventual socialist society – was put on the backburner, perhaps
forever, although many members still looked east for an alternative model of the world.

There were times when the PCI leadership spoke the language
of class war. When 500 workers demonstrated outside their factory against job losses in Modena in January 1950, the police
opened fire. Two hundred shots were fired. After the dust had
cleared, six workers lay dead. Togliatti's speech to the workers of
Modena during the funerals that followed the shootings was an
angry one:

> Who condemned you to death? Who killed you? A prefect,
> an irresponsible and wicked police chief? A cynical interior
> minister? A Prime Minister who boasts – sadly – about having
> destroyed the unity of the nation which had been formed dur-
> ing the glorious struggle against the foreign invader.[95]

Togliatti later 'adopted' the sister of one of the workers killed in
Modena, who came to study in Rome, although she kept in close
contact with her own family in Modena.

Togliatti is painted at times as a defender of democracy, at others as a supporter – or even an agent – of dictatorship. He was an
anti-fascist from the 1920s, a Stalinist in Moscow in the 1930s, and
then an Italian Communist in the West after 1944. But Togliatti
was not the entire party. Communism in Italy after 1945 was a
mass movement that reached into every corner of Italian society.

For the historian Paul Ginsborg 'The history of the PCI as a mass party ... provided a crucial link between major sections of the working class and modern politics, it taught a vision of politics based on self-sacrifice, honesty, social equity and efficiency ... it demanded respect for the Constitution and the rule of law.'[96]

A Mass Party

The figures for membership of the PCI are striking. The party had around two million members after 1945 and a large part of the 1950s. In 1954 the membership reached an official peak of 2,145,327.[97] As a reflection of this mass nature of the party, the Communist organisational apparatus was far-reaching. There were full-time party workers all over Italy, and the daily newspaper *L'Unità* ('Founded by Antonio Gramsci') had offices in most major cities and even in minor ones, as well as foreign and sports correspondents. Regular PCI publications included weekly and monthly magazines, and specialist propaganda outlets and book clubs. There were organisations for pensioners and young people and sporting activities, as well as a large women's group, a big youth wing, extensive groups of former partisans (the ANPI) and an extensive trade union federation (the CGIL) 'within the orbit' of the PCI.

Militants lived and died a communist life. Funerals were often 'red', accompanied by flags and the singing of the *Internazionale* and/or *Bandiera rossa*, although the relationship with Catholic rituals was ambiguous and often intertwined with daily life. David Kertzer has argued that 'The Party has attempted to create its own system of sacred symbols, serving to bind together the Communist community and attract outsiders to the Communist world.'[98]

Ordinary communist culture and practice was expressed through the *Feste de l'Unità*, which were held across Italy, usually in the summer (and amongst emigrant communities across the world). These events were run by volunteers complete with aprons with party symbols, and included restaurants and bars, dance floors (usually for *ballo liscio* – uncostumed ballroom dancing – by couples), a few political meetings and stalls of various kinds. These festivals were popular and fun, drawing on local traditions of the village fete. Communists also created networks of 'people's houses' – bars and meeting places for sympathisers to hang out in. Many of these had been eliminated by fascism, but were reopened in the post-war period. Some have argued that it was through these festivals that the Communist Party could 'successfully challenge the traditional supremacy of the Church' in terms of 'community rites', although the Church 'retained control over the traditional rites of passage, i.e., those celebrating the change of status of a person, such as baptisms, weddings, funerals, and holy communions'.[99]

May Day was a big workers' holiday, as was 25 April. Communists turned out on Liberation Day (and other anniversaries), in force, to remember their dead from the past (especially those killed under fascism) and from the post-war period. Resistance martyrs and history were central to the legitimacy of the party after 1945. But there were also communist martyrs under Italian democracy, such as the five communists – four workers and a shepherd (Lauro Farioli, Ovidio Franchi, Emilio Reverberi, Marino Serri and Afro Tondelli) – shot dead by police and *carabinieri* in Reggio Emilia in July 1960. Celebrations of martyrs (from the Resistance and the post-war period) were ritualistic and emotional and often locally based – with the laying of wreaths at small plaques.[100] But there were also a series of much bigger and more spectacular set-piece events.

Legacies of War: Trieste

Cold War, post-war and post-fascist tensions continued to pattern life on Italy's borders. As a contested zone, Trieste and its environs had been divided into occupied zones under different powers, such as Berlin and Vienna. There were moments of high tension on the border, especially in October–November 1953, when Tito upped the ante, and threatened to 'invade' from Yugoslavia. Meanwhile, Italians demonstrated in Trieste itself. On 5 November 1953 shots were fired (in the main by Italian police under the command of the British army) at a nationalist gathering in the city, killing two people and injuring forty, followed by clashes that resulted in a further four deaths.

In the end, Tito accepted a compromise, and borders were (provisionally) fixed. Trieste came back under Italian sovereignty. Agreement was finally reached on 5 October 1954 in London and, although some posturing followed, this accord would hold and was later confirmed by further talks in 1975. Trieste was proclaimed a 'free port'. The Allied troops, who had presided over this delicate area of competing claims and ideologies for nearly ten years, finally went home. For Trieste, the war was over, at last, more than thirteen years after Mussolini's declaration of war in 1940. An enormous and joyous demonstration followed, with crowds packing the beautiful and enormous Piazza Unità d'Italia, which faces straight onto the sea. Successive governments pumped funds into Trieste for political reasons, although the city's strategic and economic importance faded quite quickly. New flashpoints, however, soon emerged in the ongoing Cold War.

1956: The Secret Speech and Hungary

It was only with changing events in the East itself that the PCI's monolithic approach to the Soviet Union began to change. The year 1956 was a turning point, with the leaking of Nikita Khruschev's 'secret speech' denouncing Stalin's crimes. The *New York Times* published the text of the speech on 4 June, and this led to a long discussion within the Italian Communist Party and across society about the relationship with the USSR. Dramatic events in Hungary in the same year sent further shock waves through the communist world.

The Italian Communist Party's first reaction to the events in Hungary, and the brutal suppression of a popular revolt by Soviet forces, was an orthodox defence of the Soviet Union. *L'Unità* wrote that 'we must choose either to defend the socialist revolution, or the ... counter-revolution supported by the fascist and reactionary Hungary of the past'. However, this was not the opinion of everyone by any means, and not even of all those within the party.

Open dissent soon began to dent the surface of conformity. In October 1956 a group of influential communist intellectuals wrote a celebrated collective letter to the party's Central Committee. It later became known as the 'Letter of the 101'. This group included writers and artists such as the academic Alberto Asor Rosa, the film-maker Elio Petri, and historians Paolo Spriano (the official historian of the PCI) and Luciano Cafagna. After collecting signatures in Rome, the letter was taken along to the offices of *L'Unità*. The authors asked for it to be published and called for a debate within the party over Hungary. This request was refused. One of the PCI's more hard-line leaders – Giancarlo Pajetta – told the letter-writers that they were 'being unrealistic'. 'The world,' he said, 'is divided into two blocks.'[101] At that point the authors of the so-called 'Manifesto' went to the national press agency. The letter soon became big news. Those who had signed the document were accused of betrayal, and some backed down immediately.

There were also signs of strong dissent in the trade union movement. The big CGIL federation, always close to the Communists, issued a powerful statement on 26 October, which made clear the position of its charismatic leader Giuseppe Di Vittorio: 'The CGIL Secretary, in the face of the situation in Hungary ... notes that these sad events represent an historical judgement concerning anti-democratic governmental methods and political leadership which creates a gap between leaders and the popular masses.'[102] A violent debate broke out within the party and Di Vittorio was later forced to partly and publicly withdraw his criticisms of the Soviets. Togliatti was clear-cut: 'How can we express solidarity with those who are shooting at us?'[103] The official party line was conformist and used Stalinist language: 'Italian Communists ... are unhappy with ... the fact that the Hungarian government has not been able to fight off this counter-revolutionary attack by using its own means and has had to ask for Soviet help.'[104]

Official figures showed that some 200,000 members left the PCI in 1956–7 (the real number was probably much higher). Right across Italy there were fiery meetings, contrasting statements and

angry debates. Much of this was suppressed. Togliatti kept hold of
the party, and maintained a pro-Soviet line. Nonetheless, the seeds
had been planted for a future break with Moscow – much further
down the line. Some left to join the Socialists, others became independent leftists, while a number would later rejoin the party. A few
were given space to express dissident views but this usually cost
them positions of power. Many of those who had abandoned the
party became part of a growing 'new left', and many would turn
up in the movements of the 1960s. Others would later move to the
right. Some of those who signed the Manifesto of the 101 became
leading anti-communist intellectuals, such as the historian Renzo
De Felice.

But there were also intellectuals in the PCI loyal to the Soviet
Union. Concetto Marchesi, for example, a retired professor from
Padua University and leading party member, complained about
the 'secret speech' and the way in which 'one of the great builders
of the USSR [Stalin] has been destroyed ... Tiberius, one of the
greatest ... Emperors of Rome had an implacable critic in Cornelio
Tacito. Stalin was not so lucky. He has had Nikita Khrushchev
as his critic. Capitalism has never ceased to hate these socialist
regimes, but did we really need to add our curse to this chorus, as
a way of curing our own ills. More can be done with the work of
the living than in the condemnation of the dead.'[105]

It was a traumatic time for the PCI. Years later, the communist
intellectual Rossana Rossanda remembered the ordeal of 1956.
'Things,' she wrote 'were never the same in the party after that ...
My hair turned grey then – it's true, it really does happen. I was
thirty-two years old.'[106] Behind the scenes, Togliatti was worried.
He wrote in a cable to Moscow that 'events in Hungary have
created a difficult situation inside the Italian labour movement,
and in our party'. He pointed out that the distance between the
Communists and Socialists had widened considerably, and that
there was a challenge to his leadership.[107]

Socialist Party adherence to the Soviet model was deeply
affected by the dramatic events of 1956. Hungary proved to be the
spark for the Socialists to break with the PCI and Stalinism at the
same time. This break was not a complete one – many Socialists

remained wedded to the idea of the USSR as an alternative to capitalism. Memories were still fresh of the disastrous divisions on the left that had helped facilitate the rise of fascism. There were some within the PSI who were dubbed 'tankies', due to their enthusiasm for Soviet tanks during the Hungarian Revolution.

But party leader Pietro Nenni, their most charismatic postwar politician, condemned the Soviet invasion of Hungary in November 1956. He also returned his prestigious 'International Stalin Prize for Strengthening Peace Among Peoples' that he had been awarded in 1951, and which he had gone to collect personally in Moscow (when he had met Stalin). This was the beginning of the end of his party's suffocating coalition with the Communists, which had done them so much electoral damage in April 1948. The Socialist newspaper *Avanti!* argued that the 'Communist Hungarian leadership has lost the faith of the workers and the people and it is under the illusion that it can keep power through tanks.'[108] The lines of the Cold War, within Italy, had been redrawn. A 'third way' now appeared a possibility. This was a crucial moment in the shift towards a reformist centre-left coalition, in the early 1960s, between the Christian Democrats and the PSI. This political configuration would be known as 'the centre-left'.

Heart of Europe: Altiero Spinelli, Italy and European Integration

Europe had been at war twice in living memory, and Italy had been a battlefield for both of those wars. Coming out of the conflict, there were many who looked towards former allies and enemies to unite to prevent future war. It was therefore not surprising that Italy was at the very centre of plans for European integration. A crucial role in this entire process was played by a man called Altiero Spinelli, who would go on to co-write one of the central documents from the early period of the European project. After growing up in South America (the son of a diplomat), Spinelli studied law in Rome and – in the 1920s – moved up the ranks of the Communist movement as fascism took hold. Arrested in

1927 (just nineteen years old at the time), he spent the next sixteen years in jail and internal exile.

The small island of Ventotene off the western coast of Italy on the border between Lazio and Campania played host to one of the largest fascist confinement centres, and many anti-fascists were held there. Ventotene developed into a 'school of anti-fascism' for those inside, with exchanges of ideas and experiences within confinement.[109] Spinelli was one of the internees held there. It was on that island that Spinelli penned the celebrated *Ventotene Manifesto* along with fellow intellectual and anti-fascist Ernesto Rossi. This document also went under the title *A Draft Manifesto: For a Free and United Europe*. The 'manifesto' was scrawled on cigarette papers and smuggled out of Ventotene, and was to prove an essential text and reference point in the move towards European union in the post-war period.

For Spinelli and Rossi, 'A free and united Europe' was 'the necessary premise to the strengthening of modern civilization, for which the totalitarian era represented a standstill'. Their vision, at the time, was a socialist one, although of course this would not be the ideology at the heart of the nascent European Economic Community. Spinelli and Rossi argued for 'the creation of a solid international State'. One of the main aims of this 'international state' would be the avoidance of war.

As soon as they were released from the camps, with the fall of Mussolini in July 1943, Spinelli, Rossi and others set up a European Federalist Movement. This organisation was a minor player in post-war Italy compared to other mass parties (the Socialists, Communists and Christian Democrats), but its intellectual output was highly influential. Spinelli later became a key figure in the creation of various European institutions (often as a critic), both from the outside and the inside. It has been argued that he was 'the most important supporter of the European ideal in Italy in the post-war period'.[110] Others have gone even further, claiming that 'together with [Jean] Monnet he [Spinelli] was probably the single person with the largest influence on the European integration process'.[111]

With figures like Spinelli, and the contradictory outcome of the war (as neither clear victor nor loser), Italy developed into a core country in the processes that led to European integration. She was one of six countries to set up the nascent European Economic Community in the 1950s. Italy's Senate approved the country's membership of the Iron and Steel federation in March 1952, and the Lower House did the same in June of that year. Italy was a significant site for discussions over the future of Europe. Negotiations were held in Messina in Sicily in 1955 and Venice in 1956, and the celebrated final founding Treaty of the EEC was signed in Rome in 1957 – the Treaty of Rome.[112] In the early years of European integration, economic growth helped to keep 'Europe' popular, although most people were relatively unaware of the actual workings of the European Community and Commission. The European project remained almost entirely uncontroversial within Italy for decades. Links with Europe patterned Italy's understanding of the world and its international role as she stood on the brink of a boom that would transform every aspect of her social, economic and cultural life.

2

Takeoff: Italy in the Boom Years

'A country of 50 million people is undergoing the deepest cultural change in its history – which is coinciding with its first real unification.'

Pier Paolo Pasolini[1]

'The DNA of a nation changed, the geography of minds, mentalities, lifestyles, values. But, deep down, did it really change?'

Simonetta Fiori[2]

It was called an 'economic miracle', but others referred to it as *il Boom*. Italy was still a relatively poor country as the 1950s began, but by the end of that decade a 'great transformation' was in full swing. Soon Italy would be unrecognisable. Lives were uprooted on a vast scale. Emigration of Italians abroad, to find work, continued, but the most important population movements were internal, towards the northern industrial cities. Milan's population increased by a quarter in the 1950s, and Turin's by an incredible 42 per cent. The South and the countryside in general, meanwhile, haemorrhaged people. A total of 1.7 million left the South in the same decade. And this all seemed to happen suddenly, unexpectedly, and with extraordinary speed. This wasn't a Gattopardian moment – as in the famous motto from Giuseppe Tomasi di Lampedusa's novel, *Il Gattopardo* (*The Leopard*) – about 'things changing, so that things could remain the same'. Nothing *would* ever be the same again. Italy was on fast forward.

Il Boom affected every aspect of economic and social life. Large swathes of rural Italy, which had provided employment and sustenance for thousands of years, became deserted by those seeking work. Entire categories of employment disappeared. The miracle revolutionised language and rhythms. Land was abandoned as urban or semi-urban life became the norm. A new Italy was on the way, with new Italians. Some 10,860,000 children were born in Italy between 1953 and 1964. This was the baby-boom generation – and they were the children of the boom.[3] The Italy of the 1960s would be unrecognisable from that of just ten years earlier.

Italy was at a perfect stage to profit from the global upturn in the 1950s. It had an almost limitless supply of cheap labour, and its industries could make cheap consumer goods to sell to a lucrative new market of families who did not yet have fridges, TVs, cars or washing machines, and wanted them. It was during the boom years that Italy developed what has been called 'a new consumer culture ... on an everyday level [that gave] voice to new subjects, and [led to] new kinds of language and symbolism'.[4] By the mid-1970s 'white' goods and other consumer items were everywhere. Very few people now didn't have these items. Only 6 per cent of Italian families were without a fridge, and only 8 per cent had no television.[5]

Millions of houses and apartments were also required for those moving to the cities, leading to a building boom of vast proportions, funded by both public and private money. Moreover, Italy developed an innovative class of entrepreneurs in key sectors – design, technology, fashion – to take advantage of the opportunities offered by the boom. Only Japan grew as fast as Italy in the late 1950s and early 1960s, and the lira was one of the most stable currencies around. Italy's gross national product rose by over 7.5 per cent between 1958 and 1961, at the peak of the boom. There were labour shortages. It wasn't difficult to find a job, if you were willing to move to get one. As the boom took hold, it swept away much of what had been traditional about Italy with a speed that many found bewildering. The most tumultuous changes had begun to take root in rural Italy at the beginning of the decade.

Final Act? Post-War Peasant
Struggles and Reform

There was a strange historical irony in the fact that, as the Italian peasantry disappeared, it also won unprecedented victories right across Italy. These gains, however, merely hastened the end of rural Italy as a place employing large numbers of labourers. In the South, extensive land occupations and other protests had already begun towards the end of the war and continued right through the 1940s. Often these protests were met with violence reminiscent of earlier periods of repression – both Liberal and Fascist. The bitter battles over land and contracts in the 1940s and 1950s led to historic concessions, and many of those struggles took inspiration from the great strikes and occupations of the 'red years' of 1919–20, when unions had taken on the agrarian elites and had later been crushed by the landowners and the Fascist squads. Now, it was payback time.

Southern peasants rose up time and again in the post-war period. Their demands were clear: land and work. This movement took on vast proportions in the 1940s and in the early 1950s. Its weapons were those utilised in other periods of the early twentieth century – collective land occupations and demonstrations. But there were also more innovative tactics, such as 'the reverse strike', where peasants would gather to work on uncultivated land or to fix roads that had been left in a neglected state.

In response to these struggles, the Christian Democrats set up the *Cassa per il Mezzogiorno* (Southern Development Fund) in August 1950. This was a body that used public funds to encourage and create development in the South. It soon became a formidable source of political patronage and corruption. A total of 120 billion lire was originally set aside for use by the *Cassa*. This money was designed, in theory, to build roads, aqueducts and facilities for tourism and agriculture. Alongside the *Cassa*, the government passed an extensive land reform law in the same year, which handed over extensive quantities of land to the Southern peasantry in particular – but also to those in other areas marked down as 'underdeveloped' such as the Tuscan Maremma region. However, this was a law that was out of step with the times. Many Southern peasants simply did not want to be peasants any more. They were buying a train or a boat ticket and leaving the countryside altogether – heading for the southern cities (Bari, Naples, Palermo, Catania) or for the industrial north, or out of Italy. A few came back, but most did not return. They did not want land, they wanted to be liberated from the land.

Some of the more striking aspects of the 'backward' South were redeveloped around this time. For example, people had lived within cave-like dwellings known as the *sassi* in the city of Matera, in the deep South, for hundreds of years – in difficult and often unhealthy conditions. Now, the *sassi* were cleared and new, model, villages were built in open countryside, with the participation of leading architects. These places looked beautiful, and their facilities were state of the art, but socially they were not deemed to be a success. The *sassi* had been unhygienic and dark, but they had fostered over many centuries a sense of community. Out in the open countryside, this was no longer there.

The 1950s also saw the final break-up of the southern great estates – the *latifondi*. Land was distributed in a democratic way, but also through methods that were clearly aimed at the reinforcement of Christian Democratic hegemony. Party gatekeepers controlled resources in the countryside and exchanged them for political support. But these were also structures and practices that were out of step with the times. Italy's history and its economy were shifting focus decisively towards the city, and the factory. Reform came too late to save rural Italy in the South.

Exodus: Stories from the Great Migration

'We were seen as foreigners at the time.'[6]
    Alfonso Tesoro, a migrant to Rome during the boom

Italians had always been willing to move to find work. For years they had been forced to do so. In 1913 an astonishing 800,000 had migrated abroad – in one year. In November 1951 the banks of the Po River broke across the Veneto region in the north-east of Italy. Some 180,000 people were evacuated or forced off the land. A total of 100,000 hectares of land were inundated and one hundred or so people died, many in one incident where a lorry carrying those fleeing from the floods was swept away. Large numbers of farm animals were lost. This disaster was a central factor in the abandonment of vast tracts of land in the Veneto region by the peasantry. They moved en masse to Milan and Lombardy – where they often purchased strips of land and built their own houses using a kind of rural-urban hybrid mix. Later, many would become factory workers. The images from that disaster marked the end of an era.

Yet it was the economic boom in the late 1950s and 1960s that led to Italy's second great migration – and it took place largely within her own borders. For the first time in her history, Italy could provide work for most of her citizens. Shangri-La, for many potential Italian migrants of the 1950s and the 1960s, was no longer New York or Buenos Aires or Paris or Sydney. Now the destinations of choice were the cities of the industrial triangle – Genoa, Milan, Turin.

Migrants usually turned up with contacts for family or friends. The migrant chain did its job – as in New York or Buenos Aires – in Milan, Genoa and Turin. This process tended to create tight-knit communities, and stigmatisation. For example, hundreds of Sicilians from the town of Milocca settled in the post-war period in Asti near Turin. These migrants were studied by Giuseppe Virciglio in his book from 1991, *Milocca al nord* (*Milocca in the North*). He discovered that 'thousands' of these migrants were 'ghettoised' in what was known as a 'very big house'. As time wore on, new housing was built on the edge of town. But this also carried dangers of 're-ghettoisation'. Many moved to a neighbourhood known as Praia, but as Virciglio wrote: 'Even today the label "praiano" ... often takes on negative and prejudicial connotations.'[7]

Italian society was revolutionised by this mass population movement. Every morning, in the vast, cavernous stations of Milan and Turin, new migrants poured out onto the lengthy

platforms. Thousands arrived, every day. Social change could
be seen, touched, smelt on every street corner and every train
platform. It was almost biblical. In 1962 alone, at least 100,000
migrants – many from the South – turned up in the city of Milan.[8]

Not all migrants were lost in the metropolis, unable to tell
night from day, as in some representations of their arrival. Very
few had no contacts at all in the big city. Almost everyone had a
cousin, a husband, a son or daughter, a neighbour already there.
They had somewhere to go – a first port of call. Immigrant networks were often on hand to help. Locals quickly saw the possibilities for making money from these new arrivals – both as cheap
labour and as consumers. It was a good time to make mattresses,
for example, or to sell agricultural land, or to work as a notary
or a surveyor. It was a very good time to be a bricklayer or occasional builder. Migrants with savings could buy plots of land and
construct their own houses – for example on the edge of Milan.

These neighbourhoods were known as *coree*, probably because
of their appearance around the time of the Korean War. The buildings these migrants built, with their own hands, at weekends and
in the evenings, were not illegal, but they often only had to adhere
to a very basic street plan. Public services such as water, electricity, schools and pavements were usually installed later, and many
villages and peripheral towns struggled to cope with the influx of
migrants. Schools in Turin had to adopt a shift system to accommodate all the new children.

After the first wave of migrants built their own houses, they
would then add two or three floors to the original structure, let-
ting out the lower floors to other migrants, usually from the South.
Migrants thus lived off the proceeds of migration. Sometimes, in
this second wave, there would be six or seven people to a room.
For young women, often just married, this phase was traumatic.
The contrast with their home villages, the fog and grime of Milan,
and the lack of privacy, was brutal. Ethnicity played its part in
the layout of these new migrant semi-cities. In the vast Bollate
'sud' *corea*, to the north of Milan, most immigrants were from the
South, whereas in the Bollate 'nord' they usually hailed from the
northern Veneto region. Italy thus urbanised and industrialised

at the same time. All of this was exciting and it all took place at breakneck speed. Time seemed compressed, as Italy hurtled towards modernity.

These migrants had one powerful weapon on their side – the ability to vote. Political parties were interested in this new and shifting electorate, and their needs could not be ignored completely. They had to be provided for, housed and educated in some way. Ghettoes were created, and entire cities constructed for these new populations. But there was also strong investment in integration and housing. Daily life could often be a struggle, however, and forms of racism were common. Other migrants with little or no capital behind them were forced into rented accommodation elsewhere in the city. Many ended up in poor-quality flats in the centre or inner suburbs of Milan, Turin and Genoa.

A series of myths developed at the time – and have been reinforced since – about the migrants of the 1950s and 1960s and their behaviour. Stereotyping was rife, as was discrimination, particularly against southern migrants. It was said that southerners used their bidets to grow tomatoes, that their suitcases were always wrapped with string, and that the men were 'hot-blooded' and often linked to various kinds of criminality. Local press reports labelled criminals with regional 'characteristics'. It was also said that signs were exhibited by landlords that warned: 'We don't rent to southerners'. In general, this story of hostility is usually replaced with one linked to integration and community in the period that followed the boom. Nostalgia also softened the harsh memories of the past, as a golden age was invoked that harked back to a time of plenty. The conflicts of that period were largely forgotten.

The End of Rural Italy

For hundreds of years, family and working lives had been focused, for the vast majority of Italians, around the tempos and productive processes associated with rural life. Of course, rural Italy was not an unchanging world – and nor were its systems by any means the same in different parts of the country. But some of its forms – such as sharecropping, where families worked and lived on the land and handed over part of the crop to the landowner – had features that had remained stable for hundreds of years. Quickly, they were about to become part of history.

The number of families working in agriculture, or mainly in agriculture, had remained more or less the same between 1901 and 1951 (at about 3.5 million). However, the overall number of families in Italy increased from 7.1 million to 11.8 million in the same period. In 1958 industrial employees overtook those in agriculture for the first time. Italy lost 5 million agricultural workers in the twenty years between 1951 and 1971. In 1951, 42 per cent of Italians had worked in the countryside. By 1996, only 7 per cent of the workforce was employed on the land.

As the prominent Italian historian Vittorio Vidotto states, 'Social classes who had dominated history for centuries simply disappeared. And with them a system of social relations and production based on the key role of human labour and the peasant family also left the scene.'9 As the peasants left, machines arrived. There were only 57,000 tractors in Italy in 1957. By 1980 this figure had risen to over a million. Some areas were unrecognisable physically and socially from the same spaces just twenty years earlier. Italy's landscape was redrawn.

This was such a deep and total transformation that the effects are still being felt. Seasons and weather had always dictated peasant and rural life. With the great transformation, a deep-rooted link to the seasons was also lost. This was a connection that had marked key moments in the year for the peasant family – both 'natural' – the harvest, sowing of seeds – and 'productive' – such as the negotiation of annual contracts and rents. Urban and industrial worlds, on the other hand, were largely detached from nature. Their rhythms were those of the working day, as regulated by factory sirens. The only season that existed for the factory worker was that of the summer holiday, the two or three weeks when the workers departed for their home town, or the seaside.

In former sharecropping areas there were deep changes to culture and family forms.

The idea – or dream – of a private home and a job in a factory or a building site quickly replaced the myth of land ownership. Bitter battles had been fought in Italy over rural property – both collectively and at the level of the family – during the nineteenth and twentieth centuries. But during and after the boom the centrality of land ownership faded. For the historian Agopik Manoukian, 'The land was no longer seen as something to grow things on' and 'a house in town became the new ideal for investment – the symbol of a common family enterprise'.[10] This was not the type of working house that had been the norm on the land, but 'a ... house ... which could be filled with new furniture and objects ... things which weren't necessarily used, but they were all important to show others and themselves that they had arrived – and had escaped from a situation which had been theirs for centuries'.[11] Houses and other dwellings were transformed. The long and traditional relationship with animals and their products, experienced in many rural areas, was abandoned. Bread was no longer made, it was purchased. Italians were becoming urbanised.

Gender structures within rural families had been patterned by spatial separation of the sexes and various rituals. The 'head of the table' at mealtime – for example – was almost always a man. In some households women never shared meals in the same space as men. As well as gender, these positions and rituals were also connected to social hierarchies, wrapped around age and authority. Certain women exercised great power over other women, and in specific parts of the household. However, as the country changed these structures were up for grabs as rules and social and gender mores were modified.

None of the changes during the time of the economic miracle seemed ordered or predestined. The family, after all, was and is a malleable entity, and it was also an ideology, a belief system – a way of being that could move across time and space and interact through changing forms of technology. For Manoukian, 'On the one side family connections could ... change in line with external conditions ... [but they also] resisted change and reproduced themselves in different places and situations. On the one hand the family was something to free yourself from ... and on the other it was reborn and reconstructed.'[12] Yet the 'death' of the peasantry did not entirely kill off the cultures and mores of that world. Traces of rural cultural forms often survived and were adapted to urban settings. Houses built by the immigrants on former agricultural land around cities (which was divided into strips and sold off) were often modelled on rural dwellings, with large gardens and vegetable plots. Meanwhile, links to the land were often kept alive through second homes and family ties, and revisited on weekends or on holiday. Nostalgia for Italy's rural past became a potent resource for advertisers and copywriters.[13]

The End of Sharecropping

In the centre of the country, meanwhile, the sharecropping system also witnessed its last great social uprising. This was an ancient system of land use whereby families worked the fields and shared their produce with landowners as payment in kind. The exact share of the crop to be handed over had always been a matter for debate and negotiation. After the war, sharecroppers obtained stunning concessions following a long and bitter strike. In 1947 they won 53 per cent of their produce for themselves (it had traditionally been 50 per cent) and this share rose to an unprecedented 58 per cent in 1964. But these were pyrrhic victories. Sharecropping itself was in its death throes.

A way of life that had patterned much of Italy's landscapes and rhythms, and that had proved relatively stable for hundreds of years, was cast quickly into oblivion. Sharecropping systems no longer made sense for either the families or the landowners. As the systems broke down or were phased out, people abandoned the land.[14] Farms and extensive sharecropping farmhouses were abandoned, or transformed into agro-tourist hotels and guest houses. Entire areas saw a population exodus. Once the local church had gone, its roof falling inwards through disrepair, a village effectively ceased to exist. Right across central Italy vast rural buildings, courtyards, barns, storehouses and peasant dwellings were left at the mercy of the weather and vegetation – potent and melancholic symbols of a past that had passed. The novelist Gianni Celati later made a beautiful documentary about these places called, quite simply, *Visioni di case che crollano* (*Visions of Houses that are Falling Down*).[15]

Change was dramatic on a local level. In Umbria, a region where sharecropping had been dominant, 137,000 people left agricultural work between 1951 and 1971. In 1951, 60 per cent of employees in Umbria had worked on the land. By 1981 this figure had fallen to a mere 9 per cent. The land, of course, was still there, and much of it was still cultivated. But the peasants and sharecroppers who had worked and lived on that land no longer existed.

Legal changes reflected and hastened these transformations. In 1964 a law was passed that made it illegal to create any new sharecropping contracts. And in 1982 another law allowed for existing sharecropping contracts to be wound up if just one of the parties involved requested a change. The binding partnerships and in-kind agreements that had held this system together for so long were no more. Sharecropping disappeared completely as a form of production and exchange. But the cultural and economic legacy of that system is still being felt.[16]

Former Jobs and Nostalgia

In the rice fields of the North, mechanisation replaced the intensive and seasonal use of (largely female) labour (known as the *mondine*) that worked these areas right up to the 1960s. Immortalised in the popular post-war film *Riso Amaro* (1949; *Bitter Rice*), written and directed by Giuseppe De Santis (a member of the Communist Party), these women would work bent over for long hours, wearing large hats in the baking sun, planting the rice by hand, their feet deep in water. The *mondine* had a rich history of resistance and rebellion. The disappearance of these seasonal workers in the boom years of the early 1950s left behind a desolate but beautiful landscape where massive farms were run by a tiny workforce that was now able to cope with the production cycle only thanks to the increased use of machinery. One family could now manage entire rice fields. The combative counter-culture of the *mondine*, meanwhile, was kept alive through songs and popular memory.

In the meantime, entire regions turned away from more traditional forms of mixed production towards lucrative export-led goods – above all wine and cheese, but also clothing and speciality high-quality production. The gentle hills of the Langhe region to the north of Turin later began to specialise entirely in high-priced wine – and the once ubiquitous oxen disappeared from the landscape. With the boom in the international wine trade, grapes became the dominant crop. Soon, wealthy tourists were flocking to the region in search of expensive bottles of Barolo and Barbaresco. Grinding poverty, as described in Beppe Fenoglio's novel *La Malora* (1954) set in the Langhe, was replaced with flashy forms of wealth.[17]

Money, Money, Money

Huge profits were made during the boom. New inventors and entrepreneurs emerged, and sometimes, it seemed, they had come from nowhere. A few were self-made people, who were living the American dream. Others represented firms with long traditions of manufacture and production. Creativity exploded and barriers and hierarchies came down, as designers, architects and writers collaborated with producers and engineers. These companies and individuals were in a perfect position to take advantage of the opportunities offered by the post-war miracle.

The architect Gio Ponti worked closely during this period with a furniture company called Cassina, based in the small town of Meda just outside Milan. Ponti's brief at one point was to produce a chair that combined high-quality design with mass-production values – an object that would be available to all, but would also carry status. The result was a sleek seat called the *superleggera* – the *superlight* – first produced in 1957. Cassina tested it by dropping it from the upper floors of their factory. Ponti and Cassina's collaboration was a roaring success. The *superleggera* sold in the millions. Every home seemed to have one, or even a whole set. Italian design, at this precise moment in the 1950s, became the envy of the world. Years before IKEA, Italian architects and designers were producing self-build furniture. The fact that most Italians in the big cities lived in smallish flats meant that designers had to be extremely creative in terms of their use of space.

Giovanni Borghi opened his first factory just outside Milan in 1951. His company was called Ignis and he soon became known as Mister Ignis. Borghi came from an entrepreneurial family but he had grand designs that far outstripped his own relatives. Ignis made washing machines and fridges, key consumer durables for Italian homes during the boom. These items were soon ubiquitous in Italian kitchens and *tinelli* – small semi-rooms used for everyday family or individual meals (without guests).[18] The *tinello* was usually found right next to the kitchen. Ignis became one of the biggest fridge producers in Europe. At one point the company was churning out 8,000 fridges a day.

Borghi was a kind of archetype of the Milanese industrialist of the boom years. 'An ex-artisan, barely educated, he had a gruff voice, and liked to talk in Milanese dialect. He was rude and uninterested in manners, and he liked to underline the fact that everything and every human being has a price.'[19] Known as '*cumenda*', a Milanese version of 'commander', Borghi was both modern and traditional at the same time. He was paternalistic in his view of 'his' workers and would always ask – in Milanese dialect – how much things were worth. His use of sponsorship – often of sporting teams and stars – was innovative and highly successful. With Ignis the Varese-based basketball club unexpectedly became one of the best teams in Europe. The company also used advertising through boxing, cycling, rowing and other sports to great effect. Boom millionaires such as Borghi competed for power and influence across Italy during the years of the economic miracle, and their products entered Italian homes and filled her cities and roads.

Factories and Workers

Italy's second industrial revolution (the first had been at the end of the nineteenth century) that accompanied and created the boom was extremely short-lived – ending almost as soon as it began. Yet it was a moment of tumultuous change and development. Big factories became a key part of the landscape across the country in a period that only ran from the 1950s to the 1970s, although there had been large firms in operation in some parts of Italy before that date, most notably in the northern industrial triangle in the late nineteenth and early twentieth centuries. Italy's new industrial working class thus provided the raw material, while both producing and consuming goods, that stood at the heart of the economic miracle.

During the boom, Italians put on their blue overalls, discarding their peasant clothes. They became regimented workers, their lives determined by the regulations and rules of the factory – a working class. Where once they toiled outdoors, in the fields, they now worked inside, in places where the seasons and the days merged into each other. Work itself was back-breaking. In many factories in Milan there were three shifts, all accompanied by masses of workers moving back and forth to and from the factory gates. Sirens marked the tempo of the working day (and night). Smoke billowed out of numerous chimneys. A short stop for a cigarette (purchased individually) and a glass of potent green Fernet Branca liquor at a local bar would often precede the start and follow the end of the working day. Municipal clocks placed everywhere made sure the workers knew what time it was, at any moment of the day.

Workers streamed into (and back out of) the cities on trams, bicycles or scooters, or, around Milan, often on the extensive Ferrovie Nord commuter network, which brought them into town from the hinterland, where so-called 'dormitory towns' were created. Lunchtime would take place in a local bar, with a packed lunch held in a metal case with a clasp (*la schiscetta*), and a glass or two of rough wine. Later in the day it would be home again, and almost straight to bed. Next day, the whole thing would start again.

Factory work was tough, repetitive and often dangerous, but it was also relatively well paid, and secure. A new working class could soon afford consumer durables, often on credit – a car, a fridge, a washing machine and, a bit later on, a television. This working class could buy things, and put food on their family's plates. In August many factories shut down, and workers set off back home (if they were migrants) or went on holiday. The expanding city and its infrastructure, with its metro lines and tower blocks, was built by these migrants. Work was available everywhere.

Inevitably, unionisation and harsh working conditions led to protests and demands for improvement. Strikes and protests marked the end of the 1950s and early 1960s in some of the more industrialised parts of the country (where there was a long tradition of organisation and militancy). In 1962 younger, mainly southern workers rioted in the centre of Turin, causing a kind of moral panic in the local press. The rioters were quickly tried and convicted. Some began to depict these southern migrant youths as part of a class of so-called 'mass workers'. They saw the potential, here, for a new revolutionary subject, excluded from the riches of industrial society. Thanks to the economic miracle, the city of Turin had developed an explosive mix of social and economic unrest as the boom uprooted the social structures of both northern and southern Italy. Housing, schools, hospitals all came under intense pressure as mass migration almost doubled the urban population.[20]

A Love Affair: Italians and Cars

'The car was the contemporary icon of the new urban and industrial landscape. It expressed spatial and social mobility. It attested to the value of individuality. It inaugurated new ways of working and consuming.'

Emanuela Scarpellini[21]

Before the 1950s, cars were still a rarity in Italy. Long journeys were largely taken by train or boat, while pedal bikes were used by millions. Factories had bike parks instead of car parks. Then the boom began. Motorisation exploded, expanding the horizons of Italians and introducing forms of mobility that revolutionised everyday life. The boom and the motor car were inextricably linked.

Scooters were the first mass-motorised vehicles to conquer Italian roads. Vespas, made in Pontedera near Pisa by a company called Piaggio and named after the Italian word for 'wasp', were sleek and smooth. Lambrettas, meanwhile, manufactured in Milan and named after the area of the city where the Innocenti factory was sited (Lambrate), were more industrial and 'urban'. Both became international icons of Italian style and design. Gregory Peck and Audrey Hepburn drove around Rome on a Vespa in the classic 'postcard' film, *Roman Holiday* (1953).

Scooters freed young people from the suffocating smallness of their village or neighbourhood. They were cheap, noisy, uncomfortable and dangerous, but also liberating. Anyone could drive them and they could travel long distances. In their initial phase, Vespas and Lambrettas were made with wide seats and designed as family vehicles, for days out of the city to the sea, the lakes or the mountains. They could be ridden by two or even three people at a time. There was nowhere to put luggage, however, and, if it rained, you got soaked.

Italians quickly fell in love with cars. The motor vehicle performed both real and symbolic functions. A series of cheap FIAT cars were produced and the company's profits went through the roof. These cars carried Italians across cities and up and down sparkling new motorways. By 1970 there were 10 million cars in Italy.[22] Some were known just by their numbers, such as the 600 (1955), the 500 (1957), the 850 (1964), the 127 (1971), the 126 (1972). Others (not always made by FIAT) were given proper brand names – the Alfetta, the Spider, the Uno, the Punto. The 500 was relatively cheap – costing just 415,000 lire at the time. Nearly four million 500s would roll off the production lines up to the 1970s. This was a car that became an icon, an emblem of a whole historical epoch.

These 'utilitarian' cars were durable, beautifully designed, and aimed at the family unit across a wide range of social classes. They could be purchased on credit and were the ultimate status symbol for Italians during the boom, when many finally had enough money and the time for a summer holiday. In August, once the factories had closed, Italians were 'free' to sit in traffic jams – but they could also pile their baggage on top of their *cinquecento*, put the kids in the back, and head south, or to the beach for the day.

For the sociologist Giampaolo Fabris, 'The car had a social dimension, but it was also a kind of house.' Fabris claims, for example, that many Italians first had sex – in the 1950s and 1960s – inside a 600 or a 500 (the seats, he points out, could be folded right down).[23] FIAT was not the only car manufacturer to ride and profit from Italy's intense and motorised boom. Alfa Romeo in Milan cornered the luxury end of the market with sleek designs. In the ultimate bitter-sweet 'boom' road-movie, *Il Sorpasso* (1962; *The Overtaking*), the handsome star Vittorio Gassman drives a 'spider' car at great speed across Italy. Fabris claims that the car was often treated as part of the family itself. It was a kind of pet, or even a superior kind of human being. It needed care, regular cleaning and polishing. It represented rebellion, speed, masculinity, but also conformism (in the end, everyone had one). The history of the car was highly emotional and packed with triggers to memories of the past. Car use was gendered, rendering men and family units more mobile but, in the early period at least, women and children more dependent on their husband-driver.[24]

Motorway of the Sun

On 7 December 1958 the diminutive Christian Democratic grandee Amintore Fanfani opened the first 100 kilometres of a new motorway. This monster road would snake up and down the country, crossing ravines and blasting through entire mountain ranges.

It began in a nondescript place called San Donato Milanese (whose population had mushroomed during the boom) just to the south of Milan, and it was due to end in Naples. It was given an exotic name – 'Motorway of the Sun'.

Italy's arterial motorway changed the way the country understood itself. This magnificent road axis would eventually link northern and southern Italy. It was the stuff of dreams and holidays, of memories and nightmares, and of mobility and stasis. Its route rewrote the geography of Italy, highlighting places that were to become famous as exits and pay stations – such as the massive toll gate at Melegnano, to the south of Milan, where queues to pay on return from holiday sometimes reached biblical proportions. In the 1990s the satirical magazine *Cuore* issued fake postcards, showing a packed traffic jam and the phrase 'Greetings from Melegnano'.

In other places the very route of the motorway was adjusted for political reasons, as with the celebrated 'Fanfani curve' which took the road close to Arezzo, where the politician Amintore Fanfani had gone to school, for no reason other than the patronage, influence and power he exerted. Motorway exits brought business, tourism and visibility. The first phase of this building enterprise was relatively successful, but the extension of the motorway right down to Reggio Calabria has been seen, almost universally, as a disaster – where corruption and organised crime created a monster that devoured public money, and a road that was extremely dangerous and in continual need of repair.

Mass motorisation had a bloody and smoky downside. Car accidents soon became a big killer of Italians. Sad little memorials, flowers and plaques were often to be found at roadsides, in memory of those who had died there. Public space began to be dominated by the ubiquitous 'right' to drive a car and look for a parking place. Naples' vast Piazza Plebiscito became a car park, while vehicles buzzed around the Duomo in the centre of Milan, or close to the Colosseum in Rome. Nightmarish ring roads and overpasses were built around and straight through the middle of cities such as Rome, Milan and Genoa (where the motorway still cuts the city in half). Federico Fellini depicted Rome's outer ring road in his film *Roma* (1972) as a vision of hell.

Film directors often poked fun at Italian consumerism, using the car as a leitmotif for the headlong rush to buy. In *I Mostri* (1963; *The Monsters*), a ferocious episode-film directed by Dino Risi, a character played by Ugo Tognazzi buys a sparkling FIAT 600 on credit. His first drive, however, is not home to his family, but a visit to street prostitutes. In another scene a traffic warden masters the art of giving quick tickets while drivers park briefly to buy a newspaper. It wasn't just cars that were presented as a problem. In one sequence a husband is so entranced by his television that he fails to notice his wife having an affair in the bedroom next door.

Fiataly

Thanks to this mass motorisation, the FIAT company – founded in Turin in 1899 – extended its power and influence into all areas of Italian life. The journalist Enrico Deaglio has written that 'FIAT, in reality, was the state.'[25] A biographer of the Agnelli family (founders of the company) has argued that 'To tell the story of the Agnellis and FIAT ... is to reconstruct the path taken by national identity.'[26] This was no ordinary business, or family. Its culture, politics and strategies intersected with those of Italy itself, and the city where FIAT had its nerve centre: Turin.

The Agnelli family controlled many aspects of urban and industrial life in the city where many of their factories operated. Their rituals, their houses, their pronouncements were all part of the way they exercised their power. Later, this was mediated through new means of communication. Giovanni Agnelli, the founder of the company, would walk to the factory from his home in Turin's city centre, carrying a walking stick. But the post-war history of the family and the company didn't begin well. Giovanni was buried almost in silence in December 1945. He had been accused of being a collaborator after the war. But this black mark over the family was soon forgotten.

After 1946, Italy no longer had a royal family, but it did have the Agnelli dynasty. Some called Gianni Agnelli – Giovanni's grandson – 'a King who reigns but does not govern', while the journalist Eugenio Scalfari described the car magnate as 'the King of Republican Italy'.[27] Unlike his grandfather, Gianni Agnelli often preferred a helicopter or a fast sports car. The Agnellis modernised Italy and their own lives changed with the times. Gianni wore various hats – as befitting a businessman of his importance – from his largely symbolic role as mayor of the small town of Villar Perosa (current population: 4,019) to his presence on the boards of numerous other companies. His degree in law led to his nickname as 'the lawyer'. This extended family were role models and anti-role models, often good-looking and also seen as hard-working. Some became 'black sheep', others followed more traditional pathways.

At times FIAT seemed so powerful as to be able to avoid the edicts of the Cold War. In 1966 an agreement was ratified between the Soviet government and the Italian car company. This led to the construction of a car factory in a place called Togliatti (named after the former leader of the Italian Communist Party) in the south-west of the USSR. FIAT also arrived at a similar accord in Poland. The boom years were good for the company, as its cheap, well-designed cars sold in their millions. The company expanded and the giant Mirafiori plant in Turin operated at full capacity.

FIAT was not just a company. It was also a political powerhouse, with a fast track right to the heart of government. Seventimes Prime Minister Giulio Andreotti recalled how the General Manager of the company, Vittorio Valletta, 'would come to Rome often and meet with Prime Minister De Gasperi. There was mutual respect between them. Everyone knew that – despite being a private company – FIAT had a huge influence on the economy in general.'[28] But Andreotti was anxious to underline that the government made independent choices. Some politicians claimed that 'that which is good for FIAT is good for Italy', although not everyone agreed.

FIAT was never just a business – it was an empire, a way of life. Its primary role of course was to manufacture cars and lorries for ordinary people and luxury vehicles for the very rich. But FIAT was inter-class (like the Church and the Christian Democrats) and paternalistic. It cared for its workers from the cradle to the grave – through its own schools, summer camps, retirement homes. Many employees read the FIAT-owned Turin-based quality newspaper *La Stampa* from the 1920s onwards and supported a FIAT-owned football team (Juventus) with its millions of fans and dozens of trophies. The company made sure it looked after its loyal staff (although, for many, this cosy relationship broke down in the 1960s and 1970s). FIAT was loved – and hated. Some of its workers adored the Agnellis as benevolent gods. When Gianni Agnelli died there were queues around the block of the old factory to pay respects at his coffin.[29] But other workers came to despise the factory and those who owned it. They rejected the entire system (in some cases) or felt highly exploited and angry (a much greater number).

Riding the Tiger? Planning and Cities

'We would often go and see our city grow. It moved forward victoriously, into the countryside, against the countryside, conquering other lands. It moved. You could watch our city move.'
Luciano Bianciardi[30]

Italy is one of the most beautiful countries in the world. It is also a country that has systematically failed to defend its own environment. The main driving forces behind the 'concretisation' of Italy have been building speculation and tourist-led expansion. Whole coastlines were built up and hidden from view through this process, and large areas became much more vulnerable to damage after earthquakes, floods and landslips.

Politicians struggled to manage the powerful forces unleashed by the economic boom. A wide-ranging urban council house-building programme tried to meet demand, but there were places where migration pressures overwhelmed local services. Was the economy planned? Up to a point. There were plans, but they were often overtaken by events, or not adhered to, or out of date by the time they had gone through the political process. Urban expansion was certainly out of control in many parts of Italy by the 1960s. Formal procedures were often followed, but the reality was that cities sprawled across the countryside, eating up land and farms in their wake. When seen from above the shape that these developments made on the ground was most commonly compared to an oil slick spreading inexorably across the landscape.

Right across Italy, corruption and speculation allowed for rules to be broken, and plans to be ignored or modified. This was most obvious in the areas where organised crime was strongest. The 'rape of Palermo' saw large tracts of the hinterland covered in cement, as well as vast swathes of beautiful coastline. Much of this was linked to the Mafia – who had placed key figures inside the local administration. Naples also saw a startling construction boom.

It was difficult to understand what was happening, especially for those caught up in rapid urbanisation. In Rome semi-peripheral *'borgate'* neighbourhoods were incorporated into the city, but traces of the older city were everywhere. This was particularly true of those places where countryside met the city. Former peasant dwellings remained within the urban fabric, but their agricultural production soon became a distant memory, and then disappeared even from that realm. These neighbourhoods often grew in a spontaneous way, like mushrooms. Centocelle to the south-east of the city was and is a fairly typical Roman peripheral zone. For one resident '[this place] was built by what we call small building entrepreneurs [*palazzinari*] ... They built a house here, a house there etc. etc.'[31] The speed of change was often bewildering for those who lived through it – hence clichés such as 'once upon a time, this was all countryside'. Another local said that 'Centocelle was not born with a plan; it was born, with a sense of "Where shall we live? On the edge."'[32] In Milan, 600 or so kilometres further north, the tendency to adjust planning rules and regulations to suit the needs of building entrepreneurs became known as the '*rito ambrosiano*' (the *Ambrosian ritual*, referring to Milan's patron saint – Ambrose). Final planning outcomes often bore little resemblance to the original blueprints.

Amidst the chaos there were many examples of enlightened public planning and of resistance to the destruction of traditional neighbourhoods, vistas and buildings. A notable campaign, for example, ensued over a 1950s project for a new Hilton Hotel in Rome. And there were areas where the story was a different one. Bologna managed to preserve one of the most exquisite medieval city centres in the world, and attempted to keep a social mix through rent controls, innovative reforms and attention to land and building use. Elsewhere, innovative architects and planners attempted to chart a different path towards urban development, as with Giancarlo De Carlo's participatory housing estate in the industrial city of Terni, or Aldo Rossi's visionary housing blocks in Milan.

But these were exceptions to the rule. Italy's environmental movement was weak and the possibilities of making a quick buck were many. Italy's coasts were perhaps the areas that suffered the most in the rush to build. The Ligurian seaside was swathed in hotels and second homes. By the end of the 1960s a visitor who had not seen Italy for ten years would have struggled to recognise many of its cities.

1963: Vajont

Sometimes the costs of this kind of development became obvious to all, as man-made disasters led to considerable loss of life. Hydro-electric power had been Italy's 'white coal' in the nineteenth and twentieth centuries, a major provider of energy since the industrial revolution in Lombardy and in a country with tiny amounts of real, black coal supplies. Energy companies were always on the hunt for areas to dam so that they could create and sell energy to the state from the ensuing water flows. In the late 1950s the SADE company identified a steep valley in the

Friuli region as a possible site for a dam. The area was known as Vajont.

Despite numerous warnings about the safety of the project (geologists reported that the land around the proposed dam was too fragile and liable to slippage) the huge dam went ahead. Local protests were ignored. On 9 October 1963, at 10.39 p.m., all the warnings were proved correct as a significant section of the mountain collapsed into a lake behind the dam. About 50 million cubic metres of water then poured over the dam structure (which survived intact) and down into the valley below. An entire town called Longarone was obliterated, as well as some nearby villages. The final death toll amounted to 1,917 victims, 1,450 from Longarone alone. The after-effects of the disaster resembled a moonscape. The great journalist Dino Buzzati, who knew the area well, wrote a celebrated piece about the tragedy. 'The mountain which broke and which created the massacre is one of the mountains of my life. Its profile is etched on my soul, and it will be there for ever. For this reason my throat is dry and I cannot come up with the usual words for such circumstances. Words like anger, incredulity, horror, pity, consternation, tears, mourning are stuck there, weighing heavily.' Buzzati concluded that 'Once again the fantasy of nature has been greater and more astute than the fantasy of science.'[33]

Vajont was a potent cautionary tale for Italy. It showed that unfettered development and a rush to profit could have catastrophic consequences. It also demonstrated how the environment was expendable, and fragile. There was a long battle for justice. On the thirty-fourth anniversary of the disaster, in an audacious piece of television, the actor and playwright Marco Paolini performed a one-man play live on TV, in a specially built theatre close to the dam itself. Viewers were engrossed as Paolini reconstructed the human tragedy behind Vajont. The success of this show (three and a half million spectators were glued to their television sets deep into the night) renewed interest in the case and led to further books, exhibitions and a feature film.[34]

Landslip: Agrigento – July 1966

Further signs of ecological disaster could be seen in the South. Agrigento in Sicily is still best known for its stunning Greek ruins, which stand in the 'Valley of the Temples'. In the post-war period the city of Agrigento expanded through the spread of unsightly modern constructions that sat precariously on top of a hill overlooking the temples. Seen from afar, this area appeared as a mass of concrete. From close-up it was an agglomeration of housing without any sense of order. Photographs of the city's new skyline were enough to transmit the full horror of what had happened.

In the summer of 1966 this lack of planning and rush to build bore bitter fruit. Nobody had taken notice of the effects of uncontrolled building on the terrain itself, which began to give way in a series of dramatic landslips. At 6.30 in the morning on 19 July cracks suddenly appeared in roads. Some buildings collapsed, while others took on strange misshapen forms. Many thought it was an earthquake and residents fled. Thousands of people (at least 8,000 according to some estimates) were made homeless and their houses rendered unsafe. Two 'tent-cities' were set up for those without anywhere to live (under the baking hot sun). Slow responses to similar disasters were a sad feature of Italian life, and would be seen on other occasions in subsequent decades.

As with many such disasters before, and since, the events in Agrigento quickly took on a national focus. Italy's President and Prime Minister both turned up to offer moral support. Money poured in for the aid effort. Journalists visited from right across Italy. In his report to Parliament the Minister of Public Works stated that 'serious, alarming and outrageous things have taken place in Agrigento – and all this shows that, for years, it has not been the law which has ruled here, but uncontested illegality'.[35]

The series of landslips in Agrigento led to a national debate over the role of politicians and the Mafia in allowing or promoting illegal construction of houses and other buildings. In 1967 the city's local administration was wound up under central government orders, and Agrigento was run centrally until 1970. In the end, however, all the judicial investigations into the facts surrounding the disaster and its causes came to nothing. Everyone was cleared. In 1968 a new neighbourhood was built on the edge of the city – which ended up taking in many of those left homeless by the 1966 landslips. An unsightly flyover was built to connect the city to this new zone. Agrigento remained a symbol of the damage of uncontrolled construction, but very little was done to halt further developments of this kind. Outside of the planning system, the South became criss-crossed by hundreds of thousands of unfinished buildings, with their familiar metal rods sticking out of concrete blocks, heralding the possible construction of yet another floor. Families would prepare for these new sections of their houses ahead of time, so that they never seemed to be complete. Many were awaiting one of the numerous amnesties for illegal buildings, whereby a fine could be paid to 'legalise' their situation. Of course, the message sent out by this kind of policy was a simple one: crime pays.

1966: Mud Angels

In the winter of 1966 heavy rain had been falling for days. Rivers rose alarmingly right across Italy. November saw disaster strike in a series of places almost at the same time. This was a national tragedy, but much of the focus fell on two beautiful, tourist cities – Florence and Venice. In the former, the Arno's waters submerged entire neighbourhoods, ruined priceless works of art, and damaged thousands of books from the national library, which stood (and stands) right by the river. An estimated 12,000 people were made homeless, and dozens were killed in Florence and other places in Tuscany thanks to the floods. The official figure, compiled many years later, was of thirty-five deaths. Many of these victims were old people who were unable to save themselves in time, but in nearby Sesto Fiorentino two three-year-old children were swept away by the rising water. Half the city was cut off. Florence's flood was also a spark for solidarity on a vast scale.

Thousands of young people turned up in the city to help with the clean-up effort. Their generosity earned them the collective name of 'the mud angels'.

In Venice unheard – of levels of high water – over 1.9 metres in places – caused immense damage. Many lower floors of buildings were abandoned forever. As the historian Richard Bosworth writes, 'the flood receded with violent rapidity, leaving dead pigeons and rats in every square as a token of mortality, while viscous black mud lay a metre deep … It was estimated that 200,000 tonnes of rubbish needed collecting (it was still rotting a week later).'[36] In retrospect, November 1966 has often been described as a turning point for the city, as many residents left, never to return, the moment when it was transformed from a real, living place to a kind of Italian Disneyland, populated mainly by short-stay visitors. Venice lost much of its active population, and set itself on a road toward being a place that attracts 26 million tourists a year, but only has 55,000 actual residents. In theory, lessons were learnt from the 1963 and 1966 disasters. However, very little changed. The damage had been done. Uncontrolled urban sprawl had left Italy's cities with little protection against earthquakes and the vagaries of the weather. The boom had a dark side.

The Brick Kings

A new generation of powerful building entrepreneurs was born on the back of the boom, from 'Don' Salvatore Ligresti (an immigrant from Sicily to Milan) to a businessman called Silvio Berlusconi, who made his first fortune thanks to housing investment in Milan in the 1960s. Italy's central government and local authorities all over the country tried to deal with the mass movement of its citizens through the construction of large-scale housing estates. This was often accompanied by high-quality architecture and sophisticated planning. It was a time of experimentation – when the influence of Le Corbusier was high.

In the 1950s, for example, a sizeable estate was built on the edge of Milan, in open countryside in a place called Comasina.

The Comasina estate contained various forms of housing, a futur-
istic church, shops, a community centre, parks and other services.
Comasina was designed as a 'self-sufficient' neighbourhood –
not, in theory, dependent on the city of Milan for jobs, transport
and services. This self-sufficiency did not proceed as planned, and
most of those employed there commuted to the city or nearby
factories. Housing was of high quality but there were powerful
social and regional differences in the estate. A 'playground war'
saw families clash over the behaviour of their children and the use
of public space. Comasina was a step up for many – a sign of social
mobility – but also stigmatised as a place of crime and a kind of
'Bronx'. Life was not easy for those in Comasina. As a journalist
reported at the time, 'on Sunday mornings the sordid working-
class tower blocks resound with shouts, insults, swearing, furious
outpourings of the tensions repressed for a whole week'.[37]

But all this appeared to be a price that people felt was worth
paying. As one immigrant (a schoolteacher from Apulia) to Milan
recalled from those years, 'I remember that first winter. It was
terrible looking out of the window: fog everywhere, you could
never see the sky ... we were forced to spend day after day at
home ... we were six children in three rooms. My father had a
job at Alfa Romeo found for him by his brother. My mother was
scared to go shopping. But it was our first happy year. There were
no longer arguments at home ... we ate well and we had a home
which for us was like that of a lord.'[38]

Other projects, however, proved a costly disaster, and some
became symbols of the failures of central and local government, and even of architecture and planning itself. This was the
case of the celebrated (but not in a positive way) ZEN (*Zona
Espansione Nord*) neighbourhood outside Palermo. Designed
by architect Vittorio Gregotti (his project won a public competition in 1971) and supposedly based, in part, on the layout
of African villages, the ZEN story became a well-documented
and notorious saga of mismanagement and corruption, and was
never properly finished. Construction only began in 1976. None
of the services from the original plan (schools, sports grounds,
social centres, workshops) were built. Gregotti later argued that

the neighbourhood should be 'knocked down and rebuilt as it was originally planned'.[39] Although critics have often blamed the architect for the outcome of the ZEN story, the responsibility really lay with the local authorities whose botched execution of the plans failed both their designer and – above all – the long-suffering residents (of which there are still some 16,000).

Cultural Change and the Boom:
Italy's Soundtrack

Italy's transformations had their own, distinctive, soundtrack. A group of talented and radical singer-songwriters emerged in the post-war period – taking the conservative world of Italian music by storm. Many were from Genoa, a port city going through tough times. Their songs told of dark alleys, prostitutes and daily life in the labyrinths of the old city. Often inspired by French singer-songwriters such as Georges Brassens, these musicians were highly controversial and often political in their outlook.

Fabrizio De André, a striking man (also a heavy smoker and drinker) with a memorable deep voice and a poetic turn of phrase, quickly became the leading light of this self-acknowledged group. His songs became anthems for a generation, whether sung by him or – on one particularly famous occasion – by a young, tall and feisty woman with a magnificent voice, who became known as Mina. De André's lyrics told of prostitutes drummed out of town, or of the forgotten dead of the First World War, and, as the 1960s and 1970s wore on, they delved further and further into contemporary politics – as in his concept album *Storia di un impiegato* (1973; *The Story of an Administrative Worker*). In 1979 De André (and his partner Dori Ghezzi) were kidnapped by Sardinian 'bandits' (he had a house on the island) who demanded a ransom. Unlike almost all other victims of similar kidnappings, De André identified strongly with his captors. His later song about those experiences – 'Hotel Aspromonte' – created poetry from that terrifying event.

External musical influences played a strong part in the Italian music scene, but they were never simply accepted or copied. Rock and roll came to Italy via musicians in Rome and Milan in the 1950s, and it soon made some of its protagonists into big stars. Adriano Celentano, a son of southern migrants born and brought up in Milan, was the most successful of the early rock-and-rollers, and his remarkable career continued well into the twenty-first century. Celentano, the 'rubber-legged-one' (*il molleggiato*), developed from a cover-song merchant into a talented songwriter who initially wrote about the things he knew best – the inner suburbs of Milan. His songs were often a description of the boom years, as with 'Il ragazzo della via Gluck' (1964) ('The Boy from Gluck Street', where Celentano was born). In the video to this song, Celentano was filmed strolling on the edge of Milan, while he remembered the grass of his childhood that had been replaced by constant house-building.

Celentano experimented with musicial styles, and was sensitive to environmental themes (well before they became fashionable). When he was made presenter of one of Italy's most popular afternoon television shows – *Fantastico* – in the 1980s, he resorted to long (live) monologues that hypnotised his audience. Lengthy pauses were followed by his opinions on hunting, love, music and the destruction of Italy's landscape. This tactic was also a sign of the increasing power (and dangers) of television. Celentano was speaking directly to millions of Italians, live – and bypassing other forms of mediation or even traditional control mechanisms. It was a messianic moment – others (most notably Silvio Berlusconi) would later use very similar forms of communication.

Celentano sang in a famous 1957 concert held at Milan's ice-rink that was a founding moment for Italian rock and roll. Other members of that improvised 1957 group included Giorgio Gaber and Enzo Jannacci. Gaber had been brought up fairly near to Milan's city centre, and he also began to write about his immediate surroundings during the economic miracle. Some of his best-loved early and popular songs described the bar life of the city at the time. In 'Trani a gogo', for example, he painted a picture of the 'Trani' bars that sold Southern wine and where the Milanese working class would go at lunchtime (with their packed lunches in tin boxes) and in the evenings: *Si passa la sera scolando Barbera/ Nel Trani a gogo* – 'The evening goes by, drinking Barbera/In the Trani a gogo.'

Gaber quickly became famous and appeared frequently on national television, but his music was evolving in new and interesting ways. In the 1960s and 1970s he created a hybrid art form – the *teatro-canzone* (song-theatre) – which enjoyed enormous success and made him into a cult figure. Gaber's regular theatre shows were carefully constructed, including written monologues interwoven with songs. These events also became concept albums written from scratch for each show. As a wave of protest movements swept across Italy, Gaber became a critical voice. He was a man of the left, but he analysed and deconstructed the movement, its foibles and its language. Gaber managed to make poetry out of politics, as in the song 'La libertà' ('Freedom').

Gaber's most celebrated work was *Il Signor G* (1970), which aimed to critique and understand middle-class Italian attitudes at the time. Gaber created an alter ego for this double album and theatre-show called *Mr G*. Gaber's own father had been an *impiegato*. Gaber described Mr G as 'ordinary' and as 'full of contradictions and pain'.[40] After a sell-out month of performances in Milan every year, Gaber would bring out records of the live performances and studio recordings. He also took control of his own career – and had his own record label. Gaber's shows and albums reflected a changing Italy after the hope provided to many by the movements of the 1960s. His tone was increasingly pessimistic – as in the songs and albums *Far finta di essere sani* (*Pretending to be Healthy*) and *La mia generazione ha perso* (*My Generation has Lost*).

The final member of that early rock-and-roll group was Enzo Jannacci. A cardiologist by trade (he continued to practise for most of his life, and trained with the celebrated heart surgeon Christiaan Barnard in South Africa), Jannacci was an eccentric singer with an unusual and gravelly voice. His songs were often written in Milanese dialect. Many of his early compositions once again told stories about those he saw around him in the Milan of

the boom – with bawdy humour and often farcical tales linked
to the criminals and drunks of the Milanese lumpen-proletariat.
Jannacci told tales of failed robberies, of standing-up sex in cinemas, and of falling-down alcoholic stupors. As his music evolved,
he began to work with Beppe Viola, a sports commentator and
writer with an unusual capacity for lyric-writing. In their masterpiece, 'Quelli che . . .', Jannacci and Viola created a new kind of
'song', made up of repetitive music and the unpacking of phrases
and stupidities from everyday Italian life, including the world of
sport. 'Quelli che . . .' was a flexible song, which could be adapted
to the current political context – an early form of Milanese rap.

Another key figure on the Milanese scene at the time was
Dario Fo: actor, playwright, political militant and singer. Fo and
Jannacci sometimes wrote songs together, bringing in elements
of Italian popular theatre and slapstick alongside political comment and humour. 'Ho visto un re' ('I have Seen a King') was a
satirical take on the nature of power, which also took sideswipes
at the Church. Much of this was, of course, great fun – but there
was also an edge to their music that would intensify as the 1960s
drew to a close. Fo would go on to become a notable international
figure through his satirical work and popular theatre with his wife
Franca Rame and in one-man shows, including the masterpiece
Mistero Buffo. Fo's music and theatre represented a hybrid of
styles, and an innovative mix of tradition, political protest and
audience participation. His success amongst the public showed
how there was an increasing desire for new forms of culture as
the 1960s wore on.

San Remo, a small seaside town in Liguria famous for its
flowers, hosted Italy's first Festival of Song in 1951. Originally
intended for radio, this annual event became a TV spectacular,
attracting massive audiences. As with the annual Giro d'Italia
cycling race, the games played by the Italian national football
team, Ferrari during Formula One racing, and the opening
night of La Scala, San Remo became part of the national cal-
endar or of Italian identity itself. Its songs and controversies
marked the history of the nation, and individual lifetimes and
careers.

San Remo was also a competitive event. A 'best' song was chosen in every festival, alongside other categories that changed over time. This led to endless debate, as well as conspiracy theories about its ever-changing and byzantine rules and voting systems. 'San Remo', as it quickly became known, was held over a number of days in January, although this was later moved to late February or early March. It was first shown live on TV in 1955, shortly after the birth of Italian television itself. The 1955 festival was won by a popular singer called Claudio Villa, although he had been forced to mime over a record because of a sore throat. The songs were almost always meant to be original, although later editions began to invite guests including big stars from abroad (who sang out of competition).

Italians soon began to gather around their television sets to watch San Remo – and this became an annual ritual – something that combined low and high culture. It was also a mirror of changes to the country itself, with the arrival of different forms of music (some influenced by the musical cultures of other countries, some not), arguments, discussions, rebellions, accusations of censorship, scandals and even suicides. The composition of, and decisions made by, the 'jury' who usually decided on the winners of the various categories, were always subject to debate and often there were accusations of corruption. The winners at the festival, after all, were guaranteed sales and stardom.

In the early years, different presenters were involved in the festival, but from 1963 onwards this high-profile role was dominated by two celebrated television stars – Mike Bongiorno and Pippo Baudo – who ran twenty-four editions of the festival between them (thirteen for Baudo and eleven for Bongiorno). There is now even a statue of Mike Bongiorno in San Remo. Over the years the presenters were almost always men, and their 'assistants' were usually women. San Remo attracted massive audiences. In 1987, for example, nearly 16 million Italians watched the festival. In recent years these figures have been in decline.

Certain key moments in San Remo's history became part of popular memory. The Pugliese singer Domenico Modugno's global success with 'Nel blu dipinto di blu' ('Volare') in 1958 was

a crucial moment – a kind of harbinger of the economic miracle.
Modugno became world-famous with this song, and was known
as 'Mister Volare'. 'Volare' reached number 1 in the charts in the
United States and France and sold 22 million copies, including
800,000 in Italy. When Modugno spread his arms out wide and
blasted out the chorus, the public was won over immediately,
both in the theatre and – most importantly – at home in front of
the television. Gianni Borgna later wrote that this moment was
one of 'collective drunkenness. Everywhere people sang Volare
together – even in football stadiums, at half time.'[41] Historians
of Italian music have divided the post-war period into a pre- and
post-Modugno phase. San Remo was a key component in a boom
in record sales. In 1958 Italians purchased 16 million records (by
that time there were jukeboxes in many bars). This was an increase
of 13 million from 1951.

In 1961 Adriano Celentano scandalised part of Italy by turning
his back on the audience during his performance of '24.000 baci'
('24,000 Kisses'). Celentano was simply copying the legendary
Eddie Cochran, but this did not lessen the impact of his gesture,
which was interpreted by some as a sign of disrespect towards the
public. Later, in 1970, he annoyed the left with his victory at the
San Remo festival with a song seen as anti-union and anti-strike
called 'Chi non lavora non fa l'amore' ('Who Does not Work,
won't Make Love'). By the 1960s San Remo had become very
important indeed – making and breaking careers. In 1967 a talented young singer-songwriter from Genoa, Luigi Tenco, shot
himself in the head in his hotel room after his song failed to make
it through to the next round. His death (and his suicide note,
which made reference to the decisions of the festival jury) caused
widespread shock – but the show went on.

Over time the songs themselves became less important – it was
the 'show' that mattered. 'San Remo,' as Stephen Gundle argues,
'became almost entirely a television event, the success or otherwise of which was measured in terms of viewing figures. The stars
of the show were not the singers but the avuncular male presenter
… and his beautiful female assistants … [it was] a ritual without
content, a "non-place" of popular culture which everyone passed

through passively: there was no creative appropriation or absorption of the songs into a patrimony of memory.'[42]

The biggest star of all from the 1960s and 1970s, however, was the aforementioned Mina, from Cremona (although she was born in Busto Arsizio, just outside Milan) in the north of Italy. Her first records were light rock and roll covers – with titles such as 'Juke Box urli d'amore' ('Juke Box Cries of Love') – but Mina soon moved on to more meaty numbers. Her success was enormous, and she became a household name. As a celebrity, her private life came under intense scrutiny. Her decision not to marry when she became pregnant in 1962 after an affair with the actor Corrado Pani caused scandal (while many admired her courage). Her voice was extraordinary – powerful and yet delicate – and her stage presence electric. Tired of her celebrity status, she retired completely from public life and live performance in 1974, although she continued to produce records on a regular basis. Celentano and Mina were also sex symbols. Mina often sang alongside another hugely popular male singing star of the 1960s and 1970s – Lucio Battisti. As Borgna has written, Battisti was 'a bit like Italy's Bob Dylan ... who was able to interpret changes of mood and the climate [of the 1970s]'.[43]

These songwriters and musicians provided a soundtrack to a changing country, for those who bought and listened to their music but also for those studying and reflecting on those transformations. The festival of San Remo was a key stage for musicians, but music reached deep into society and reflected new forms of youth and mass culture emerging within Italy, some of which were influenced by foreign stars, while others were homegrown and intensely local. New technology – record players, cassette recorders, jukeboxes – allowed music to become portable and reach new audiences. Italy's cultural ferment could be heard, as well as seen.

Cultural Change and the Boom: The Magic Rectangle – Italy and Television

Television entered the lives of Italians in January 1954, with the first transmission from studios in Milan. The beginnings were slow – very few families possessed sets, which were expensive and extremely large. Hardly anybody saw that first programme. There were a mere 24,000 licence-holders in the entire country. But things changed swiftly. As with music, television created and reflected the heady sense of change of the boom years. It symbolised the new, and it was a place where the transformations of the economic miracle were played out, performed and watched.

In November 1955 a quiz-game show called *Lascia o raddoppia?* (*Double or Quits?*) gained vast audiences and became front-page news. The format was simple – contestants answered questions on a specialist subject, and if they answered enough of them correctly, they could eventually win a car (a FIAT 500, of course, the ultimate symbol of the boom). Lesser prizes could be collected at any time by bailing out of the quiz. *Lascia o raddoppia?* was presented by a charismatic Italian-American who went under the name of (the aforementioned) Mike Bongiorno. A succession of female assistants were employed as window-dressing to his fast-talking delivery, although they were rarely allowed to actually say anything. Italy was hooked. As one commentator wrote at the time, 'At nine o'clock on Thursday nights, Italy comes to a halt.'

Why was *Lascia o raddoppia?* so popular? The programme worked on a series of levels. On the one hand it created controversy and debate over the questions and the answers, something that kept interest going well after the programme was actually over. A second key feature was the consumerist or 'American' thrust of the show – the glamour – the chance to become famous and win something valuable. *Lascia o raddoppia?* tapped into aspirations – at a time when real social mobility appeared possible, at last, for an entire generation. Finally, the real stars of the programme were ordinary people – with whom the public could identify, and they soon became instant stars. Viewers commented on their dress sense, their accent, their bodies, their voices, their knowledge of specialist subjects. *Lascia o raddoppia?* encapsulated a kind of cosy, Italian version of the American dream.

For Italian TV, *Lascia o raddoppia?* was a game-changer. Everyone suddenly wanted to watch it, or just know what had happened last night. Television sets were put in cinemas, people crowded into bars or into the houses of friends or family members. It also created its own mythologies. Newspapers reprinted the entire 'script' of the programme for those who hadn't seen it. Italian TV was funded in two ways – through a television licence tax (the much-hated *canone*, which also applied to radio sets) and through advertising revenue. Mike Bongiorno sold TV sets and TV licences. But not everyone was a fan. Television in general, including Bongiorno himself, attracted criticism and ridicule from many intellectuals. Some said his entire vocabulary consisted of just fifteen words. Umberto Eco in a celebrated article, 'Fenomenologia di Mike Bongiorno' ('The Phenomenology of Mike Bongiorno'), called his Italian 'basic'.[44]

Television helped unify Italians around a common language – something that had been the dream of the nation-builders of the country in the nineteenth and twentieth centuries. As the linguistic expert Tullio De Mauro put it, 'The use of a national language in our country was carried forward not thanks to the school or national planning, but thanks to tragic events, such as trench warfare in World War One, or unexpected and extra-educational moments, such as the great emigration of Italians in the Nineteenth Century, the internal migrations of the 1950s, or cinema, radio and television.'[45]

But television also created and spread its own language. When Bongiorno talked about ordinary contestants on *Lascia o Raddoppia?* as 'personaggi', he was not simply using that word in the wrong manner (as many of his critics claimed) but inventing a different way of understanding the term. Traditionally, the word 'personaggio' had signified a character, as in a play. But Bongiorno used the word to mean 'personality' – a TV personality – and this usage stuck.

Television by the early 1960s had become part of everyday life in Italy, in the countryside and the city. There were 10 million licence holders in Italy in 1970. This rapid diffusion led to a rearrangement of people's front rooms and patterned behaviour. As a critic wrote in 1963, 'television had become a truly popular pastime, and it was also one of the many forms upon which the image of an Italian miracle was constructed'.[46] But Italian TV was not just about quiz shows. It was also a heavily controlled political and pedagogical project – at least for the early period. Christian Democrats, and the Church, controlled much of the scheduling and the content. High culture was as important as low culture. Operas were shown live, there were productions of Dante and Manzoni, and didactic programmes dedicated to agriculture and education. Later, the great film director Roberto Rossellini worked extensively for Italian TV. Even *Lascia o Raddoppia?* was a potent combination of high and low culture. Its first and soon-to-be famous contestant inspired a debate across the country around a question concerning musical instruments used in opera.[47]

To 'protect' the public, advertising was confined to a restrictive set-up and crushed into a specific time of day. Short films were the only format allowed, and the product could only be mentioned right at the end. These tiny films were shown within a single package (known as *Carosello*) at the same time every evening. Top directors were involved – and the films were often highly entertaining. Creative animators also worked in this sphere, creating popular characters such as the little cartoon chick Calimero, who would be washed by a detergent called Ava. Pressure cookers were sold through an innovative cartoon known as 'The line', drawn by Osvaldo Cavandoli. In 'The line' the character often spoke to the designer himself to ask for different types of drawing. *Carosello* launched a series of characters and 'personalities' that became household names. It also employed film stars (including many from abroad) as well as top cyclists and footballers.

Television has often been assigned astounding powers in terms of its transformative power in Italy. Most of the effects attributed to TV have been negative ones. Television has been described as a destroyer of 'authentic' culture, a purveyor of mass dumbing-down, a de-motivator, an individualising force, a destroyer of childhood and of family life. This analysis was already there, amongst many intellectuals, in the 1960s. Often, the fact that poor people appeared to possess television sets was commented upon. Television was also marked out as the opium of the people, a kind of propaganda machine. Anti-television narratives were cemented by the polemical writings of the poet, novelist and film-maker Pier Paolo Pasolini in the 1970s. He referred to 'the damned who watch television every evening'. Some claimed that TV simply replaced political activism. 'Television took over', remembered one former militant, 'and the Communist Party is no longer a mass party.'[48] For the journalist Indro Montanelli, 'television … ruined everything'.[49]

Yet television (like consumerism and affluence itself) was always a contradictory medium. It had collective and individualising effects. It was neither 'bad' nor 'good'. It reflected change, as well as creating it. The television critic Beniamino Placido poked fun at the intellectual's attitude towards television. 'You can't. You must not. What kind of intellectual would you be if you had one [a TV set]? You would have given in to mass communication, to the cultural industry. Adorno would look down on you. Horkheimer would tell you off. And I can't even begin to think how Lukács would react.'[50] Television could liberate as well as oppress; it opened minds as well as closed them. To quote De Mauro again: 'For the poorest classes in Italy, such as the peasantry, television was a cultural model which also represented … an incentive to overcome ancient forms of inertia, to break old silences.'[51]

Television quickly became an object of discussion. The medium was as important as what was seen on screen, or the presumed object of any single programme. The transmission of the moon landings in 1969 was remembered not so much for the historic nature of that historic event, but rather because of a feisty and lengthy spat between two presenters. When Italian state television's monopoly began to break down in the 1970s, new forms of TV culture appeared in Italy. These would spawn further discussion over the ways that television was affecting all areas of Italian public life, including politics. Whatever the outcome of these debates, television was here to stay, and would play an increasingly central political and cultural role in the years to come.

Love and Marriage before and during
the Boom: Public Sinners?

The boom years saw powerful tensions emerge in Italian society between the forces of modernity and tradition. In this period of great change, there were those who tried desperately to preserve what they saw as central pillars of Italian life. One of these institutions was that of marriage – both in terms of the possibility of divorce and that of civil as opposed to religious union.

In the late 1950s the actions of a local priest led to a national debate over the role and values of the Church, and around marriage itself. Mauro Bellandi and Loriana Nunziati were a young couple from Prato, in Tuscany, who had been married in 1956 with a civil ceremony. They had both been baptised as Catholics – as was common in Italy at the time. Prato's bishop was scandalised by the decision taken by the couple, and sent a letter to a parish priest on the couple's wedding day. This letter was also pinned to the doors of local churches. It read as follows:

> Today, the 12 August, two of your parishioners are celebrating their wedding at the Town Hall and have refused a religious wedding. The ecclesiastical authorities have done all they can to prevent this very serious sin taking place. This gesture of open repudiation of religion is something that causes immense pain for the clergy and believers. A so-called civil marriage for two baptised people is not a marriage, but only the beginning of a scandalous form of concubinage [co-habitation].[52]

'For this reason,' the bishop continued, 'you ... and in the light of Christian morals and the laws of the Church [and] in line with the Canonical Code, will consider Mr Mauro Bellandi and Miss Loriana Nunziati as public sinners. They will not be allowed to have their house blessed, they cannot act as godparents during baptisms ... and they cannot have a religious funeral. We will pray for them so that this terrible scandal is resolved.'

But the bishop was not yet satisfied with his work. He also extended the definition of sinners to the families of the couple: 'Because the ecclesiastical authorities have noted that their parents have failed to fulfill their duties as Christian parents, and have allowed this sinful and scandalous act to take place, during Easter, the Bellandi family and the parents of Loriana Nunziati will not be allowed to take the holy waters. This letter will be read to the congregation.'

This very public dispute soon escalated. The couple took the unprecedented step of suing the bishop for defamation, and at this point a local scandal became a national cause célèbre. Politicians, writers, legal experts, Church leaders and many members of the ordinary public weighed in on either side of the debate. Aldo Capitini, a well-known peace campaigner and writer from Perugia, wrote to his own local priest to ask to be 'de-baptised' in protest.[53] After the Bishop of Prato was initially found guilty and ordered to pay 40,000 lire in damages, the Church launched a further protest, which, in some areas, included the ringing of bells and the laying out of black, mourning material around churches. The bishop was later cleared on appeal (with reference to the famous, or infamous, Article 7 of the constitution, which had fixed relationships between Church and State).

Prato's bishop saw himself as a Cold Warrior, a defender of values that he saw as being eroded all around him. In 1958 he wrote that 'I will never praise atheist Marxism, which is oppressive and inhuman – I will always describe it as evil ... I will never see light in ... that unhappy form of secular anti-Catholicism, which is ruining our country, which lives and breathes hatred ... and whose methods are rooted in insults, and whose sad mission is only to demolish all Christian values present in Italian society ... in order to open the road to the ugly forces of materialism.' The couple themselves later said that their lives had been deeply affected by the whole debate and legal process. Years later, the bishop was still defending his actions from the 1950s.[54] For those not directly involved, it seemed as if two Italies were at war. Many were forced to choose which side they were on.

Marriage, Divorce and the Law

It wasn't just *how* people got married – in a church, or through a civil ceremony – that caused controversy in democratic Italy. The behaviour of husbands and wives was also subject to public scrutiny and legal redress. The 1948 Constitution had stated that 'The Republic recognises the rights of the family as a natural society founded on marriage', but added that 'Marriage is based on the moral and legal equality of the spouses within the limits laid down by law to guarantee the unity of the family.' There was some ambiguity in these two articles, and it would be the constitutional courts and other courts that would be called upon to interpret various laws and customs from the past in a more modern Italy. Divorce was illegal, and the legal system still contained punishments for those who lived in ways that were seen by some as 'immoral'. Yet the application of these laws was inconsistent. A series of high-profile 'scandals' in the 1950s opened up the debate around divorce and led to reform.

The Cyclist and the 'White Lady'

In August 1954 two *carabinieri* and three other men turned up at a villa in Novi Ligure in northern Italy. It was 3 a.m. The *carabinieri* entered the house and checked the bedsheets and the wardrobes. It was said that they even tried to see whether the mattress was still warm. What were they looking for? The villa was owned by the world-famous cyclist Fausto Coppi, a sporting superstar of the time and one of the most well-known and recognisable people in Italy. A woman called Giulia Occhini was also in the house. Coppi was married, but not to Occhini, who later said that the couple were prepared for the arrival of the *carabinieri*. To try to avoid being caught sleeping in the same bed (a *crime*, at the time, as we will see), Coppi and Occhini had created a wardrobe with two sides through which she could escape if necessary. One of the men waiting outside was Occhini's husband, Enrico Locatelli.

A few weeks later – in September 1954 – the *carabinieri* returned at dinner time and arrested Giulia Occhini. She would spend the next four days and nights in prison, and was interrogated there concerning possible charges linked to the crimes of 'adultery' and 'abandonment of the conjugal bed'. She was only released with the provision that she reside in Ancona, far away from Coppi. She was also obliged to sign in at a police station every Sunday. Photographs published in the press showed her leaving prison with her belongings in a pillowcase.

Coppi was a cyclist of enormous talent and charisma who had won the Tour de France and Giro d'Italia in the same season just two years earlier, in 1952, and had been crowned world champion in 1953. Coppi and Occhini both had children. Their affair caused an enormous scandal, but so did the way they were treated. This was a front-page story, which dominated discussion in the popular and quality press and the gossip magazines, as well as in bars and living rooms across the country. Coppi had his passport taken away, and had to fight to get it back. It appeared that the authorities were attempting to make an example of this famous couple.

In March 1955 Occhini and Coppi were tried and convicted of the 'crime' of 'failure to satisfy family obligations' ('Violazione degli obblighi di assistenza familiare'). In the meantime, the charge of adultery had been dropped. Coppi's maid, Tilde Sartini, was cleared of having aided and abetted them at the same trial. The tone of the trial can be seen in this extract from the prosecutor's summing up: 'The beautiful Giulia waited for her man at the crossroads – not only because he was a star of world cycling but also because he was an ace of diamonds [a reference to his wealth].' Coppi was given a two-month sentence, while Occhini (who was pregnant) received three months. Both sentences were suspended.

The trial was widely reported, and the press demonised Occhini as a man-eater and gold-digger (who was referred to exotically as 'the white lady' – originally because of a white coat she wore). Two young children were also called to testify (Coppi's daughter was eight years old at the time). *L'Unità*, the Communist daily, wrote that 'this useless trial could have been avoided' and asked whether 'Italian magistrates don't have anything better to do with their time'. Other papers, however, feasted over the whole process, with word-by-word reports from the trial on their front pages.

The couple were released as the sentence was suspended, but the whole case had been a humiliating experience and there were further consequences, including those linked to the child they would later have. Coppi and Occhini married (secretly) in Mexico but that union was never recognised legally by the Italian state. Occhini was then advised to travel to Argentina when pregnant to avoid further repressive measures against her. In addition, she was barred from seeing her two children from her marriage with Locatelli. In 1957 Occhini finally won the legal right to visit those children every two months, but she was only allowed to see them inside a religious institution, in the presence of the Mother Superior (or 'a similar religious figure'). Her husband, who had been given custody of the children, had asked for these meetings to be restricted to once every six months. Coppi died of malaria in 1960. He was just forty years old. Newspapers published a banner photo of Occhini crying over his body on their front pages.

In the early 1970s, when the divorce law changed, Locatelli started proceedings to divorce Occhini, but he died before this procedure could be completed. Coppi's death had not ended Occhini's legal torment. Long battles over names and parental control dragged on for years, as they did over the cyclist's estate and the use of his name for marketing purposes. If Occhini had given birth in Italy her son with Coppi would have automatically taken the name of her husband, Locatelli. Argentinean law was different but did not override Italian legislation. It was not until 1978 that this battle was resolved – and Coppi and Occhini's son could legally call himself Faustino Coppi. For many, the whole affair (in every sense) exposed Italy's legal approach to marriage and adultery as grotesquely out of date. The sports journalist and writer Gianni Brera argued that 'by supporting Fausto and her it felt like we were part of a battle against centuries of traditionalism in our stupid and listless country'.[55]

Communist Morality

The Coppi case was the most high-profile legal drama of its kind in the 1950s, but it was certainly not the only such scandal. We have already noted the disquiet caused in the Communist Party when its leader Palmiro Togliatti left his wife for a much younger woman (Nilde Iotti, also a politician) after the war. The couple lived together for the rest of his life. This union led to gossip and 'outrage' but not to legal proceedings as nobody took the case to the police – unlike Occhini's husband.

Further scandals were to hit another high-level Communist married couple, Luigi Longo and Teresa Noce. Both Longo and Noce had fought in the Spanish Civil War and in the Italian anti-fascist Resistance, and in 1946 had been elected as Communists to the Constituent Assembly. In 1953 Longo took out residency in the tiny state of San Marino, where divorce was legal. His aim was to try to obtain a legal separation from Noce. This controversy then went public, embarrassing the party. Noce wrote to the *Corriere della Sera* saying that she knew nothing about the divorce. It later turned out that Longo had forged her signature. She noted that the Communist Party had opposed divorce during debates over the constitution, and added that 'Communists cannot have two kinds of politics – one personal, and one public.' She also noted that she was the leader of a large trade union with 'a majority of its members who are against divorce'.[56]

Noce's public statements were uncomfortable reading for the party on two levels. They brought into focus what they hoped would remain a private matter between two of its most important figures, and the comparisons with Togliatti's own personal life were obvious. There seemed to be one law for the party leaders and another for the masses. Yet Noce paid a heavy price for going public. She was marginalised within the party and shifted away from positions of influence.

Similar stories involved the famous footballer Valentino Mazzola in the 1940s, the millionaire publisher Giangiacomo Feltrinelli (rich people could get marriages annulled through special deals with the Church), the singer Mina who had a child out of wedlock, and Roberto Rossellini's high-profile affair with Ingrid Bergman in the 1940s and 1950s. There was also the relationship between the married film producer Carlo Ponti and Sofia Loren, or that involving Maria Callas (who married an Italian in 1949) and Aristotle Onassis. Gossip magazines pretended to take the high moral ground, but also sold copies through salacious reporting of affairs and legal processes.

Responding to the Boom: The Church

The boom presented the Church with serious challenges. Society was changing with speed, and the Church struggled to keep up. Before 1958 it had refused to modernise in any meaningful way apart from a little tinkering with liturgical practice. Change was painfully slow. Then in October of that year a new Pope was elected. He took the name of John XXIII. Born in 1881, his real name was Angelo Giuseppe Roncalli and he came from a large sharecropping family in the Lombard countryside. He served as a military chaplain in the army during the First World War, and was widely seen as having saved numerous Jews from persecution during the Second World War. From his first speech and acts, the new Pope – who would become known in Italy as 'the good Pope' – did things differently. He visited children in a hospital in Rome and used informal language to refer to himself. His (short) reign would be revolutionary, opening up the possibility of renewal within the Church in response to intense and transformative social, economic and political challenges.

The new Pope moved fast. In January 1959 he stated that there would be a reform process to examine all aspects of Church practice. He saw the 'modern age' as containing problems, 'deviations' but also 'opportunities'. This elaborate series of discussions and meetings was known as the Second Vatican Council (or the Twenty-First Ecumenical Church Council) and officially began in October 1962. It was a spectacular event, bringing together Catholics from across the world. For the opening of the Council hundreds of clerics paraded through the vast spaces of Piazza San Pietro in Rome. Ten commissions were set up, and the Council ran right through until 1965. A total of 2,500 bishops were involved in the Council's work. The very fact that the Church was discussing policy and age-old traditions was an important symbolic moment.

Documentation produced by the Council ranged from formal constitutions that had binding power of authority to practice and decrees that were more oriented towards directing or advising on the work of priests. But, in practical terms, what did the Vatican Council propose? There were changes that brought the Church closer to the people in an everyday sense. Mass no longer had to be performed in Latin, or with the priest's back turned towards the congregation, and the position of the altar was changed. The Vatican Council also stated that 'Access to sacred Scripture ought to be open wide to the Christian faithful.' More generally, the discussions by the Council led to great ferment in the Church.

Pope John broke with tradition. In 1962 he visited the cities of Loreto and Assisi in central Italy. He travelled like anyone else – by train. It was lent to the Pope by the Italian President, and departed from the old – and almost unused – station in the Vatican itself. Incredibly, this was the first time since 1857 that a sitting Pope had left the city of Rome. Enormous crowds turned out to see and often try to touch the Pope along the route. He also met with important Christian Democratic politicians. In one station the Pope told the crowd that 'you ask to kiss my hand, but I cannot do so with everyone. I raise my hand and bless you.' This was a Pope at home amongst the people. In one speech he advised parents to 'go home and give your children a hug'. Pope John's train journey set the tone. Subsequent Popes would become veritable globe-trotters.

Pope John XXIII died of stomach cancer in June 1963. He had been in charge for just under five years, but his influence was immense. After his death he quickly inspired a popular cult, especially in his home town that was renamed after him as Sotto il Monte Giovanni XXIII. Pope John was made a saint in 2013 despite only one confirmed 'miracle' – normally you need two – the curing of a nun in Naples in 1966 who saw a vision of the Pope in her prayers.

Pope John was succeeded by Pope Paul VI, another Italian who had previously been Archbishop of Milan. In that city, as Cardinal Montini (his name before he became Pope) he had reached out to the workers of the 'miracle', visiting numerous factories and preaching outside the gates. Internal immigration had led to significant urban growth, and new neighbourhoods appeared as if from nowhere. One of the consequences of this was the constant need for new churches. More than 120 new churches were planned or built by Montini during his time in Milan in the 1950s. Priests had always been key figures in villages and towns – now they took on this same pastoral and social role in the new city spaces that had grown 'like mushrooms' across Italy. The Church was right there, in the heart of the boom, setting out its stall amongst the new migrants to the big cities – providing services and playgrounds and advice.

Responding to the Boom: Politics

The Christian Democratic slogan for the 1958 elections, just as the boom was about to take off, was 'Progress without risk'. This encapsulated the party's idea of power. Successive Christian Democratic governments attempted to manage the epoch-changing developments of the boom years. They also put down deep roots across the country. Clientelistic networks of exchange were encouraged by the fact that the Christian Democrats were guaranteed political power after 1948. The party soon became a state within a state, with unlimited access to public resources that could be exchanged for electoral support. With clientelism came widespread patronage and nepotism. People were often placed in public roles not because they deserved to be there, on merit, but because of politics, friendship or family connections. Occasionally this led to quite grotesque networks of power-family-relationships. A system of 'recommendations' was built upon and sometimes consolidated. Jobs were dependent on mediators who guaranteed the 'provenance' of the candidate, as well as local power bases and gatekeepers. Without this kind of mediation, access to resources was almost impossible. An anti-meritocratic system influenced all institutions, not just those linked to pure politics – from universities to opera houses to telephone companies.

In the late 1960s Percy Allum, a British academic, set out to analyse the political power structures of Italy. He decided to look in depth at Naples, the most 'southern' of southern cities. Chapter 1 of his subsequent book started with what he called an 'Italian proverb' which, translated, read as follows: 'When a horse shits, a hundred sparrows dine.'[57] Much of Allum's book was dedicated to a detailed and concrete study of the political system in the city. Allum laid bare the machines that organised and controlled elections in Naples and distributed public funding. The city was electorally stable, something that Allum called 'part and parcel of the peculiar structure of Neapolitan society'.[58] To be elected in Naples, a politician required 'a following or a clientele'.[59] The construction of a *clientela* was a complicated process, which required political connections, resources and personal ties. Intermediaries built up links and got the vote out at election time. 'An individual politician's position,' Allum wrote, 'is measured in terms not only of the votes he can mobilise but the number of political messengers and "go-betweens" he can command.'[60]

But this was not just an academic analysis. Unusually, Allum named names. The Gava family, who had begun their rise up the local Christian Democratic Party in the 1950s, were the protagonists of the last part of the book. Allum listed the economic and public bodies controlled by various members of the Gava clan-family. Their interests ranged from the building trade (all the rage in Naples at the time) to tourism, public infrastructure and banking. Silvio Gava used his roles as a minister in the national government at various times to pass down appointments or influence their outcome. He held a number of ministerial positions and presidencies of commissions over the period between 1953 and 1972, and was elected in every election from 1948 to 1972.[61]

A fellow party member described him as 'a boss ... a man of power'.

Nationally, politics were built around a galaxy of small parties linked to the Christian Democrats. Italy had an extensive range of ministers and under-ministers, and these institutional figures exercised power and influence, with access to resources that could be handed down to potential and actual voters. The Christian Democratic Party itself created a series of factions that were almost mini-parties, and leaders and aspirant leaders jockeyed for position within coalitions. These factions were partly built around individuals (as with the so-called *Andreottiani* and *Fanfaniani*, linked to Christian Democratic grandees Giulio Andreotti and Amintore Fanfani), but they were also linked to broad political positions – there was a left, a right and a centre, as well as local power bases and parallel Church factions. Within these power structures, there were intense rivalries and the political war was extremely dirty.

1960: Riots and the Return of Anti-Fascism

As Italy entered the 1960s, Christian Democratic support was in slow if steady decline. The party needed new allies. It was at this point that it decided to seek the votes of the neo-fascist party – the Movimento Sociale Italiano – to prop up a government. This had never happened so explicitly before, and led to a revival of militant anti-fascism across Italy.

Anger at this strategy tapped into legacies remaining from the post-war settlement. Few former fascists had been punished in any way, while former partisans were seemingly being penalised for their past. In the 1950s Pier Paolo Pasolini saw Rossellini's famous wartime film, *Rome, Open City*, in a cinema in the capital. He then wrote a bitter poem about his feelings that day:

They are adults now [the children of *Roma Città Aperta*]: they've lived through/their appalling post-war corruption/[...] and they are all around me, poor little men/for whom each martyrdom has been useless/slaves of time, in these days/in which awakens the sad stupor of knowing/that all the light for which we lived/ was only a dream/unjustified, unobjective/source now of solitary, shameful tears.[62]

Memory was also being manipulated. Despite 25 April (Liberation Day) being a national holiday, the Christian Democrats tried to ban public demonstrations on 25 April 1948, just after their crushing victory in the general election of that year. Later, during the 1950s, the Christian Democrats inaugurated somewhat tepid celebrations. The government was keen to see the radical aspects of the Resistance marginalised, or ignored. The historian Phil Cooke has described 'the period following the attack on Palmiro Togliatti's life in July 1948 through the early 1950s' as when the Resistance was 'put on trial'. Thousands of former partisans were arrested, and there was also a backlash against the whole idea of militant anti-fascism.[63] Partisans often found it difficult to adapt to civilian life. A few took to crime. Others continued to dream of revolution. Meanwhile, on the left, and locally, the memory of the Resistance was kept alive through monuments, celebrations and cultural activities.

The frustration at the post-war agreements and amnesties boiled over in the summer of 1960. Anti-fascism was reborn in the streets. Fernando Tambroni was a powerful politician who had been Interior Minister for most of the second half of the 1950s. He then rose to the position of Prime Minister, but his slim majority in both houses in March and April 1960 relied on the support of the neo-fascists. Protests against the Tambroni government initially took place within the Christian Democratic Party itself, but they soon spread to the country at large.

Striped Shirts on the Streets

In June 1960 the Movimento Sociale Italiano decided to hold its annual congress in Genoa – a city with a powerful anti-fascist and Socialist tradition and where many had died during the

Resistance. To add to the provocative nature of this decision, the neo-fascist MSI party announced that the congress would be presided over by a man called Carlo Emanuele Basile. As Prefect of the City of Genoa under Nazi occupation, Basile was despised locally for his role in the repression of anti-fascism and his overseeing of wartime deportations. Not surprisingly, the news of the impending congress led to demonstrations.

The Socialist and future Italian President Sandro Pertini made an incendiary speech to gathering crowds in Genoa:

> We have been too kind to our enemies. This kindness has meant that today the fascists act as if they are in charge, and they have even said that the execution of Mussolini was murder. Yet, to the neo-fascists who are still out there I say – I am proud of having ordered the execution of Mussolini – because I, along with others, merely carried out that death sentence which had been pronounced by the Italian people twenty years earlier.[64]

Over the years there had been frequent calls for the MSI to be banned. Anti-fascists saw the very existence of that party as a crime in a constitutional democracy. When riots broke out in Genoa at the end of June, many of those who took to the streets were young people from the post-war, boom generation. These demonstrators were described generically as 'those in striped T-shirts' thanks to the clothes some of them wore. Others had taken part in the Resistance. Port workers were also out on the streets. The riots lasted for days and the MSI cancelled its planned congress.

As protests spread, the Tambroni government resorted to the violent suppression of demonstrations, which were attacked by police and fired upon right across Italy. In Rome on 6 July *carabinieri* on horseback charged an anti-fascist demonstration at a highly symbolic location – Porta San Paolo – the place where the Italian Resistance had officially begun in September 1943. Numerous plaques at that place attest to its importance as a historical site of anti-fascism. It is said that the *carabinieri* were led by a famous show-jumper on his horse, Raimondo D'Inzeo. In the Olympics held in Rome later that year, D'Inzeo would win a gold medal.

The Communist politician Pietro Ingrao, who was arrested during the clashes in Rome, told Parliament on 7 July that 'many of us saw the violence, the charges by the cavalry, mass beatings, house to house searches. A non-communist establishment newspaper has made a reference to "other times". And when we are close to the fallen of Porta San Paolo, we know what times we are talking about.'[65] Things would soon get even worse, confirming the darkest predictions of those who said that the Fascists were on their way back to power.

Also on 7 July an anti-fascist demonstration was planned for Reggio Emilia, a city governed by the Communist Party. In what appeared to be a premeditated attack, police shot into the crowd, killing five unarmed protestors. A total of 182 shots were fired. Another four people were killed in Sicily on 8 July. The 'dead of Reggio Emilia' became a powerful symbol of the 'new resistance', inspiring a well-known anti-fascist song:

> Compagno cittadino fratello partigiano
> teniamoci per mano in questi giorni tristi
> di nuovo a Reggio Emilia di nuovo là in Sicilia
> son morti dei compagni per mano dei fascisti
> di nuovo come un tempo sopra l'Italia intera
> Fischia il vento infuria la bufera.

> (Comrade citizen brother partisan
> let us stick together in these sad days
> Once again in Reggio Emilia and in Sicily
> Comrades have been killed by the fascists
> Once again a storm is brewing and the wind is screaming
> Across the whole of Italy.)

'Per i morti di Reggio Emilia' by Fausto Amodei, 1961.[66]

Government officials defended the repressive activities of the forces of law and order, and claimed that (in the face of all the evidence) there was a 'pre-established' plan to organise an 'insurrection' in Italy which also involved 'international forces' (or 'Moscow'). On 19 July, under intense pressure from elements within his own party, Tambroni resigned. A new government was sworn in during August, without MSI votes. Nobody would attempt to use neo-fascist votes again until the 1990s (when the MSI would effectively cease to exist). If they were to remain in power, the Christian Democrats would now have to look to the left. A new period of political alliances was inevitable. Meanwhile, Italy was about to become a global stage for the first time since the era of Fascism.

1960: The World Comes to Rome

The year 1960 was a tumultuous one for Italy. It was the peak of the boom (although nobody knew it at the time) with near full-employment in parts of the country. In August and September, Italy hosted the Olympic Games in Rome, its first major international event since the fall of Mussolini's regime. Eighty-three nations took part. A sparkling new stadium was built, and vast areas of the city were expropriated to construct the Olympic village and other sites. Many years later (in 2015), the Mayor of Rome, Ignazio Marino, revealed that the city had still not paid for all the costs of the 1960 games.

Cassius Clay – later Muhammed Ali – won a gold medal in Rome (which he later claimed to have thrown into the Ohio river after a racist incident back home) and there was enough Italian success to make a few individuals into household names. Imaginative use was made of Rome's unique settings – with gymnastics being staged in the Caracalla Baths. Not everything was focused on the capital city. Yachting was held in the Bay of Naples and rowing in Lake Albano near the Pope's summer residence.

One non-Italian victory was highly symbolic. The barefoot runner Abebe Bikila won the marathon – held partly at night, to avoid the heat, with spotlights and torches picking out the leaders. After Bikila had crossed the finish line, he launched into a series of vigorous exercises. His run through Rome's monuments – some of which had been stolen from his home nation – was epic and beautiful. Bikila was a soldier in Haile Selassie's army, and his father, it was said, had fought against Mussolini's troops in the 1930s. Selassie, the Emperor of Ethiopia, had been forced into exile by Mussolini's Fascist invasion in 1935–6.

Centre-Left

In the early 1960s a series of experimental centre-left administrations (with Christian Democrats and Socialists) were tried out at a local level – in Milan, Florence and Genoa – and this model would now take root in central government. Moderate, reformist and anti-fascist Christian Democratic politicians were happy to propose a shift to the left as part of a new strategy in the wake of the disastrous Tambroni experiment. Thus, the centre-left was born. These alliances would not be with the Communists – the Cold War ruled out that kind of link until the 1970s and beyond – but with the more moderate and Western-supporting Partito Socialista Italiano (PSI). Centre-left governments after 1962 (some with 'external support' from the PSI, some with Socialist ministers in the cabinet itself) finally carried through long-awaited reforms to the education system and instituted other policies such as the nationalisation of the electricity network.

Aldo Moro, a moderate but modern Christian Democratic politician with a strong sense of religious belief and a power base in the South (and specifically Apulia), was the architect of the centre-left. Moro was also a respected academic who taught in the Department of Political Science in Rome's La Sapienza University – part of which is now named after him. His interminable speeches to Christian Democratic congresses (in 1962 he kept his audience in their seats for seven hours) were masterpieces of 'political speak'. In December 1963 the first fully fledged centre-left government was sworn into office.

This caused protest both within the Christian Democratic Party and amongst Socialists. Many left-wing Socialists opposed to an alliance with the Christian Democrats left the party in 1964, forming a new party known as the Partito Socialista Italiano di Unità Proletaria or PSIUP. This grouping contained many important intellectuals and activists and historic members of the PSI, such as Lelio Basso, Emilio Lussu and Vittorio Foa. However, it failed to make much of an impression on the electorate and in 1972 it split again – this time three ways (some went back to the PSI, some to the Communists, and some to a new, smaller party called the Partito di Unità Proletaria or PdUP) – and disappeared completely. Nonetheless, the Socialists were crucial in modernising Italy in the 1960s – and especially in terms of its institutions. The Communists, meanwhile, were still excluded from national power.

1964: Rome – End of an Era

Thousands lined the streets for Togliatti's funeral in Rome in 1964. He had died in Yalta in the Soviet Union while on holiday in August. People held up clenched fists, and were crying. Mourners filed past the coffin, many also making the sign of the cross as they did so. Later, sequences from this funeral appeared in films by well-known directors Pier Paolo Pasolini and the Taviani brothers. Renato Guttuso, a communist artist, created a huge mural called *Togliatti's Funeral*, with massed red flags around a sea of figures, and with a number of Lenins, a Stalin, a figure of the American communist Angela Davis and nearly all of the PCI leadership from the time.

Togliatti's coffin had been brought back to Italy on an Aeroflot plane. 'Even in death,' wrote Rossana Rossanda, 'he couldn't escape the Soviet mantle.'[67] 'At his funeral,' she remembered, 'a vast crowd walked for hours and hours, trampling the fading petals from the wreaths that shed more and more of them as the procession made its way to San Giovanni [a large piazza in Rome often used for left-wing demonstrations].'[68] The Soviet leader Leonid Brezhnev and the Spanish Civil War heroine La Pasionaria (Dolores Ibárruri) spoke from the platform. The poet Paolo Neruda sent a message that asked people to 'Consider me amongst those who are crying.'

During his life, and even after his death, Togliatti's private life was something of an embarrassment for the party. His wife (from whom he had been separated for years) and son Aldo were asked to stay in a car during the funeral, while his partner Nilde Iotti was seen in public amongst the front row of mourners, dressed in black, alongside the couple's adopted daughter, Marisa. In some ways, Iotti was only allowed to become Togliatti's official partner after his death. Her role as widow overshadowed her complicated position as unmarried 'companion'.

The journalist and author Giorgio Bocca described Togliatti's funeral as 'incredible! ... A million people followed the coffin, arriving from all over Italy, Communists and non-Communists, people who took their first train, their first plane, to see his body laid out for the last time where great figures from world communism stood guard ... they saluted him with a clenched fist, or by bowing their heads, or with the sign of the cross ... men and women were in tears, as if their own father had passed away'.[69]

The brief appearance of Togliatti's son on that day underlined one of the dark sides of the Togliatti story. Aldo suffered from mental-health problems, and would be confined to a clinic for the last thirty years of his life, in Modena. The party decided to keep Aldo's fate a secret, and he wasn't registered in the clinic under his own surname – just as 'Aldo'. In the 1990s a local journalist 'discovered' him there. 1964 had been, according to some journalists, the last time Aldo was glimpsed in public.[70]

Togliatti's funeral also took on deeper historical meaning. The historian Giuliano Procacci concluded that 'In the sadness of the crowds who accompanied him for the last time, there was an understanding that certain aims had not been achieved, [and] the foreboding of a long and difficult road ahead.'[71] But the historian of the Communist Party, Paolo Spriano, argued that Togliatti 'was also, and perhaps above all, a man who took sides, that of the workers, the poor, those who did not have power', and in this sense he had not been 'defeated'.[72] Whatever the truth, Togliatti's death seemed to signal the end of an era.

Moral Panic: Censorship and Modernisation

The boom led to intense debate over all aspects of Italian society. It was a time of hope, but also a period of fear. Many wanted to modernise Italy, others were worried about the pace of change, and the disappearance of traditional values. There were attempts to stem the tide of progress. The boom was a time when institutional figures took a stand as 'defenders of public morality'. In 1960 the celebrated film director Luchino Visconti released his explosive three-hour epic, *Rocco and his Brothers*. A sweeping melodrama set in the time it was made, *Rocco* told the story of five brothers, and their mother, and the outcome of that family's migration from the deep south of Basilicata to Milan. The film was dominated by a powerful and violent love triangle involving two of the brothers, Simone and Rocco (played by a young and stunning Alain Delon), and a prostitute, Nadia, played by Annie Girardot. In one shocking scene, Girardot is raped by Simone in front of Rocco. Simone taunts his brother by throwing Girardot's knickers at him – which land on Rocco's head. This scene – and others in the film – led to a censorship scandal.

Censors demanded extensive cuts to the film, which Visconti refused to make. The arguments of the censors were, however, a little confused. On the one hand, they accused Visconti of throwing mud at Italy, of defaming the country's reputation, of distorting reality. On the other, however, they claimed that the scenes were 'too real', too close to the bone. In the end a compromise was reached. The offending scene was 'blacked out' with darkened film – but kept in the movie. Crowds flocked to see the film, and it was said that many tried to sit in the front row to try and get as good a view of the offending scenes as possible. *Rocco* was a big hit, in part thanks to the censorship row. A fully restored version would only be recreated in the 1990s.

Censorship debates or moral panics were attached to a series of other films in the same period, from Michelangelo Antonioni's masterpieces *L'Avventura* and *La Notte* to Federico Fellini's international smash hit *La Dolce Vita*. Pasolini's work was also heavily censored and the object of political attack from the right, and theatre was caught up in the controversy. In 1960 Visconti directed a play based on a novel by Giovanni Testori, *L'Arialda*, set in a working-class housing block in Milan. The play opened for over-18s only in Rome, with cuts imposed. When it moved to

Milan in 1961, the play was closed after just one night following an intervention by the same censor who had blocked *Rocco and his Brothers*. Court cases and seizures of copies of Testori's books were to follow. Many felt that Italian society was modernising at such a speed that crucial values were being lost. Others argued that modernisation was proceeding far too slowly. Here, as in other spheres, two Italys stood on either side of the fence, with different visions of their country and its institutions. The next decade would see a heady mixture of reform and violence.

3

Blood and Reform: Institutional Change and Violence in the 1960s and 1970s

The late 1960s and 1970s in Italy were a time of confrontation, violence and bloodshed. Yet this was also a period of epochal and peaceful reform, which saw Italy's institutions dragged into the twentieth century. Italy experienced a 'long May' of protest, focused around the key year of 1968. The state and political parties responded, at last, by passing a series of reforms. There were major changes to family law (1975), radical changes to the prison system (1975), psychiatric hospitals were abolished altogether (1978), while divorce (1970) and abortion (1978) were legalised. Workers won major rights in the workplace and beyond (1970). A national health service was put in place, alongside other parts of the welfare state.

While battles raged on the streets, and in the courtrooms, with bombs, assassinations, conspiracies and plots, Italy and her institutions were modernised as pressure from all sides, but in particular the movements emerging from 1968, saw lawmakers put together organic and modern reforms, which often anticipated changes in other countries. The 1970s were thus a period of exceptional reform, giving the lie to the idea that Italy would never change, or was 'unreformable'. A 'long march' through the institutions took place, right across Italy. And one of the sparks for this revolution was seen in the most unlikely of places – a psychiatric hospital in a town on the border with Communist Yugoslavia.

Concrete Utopias: Franco Basaglia and the Revolution in Psychiatry

In 1961 a psychiatrist called Franco Basaglia took over as Director of the Psychiatric Hospital in Gorizia, right on the edge of north-east Italy. The grounds of the hospital were marked by the same border that signalled the edge of the West itself – the Iron Curtain. On the other side stood Tito's Yugoslavia. An anti-fascist who had been in prison in Venice under Nazi occupation, Basaglia quickly decided that the institution of which he was in charge was both useless and morally wrong. His first act was to refuse to give permission for the tying-up of patients at night. This physical restraint for patients was so much part of the asylum's routine that it was normally given retrospectively. Basaglia said no. Later, he wrote that the hospital smelt 'of shit, and of death'. Those smells took him back to his time in prison in wartime Venice. Asylums were forbidding and frightening places.

In 1949 Ugo Cerletti, the Italian psychiatrist who invented electro-shock treatment (by experimenting on pigs) visited a psychiatric hospital in the south of Italy. Inside, he found a vision of hell. 'A bunch of a hundred or so human bare-footed and dishevelled creatures, dressed in shapeless uniforms … [were] crushed together … From within came cries and shouts of all kinds.'[1] Italy's health minister used Dante's *Inferno* to invoke conditions inside many asylums. Photographers capture the battered bodies and prison-like architecture that featured in these so-called 'hospitals'. In some places, militants 'descended' on their local asylum, demanding to be allowed in to see how their relatives and friends were being treated.

After 1961, Basaglia set about reforming Gorizia's asylum from the inside, freeing patients from restraint and organising general meetings. Patients knocked down their own walls and fences, and were filmed doing so. Psychiatrists abandoned their white coats. Patients were listened to, often for the first time, and treated as human beings. Basaglia's office door was 'always open'. In 1968–9 this experience of radical reform suddenly became famous, thanks to a best-selling collective book, *L'istituzione negata* (*The Institution Denied*), and a prime-time television documentary, seen by millions, called *I giardini di Abele* (*The Gardens of Abel*). Gorizia's 'overturned' psychiatric hospital seemed to prefigure real institutional change. It represented a 'practical utopia' that could be visited, listened to, photographed and filmed. Many who visited the asylum were amazed. They couldn't, they said, tell who 'the mad' were. Soon, the movement for the reform of psychiatric institutions spawned similar radical experiments right across Italy. Critical texts about madness and psychiatric care became best-sellers. The Canadian sociologist Erving Goffman's study, *Asylums*, for example, was widely read, and its definition of 'total institutions' was then applied to other places – from schools to prisons.

There were over 100,000 people inside psychiatric hospitals in Italy in the early 1960s. Most asylums were conceived on a large scale and deliberately located outside of city centres. The organisation and running of these hospitals was still governed by a law from 1904 and by Fascist legislation. Patients were registered with local judges and denied the right to vote, but they had committed no crime (although there was also a criminal asylum system). Once admitted, it was frequently difficult to leave. Treatment often seemed more like punishment, and repressive methods bordering on institutionalised torture were common.

Basaglia's practical utopia was taken further in the 1970s when he was appointed director of the asylum in Trieste, a bigger and more metropolitan city – but still a place very much linked to the Cold War. By 1971 when Basaglia arrived in Trieste, ten years after his appointment in Gorizia, there was a nationwide and global movement solidly in favour of change in terms of mental health care. Basaglia himself helped to set up a national organisation called *Psichiatria democratica*. Local politicians gave the reformers support – many were shocked by what they had seen inside the psychiatric hospitals under their control.

Many asylums soon became more humane and democratic, and patients were returned to the community. New forms of treatment were attempted, including anti-psychotic drugs but also creative techniques involving theatrical experimentation and art therapy. But this process was not without risks. Occasionally former patients murdered partners or parents, while others committed suicide. Basaglia himself was twice accused of manslaughter (and twice cleared).

In Trieste, Basaglia managed to empty the mental hospital in a few, brief, exciting years of change. He set up cooperatives to move people back into the world of work, as well as innovative daycare centres across the city. The asylum even became a centre for cultural activity – with concerts, debates, art projects and exhibitions. Jazz legend Ornette Coleman played a celebrated concert in the grounds. Barriers between the city and the 'city of the mad' were broken down. A large blue papier-maché horse (called Marco Cavallo, after the horse that used to pull the laundry truck inside the asylum) was designed by artists (including Basaglia's cousin Vittorio) inside the asylum and paraded through the streets of Trieste. The symbolic exit of the horse prefigured the release of thousands of patients across the country.

The forgotten people inside asylums were given a voice. In Arezzo's psychiatric hospital, a patient – Adalgisa Conti – was 'discovered' in the 1970s. She had been inside that institution for nearly sixty years (since 1913). Her life story became a book.[2] Another patient, in Gorizia, had not seen the city centre (a mere ten minutes' walk away) for decades. Meetings were held inside asylums where patients could discuss their treatment and the running of the hospital itself. Arezzo witnessed over five hundred patient meetings in eleven years of reform activity. The journalist Franco Pierini wrote about the meetings he witnessed:

It would be wrong, very wrong, to report that these men and women talk like us and can argue like us. They do it better, their way of discussing things, their dialectic of opposing views, their skill in reaching conclusions without scapegoating or making anyone feel defeated, is superior to ours.[3]

People who had never spoken before were speaking out. There was an 'explosion of orality'. The possession of words and the taking the floor was something that would be seen everywhere in the late 1960s – as institutions were challenged by students and workers, and even by artists and architects. This challenge reached down into the family itself, as children rejected parental authority. Women demanded more power and equal rights inside the family, and in society as a whole. Many were attracted by the idea of going 'on the road', in a desire to escape from the suffocating conservatism of much of provincial Italy. This desire for liberty was accompanied by experiments in sexual liberation, musical tastes, literature and art, and the setting up of alternative spaces to the family and the school.

Pressure for radical reform of the entire system thus built up from below. All the major parties eventually accepted that something had to be done. In 1968 reforms to the outdated 1904 law allowed for guest status in asylums and the formation of mental health centres. Ten years later, during the 'age of reform', and with the backing of both the Christian Democrats and the Communist Party, the so-called 'Basaglia law' was passed. Law 180 (178) was a historic piece of legislation.

The circumstances around the passing of the 'Basaglia law' were unique – but the climate of change was not. A referendum pushed by the Radical Party (a small organisation dedicated to radical reform) to get rid of the 1904 law collected hundreds of thousands of signatures. There was a real danger of a legislative vacuum, and it was this threat that finally forced the political class into action. An agreement was found in record time to avoid a referendum – and (exceptionally) this legislation was passed in committee and without even being voted on by Parliament itself. The law was a compromise, but it was also revolutionary. All asylums (apart from criminal psychiatric hospitals, which are currently being disbanded) were to be closed. No new asylums could be built. Emergency mental health care centres were to be opened in general hospitals, and these were designed to be small (to avoid the creation of new, 'mini-asylums'). Mental health was no longer separated from other illnesses. Mental health patients were thus integrated into the world of health in general. Their position was (finally) brought into line with the constitution. They were to be citizens, with rights. Forced treatment – which was only to be allowed under exceptional circumstances – was very carefully regulated.

Once the reform was passed, it quickly became part of general health care reforms that were passed in the late 1970s, instituting Italy's national health service. Later, health care was decentralised to regional governments. This led to considerable variations from region to region in terms of mental health care. Despite the 1978 law, asylums remained open for some time. It took decades to deal with the so-called 'residual' asylum population. Many people simply could not function outside of the institution they knew so well. Others did not want to leave at all.

Moreover, reformed asylums had often developed into more humane places, greatly preferable to the pre-Basaglia era. A long battle ensued for the implementation of the reforms – and there were constant proposals for the abrogation of Law 180 and the retention of psychiatric hospitals. Basaglia's wife, Franca Ongaro, who was twice elected as a senator in the 1980s and 1990s, was one of the leaders of this struggle – although by then the movement that had sustained Basaglia was far weaker than it had been in the 1970s.

Those opposed to reform and closure – such as the writer and psychiatrist Mario Tobino – complained that patients had 'been abandoned' and families been forced to carry the burden of problems caused by mental illness. There was talk of 'hundreds of suicides'. Tragedies linked to mental illness were blamed on the law and on the Basaglian movement. Yet, by the end of the 1990s, nearly all the old asylums had been closed. Some are now in ruins, while others have become universities, flats or schools. Beautiful parks have, in some cases, been opened where once there were sites of institutionalised suffering and exclusion. Other former asylums are still linked to mental health care. An entire system had been transformed. This was a sector where Italy led the world, and many still visit Trieste (designated as a model for mental health care by the World Health Organisation) to try and understand how to close or reform their own systems. The story of the radical psychiatry movement in the 1960s and 1970s and

Piazzale Loreto, Milan, 29 April 1945. The bodies of Fascist leaders are hung by their feet from a petrol station so the crowd can see them. Mussolini and his lover, Claretta Petacci, are third and fourth from the left respectively. The other bodies include – from left to right – Nicola Bombacci (to the left of Mussolini) and Alessandro Pavolini and Achille Starace (to the right of Petacci).

Poster for the film *Paisà*, Roberto Rossellini, 1946.

Peasants ploughing, 1950s.

The FALCK factory, Sesto San Giovanni, Milan, 1971.

Men reading the results of the 2 June 1946 referendum in the newspapers. The middle headline reads: 'The Republic has won'.

Mourners visiting Palmiro Togliatti's body, Communist Party headquarters, central Rome, 23 August 1964. The photo is of Togliatti.

Silvestre Loconsolo (Archivio del Lavoro, Milan, Italy)

The Pirelli Tower, Milan, 1964.

Enzo Ferrari in front of the Ferrari factory in
Maranello, near Modena, central Italy, 1960s. The car
is a 330 GT 2+2, first produced in 1964.

Touring Club Italiano/Alinari Archives Management

The A6 between Turin and Savona, 1970.

Vatican Council II, St Peter's Basilica, Rome, 1960s.

Gianni Agnelli near the factory gates of FIAT's Mirafiori factory, Turin, 1966.

Italian emigrant worker in Germany, 1972.

Vajont, 1963: the aftermath of the tragedy in the area where the town of Longarone once stood.

Cars recovered after the flood in Florence, 1966.

Funeral for the victims of the Piazza Fontana bombing, Piazza del Duomo, Milan, 15 December 1969.

the 'Basaglia law' in the 1970s reveal how this period was one of great ferment and change, and concrete reform, which revolutionised Italy's institutions. There was more to come.

Schools, Exams and Experiments

Italy's school system had last undergone systematic reform in 1923, right at the beginning of the Fascist era. Post-war Italian education was in dire need of change, but as with so many other public institutions this was slow to materialise. Education was, not surprisingly, a hot political battleground, and the Church was a crucial part of the system. Until 1962–3 most children just went to elementary school, and many left education altogether at that point to go to work. The physical state of many schools was dire, and teachers had often learnt their trade under the Fascist regime. Photographs published in the post-war period showed schools in the South where children had no shoes and rooms were filthy.

Children who remained within the system went on to *licei* – schools of excellence directed largely towards either a classical or a scientific education – or technical institutes where a trade could be learnt. In the early 1960s centre-left coalitions attempted to reform the education system. After a lengthy debate, a new 'middle-school' system was set up for children between eleven and fourteen and the school leaving age was raised to fourteen. Experimentation was encouraged at some levels of the system. A new generation of teachers entered the profession.

Italy's elites continued to be formed in the prestigious urban *licei*, often in the classical wing of the system: the Liceo d'Azeglio in Turin, the Liceo Mameli in Rome, the Liceo Machiavelli in Florence. In general, as in France, it was the state school system that attracted and reproduced privilege in the economic and political spheres. Private schools were of a lower standard and prestige, and carried stigma as institutions that were for those who couldn't hack it in state schools. Large numbers of institutions were run by and for the Catholic Church – who also attracted children to after-school clubs or summer (Italian kids had three months off in the summer) play–pray places called *oratori* or *colonie estive* (with services generally not provided by the state itself).

In most schools education was based around learning by rote and tough oral exams. Hierarchies were rigid and curriculums traditional. Progression from year to year was difficult and selective. Many students were 'knocked back' or '*bocciati*' at the end of the year, and forced to repeat an entire year with younger children (or change to an 'easier' school to complete their studies). This system invested individual teachers with great power. Teaching was a profession with a high status in Italy (something that remains to some extent true today).

The *licei* and other schools were places that were often hostile to the poor – and where Italian had always been obligatory (thus discriminating against and marginalising those who spoke in dialect). These institutions were run through authoritarian sets of rules and regulations, including an emphasis on 'good behaviour' for which a mark was received at the end of the year. Discrimination within this system was rife. For example, in some schools frequented by southern immigrants around Milan in the 1950s and 1960s, around half the children were being knocked back every year. In many cases this was the result of decisions taken by northern teachers in the face of children from a different culture. Separate classes – known as *differential* classes – were set up through a 1962 law for so-called 'unruly' (*disadattati*) children. In 1967 a further decree established that 'students who have anomalies or psychological-physical abnormalities which do not allow them to attend normal schools in a regular way and who require particular treatment or medical-education assistance will be sent to "special schools". Those who are marked by a non-serious level of "intellectual backwardness", or are "unsuited to their environment", or those with behavioural problems, and who can be reintegrated into normal schools, will be sent to "differential classes".' Thus 'slow' or 'difficult' students (who were often identified amongst the children of migrants, especially from the South) were often transferred to these so-called 'special' classes – a form of institutional segregation that condemned many of them to educational failure. Alongside this system there were special institutions for children designated as having mental or physical handicaps. Some of these schools had been set up much earlier in the nineteenth and twentieth centuries. The 'differential' classes were abolished in 1977 and replaced with support or special-needs teachers – a reform that allowed for the integration of all children into the same class.[4]

Letter to a Teacher

A backlash against the more antiquated features of the school system began to take root in the 1960s. A key aspect of this radical critique came from an unlikely source in rural Tuscany. Lorenzo Milani was born in 1923 in Florence to a Jewish mother and a Catholic father. He became a priest in 1947 and was soon in trouble for his critical attitude to Church hierarchies and his attempt to set up a local 'popular' school open to all – and not just Catholics.

To punish Don Milani for his unorthodox behaviour, in 1954 he was sent by the Church authorities to a tiny rural hamlet in Tuscany, a backwater known as Barbiana. Undaunted by this attempt to sideline him, Don Milani set up another school in the grounds of a church for local children, with a focus on those who had struggled within traditional institutions. Milani's alternative and utopian 'school' ran all day and at weekends, and throughout the holidays. It used the Italian constitution as a text. On the walls Milani wrote slogans that subverted those of fascism – such as 'I care' (one of the slogans under the regime had been 'I don't care'). Children were encouraged to talk about their own lives, not study abstract subjects that had little connection to the realities of the everyday. All children could attend – and the pupils in some ways 'taught themselves'. Another aspect of their education was that there was the reading out loud of the daily newspaper, every day. Classes were often held outside.

In 1967 a book was published with a simple white cover. The 'authors' were eight children from the Barbiana school themselves – but Don Milani was a crucial figure behind the publication. This short book would soon take Italy by storm. Its title was *Letter to a Teacher* and its language was clear, direct, angry. 'This book', it began, 'has not been written for teachers, but for parents. It is a call for them to organise.' The text was in the form of a letter, as the title suggested. It started like this:

Dear Miss,

You won't remember me or my name. You have failed so many of us. On the other hand I have often had thoughts about you, and the other teachers, and about the institution which you call 'school' and about the boys that you fail. You fail us right out into the fields and factories and there you forget us.[5]

Letter to a Teacher was a combination of many features that would soon take root in 1968 and beyond. It contained a kind of sociological enquiry into the way traditional schools were run (a form of counter-information); it attacked structures of power in the school system, and it provided or pointed towards alternatives to that system. For the children and teachers in Barbiana, Italy's state schools were based around class discrimination. They supported the rich but humiliated and excluded the poor. *Letter to a Teacher* compared schools to hospitals 'which cure the healthy and reject the ill'. Don Milani was very clear about one aspect of the school system – exams – they were to 'be abolished'. The message to teachers was blunt: 'most of your children hate school'.

Barbiana itself was a practical utopia and – like Basaglia's Gorizia – its influence was enormous. This was a new kind of school, where children were active participants, and where nobody was knocked back. 'Give a full-time school to children who seem stupid ... Give a purpose to the lazy.'[6] The book became a kind of bible for a new generation of students, teachers and educators. But even Barbiana couldn't work miracles. Some kids dropped out, despite the best efforts of the priest and the other children. Others were forced to work – their toil was needed in the fields. Don Milani could also be very strict.

With the success of the book, followers flocked to Barbiana to see the school in action. Although Don Milani died of cancer in 1967 at the age of forty-four (an early death that confirmed his mythical-martyr status), the example of 'Barbiana' lived on. A wave of innovation spread through the education system – as demand for change affected students and teachers alike, as well as parents. *Letter to a Teacher*, like the work of Basaglia and his radical psychiatrists, prepared the ground both for the movements of 1968 and for the legal reforms of the 1970s. There was also a dark side to *Letter to a Teacher*. In some people's hands it turned all teachers into a class enemy. Its language was radical and totalising. It was an incendiary text.[7]

Don Milani also played a key role in another institutional set of reforms. Military service had been a cornerstone of Italy's military state since unification in the nineteenth century. All men (with some exceptions) had to serve in the army for varying periods and there was no 'civil' option. Those who refused without a legitimate reason were given prison sentences – and treated as deserters. Military service was commonly known by the term *La Naja*, which seemed to indicate (in a negative sense) a kind of trap or web.

In 1972 conscientious objectors were finally allowed to opt out of full-blown military service. After the reforms of that year, young men had a choice between the military and something called 'civil service'. In the latter case, they could work in schools or in various other public institutions. This change to the law followed a long battle on the part of pacifists, the left, as well as priests and Catholics. Don Milani published a pamphlet in opposition to military service entitled 'Obedience is no Longer a Virtue'. It took the form of a letter to 'military priests' who had dubbed 'conscientious objectors' an insult to the nation. If this was the case, Milani wrote, 'I have no fatherland and I believe I have the right to divide the world into the poor and the needy on the one hand, and the privileged and the oppressors on the other. The first group represent my fatherland, the other group represent my foreigners.'[8] The priest from Florence was tried and condemned (on appeal) for encouraging desertion and 'insulting the armed forces', but in the meantime he had passed away.

There is Hope, if this Can Happen in Vho

In a tiny northern town called Vho, near Cremona in the north of Italy, a teacher called Mario Lodi began to experiment with alternative methods in the elementary school where he taught from 1956 onwards. Lodi visited Barbiana in 1963. He later published an account of his experiences in the classroom in a series of books, using the same direct and clear form as *Letter to a Teacher*. One of his books was called *C'è speranza se questo accade al Vho* (*There is Hope, if this Can Happen in Vho*). For Lodi, there was 'nothing ... like an institution to show what condition people are in'.[9] Lodi took Don Milani's revolution into the state school system. He was one of many idealistic teachers who were to transform the profession in the post-war period.

One of Lodi's first acts in his new school was to physically rearrange the classroom. The desk at the front – symbol of the teacher's power – was removed. He tried to create space for interaction and play. Lodi would also sit down, so to be at the same height as the students. He felt that 'the school is designed for slaves, not free people' and 'the freedom to educate is non-existent'.[10] Like Don Milani, he wanted to abolish exams and liberate students from the hierarchies in the system. Lodi compared school students to factory workers.

School students were educated 'in an authoritarian system based on exams ... if the teacher no longer has the power to give out marks, the whole system will collapse. It would be like taking away weapons from the police in an oppressive state. In the schoolroom – a place which looks like a prison or a factory – there is a simple, functional and terrible set of rules: explanation, repetition, mark.'[11]

For Lodi and other radical educators the school needed to be overturned from within, and reformed from without. An entirely new educational system was required. Schools were class-based systems, 'which tend to create docile and passive people, who know little about the important things in life'. 'Children,' he added 'need to be put at the centre of things, free of all fear.'[12] Lodi's books were widely read and highly influential, like those based on the Barbiana experiment. This type of critique of educational institutions and experimental practice led directly to a series of other innovative experiences that ranged from nurseries right up to universities and adult education.

The psychoanalyst Elvio Fachinelli dubbed this type of activity 'non-authoritarian practice in schools'. Students should, Fachinelli argued, be allowed to 'eat when they want, sit on tables, talk in dialect, have dirty knees or wear see-through shirts, play cards ... all things which many people believe are incompatible with schooling and education'.[13] But the problem was not just the school itself – it also included the family. For these alternative educators, 'authoritarianism starts in infancy through the family'.[14] Part of the strategy for change was that of revealing the true face of institutions and how they worked. They needed to be 'unmasked' to provoke change.

Exam Factories?

School exam systems in the Republic were still governed by Giovanni Gentile's reforms, passed way back in 1923. Gentile had introduced national state exams. If these were passed – by *licei* students – access to university was guaranteed. But only those who went to the *Liceo Classico* could choose from all university courses on offer, while those from the *Licei Scientifici* were able to access scientific subjects. Other school graduates were not admitted to university at all. This state exam was known as *La Maturità* and was also a rite of passage for many young people.

In December 1969, in the wake of the university student and school student movements of 1967–8, a change to the law loosened up the exam system. Access to universities was opened up both in terms of courses and qualifications. This 'urgent' university/school reform liberalised access for school students from different kinds of institutions. It was an important victory. A university place was no longer the reserve of the elite, and this was a measure that clearly favoured social mobility. Italy's school system had modernised and become more democratic. But critics of this new system saw the reformed exams as excessively easy. Pass rates stood at 70 per cent or so in the 1950s and 1960s, but rose considerably to around 90 per cent in 1971 and 94 per cent in 1981. Since then, they have risen still further.

Much debate focused on technical matters linked to the state exam. Final results were usually decided upon by a so-called commission with teachers from the student's school plus externals. The precise make-up of these commissions was linked to the 'objectivity' or otherwise of the final results. Outside commissioners guaranteed some sort of objectivity. The *maturità* exam was a vast national logistical operation, with deep cultural and social implications, which saw thousands of students across Italy stay up for nights on end as they revised for possible questions from a vast range of topics. As the *maturità* approached at the end of the school year, feverish speculation gathered pace about which subjects would 'come up' in the exam.[15] On some occasions there were leaks, and the Internet has only made this speculation worse. Finally, the day of the *maturità* came (or days, as it lasted for some time).

Exams were long and gruelling. Some tried to cheat. Some had believed rumours about topics that later turned out to be incorrect. Then it was all over and it was time to wait for the results. The long years of school were finished. But given the structure of the Italian family, and the fact that many students attended university in their own towns or cities, and thus stayed at home, the friends made at school ('bench companions', as they were known) were often friends for life, often in a far deeper way than those encountered at university.

Italian school and university students received a rounded and 'general' education, and the oral exams system meant that they learnt to think on their feet and synthesise vast amounts of material. What they were not encouraged to do (in the main) was take a critical approach to the texts they studied. The university exams system was very much in continuity with the way schools were run. It was a physical endurance test as much as an exercise of the mind.[16] Many dropped out of university, or felt alienated by its hierarchical structures or by courses that seemed to bear little relationship to everyday life. When 1967–8 came around, these students would rebel against the entire university system.

The Battle over Divorce

Change also affected institutions relating to private life and morality. Slowly, thanks to the fallout from the Coppi case and shifting social attitudes, things started to change even within the family. First discussions over a divorce law took place in 1965. In 1967 it was established that a divorce reform would not require a change to the constitution, but could be brought in through a normal law.[17] At the end of November 1969 a divorce law passed in the Lower House with a slim majority (most Christian Democrats voted against). A final vote in the Senate saw divorce become law in December 1970. Divorce was not, however, made easy, even if it was now possible. To obtain a divorce, married couples first had to go before a judge and ask for what was called a legal separation. After three years in this limbo (and still married) state, they could then go before a judge (again) and request a divorce.

Not surprisingly, the Catholic Church was bitterly opposed to divorce, and fought reform with all the means at its disposal. This was an area around which the Church hierarchy was not willing to budge an inch. But not all Catholics were against change, and there were public pronouncements by Catholics (and even some priests) in favour of the legislation. The Church leadership, however, felt that it could not simply stand by and allow divorce to go through. Their zeal led them towards a political error of great magnitude. Italy's constitution had provided for the use of referendums against laws. If 500,000 certified signatures were collected in opposition to a law, a vote could be held to abrogate a specific piece of legislation. For the first twenty-five years or so of the Republic's life, this political weapon had lain dormant.

It was the Church and the Christian Democrats who decided to trigger the referendum clause for the first time in 1974 – against the divorce law passed in 1970. The anti-divorce campaign began in earnest with the collection of signatures. Some 1.3 million people were signed up to abrogate the legislation. In the long run-up to the referendum, there had been various attempts to reach a compromise on a different law (such as restricting divorce to those who married with a civil ceremony), but all of these intermediate proposals were in vain.

After a long and often bitter campaign, the divorce referendum was held over two days in May 1974. All over Italy people watched their television sets as the results came in. In Milan, the actor and writer Dario Fo held a long public meeting-demonstration-happening in the piazza outside his theatre with constant comments and debates. It was a time of great mobilisation and hope. A total of 32 million valid votes were cast. Some 88 per cent of those who could vote did so. This was an extremely high turnout for a referendum concerning just one law. If you voted 'Yes', you were against divorce, whereas a 'No' vote was in favour of keeping the reform in place. The results were striking. Some 59 per cent (19 million voters) defied the orders of the Church and backed divorce. There were just over 13 million on the other side of the divide. But there were, as ever, geographical divisions. A number of regions in the south of Italy and up in the north-east, where Catholic sub-cultures were still powerful, voted narrowly against divorce. Nonetheless, the islands of Sicily and Sardinia both voted No (and therefore Yes to maintaining the reform). Even the South was changing.

After the results had come in, the journalist Oriana Fallaci wrote that 'I was sure that we were going to lose ... today I am proud to be a woman in Italy.' She joined the street party in Rome. 'In Piazza Navona everyone was waving flags.'[18] Meanwhile, Pier Paolo Pasolini saw the referendum result as a sign that Italy's middle classes were 'radically – anthropologically – changed'. Their values were now 'the hedonistic ideology of consumerism and a kind of American-style modernist tolerance'.[19] The referendum that they had forced through had ended with a crushing defeat for the Church. Italy had changed, and the family, although still central, was no longer sacred. As the historian John Pollard argues, 'The chickens of secularisation came home to roost in a spectacular way in the referendum on the Divorce Law in 1974.'[20] The dramatic divorce referendum was 'the beginning of the end of the Church's hold on the thinking of the Italian people in terms of sexual behaviour, marriage and family relationships'.[21] It was crisis time – and not just for the Church. The political strategy of the Christian Democrats had proved to be disastrous, and the party's politicians seemed out of touch with the desires of the majority of Italians. This defeat was also procedural, and would have lasting consequences. The use of the referendum tactic had proved to be an own goal, and in using it the Church and the Christian Democrats had unwittingly provided their enemies with a potent weapon. Referendums would subsequently be used by other reforming parties to push through a series of changes throughout the 1970s, 1980s and 1990s.

Inside the Family – Parents and Children, Husbands and Wives

Legal systems and codes in Italy codified discrimination within the heart of the family. Fascism's 1930 penal code, left largely in place in 1948, was very much at the core of the problem. Italy's 1948 Constitution was both radical and conservative – often because of compromise with the Church and the Christian Democrats. The constitution attempted to provide equality, although this was quite limited, and often in conflict with earlier rules, which were passionately protected by the Church. Article 29 stated that 'The Republic recognises the rights of the family as a natural society founded on marriage', but also that 'Marriage is based on the moral and legal equality of the spouses within the limits laid down by law to guarantee the unity of the family.' Equality was supposedly guaranteed, therefore, but within the family unit and only in a legal marriage.

Article 30, however, seemed to move in a slightly different direction. It dealt with parenthood and children. 'It is the duty', it said, 'and right of parents to support, raise and educate their children, even if born out of wedlock. The law ensures such legal and social protection measures as are compatible with the rights of the members of the legitimate family to any children born out of wedlock.' Finally, Article 37 made further (if indirect) reference to the family: 'Working women', it said, 'are entitled to equal rights and, for comparable jobs, equal pay as men. Working conditions must allow women to fulfil their essential role in the family and ensure appropriate protection for the mother and child.'[22]

Despite some of the rights laid down in the new constitution, many judges who applied the law in the post-war period did so in ways that underlined and at times even made worse legally binding gender- and marriage-based inequalities. It took years for many of the clauses in the codes and other laws to be brought in line with the constitution. It was only in 1955, for example, that 'a note about fatherhood and motherhood' was removed from documents required for marriage. This finally got rid of the 'humiliating indication of N.N. [from the Latin *Nomen nescio*, 'no name' or 'I do not know the name'] for those who had not been officially "recognised" by their parents, and were therefore "illegitimate"'.[23]

It was not until the 1960s and 1970s that things began to change in a more positive and radical way. The gentle but inevitable turnover of the judiciary, plus the effect of reform movements outside – in the real world – had a decisive influence on this modernisation. But progress was slow and contradictory. Often, the courts applied the constitution to reimpose or codify inequalities and injustices, such as the 'right' of a husband to ask his wife to give up her job for the 'well-being of the family'.[24] In 1968 the idea that adultery was worse when committed by women than by men (and still illegal) was finally struck down. This date was not a coincidence. The Constitutional Court 'took note of the new ethical and social climate created by the economic boom'.[25] Six more years would pass before extra-marital affairs were taken out of the legal process altogether (apart from when they were used in divorce proceedings).

It was also important that women were permitted to enter a series of professions, something not guaranteed in Italy. The legal profession was one of the least permeable of all to gender equality. In 1961 the Constitutional Court cancelled a 1919 law banning women from the judiciary. This led to a February 1963 law that finally opened this profession up to women.[26] Before that, public competitions for these posts were restricted to men (in a way that was clearly unconstitutional). The first competition for magistrates that was open to women was held in May 1963. A total of 200 posts were available – and a mere eight women were judged to be admissible. They began working with 5,647 male magistrates in 1965. A debate at the Constituent Assembly in 1947 had concentrated on this very point. Then, a tactical decision had been taken to allow legal changes to these measures in the future, and not enshrine discrimination in the constitution itself (something that would have been, in any case, in contradiction with other articles). But it still took years before this anomaly was corrected.

By the time a law was finally passed admitting women to the judiciary, numerous rounds of competitions had been held that had excluded them merely on the basis of their gender.[27] At a lower level, there are now many women magistrates, but the higher levels still appear to have a strong glass ceiling. Of the 107 judges who served on the Constitutional Court from 1955 (when the court was set up) to 2015, only five were women. Other victories also took time. In 1957 women were admitted to juries in certain courts. Glass ceilings were also dented by powerful women such as Nilde Iotti, who became Speaker of the House in 1979.[28]

The Workers' Statute

As the 1960s wore on the level of organisation and militancy amongst the workers, especially in the big production line factories in the north, reached levels not seen since the 'two red years' of 1919–20 or the dramatic strikes of 1943 that hastened the end

of Mussolini's regime. Discipline within many factories broke
down completely, as wildcat strikes and spontaneous sit-downs
brought production swiftly to a halt on numerous occasions. This
'refusal to work' in the late 1960s and 1970s was seen by some
as a rejection of capitalism itself.[29] Others, however, understood
the struggle of the workers as one linked above all to forms of
dignity and progress – economic, social, and in terms of work
conditions. Once these gains were consolidated, the waves of protest died down. Workers veered between revolutionary demands
(and rhetoric) and reformist outcomes. One of the slogans of the
movement was 'More money, less work', while another was 'We
want everything'.

In 1969 workers' protests spread like wildfire. During the
period up to November of that year some 250 million hours of
work were lost to strikes across Italy. What became known as the
'hot autumn' saw workers all over Italy engage in struggles over
pay, hours, conditions and rights. If we just take metalworkers
in September of that year, there were 72 hours of strikes in that
month across the country, two national 24-hour stoppages and
a 48-hour strike in Turin and its surrounding area. The outcome
of this dramatic period where strikes reached unprecedented levels was a new set of laws and rights, passed in 1970, and known
collectively as 'The Workers' Statute'. Alongside this package of
measures, workers also achieved wage rises and cuts in working
hours, as well as improvements to conditions.[30]

The Workers' Statute enshrined a series of rights for the
organised working class. Some of these rights were simply the
application of the constitution – the right to strike, the right to
join a union, the right not be victimised. Other measures went
further than the principles outlined in the 1948 constitution,
such as the right to periods of free education for workers (for
which employers were obliged to give them paid time off). This
was known as the '150 hours scheme', and led to a flourishing of
adult education across the country. Clauses in the statute were
aimed at so-called worker-students, who were often studying
hard to obtain qualifications they had failed to achieve at school,
usually in out-of-work hours. Worker-students had the right to

demand shifts that helped their studies, and could ask for time off to take exams.

Passed in May 1970, the Statute also contained a celebrated article – Article 18 – that protected employment rights for workers in large-scale businesses. Employees of these companies could only be sacked if 'reasonable cause' could be proven against them. Article 18 would lead to endless discussions and demonstrations over the following forty years or so, until much of it was modified through a series of reforms and other measures (which were challenged in the courts) in the second decade of the twenty-first century.

Many of the articles and measures included in the Workers' Statute were inspired by the struggle against discrimination suffered by militant workers within factories and workplaces in the post-war period. Many communist workers employed by FIAT in Turin had been forced to work in isolated plants to lessen the impact of their political convictions on others. These areas became known as 'FIAT Confino' – a reference to the internal exile policies imposed by fascism in the 1920s and 1930s (where anti-fascists were dispatched to remote islands). With the Statute, marginalisation of militant employees was effectively outlawed. In addition, the surveillance of workers (another widespread feature of the boom period within factories) was severely limited.

Factory life sometimes had its liberating side, but it was also repressive and repetitive. The production line was a tough place to be. Rules governed every aspect of life. In Mario Monicelli's short film, *Renzo e Luciana*, released in 1962, two workers from the Pirelli factory in Milan get married in their lunch hour, in secret, to avoid discrimination. The wedding takes place in a kind of shack, with music provided by a jukebox. Afterwards, the couple go straight back to work – ignoring each other to avoid detection. After the Statute was passed, workers could not be paid more if they didn't join a union, nor could they be sacked for taking part in strikes. Women could no longer be laid off if they got married (which was common practice at the time).

During Italy's brief industrial age, film-makers and writers turned their attention to the life of the factory. In Elio Petri's powerful movie, *The Working Class Goes to Heaven*,[31] Gian Maria Volonté plays a factory worker (Lulù) whose home is packed with useless consumer goods. Lulù begins the film as a Stakhonovite, a model worker, who toils at great speed to produce metal parts with repetitive movements (in scenes reminiscent of Charlie Chaplin's *Modern Times*) to earn extra to pay for his family's 'needs'. New workers are assigned to Lulù for 'training'. After work, Lulù goes home and falls asleep almost immediately, often in front of the television. He ignores protesting students who leaflet at the factory gates, in the snow, every morning. Then, Lulù cuts his finger off in his machine. He is transformed, becoming radicalised by the students and joining the 'movement'. But there is no escape for Lulù. He ends up back on the production line.

Prisons and Riots

Prisons were another institution in urgent need of reform, out of touch with the modern world and still governed by a combination of fascist and liberal laws. Every aspect of the lives of inmates was regulated and controlled by an extensive range of oppressive rules. Life inside Italian prisons in the 1960s had changed very little despite the transition to democracy. There was little sense of rehabilitation or an alternative to punishment and isolation. Letters were censored. Punishments were brutal and institutionalised. Dark cells contained special beds where prisoners were tied up for long periods. Inmates were isolated from each other and from the outside world. Meanwhile, the prison buildings themselves were old and crumbling, and increasingly overcrowded. Inmates were forced to work for tiny wages.

Traumatic riots spread throughout the system and across Italy in the late 1960s, leading to the destruction of some prisons and dramatic face-offs with the army and the police, as well as loss of life. Turin's Le Nuove prison was so badly damaged by a riot in April 1969 that many of the inmates were transferred to Sardinia. This riot marked a turning point in Italy's prison system. As the historian Eleanor Chiari has written, 'The riot of 1969 [in Turin] lasted four days. It involved the destruction of three wings, the kitchens, the priest's offices, the matriculation office and the workshops for industrial works with damages of several hundred million lire.' The police re-entered the prison on Easter Monday and 'inmates were dragged in chains, kept for hours face down in the courtyard and then taken by three carrier planes ... to far-off islands'.[32]

In the wake of some riots prisoners effectively took over some prisons for a time, and political militants were involved (from the inside and the outside). Slogans called for 'everyone to be freed' and the closing down of the entire system. Some political movements saw these prisoners as the vanguard of a possible revolution, describing them as the anti-colonialist writer Frantz Fanon might have done as the 'wretched of the earth'. Prisoners poured onto the roof of the prisons they had been held within, waving clenched fists at supporters and family members on the streets outside, beyond the walls.

Across Italy the state responded with repression, sending in armed police or even the army to quell revolts. Once the riots were over, the prisoners were often beaten and humiliated. Women prisoners also carried out their own protests. Further riots broke out sporadically in the 1970s. In 1974 hostages were taken inside the prison in Alessandria, a city in Piedmont, the north of the country. After a long and failed negotiation, there was an attempt to free the hostages. The outcome was a bloodbath, with seven people killed.

Prisons thus came under attack from both the inside and the outside of the institution's walls in the 1960s and 1970s. In a celebrated book Aldo Ricci and Giulio Salierno (a former fascist who had spent years inside prison in various countries) described prisons as 'total institutions' (following the work of the Canadian sociologist Erving Goffman). Their book included detailed descriptions of prison riots and their aftermath. The two authors concluded that 'there can be no freedom as long as there are still prisoners'.[33]

The turmoil of the 1960s and 1970s led to a root-and-branch reform of the entire prison system in 1975. Prisoners, like asylum patients, were given constitutional rights, nearly thirty years after the passing of the constitution. New measures also provided funds for rehabilitation and education, and alternatives to imprisonment. From a system that was one of the most oppressive in the world, Italy's prisons became amongst the most liberal.

Yet not all prisoners were treated the same, even under the new reforms. Special prisons were introduced under emergency laws in order – it was claimed – to deal with the increase in political violence.[34] And for some prisoners – such as certain *mafiosi* – things were always and continued to be different. Palermo's prison, for example, was often referred to as Grand Hotel Ucciardone. As the historian John Dickie writes, 'bosses came and went from their cells in silk dressing gowns, ate lobster and drank champagne'.[35] In Naples, in the Poggioreale prison, a man called Raffaele Cutolo used the institution as a base for creating a new and powerful Camorra organisation. He recognised that 'Prison was the perfect base for a criminal empire.'[36] Tough prison regimes for high-level *mafiosi* and *camorristi* would not come in until the 1990s.

Universities and 1968

'It is forbidden to forbid.'

Slogan, 1968

A heady mix of historical and political influences came to a head at the end of the 1960s. The Vietnam War, events in Mao's China, and anti-imperialist struggles across the globe alongside the peace movement provided a global backdrop. Radical strands of thought within psychiatry, the school system as well as literature, music and art created the basis for new forms of anti-authoritarianism and a cultural revolution. Mass overcrowding of the education system, lack of resources and seemingly unchanging practices within universities contributed to a dissatisfaction with how institutions and society worked. Many wanted to break away. An entire generation was politicised and ready to fight back. Writers such as Herbert Marcuse, R. D. Laing and Frantz Fanon provided a more generalised critique of the way that society worked.[37] A seemingly distant and fossilised political system seemed impervious to the desire for change. The Prague Spring in

1968 undermined the Communist Party and its hold over the left. Italy's student movement sympathised with the Czechoslovak rebels, not the regime. As a student leaflet put it in 1968, 'In front of the Soviet tanks, not behind them'.

It was thus not surprising that, as the 1960s wore on, students began to fight back against their own professors and the entire university system. Their main weapon of struggle was to occupy university spaces. These occupations began sporadically in the mid-1960s, in Rome and in Milan (architecture faculties were a centre of activity), and in the new university in Trento in the north of the country, before exploding across Italy in 1967. Italy's student movement preceded that of May 1968 in France, and lasted far longer. Some called Italy's 1968 the 'long' or 'drawn-out May', in comparison with the events in Paris. The movement quickly spread. Parts of Pisa University were occupied in February 1967, closely followed by similar acts in the centre of Turin, which were to continue in some ways throughout the year. These occupations ended in police violence and arrests.

In these occupied spaces, students issued documents, organised themselves into groups, elected leaders, and discussed a variety of themes beyond those strictly linked to university reform. In November 1967 a huge occupation blocked activity at the prestigious private Catholic University in the centre of Milan. Clashes between students and police outside the university in March 1968 led to the expulsion of many students, including one of the early leaders of the movement, a migrant from Umbria called Mario Capanna. Many of these expelled students soon signed up to the central state university in Milan, where they continued their radical activities. Protesting students complained about the content of their courses, the way they were taught and examined, and the power structures within universities. They interrupted lectures and talked back to astonished professors. In Turin a student called Guido Viale stood on the 'sacred' teaching desk and called a professor an 'imbecile'. He was later arrested and imprisoned for political activities. Viale quickly became a leader, and, as an orphan, his personal status echoed one of the most popular slogans at the time: 'I want to be an orphan' (a slogan symbolising rejection of the 'bourgeois family'). Viale also criticised the very basis of how research was carried out in the university system:

> Every periodical ... contains articles that discuss articles published in other periodicals. The publications required for academic progress are mostly collections of similar articles. In this way the circle is closed. Research simply researches itself, and Faculties ... become ivory towers that are completely isolated from the cultural and political problems of the rest of society.[38]

In 1968 Viale wrote a highly influential article with an extremely clear title: 'Against the University'. Issued as a book, it sold in large quantities.

Meanwhile, in Trento, nestled in the mountains in the far north of the country (a university only set up in 1962 – in a place so sleepy it was deemed to be 'safe'), student protesters were already moving on to more radical terrain, with 'counter-courses' and what was called 'an active strike'. Numerous universities experienced occupations and other protests around this time: Padua, Florence, Siena, Lecce, Rome, Naples, Pavia, Messina, Ferrara, Parma, Venice, Genoa, Bari, Ancona, Cagliari, Perugia, Bologna, Modena, Trieste, Milan, Palermo and Catania. This was a national movement.

A highly important set-piece moment took place in Rome in March 1968. On the first day of that month students and others clashed with the police over a sustained period in a park near the architecture faculty. This event later became known as 'The Battle of Valle Giulia'. Over six hundred injuries were reported that day, three-quarters of them amongst the students. In historical terms this 'battle' is often seen as a turning point – the moment when the students 'refused to run away any more'.[39] Violence, at least in defence against the police, became acceptable for many. The movement also galvanised many school students, leading to occupations and protests in school buildings. This radicalisation of the young was another unusual feature of the Italian movement. In other countries affected by 1968 the movement was largely confined to universities. Similar demands in Italy were made at both school and university levels – around exams, teacher power and anti-authoritarianism.

The Communist Party was torn over how to react to the rapid spread of the student protests. Luigi Longo, the party's leader after the death of Togliatti in 1964, took a positive view. Writing in May 1968, he argued that 'nobody can deny the importance and wide-ranging nature of the student movement.' 'It is clear,' he added, 'that the students will form a new generation of vanguard intellectuals.'[40] But Giorgio Amendola, who came from the right of the party, accused the students of 'infantile extremism and ... old-style anarchism' in June 1968. He argued that the struggle against what he called 'social-democratic opportunism ... only works if accompanied by coherent activities against sectarianism ... and extremism ... Lenin warned us once against the dangers of playing with the revolution.'[41]

Certainly, for many in the student movement, the Communist Party was part of the problem, not the solution. Many rebelled (initially) against their own communist parents, something that was particularly traumatic for those who had taken part in the anti-fascist Resistance. It was common for students to protest against professors with impeccable anti-fascist credentials. In turn, the older generation struggled to understand what was happening. As Nuto Revelli, former partisan and oral historian, later said:

> The generation of 1968 wanted liberty after the Liberation! They knew nothing of our generation that suffered from the war – it is good that these children did not have to live through the war ... but the students made a mistake because when they came out in the piazza, they disturbed a democratic peace![42]

The Resistance, the student movement claimed, had been betrayed, and its ritualistic commemorations had nothing to say to the young people of the 1960s. This position was made clear in the influential radical periodical *Quaderni Piacentini* in the earlier part of the decade:

> NO NO NO. We don't want the dead of the Resistance to be 'honoured' with monuments to 'the fallen of all wars'

inaugurated by the Bishop, the Prefect, the President of the Court, the District Commander, Police Commissioners ... and Superintendents. We prefer silence.[43]

'New partisans', it was later said, were required. Despite theories (and rhetoric) that identified something called 'student power', students soon moved out into the wider world – to factory gates, but also into other institutions from museums to newspaper buildings. One of the slogans of part of the movement was 'Let's occupy the city'. Italy's 1968 took on outdated institutions, and official hierarchies. It also attacked the old left, above all the Communist Party, as 'conservative' and 'part of the system'. A new left had been born.

The Church and 1968

Movements of social protest also emerged from within and against the Church hierarchy. In Milan in 1967, as we have seen, it was the private Catholic University that saw the first occupations. In Trento, a nerve centre of the student movement, a protester shouted 'it's not true' during a Mass in the Cathedral in March 1968. The dissenter's name was Paolo Sorbi, twenty-five, who was studying sociology, and he was amongst a group of protesters inside the church. The priest had decided to use his Mass to condemn the Soviet Union. At that moment Sorbi, who was wearing a black beret and a leather jacket, began to shout 'it's not true, it's all lies'. It was said that only 'his comrades saved him from a beating at the hands of furious believers'.[44]

This moment echoed that which involved the German student leader Rudi Dutschke in Berlin in 1967, when he 'stormed' a church alongside other militants and was attacked by those inside.[45] Meanwhile, in Italy, dissent from within the Catholic world intensified. In September 1968 Parma's beautiful cathedral was briefly occupied by students. The protesters called upon the Church to have 'the courage to choose to favour the poor and oppose the capitalist system'.[46] Police quickly removed the occupiers, and a further meeting was held outside, but this event had national repercussions. Priests and Catholics across Italy expressed solidarity with the Parma movement. Others within the Catholic hierarchy were horrified.

Don Mazzi was the local priest in a vast new working-class neighbourhood called Isolotto built on the edge of Florence in the 1950s and 1960s. He made a public pronouncement in support of the Parma Cathedral occupiers and sent them a letter of solidarity. This sparked a series of events that led to his suspension from the priesthood in Isolotto. The Bishop of Florence was unhappy with the priest's public expression of solidarity for the Parma occupiers. Don Mazzi was told either to withdraw what he had written or resign. Buoyed up by the support of his local community, Don Mazzi did neither.

A replacement priest was sent to Isolotto, but nobody went to hear him give mass. The reaction of the local community was remarkable. They decided to carry on as before, without the support of the official Church, forming what they called a 'community'. Mass and other religious celebrations were carried out in the square in front of the church. For years, Mazzi continued to hold Mass in the square outside the Church, in a direct challenge to Catholic hierarchies. A democratic version of the catechism was produced for publication in Isolotto (and, although banned in Italy by the Church, was translated into other languages). Don Mazzi's 'community' became one of the symbols of 1968 in Italy, and showed how the Church itself was divided over protest and democracy. Radical Catholics and priests were, in many cases, right at the centre of calls for change and reform.

Increasingly, Catholic groups and individuals began to rebel against Church authority, and often against the very structures of the Church itself. As Don Mazzi later said, 'to obey the Catholic hierarchy almost always implies disobedience in terms of the real, true and evangelical needs of the people ... on the one hand, there is the Church connected with political, economic and cultural power, on the other the Church of the unemployed, the illiterate, the marginalised, the workers'.[47]

Contesting Culture

'Contestation', a widespread sense of protest against something, spread to all kinds of traditional cultural events – such as the opening night of La Scala in Milan (in December 1968, where there were riots) and the Venice Biennale international art exhibition (when police and protesters fought in Piazza San Marco as tourists fled). Milan's prestigious architectural Triennale (three-yearly exhibition) failed to open at all in 1968 after an occupation by students. Even the fashionable nightclub La Bussola in Tuscany experienced protests, and a student was shot and paralysed by police during a demonstration there in December 1968.

Support was also withdrawn from literary prizes. In 1968 Italo Calvino refused to accept the influential Viareggio Book Prize, writing to the organisers this letter:

> Given that I believe that the epoch of prizes is over, forever, I do not intend to accept this prize because I do not want to provide support for these institutional forms which are completely lacking in meaning. In my desire to avoid any press sensation, please do not announce my name as one of the winners.[48]

Protests also targeted establishment newspapers like *Il Corriere della Sera*. In June 1969 the popular *Cantagiro* TV programme was 'contested' in Cuneo, where the slogan was 'Hell-like rhythms [work patterns] in the factory; musical rhythms during the Cantagiro: two sides of the same coin'. There were demonstrations against the RAI state channel in Milan in November 1969. Contestation also affected the rituals connected to state institutions, as with the dissent during the opening of the 'legal year' by reformist magistrates and judges in 1969. There were experiments in what were called 'counter-inaugurations'.[49] Teachers refused to set and mark exams in 1970 – delaying national exams for all school students. The sense of rebellion was contagious. Reformist organisations were set up to organise institutional protest amongst those with qualifications and institutional power. These organisations were given similar names: Democratic Magistrates, Democratic Psychiatry, Democratic Medicine.

The Merlin Law: Closing the 'Closed Houses'

Between 1883 and 1958 prostitution in Italy was legalised and regulated within so-called 'Closed Houses' – brothels licensed by the state. Prostitutes were registered with police and had the cost of items such as clean sheets, taxes, board and lodgings deducted from their wages. The women in 'closed houses' were subject to constant and humiliating medical examinations (they were given a special document allowing them to work), and had often been held as virtual slaves. After a long battle, these institutions were abolished in 1958, through a measure named after the Socialist senator Lina Merlin ('The Merlin Law'). Merlin ran a long campaign against the 'closed houses', and collected together and published a series of letters sent to her from prostitutes across Italy.[50] Her campaign was not about morality, but linked to the servitude and conditions of the women working in these institutions. Her first proposal for reform was in 1948, but it would take ten years for her campaign to take effect. Leading journalists were outraged by the possibility of reform, and parliamentary progress had been painfully slow. Many men were frequent visitors to the 'closed houses' and were appalled by any talk of their abolition. The system also kept prostitution hidden and off the streets.

By 1958 there were 560 'closed houses' in Italy, where around 2,700 prostitutes worked. A number had already closed in anticipation of the reform, becoming 'empty houses'. The exploitation of prostitution also became a crime at the same time. A moral panic followed the Merlin Law, as prostitution spilled out onto the streets. Merlin's law did not provide a regulated or safe alternative to the 'closed houses'. As with other reforms, there were constant proposals to return to the past in the years to come – with attempts to bring back state brothels and regulate prostitution further. But these efforts failed to achieve the necessary support in Parliament. Italy's parliamentary system made it very difficult to pass reform. However, once passed, these reforms were even harder to change or abrogate. Hence, many remained in their original form for years.

Franca Viola and Forced Marriage through Rape

The 1960s and 1970s were also a time when ancient patriarchal traditions were challenged for the first time. Often, it took a courageous individual to spark change. Franca Viola, born in Alcamo, Sicily, in 1947, was one such person. In 1965, on Boxing Day, Viola was kidnapped by a group of twelve men (they were said to be armed) led by someone called Filippo Melodia. She was then repeatedly raped. Viola was seventeen years old. In such circumstances, especially in Sicily, the usual outcome of this kind of event was a 'forced marriage' as the woman's 'chastity' had been compromised. Unusually, Viola refused this option. Melodia was sent to jail for the kidnapping – a conviction reduced through the legal process to two years when he had to live in another area of Italy. Melodia had family links to a local Mafia boss. At the 1966 trial Franca Viola said that 'I am nobody's property, nobody can force me to love someone for whom I have no respect. Those who do certain things lose honour, not those who are victims of those acts.'[51] Viola's story was later made into a film starring a fourteen-year-old Ornella Muti (in her first role).[52] As the historian Niamh Cullen has argued, 'The case of Franca Viola forced the Italian public to confront the issue of gender violence and its cultural and social place within the nation.'[53]

Not only was kidnapping and rape still possible at the time under Italy's legal system, murder was also more or less acceptable, as long as it preserved a sense of male 'honour'. This sense of 'honour' was cited in the infamous Article 587 of the criminal code:

Whoever causes the death of a wife, a daughter or a sister, caught in the act of an illegitimate carnal relationship, and in an angry state created by the offence against their honour or that of their family, is punished with a prison sentence of between 3 and 7 years. The same sentence should be applied to a person who causes the death of the person who is engaged in a carnal relationship with the wife, daughter or sister.

Honour killings were parodied and lambasted by public intellectuals and film-makers from the 1960s onwards. Yet legal reform took years. Despite protests and Franca Viola's courageous stance, it was not until 1981 that measures were passed which did away with the possibility of 'eliminating' a crime of sexual violence through marriage as well as 'honour killings'. Fifteen years later, in 1996, rape was finally redefined in Italian law as a crime against 'the person' as opposed to 'against public morals'. It had been a long and difficult political and legal struggle in order to achieve constitutional equality, but the battle for equality at a social and cultural level was far from over.

Feminism: The Public and the Private

Italian feminism exploded onto the political, social and cultural scene in the late 1960s and 1970s. As with the movements of 1968 in general, feminism in Italy was in part a reaction against the old left, and in part in opposition to the structures of society itself, everyday politics, and institutional and legal discrimination. Feminists – who organised within a myriad of groupings and formations – came together in the big national campaigns for divorce and abortion, but were also central to a range of changes to welfare-state provision, contraception availability and education, and family reform. Private and public spheres were often confused (deliberately) within feminism, as they were across the world. The personal became political.

Consciousness-raising or *autocoscienza* also became a key part of the movement. The discovery and discussion of subjectivities (the self) was central to the way that feminism worked. Through *autocoscienza*, as the historian Perry Willson argues, 'women ... by sharing their innermost thoughts in leaderless, small groups, could discover their own identities and put together a new vision of the world (in order to change it)'.[54] *Autocoscienza* rejected classic forms of political campaigning, such as demonstrations. The phrase 'leave the Piazza' was a common one at the time, as was the idea of 'starting from yourself'.[55] It was also influenced by Maoist practice in China, at least in the sense of its translation into Western movements (which often had little basis in Chinese reality). Later there would be a 'return to the streets' with the mass and successful campaigns for divorce, abortion and family-law reform.

Women participated fully in the 'long march' into and against the institutions. Franca Ongaro – Franco Basaglia's wife – was instrumental in the changes carried out within asylums in the 1960s and 1970s, despite her lack of psychiatric training. Later, as an independent senator in the Upper House, she campaigned for the implementation of the 'Basaglia law' and against attempts to repeal or change that legislation. The Radical Party was perhaps the only national organisation to embrace feminist demands (and, to some extent, its practice) and to take these issues into Parliament itself. Other major parties were more suspicious of feminist ideas in general, and this distrust, for many feminists, was mutual. Feminists also set up alternative institutions, such as self-managed women's health clinics. By 1975–6, in Rome alone, there were clinics of this kind 'operative in ten ... neighbourhoods [that] engaged more than four hundred volunteers'.[56] Many of these clinics were institutionalised and given official public status. A valuable public service had been created from a social and cultural movement.

Feminist texts challenged the orthodoxies of the time. In part, these were translations of key books from other languages – such as Betty Friedan's *The Feminine Mystique* (which came out in Italian in 1964) or Juliet Mitchell's *Psychoanalysis and Feminism* (published by Einaudi in 1976). But Italian feminists produced their own key texts. Carla Lonzi, an art critic, was the author of the highly influential book *Sputiamo su Hegel* (*Let's Spit on Hegel*), which appeared in 1970. In this text she called for a separatist approach to politics. 'There are no goals,' she wrote, 'there is only the present of our here and now ... we are giving shape to the present.'[57]

Debates raged within the movement about organisational forms (should they include men?) and patriarchal structures within the left itself. For example, the *Manifesto of Rivolta Femminile* (1970) argued that 'Women must not be defined in relation to men ... Man is not the model to be aspired to in women's process of self-discovery ... Equality is an ideological attempt to enslave women further.' Other feminists underlined the importance of class, calling for 'wages for housework'. Contradictions were also clear in the way that contestation within the family (thus against parents as parents) could often work against a critique of patriarchal forms (wives and mothers empowered vis-à-vis husbands and partners, but also operating as parents inside the family). The sociologist Laura Balbo later wrote convincingly of women's 'dual presence', whereby their lives were 'marked by a constant tension between the two spheres of work and family within which their presence was equally required'.[58] Sometimes, these tensions were seen in the public sphere.

On 6 December 1975 a large feminist demonstration was held in Rome and the numbers on the streets were swelled by school students. Shockingly, the demonstration was physically attacked by groups of men – mostly from the far-left group *Lotta Continua*. This led directly to a traumatic but fascinating discussion within that organisation, which disbanded itself in 1976 after a fiery congress in Rimini. It has been argued that 'the forms, the timing and the content of feminist practice was seen to be in contradiction with exclusively male-centred ways of doing politics'.[59]

Feminism fed directly into a range of central reforms, and affected the very basis of the Church's control over private lives in deep and lasting ways. In this sense feminism was the most successful and concrete of all the social movements to emerge from and play a part in Italy's 'long 1968'.

Abortion

Key reforms saw lengthy battles not just with the Church and their political representatives, the Christian Democrats, but also with the Constitutional Court. This was the case, for example, with the long history of attempts to legalise abortion in Italy. In February 1975 the Constitutional Court declared that Article 546 of the 1930 code – which criminalised abortion for the woman involved and for the abortionist – was constitutional. However, the Court did allow for abortions in certain circumstances linked to health. The 1930 criminal code had made a distinction between abortion with and without the consent of the woman involved. In the case of consent, both the pregnant woman and the abortionist were punishable by law – and could be given prison sentences.

The Radical Party (which at that point had no representation in Parliament – although its first four deputies would be elected in 1976) decided to utilise the referendum weapon, previously employed by the Church against liberal reforms, to push for abortion reform. This proved to be a brilliant and effective tactic. Referendums had the potential to act as a spark for the removal of unpopular laws in a way that accelerated change and bypassed a notoriously conservative political class. The Radicals collected over 500,000 signatures in an attempt to abrogate restrictive abortion articles from the Fascist period. Meanwhile, an alliance of neo-fascists and Christian Democrats – alongside the Church – looked to restrict abortions to only the most serious of circumstances.

Referendum proposals put pressure on the political class to get its act together. A reform was approved in January 1977, but opposition was still strong. Finally, an integrated law was passed in May 1978, just after the 'Basaglia law' that would close Italy's psychiatric hospitals (and which had also been forced through thanks to a referendum challenge). Despite their previous defeat over divorce, the Christian Democrats and the Church pushed for another referendum. But their defeat this time – in 1981 – was even heavier than before. The abortion argument had largely been won.

Over 21 million Italians turned out to support the abortion law – some 68 per cent of those who voted. Nearly 80 per cent of Italians cast a vote, a figure that showed how important this instrument of democracy had become by the early 1980s. A 'referendum season' followed, which would last well into the 1990s and bring the Radical Party to the centre of Italian politics.

Nonetheless, the new abortion law (known as Law 194) was not ideal. It contained restrictive clauses that often made it difficult for women to get an abortion at all, and could also make the whole process more traumatic than it needed to be.

Under the requirements of Law 194, for example, doctors and others could 'opt out' of carrying out abortions as 'conscientious objectors'. In some parts of Italy the numbers of such 'objectors' reached sizeable proportions (occasionally over 90 per cent), making it very hard for women to obtain an abortion locally (or forcing them to go private). Meanwhile, the number of abortions fell consistently after 1978.[60] Changes to birth-control legislation and sex education also had a positive effect. There were various attempts to roll back this law after 1978, but none of them came close to achieving a consensus across Italian society itself. The Church was forced to adapt to a changing world.

Witch Trial: The Braibanti Case, 1964–82

In late 1967 an artist, poet and writer, and expert in the study of ants – Aldo Braibanti – was arrested in Rome. His arrest related in part to a period in the late 1950s when Braibanti had run a kind of 'free artistic community' in a small town in the north of Italy. Two school students who were both in their late teens at the time had frequented Braibanti in that period. In the early 1960s one of those students, Giovanni Sanfratello, had continued to see Braibanti in Rome and elsewhere. In October 1964 Sanfratello's family went to the judicial authorities, who opened an investigation. The family claimed that Braibanti's behaviour was damaging their son.

Then, on 1 November 1964, Sanfratello was effectively kidnapped by various members of his own family and taken straight to a psychiatric hospital. Once committed, it was said that he was subjected to numerous rounds of electroshock and insulin treatment. He would only be released in February 1966 – with stringent conditions imposed upon his life by magistrates, including one that he should only read books that were at least

a hundred years old. Meanwhile, the judicial investigation
into Braibanti took three and a half years to complete. On 5
December 1967 Braibanti was picked up by police and taken
to Rome's Regina Coeli prison. He would remain behind bars
for the next two years. 'It is truly painful to find yourself in
prison,' he wrote to his mother, 'without having committed any
crime at all.'[61]

The charge against Braibanti was an extraordinary one – *plagio* (brainwashing) – a 'crime' that had been part of Italy's liberal criminal codes and had been incorporated in a modified
form into the 1930 Fascist criminal code. *Plagio* was linked to
a supposed situation where one person 'influences another person so that they are completely under their control'. Although
originally intended to deal with cases of 'slavery', in the 1930
version this 'crime' was a more ambiguous one. Like so many
of the articles from the Fascist code, Article 603 was open to
different interpretations, and in the wrong hands could be an
instrument of repression. According to the prosecution two
students had been under Braibanti's power, so much so that
it was claimed they 'hated' their own families and had been
reduced to the status of 'slaves'. The press referred to these students as 'disciples'.

Newspapers stated openly that Braibanti was gay, and the trial
soon developed into a discussion around 'appropriate' forms of
sexuality. Braibanti had also been an active communist – imprisoned and tortured under the Fascist regime because of his anti-
fascist activities. Quickly, the legal process began to resemble
a witch-hunt, and ample space was dedicated to it in the press.
Braibanti's books were picked over for supposedly 'immoral'
content. The trial would last thirty-one days.

In a violent closing speech, the prosecutor – Antonino
Loiacono – called for a fourteen-year jail sentence (critics complained that this wasn't dissimilar from a sentence given for murder).[62] Loiacono called Braibanti an 'example of degeneration,
obsession, moral poverty ... an intellectual failure, he has done
nothing, his books don't sell ... he is an evil genius ... our dear
family, the house, the church tower ... our world ... all of this has

been destroyed by this man with his cold, metallic, nasal voice ... If you let him go free you will allow him to corrupt our youth again.'[63] On 14 July 1968, at 2 a.m., Braibanti was found guilty of the 'crime' of 'brainwashing' and sentenced to nine years in prison. It was a 'moral panic', in the face of what many saw as the 'moral decline' of the 1960s.

The judges (in a ruling that ran to some 177 pages and was later published in book form) argued that Braibanti had used 'cultural and sexual pressures' to bring the two students under his power. Protests took place in the courtroom as the sentence was read out. On appeal in November 1969 there was another violent and homophobic closing statement, this time by a celebrated eighty-two-year-old neo-fascist lawyer representing the Sanfratello family.[64] This time the sentence was reduced to four years, in a kind of 'Italian-style compromise' that allowed for Braibanti's release a week after the end of the appeal.[65] He was, however, still forced to pay the costs of his time in prison and legal fees. Braibanti tried to clear his name in the High Court, but this sentence was confirmed in 1971.

Although some on the left were slow to come to Braibanti's defence (in particular the Communist Party), the case caused outrage and a campaign was begun – with the Radical Party taking the lead. The trial became a cause célèbre (as did the psychiatric treatment received by Sanfratello) and leading intellectuals rallied to Braibanti's side – including the writers Elsa Morante, Alberto Moravia and Pier Paolo Pasolini. A collective book appeared in 1969 backing Braibanti in which various authors – including Umberto Eco and the psychologist Cesare Musatti – intervened. The book argued that 'the Braibanti "case" is not a judicial affair, it is a political and civil issue'.[66] In 1981 the Constitutional Court finally struck 'plagio' from the criminal code. Ironically, the decision to remove the article from the statute books seemed to be linked to the case of a charismatic priest who had been accused of the same offence. In 1982 Braibanti's criminal conviction was invalidated by the appeal court. Braibanti was to be the only person in the history of the Italian Republic to be convicted for this specific 'crime'.

The bizarre Braibanti case exposed both the conservatism of large parts of Italian society and that of its legal system. Fascist laws were still being used to make examples of people, right through to the 1970s. Moral panics (and these were rife after 1968) were transmitted through the courts and the media. Braibanti was a scapegoat – both in terms of his sexuality and his politics. The combination of the two in this trial was particularly toxic.

Much was made of Braibanti's long black beard (for the time) during the first trial. Like the Coppi and Occhini trial and the 1966 'Zanzara' investigations (where school students had been investigated by police after publishing material relating to the sexual practices of young people), the Braibanti 'case' seemed to mark a red line between a modern and tolerant country and an anachronistic, old-fashioned and backward-looking nation. These cases divided Italians, and appeared to unmask the reactionary nature of the state machine and its legal codes. People lined up on one side or the other. As Braibanti wrote in 1968, 'this trial has laid bare a provincial Italy [*Italietta*] which is centuries behind the times, and behind which the last fascists and most backward reactionaries hide themselves'.[67]

Other Italys in the 1960s, 1970s and 1980s

Extensive institutional reforms, often, left party-political structures – and the clientelistic networks attached to them – largely untouched. While the movements of 1968 looked to influence, infiltrate, overturn and sometimes abolish many of Italy's public institutions, they were largely uninterested in the main political parties and the mechanisms that reproduced state power. Thus, even as a revolution was going on within civil society, the political hold of the parties over this machine, and its influence, continued to grow. The Christian Democratic Party, the 'white whale', continued to cast its shadow over the political structures of southern and northern Italy.

In the southern city of Naples, in the 1960s, it was the Gava family who held sway, controlling funds, voting for clienteles and political networks, along with banks and planning structures. Public works were planned strategically around election times. The Gava family-clan, with the powerful Christian Democratic grandee Silvio Gava at the top of the tree, achieved almost complete control of a major city through the systematic use of public resources. The appendix to British sociologist Percy Allum's work on Naples, published in the 1970s, included detailed lists of control positions in various companies, as well as maps laying out how the voting system worked at a local level. It was a devastating portrait – and an accurate one.

Throughout this period of local power, which lasted for decades, public works were linked to political needs. Antonio Gava (Silvio's son) pushed for the construction of a motorway along the Sorrento coastline (one of the most stunning parts of Italy). This was a costly project to say the least – requiring numerous bridges and tunnels. Neapolitans had little choice but to accept the system as it was, and to back those with more resources to hand out. There were occasional riots and urban violence, but these were generally ineffective. As one anonymous correspondent stated, 'while the principal political expression of popular ... discontent consists in throwing stones at the police, there is not much hope of serious reforms'.[68]

The power of the Christian Democrats was as strong in parts of the North as it was in much of the South. Antonio ('Toni') Bisaglia was the equivalent of Silvio Gava, but his base was in the Veneto region. Born in Rovigo in northern Italy, in 1929, Bisaglia worked his way up through the Catholic youth movement in the 1940s and 1950s after training to be a priest. He forged close links with local farmers' organisations, including the powerful Coldiretti association. By 1948, the Coldiretti had managed to recruit 711,000 families and 2.3 million members into over six thousand local branches.[69]

With a power base of this kind, Bisaglia was destined to go far. After serving in local government, he was elected as a deputy or senator in the national Parliament from 1963 until his death in 1984. Leading Christian Democratic politicians such as Bisaglia and the Gavas were near-permanent fixtures in the power structures in

post-war Italy. Only death, retirement or unexpected scandal threatened their control of resources and seats. Italy was a democracy, but
the same people almost always won. Election was guaranteed.

Bisaglia did his time as a 'bag-carrier' alongside the ultra-
powerful Veneto-based politician, Mariano Rumor (who he would
abandon in the mid-1970s). He then occupied a series of classic
ministerial positions in terms of patronage – in the Ministries of
State Participation (a perfect vector for resources and patronage,
set up in 1956), Agriculture and Industry. Bisaglia was never particularly interested in ideas or in public pronouncements, limit-
ing himself to assiduous work behind the scenes. In this he was
similar to many other grandees in the Christian Democrats. As he
often said, 'I am a moderate' ('Io sono un moderato').[70]

The journalist Giampaolo Pansa argued that Bisaglia was 'an
able manipulator of factions and head of his own highly organised and powerful stronghold'.[71] Christian Democratic bosses
were certain of re-election, but they still needed to cultivate their
voters and supporters. It was easy to slip down the resource and
power hierarchies – and there were always younger politicians
ready to take over. You had to keep abreast of change. Bisaglia
was praised for his understanding of the local and social conditions in the Veneto.[72] Always in a jacket and tie, and with the
classic heavy-framed glasses of the time, Bisaglia even looked like
a Christian Democrat.

In the 1972 elections Bisaglia's authority was laid bare by the
high number of preference votes he received – some 172,000.
Preference votes – personal votes expressed alongside a party
vote – translated into internal party power. As with other powerful
Christian Democratic politicians, Bisaglia was linked to numerous scandals – but he escaped largely unscathed. Like the Gavas in
Naples, the local power of the Christian Democrats and the need
to spend public money (whatever the cost) often led to incompre-
hensible and wasteful public projects. The most famous of these in
the case of Bisaglia was another road project – the so-called Pi-Ru-
Bi motorway – which runs through the province of Vicenza, and
owes its nickname to three politicians – Flaminio Piccoli, Mariano
Rumor and Bisaglia. Built between 1972 and 1976, this motorway

stretches for just 50 kilometres (the original plans mentioned 130 kilometres). Later, this project became known as the 'most useless motorway in Italy' due to its brevity and lack of strategic positioning. As the Italian expert Patrick McCarthy has written, 'Bisaglia's career illustrates the way that the DC held onto power ... by channeling public resources to its supporters.'[73] Meanwhile, basic needs (health, welfare, jobs) were often neglected altogether.

It was the needs of politicians that dictated how money was spent, not those of the people. The Christian Democrats welcomed and even at times managed development, but failed to modernise the country. Bisaglia married relatively late, for a politician, just a year before his death in 1984 in a bizarre boating accident. He had no children of his own, but spoke of two young and promising politicians from his party (Pier Ferdinando Casini and Marco Follini) as his 'sons'. Bisaglia's funeral was attended by all the powerful Christian Democrats of the time.

Cholera: Naples – 1973

In 1973 Naples was paralysed by a cholera epidemic. The photographer and journalist Ferdinando Scianna visited the city, and asked himself a simple question. How could this be happening, in a country as apparently rich as Italy? He started his reply with a phrase written on a wall: 'This cholera comes from Palazzo San Giacomo [City Hall].' Politicians were being blamed for the epidemic, and the city was in ferment, with demonstrations and protests of all kinds. Scianna managed to interview a local politician, Bruno Milanesi, from the Christian Democratic Party. Milanesi blamed the cholera on 'mussels imported from Tunisia' (this later turned out to be true). Lorries with disinfectant were being driven through some of the poorer parts of the city.[74]

The first cases of cholera were discovered on 24 August 1973 in a place called Torre del Greco. The mass media descended on the city, as they would do years later when the 'rubbish crisis' hit Naples.[75] Urban myths took hold. Lemons (which were thought to help prevent the disease) sold out, and their price rose to record levels. Many stopped drinking tap water altogether. An extensive vaccination programme (nearly 230,000 doses) was carried out, street by street.[76] There was (a perhaps understandable) reticence to mention the word 'cholera' (to prevent panic), but in the end the institutions were left with no choice. Naples was once again associated with stereotypes about the South – and dismissed as backward, chaotic and dangerous. In the end, once the epidemic had been contained, nobody seemed to know exactly how many victims there were. Numbers ranged from twelve to twenty-four dead, with a thousand or so who ended up in hospital. A total of 127 people were diagnosed with the disease. Italy was a modern country, yet its politicians had lined their own pockets rather than deal with the basic structural and social issues facing its people. Further disasters would expose this radical disconnect still further.

Poison Cloud: Seveso

It was a Saturday: 10 July 1976. A fire had broken out and a white cloud was seen emerging from a local factory known as the ICMESA. The cloud could still be seen on the Sunday. The factory was in a nondescript place called Seveso, just outside Milan.[77] Dioxin (a poison) was released into the air in vast quantities. People soon started to feel ill. Their eyes hurt and their skin began to go red, especially children. On the Monday the order was given to local farmers to halt work. Those animals that had eaten polluted grass started to die. Panic broke out. But it took a week for any action to be taken (the workers had gone on working in the factory, for example). On 24 July (two weeks after the leak) an evacuation finally took place. For many it was too late. There were plans to use napalm to destroy some of the vegetation in the area. Children were taken to hospital, their faces covered in bandages.[78]

Thousands of people had to be relocated. The images of the disaster were dramatic – with people in white suits and gas masks clearing up the fields, and deformed farm animals. Barbed wire was strung around the whole area, and signs indicated that nobody was to cross barriers. The army were called in. Locals and others suffered from horrific skin complaints. Pregnant women were traumatised with worry about the possible effects on their unborn babies. Over three thousand animals died in the immediate aftermath of the disaster, and tens of thousands more were slaughtered as part of a policy of containment. Seveso also led directly to a case of political violence. In February 1980 the terrorist group Prima Linea assassinated Paolo Paoletti, who worked for the ICMESA company at Seveso. But some good did come out of this horrible disaster. Seveso remained a byword for lack of regulation – a warning for future generations. Environmental legislation was passed and the disaster also changed European law (with the so-called Seveso directives on factories containing dangerous substances). As with other areas of Italian life, reform finally began to defend the environment, employees and residents, as well as nature and the animals inhabiting it, from pollution and destructive uncontrolled growth.

Earthquake: Campania – 1980

In 1980 a major earthquake hit an area around Naples as well as the city itself. Just under three thousand people died, and some 280,000 were made homeless. It was a national disaster. The Irpinia earthquake struck at 7.34 in the evening on 23 November. President Sandro Pertini turned up to observe the rescue effort, and later made an angry speech on television in which he criticised the inefficiencies of the state and made direct reference to the previous misuse of public money after the 1968 'Belice' earthquake in Sicily. Pertini asked all Italians to help, and concluded by stating that 'the best way to remember the dead is to help the living'. '*Fate Presto*' ('Come Quickly') screamed the front pages of newspapers. Volunteers streamed down to the South to help with the job of clearing up, and to bury the bodies that lay under ruins and rubble.

But despite the large numbers of volunteers, and Pertini's powerful words, amidst one disaster another soon took shape. Criminal organisations and many of those in the political party clienteles that ran the area got their hands on many of the resources that were distributed to the area. Hideous housing developments were constructed, and communities were broken up and dispersed. Expensive scaffolding – rented at a high cost – shot up all over the region, and often without any real justification. This was an ecological and human catastrophe to add to the aftermath of the earthquake itself – a dreadful example of reconstruction – a non-construction, or a deconstruction. The earthquakes of 1980 in and around Naples had revealed how badly built many constructions were. When inspectors visited housing in the wake of the earthquake, they often concluded that many buildings were unfit for human habitation quite apart from the effects of the earthquake. Illegality and lack of planning had made Naples vulnerable to natural disaster.

Blood and Lead: Bombs, Plots and Political Violence in Italy, 1969–80

The 1960s and 1970s were a time of radical and organic reform of all Italy's major technical and social institutions – from schools to universities and 'closed houses', to asylums and prisons, to the family, marriage and maternity itself. Some of these reforms went further than others, and certain institutions survived in the face of a double challenge from modernity as well as the 'years of contestation' from the movements that emerged during the 'long 1968'. In many cases reforms were supported by nationwide referendums, which confirmed significant shifts in attitudes and cultural beliefs. Yet, for many historians, these years are usually described as the 'years of lead' – as marked indelibly by political violence. The next section of this chapter will seek to understand why blood rather than reform has dominated the memory and historiography of these decades.

Has Italian history been one vast conspiracy? Should we write the history of this country as one great overarching plot carried out behind the scenes? Has Italy been a puppet, manipulated by a puppet-master? Rumours of coup plots within the state had remained largely as speculation until 1967, when the weekly news magazine *L'Espresso* led with a banner headline, under an image of a *carabinieri*'s hat. 'Finally the truth ... 14 July 1964. Conspiracy in the Quirinale. Segni and De Lorenzo were preparing for a coup.'[79] These were serious accusations, relating to events three years earlier. It was alleged that General Giovanni De Lorenzo, previously head of the Carabinieri militarised national police force, and the former President of Italy, the Christian Democrat Antonio Segni, had hatched a plan to subvert Italian democracy. It was a sensational news story.

This great political conspiracy is usually referred to as the *Piano solo* (the Solo Plan) and had, it seems, been prepared by General De Lorenzo and others in 1964. But what was the Solo Plan? De Lorenzo was also head of SIFAR – a military wing of Italy's secret services from 1962 until it was dissolved into another organisation in 1965. De Lorenzo's 'plan' looked very much like a blueprint for a coup – especially in the case of a Communist rise to national power. Named militants were to be rounded up and interned in camps in Sardinia, while major cities would be 'occupied' by *carabinieri*. Later it emerged that the Socialist Party headquarters would also be occupied as part of the Plan. De Lorenzo denied that he had drawn up such a plan, and sued the journalists who had published the story and the editor of *L'Espresso*. Both journalists were initially given jail sentences and heavy fines but later the charges were withdrawn.

For years journalists and many on the left would become familiar with the various acronyms applied to different sections of Italy's secret services: SIFAR, SISME, SID. These shady organisations were so powerful that they were sometimes seen as constituting a sort of 'double', 'underground' or 'secret state'. In addition, there was foreign interference in Italy's affairs – through NATO, the KGB and various other secret-service organisations. Parallel armed bodies were ready in case of war between East and West. Acts of violence, plots and conspiracies were often accompanied by attempts to throw police and magistrates off the scent. These false trails and cover-ups – *depistaggi* – influenced public opinion and led to constant discussions around various conspiracy theories. Different truths and 'facts' were carried forward. Consensus over what had happened and why was almost impossible to achieve.

Rumours of an imminent coup raged in Italy throughout the 1960s and 1970s. The colonels' coup in Greece in 1967, when added to the Solo Plan controversy in the same year in Italy, fuelled Italian fears of an 'authoritarian turn'. There was a widespread belief (especially on the left) that the tactics and outcomes used in Greece would be repeated in Italy and with a similar outcome. Italy, at that point, was southern Europe's only remaining democracy – with authoritarian regimes in charge in Greece, Portugal and Spain. In 1969 the radical publisher Giangiacomo Feltrinelli published a pamphlet entitled *Estate 1969* (*Summer 1969*). He was convinced that a coup was about to happen in Italy. 'For some months,' Feltrinelli wrote, 'there is a precise military and political plan in place that will aim to shift this country to the right in a radical and authoritarian way: an "Italian-style" coup.'[80] Feltrinelli was often derided at the time – and has been since – and labelled a fantasist. Nonetheless, in December 1969 a series of events took place that were not entirely removed from the scenario laid out in his book. The most serious of these moments occurred in Milan, close to the radical publisher's house.

12 December 1969: Massacre

'Piazza Fontana and that which followed was an event which marked a turning point for an entire generation. There was a before, and an after.'

Corrado Stajano[81]

'In the large bank lobby, there was a big hole in the middle of the floor. Various bodies and people who had suffered terrible injuries lay amongst the dust and rubble, while others covered in blood cried out with terror.'

Official sentence, Piazza Fontana trial judges, 1979[82]

Most of the people in the centre of Milan that Friday afternoon, on 12 December 1969, were simply doing their Christmas shopping. In the imposing rotunda of the National Agricultural Bank, a short walk from the main department stores in Piazza Fontana, farmers were making deposits. This was a Friday tradition linked to Milan's long-standing connections with the countryside and its economy. The farmers were mostly middle-aged men, although some had brought their families with them. It was a tense time. Student and worker movements were in the ascendency in the city, and recent demonstrations had seen clashes with the police. In November 1969, not far from Piazza Fontana, a young policeman and southern migrant to Milan (Antonio Annarumma), had died during clashes with students. At Annarumma's funeral, student leaders who attended were threatened with violence and had to run for their lives. Things were turning ugly.

At 4.37 p.m. a huge explosion rocked the interior of the Agricultural Bank. The vision of the aftermath was reminiscent of war. Severed limbs lay around the rubble inside the dark and smoke-filled building, and there were bodies everywhere. When the first count was made, fourteen people had been killed and nearly ninety injured. A further two victims would die by January 1970, and a man called Vittorio Mocchi died fourteen years later due to complications linked to his injuries. Some of the injuries were horrific and life-changing. A ten-year-old boy lost his leg. A priest, Don Fioravanti, was at the entrance of the bank when the explosion took place. He tried to help the victims. 'A girl without an arm came towards me,' he told the press, 'and with her other arm she pulled at my tunic. "Father, help us," she said.'[83]

Four other bombs were placed that same day in Italy (with identical timers, bags and explosives), three in Rome and one in another bank in Milan, but there were no further deaths. The bomb in the Agricultural Bank would become known by the name of its location – *Piazza Fontana*. Although the first version of the events that took place referred to an exploding boiler, the bomb attack was quickly dubbed a massacre, a *strage*: the massacre of Piazza Fontana. Others referred to this event simply by its date: 12 December.

Who had committed such an outrage, in peacetime, against people who just happened to be in a bank? Who had placed those bombs? The police had few doubts. They looked quickly towards the left and the anarchist movement. It was said that some four thousand left-wing activists were arrested in the days that followed. Interrogations carried on throughout the following days and nights in police stations across the country. Crucially, however, the working class of Milan stood firm, turning out in force for a formidable silent demonstration on the day of the victims' funerals. A message was sent out: democracy was not something that would be given away lightly.

Accidental Death? The Pinelli Case

One of those picked up in Milan on 12 December – the same day as the bomb explosion – was Giuseppe 'Pino' Pinelli, a forty-one-year-old railway worker and father of two daughters. Pinelli was an anarchist and well known to the police, but he had no criminal record. He was arrested while playing cards in a bar close to the working-class canal area of the city, and followed a police car to the central *Questura* (police station) on his scooter.

Pinelli was then held for three days and three nights without charge (a length of detention that broke the law at the time) in Milan's central police station. He slept very little and was questioned on various occasions. Proper records were not kept. On 15 December, at around midnight, a journalist in the courtyard of the police station heard something fall to the ground. It was Pinelli, who had previously been in an office on the fourth floor. Had he fallen? Was he pushed? Had he jumped? Pinelli was taken to a nearby hospital, where he died soon afterwards. A police press conference held that night claimed that Pinelli had killed himself, that there was 'strong evidence' against him, and that he had shouted 'anarchy is finished' as he plunged through the window.

Many refused to believe this story, and the police version soon unravelled. Pinelli was quickly cleared of all links to the bomb. An innocent man had died after (or during?) an illegal interrogation.

But who was responsible for this death? Blame quickly fell onto the officer in charge of the investigation, a policeman called Luigi Calabresi. Meanwhile, another anarchist, Pietro Valpreda (who worked as a dancer), was arrested in Milan on 15 December and charged with placing the bomb in the bank. He protested his innocence, and was kept for three years in prison without trial (something that led to a change in the law specifically to release him). Television reporters declared at the time that 'the guilty party' had been caught. Valpreda was eventually cleared, like Pinelli, but only in 1981.

Calabresi, meanwhile, became the subject of a hate campaign in the left-wing press. Cartoons were printed showing him pushing people off planes, without parachutes. Graffiti was daubed on walls that named him as a murderer. Eventually, Calabresi sued the left-wing newspaper *Lotta Continua* for libel, a decision that rebounded on him as the subsequent libel trial was used to denounce and interrogate those involved in the Pinelli case.

On 17 March 1972, Luigi Calabresi was shot in the back of the head outside his flat in Milan as he walked to his car in the morning. Police investigations all came to nothing, in the short term. But in 1988 a former militant from *Lotta Continua* confessed to being the driver in 1972, and accused three other militants from the group of having either carried out or sanctioned the murder. All three protested their innocence, but all were finally convicted after an interminable legal case (with some fifteen distinct sentences) in 2000.[84]

Piazza Fontana and the Pinelli case further radicalised a whole generation of Italian militants, many of whom were already part of the 1968 movement. A multi-authored book (which saw itself as a work of 'counter-information'), published a year after the bomb, pointed the finger at a shady alliance of conspirators, neo-fascists and agents provocateurs. Its title was evocative, and explosive – *Strage di stato* (*State Massacre*). A 'strategy of tension', it was argued, had been put in place that tried to use bombs and other acts of violence to undermine democracy and the left. This harked back to fears of a coup in Italy after Greece, and to memories of the *Piano solo*.

Yet the authorities continued to look to the left in their inquiries and subsequent trials, despite mounting evidence of secret-service and neo-fascist involvement in the massacre. Eventually, courageous magistrates also began to investigate the far right, and decided to question top-level politicians. After a series of inconclusive trials, some of which were televised, a thorough investigation was only and finally carried out in the 1990s.[85] By that time, many of the original protagonists were dead, and the public was far less engaged. Despite the heroic efforts of a series of magistrates, no one was eventually convicted of placing the Piazza Fontana bomb or organising a conspiracy. Some 100,000 folders of legal documents have now been digitised for posterity.

Nine 'Piazza Fontana' trials took place after 1972, with a bewildering variety of suspects, witnesses, prosecutors and evidence of various kinds. At one trial, anarchists and neo-fascists were tried together for the same crime. Many of the trials were moved to Catanzaro in the deep south of Italy, over a thousand kilometres away from Milan. The authorities were concerned about holding the trials in the city where the bomb had exploded.

Meanwhile, the separate but linked Pinelli case dragged on. Some called him the '17th victim' of the bomb. Journalists and film-makers investigated the story, almost obsessively, while Pinelli's wife, Licia, campaigned long and hard for justice. The actor and playwright Dario Fo wrote a compelling play based on the case, *Accidental Death of an Anarchist*, which drew on court cases and rolling news to satirise the more absurd versions given by the police. Fo's play was also a political event, and was updated in line with ongoing investigations. Finally, in 1975, after a long judicial inquiry (which saw lifesize dolls being thrown out of the police station window to test various theories), the state produced its final verdict. Pinelli had died 'accidentally' after 'an active illness' had caused him to fall from the window. This decision led to widespread ridicule, but it closed the case – officially at least.

Today, there are numerous memorials and plaques dedicated to Giuseppe 'Pino' Pinelli in Milan and elsewhere. A continuing struggle over the facts and the memory of those events is symbolised by two, parallel memorials in Piazza Fontana itself, right in the heart of Milan. One plaque, placed there by militants in 1977, states boldly that Pinelli was 'murdered' in the 'rooms of the police station' in 1969. Another plaque nearby (from 2006), argues that Pinelli 'died accidentally'. One plaque represents unofficial memory, the other an official, but ambiguous, version of the past. Both plaques have their own histories. These parallel versions of the same event – in marble, opposite the site of the bomb – are a stark reminder of how memory remains divided in Italy and how memory wars have marked the battle over the past in the present for long periods of time.

Piazza Fontana and its legal and political ramifications would haunt Italy for years to come. Annually, especially in the 1970s, on the anniversary of the bomb, violent demonstrations paralysed the centre of Milan. Other tragedies followed. On 12 December 1970 (the first anniversary of the bomb) a student called Saverio Saltarelli was killed during clashes in the centre of Milan by a tear-gas canister fired into his body at close range. Piazza Fontana had claimed another victim. The 1969 bomb in Milan has often been seen as a turning point for the 1960s, a moment of 'loss of innocence', a stain at the heart of Italian history. The tension created by that bomb, and the Pinelli case, would be exacerbated by events in Rome.

The Coup: 1970

Less than a year after Piazza Fontana, Italy experienced a coup attempt in Rome. It was 7 December 1970. Mystery has always surrounded the events of that night.[86] It seems that groups of neo-fascists gathered at strategic points around Rome, and that armed Forest Guards were waiting on the edge of the city. Some versions of events claim that fifty neo-fascists seized 200 rifles inside the Interior Ministry. There were reports of tanks rumbling through the centre of Rome. Leading policemen and military officers were said to be involved, as were members of the secret services. There were also farcical elements in some accounts, such as the failure of a lift in one part of the operation.

There was a supposed plan in place. First, the neo-fascists and others would occupy the offices of the central public television station. Then the leader of the coup – Junio Valerio Borghese – was to read a proclamation to the nation. He would tell the Italian people that 'our most dangerous enemies, those who would like to hand over our Fatherland to foreigners, have been nullified. Italians. We will create a State without adjectives or political banners. It will only have one flag. Our glorious tricolor!'[87]

Borghese had been a leading military officer under Mussolini's puppet government towards the end of the war.[88] He was found guilty of collaborating with the Nazis in 1949, but given a relatively mild sentence – twelve years – and a decision was taken to release him immediately. Despite this escape from justice, the 'Black Prince', as he was sometimes known, did not withdraw from public life. He threw himself into neo-fascist politics. In 1951 he was made Honorary President of the neo-fascist Movimento Sociale Italiano, and in 1968 he helped to found an extreme neo-fascist organisation called the Fronte Nazionale. The events of December 1970 in Rome are often referred to as the 'Borghese Coup'.[89]

It is a mystery as to why the coup was not carried through. Some versions of events cite a last-minute telephone call to Borghese calling the whole thing off. But nobody has ever been able to ascertain the reason for this withdrawal of support, or who made the call (or whether it even took place). Some attribute the call to the Americans, some to specific Christian Democrat politicians. Others later argued that the whole 'coup' was an elaborate trap, into which the neo-fascists had almost fallen. The realisation of this was also sometimes said to have led to the coup being abandoned *in extremis*.

Strangely, however, this coup attempt or half-coup in the centre of Italy's capital city went virtually unnoticed. It was not until some four months later that news emerged publicly in the pages of the Communist daily *Paese Sera*.[90] The newspaper ran a banner headline that day with its scoop: 'Conspiracy by the Extreme

Right against the Republic'.[91] The revelations in *Paese Sera* were quickly followed by a statement to Parliament by the Interior Minister, Franco Restivo, who denied that there had been a coup attempt, but announced investigations into a series of neo-fascist organisations. An order was placed for the arrest of Borghese and others.

From this point onwards, Borghese was – in theory – on the run from the Italian state. Nonetheless, he managed to cross the frontier into Spain. He would die in Cadiz in 1974. A complicated legal process concerning the coup dragged on right until the 1980s (and was revived in the 1990s), but ended without any guilty verdicts of note. Later, different versions emerged that also attributed a support role to various criminal organisations in Italy. Some judicial verdicts took the events of December 1970 very seriously, whereas others concluded that the coup was far from being a serious attempt to take power. For example, a 1984 sentence concerning the coup attempt dismissed the whole affair as a 'secret meeting of four or five sixty-year- olds'.[92]

In 1973 the film director Mario Monicelli made a movie based loosely on the Borghese Coup with thinly veiled characters inspired by the real-life protagonists. The whole affair was portrayed in the movie as a comical charade, but there was a twist in the tale. At the end of the film, fears of a coup inspired by those events lead to a real crackdown. The film was called *We Want the Colonels*.[93]

In the wake of these stories of plots and conspiracies, a sort of 'coup-neurosis' spread throughout the left, and was reinforced in the 1970s by events in Chile. Dario Fo and his wife Franca Rame – actors, writers and artists – played on these fears during a special performance in Turin in October 1973, just six weeks after Augusto Pinochet's coup in Chile. The show being performed was officially called *People's War in Chile*. The venue was packed – with some ten thousand people. At a pre-decided moment, the cast began to pretend that a real coup had taken place in Italy itself. It was said that telephone lines had gone dead. Fake gunshots were fired outside. Some of those present were convinced enough to panic. Fo's role in the fake coup was to pretend that it was all nonsense, something that seemed to heighten the tension amongst the public. One audience member allegedly ate ten pages of his own diary.[94] The show within a show was a great success, but Fo and Rame were making a serious political point – about the real possibility of a coup and how it could be resisted.

The Revolt of Reggio Calabria: 1970

'Reggio Regional Capital!'
                    Political slogan, Reggio Calabria, 1970[95]

When elected regional governments – as outlined in the 1948 Constitution – were finally set up across Italy in 1970, each region needed to designate a capital. This was not just a symbolic decision, but one that would lead to a steady stream of resources, offices, public spending and political influence – elements that had always been particularly important in the poorer South. In the Calabrian region the government decided to award this honour, in 1970, to Catanzaro, which was smaller and less important economically than the port-city of Reggio Calabria. A new university (Calabria lacked one) was planned for Cosenza – and not Reggio Calabria.

The bigger city was furious. A decision over the regional capital had been brewing since the 1940s and protests had been held at various moments in the post-war period, with strikes and roadblocks. A full-scale 'revolt' began in opposition to this choice in July 1970 – which soon became about many other things beyond the issue of the regional capital – poverty, politics and anti-politics, local pride. The protests began with the support of the mayor (a Christian Democrat) but were then taken over politically by the far right. Whole neighbourhoods took part in the uprising, and thousands of policemen and *carabinieri* were sent in to suppress the 'revolt'. The army was deployed to keep links open to Sicily. Barricades were erected. Trains stopped arriving in Reggio Calabria altogether. At least eight people died during clashes (across the region) that lasted for months. One man – Angelo

Campanella, a forty-three-year-old father of seven and his family's only bread-winner (he was a bus driver) – was shot dead by a *carabiniere*'s bullet while standing on his balcony. After his death most of his children were taken into care. Later, in 1971, an anti-fascist demonstrator in Catanzaro called Giuseppe Malacaria was also killed – probably by handmade bombs or grenades thrown near to local neo-fascist offices.

Very few of these deaths (some were shot, some died in more mysterious circumstances, some were policemen struck by stones) were investigated properly. Quickly, the level of the violence reached levels not seen in any other part of Italy. Some neighbourhoods introduced a kind of self-government, with identity checks. Municipal rivalries intensified, and those with different number plates were often harassed and sometimes assaulted. There were attacks on left-wing party offices and many bombs were placed or thrown across the region. Occasionally, there were shoot-outs between the forces of law and order and the protesters. The historian Guido Crainz has called the revolt 'unique in terms of its length, radicalisation and levels of violence'.[96] The film-maker Giovanni Bonfanti documented the rebellion, capturing dramatic images of a city under siege, the construction of barricades, pitched street battles, and soldiers guarding railway lines.[97]

The protest movement soon had an unlikely leader – a local neo-fascist called Ciccio Franco. He had been a head of the right-wing trade union federation CISNAL. Franco was a small balding man with a fiery temperament. At one point during the uprising he went into hiding to avoid arrest. He then gave an interview (unshaven, and dishevelled) to the celebrated journalist Oriana Fallaci in which he stated that his 'ideological champion' was the French philosopher Georges Sorel and his 'political champion' was Mussolini.[98] Franco utilised (but did not coin) the phrase 'Boia chi molla' ('Those who give up can go to hell'), a slogan that was often applied to the whole revolt.

The neo-fascist Movimento Sociale Italiano won an unprecedented 36.2 per cent of the vote in Reggio Calabria in the general elections of 1972 (becoming the biggest party) and Franco was elected senator. This was way above its results in any other previous elections in the city or at a national level. This wasn't, however, merely or only a 'fascist revolt'. The movement had many roots and causes, and was open to many interpretations. The neo-fascists had been adept at hijacking a rebellion that was also against the party system itself. Rag-doll representations of politicians were hung up from electricity wires. As one journalist wrote at the time, 'what is happening here is a complete breakdown of the relationship between the population and the political class'.[99] The MSI's attitude to violence was ambiguous. In Parliament the party defended 'law and order' and institutions such as the police, but in Reggio its militants were in the front line during clashes with those same forces. This was sometimes referred to as the politics of the 'double platform'. This 'duplicity' was carried forward throughout the 1970s and, to some extent, into the 1980s.

As the left struggled to understand what was happening, many of the participants began to see the Communists and Socialists as their enemy. In October 1972 trains packed with trade unionists and others from the North and all over Italy made the long and difficult journey down to Reggio Calabria to stage a demonstration. A boat also arrived from Genoa. It was a tense day, with the constant threat of violence in the air. A series of explosives on the railway line failed to prevent the arrival of the demonstrators. The train was also attacked en route. The train journey was later commemorated in song, there was a novel written about it and also a documentary film made.[100] In the end a compromise was reached – with Catanzaro as Regional Capital and Reggio as seat of the Regional Council (the executive body). Protests faded and the barricades were cleared away by armed vehicles (which locals remembered as 'tanks'). But a legacy of bitterness remained in popular memory and within the political and civic structures of the cities involved.[101]

The Millionaire and the Pylon

By 1972, many of Giangiacomo Feltrinelli's fears as expressed in his 1969 pamphlet appeared to have come to pass. The Piazza Fontana bomb and the Borghese Coup seemed to confirm that plans were being hatched in the upper echelons of the Italian state to subvert democracy. Feltrinelli himself was targeted for arrest and went underground. He was extremely rich (his family had made a fortune through wood) and a highly successful and ground-breaking publisher. In 1957 he had managed to publish Boris Pasternak's *Dr Zhivago* for the first time, and the book became an international best-seller. Feltrinelli's bookshops were innovative spaces – he even put a jukebox in one store.

But Feltrinelli thought that the revolution needed him. He linked up with left-wing groups in Genoa and elsewhere, and moved between Switzerland, Czechoslovakia, Austria and Italy. He started to contemplate resistance – armed resistance – and made contact with some former Second World War partisans, setting up a network of safe houses, sympathisers and communication lines. He had previously become a close friend of Fidel Castro. In 1972 Feltrinelli's body was discovered near an electric pylon outside Milan. His leg had been blown off. He was just forty-five years old. Many thought that Feltrinelli had been murdered by 'the state'. The left-wing newspaper *Potere Operaio* (*Workers' Power*) issued a communiqué stating that 'The revolutionary Comrade Feltrinelli has fallen thanks to an ambush by a class enemy.' But the most likely explanation was that Feltrinelli had died attempting to plant a bomb in order to sabotage the city's electricity supply. His life story soon became the stuff of legend, and, many years later, was beautifully told by his son, Carlo, in a book entitled *Senior Service*.[102]

Strategy of Tension

Piazza Fontana was only the first in a series of 'massacres', carried out as part of a strategy of tension involving Italy's secret services and far-right organisations. The second serious incident after the bomb in Milan was in Goia Tauro in Calabria, where an explosive device caused a train to derail resulting in six deaths in July 1970. In Peteano (in the north of Italy near Gorizia) a bomb planted in a car by neo-fascists killed three *carabinieri* in 1972. A man claiming to be an anarchist (but there are serious doubts about this claim) threw a bomb into a crowd in Via Fatebenefratelli (outside the city's central police station) in Milan in May 1973. Four people were killed. In Brescia in May 1974 a bomb left by neo-fascists in a rubbish bin in Piazza della Loggia in the centre of the city left eight dead and caused more than a hundred injuries. An anti-fascist demonstration was being held in the square at the time.[103] Later that same year, during the night of 3–4 August, a bomb placed on a passenger train exploded in a tunnel outside Bologna, killing twelve, some of whom were burned alive in the extreme heat created by the blast. In 1984 a very similar bomb killed a further sixteen people on a train. This event became known as 'the massacre of the 904 train' or the 'Christmas massacre'. These horrific attacks all led to anger, confusion and trauma. All were followed by long and often inconclusive legal processes and investigations. They did not succeed, however, in their primary aim of destroying Italian democracy and instituting a repressive or more authoritarian political system.

1977: A New 1968?

Student and social movements mushroomed again across Italy in 1977. In many cases these were creative and 'lifestyle' political struggles. Groups calling themselves 'metropolitan Indians' organised 'happenings' and meetings, and mobilised school and university students – the post-1968 generations. In part, these movements grew naturally out of the reforms created by 1968 itself – especially the opening up of university education. Local pirate and alternative radio stations became a key forum for discussion and cultural production – and some survive to this day. Music festivals were another space for alternative politics. Communes and alternative communities were set up as alternatives to the family. There was a flourishing of the underground press, some of it extremely innovative and original (such as the magazine *Re Nudo*). But drug-taking also became endemic – and in the 1980s there was a near-epidemic of deaths in Italian cities due to heroin use. Numerous people experimented with personal therapy while some turned to alternative religions. Others from the left-wing movement were elected to Parliament or local government, or worked within the media. Some of those from the left ended up on the right. There were myriad paths available for the 'veterans' of 1968 and (later) those from 1977.

Not all of what happened in 1977 was linked to creative and lifestyle forms of politics. New groupings operated within the grey area between the armed struggle and dedicated forms of political militancy. This was true of *Autonomia Operaia*, one of many groups to appear around this time. Inspired by the writings and activism of a professor of legal philosophy at the University of Padua – Antonio (Toni) Negri – *Autonomia* devised innovative ways to organise protest. Radical alliances were built around affordable housing (through occupations and rent strikes). People refused collectively to pay their bus fares, or only paid as much of their electricity or phone bills as they could manage. This strategy was summed up by Dario Fo's popular play *Non Si Paga! Non Si Paga! (Can't Pay! Won't Pay!)*.[104] Activists also occupied spaces left empty by rapid de-industrialisation or urban speculation. This led to the 'social centre' movement, where vibrant cultural spaces engaging in a range of activities were created within cities.

While the Communist Party had been able to at least communicate with the 1968 movements, and bring their reform proposals into the parliamentary setting, this proved much more difficult in 1977. In Bologna, a city governed since 1945 by the Communists, there were violent clashes between the police and students. In March 1977 a young medical student, Francesco Lorusso, was shot dead by the *carabinieri* in the street. Magistrates later decided that Lorusso had been killed by a twenty-two-year-old *carabiniere* doing his national service called Massimo Tramontani. But Tramontani escaped conviction. The magistrates held that he had acted in self-defence. In 1975 a special emergency law (the so-called Reale Law) had extended the conditions for the use of armed force by police and *carabinieri*.

Soon after Lorusso's death a plaque was placed on the wall
where he died. It reads:

THE COMRADES OF
FRANCESCO LORUSSO
HERE
ASSASSINATED BY THE ARMED FEROCITY OF
THE REGIME
11 MARCH 1977
KNOW
THAT HIS IDEA OF EQUALITY AND FREEDOM
AND LOVE WILL SURVIVE ALL CRIMES
\-
FRANCESCO IS ALIVE AND IS FIGHTING
ALONGSIDE US[105]

Nearby, bullet holes left by the police at the time have been preserved under perspex. Lorusso's killing left a bitter legacy. Graffiti
claiming that *PCI=Tanks* was seen. Some *Autonomia* militants fet-
ishised violence, exalting in the use of guns during demonstrations.
It was significant that one of the most celebrated (or denigrated,
depending on your point of view) events of 1977 took place when
self-styled 'autonomist' radicals prevented the moderate trade
union leader Luciano Lama from speaking on the University of
Rome campus. Lama, the unions and the Communist Party in
general were seen by many in the movement as 'new policemen' –
part of what they viewed as a repressive state machine.

Terrorism, Italian-Style

In the wake of Piazza Fontana, and throughout the 1970s, people
from the left and right of the political spectrum took up arms.
They believed that political ends could be achieved through what
they often called 'the armed struggle'. During the 'years of lead'
that followed, hundreds of people were killed by various forms of
political violence. Armed political groupings sprang up at regular

intervals on both the left and the right of the spectrum. The most well known of these groups on the left called itself the *Brigate Rosse* (the Red Brigades). Its symbol was a five-pointed star inside a circle. The background to this period was also linked to the end of the boom, and a period of austerity after 1973.[106]

Who were the Red Brigades and where did they come from? The first left-wing groups to advocate and use violence began to emerge at the end of the 1960s and the beginning of the 1970s. Almost all of those involved had been part of the student or workers' movements. Some were former communists (as with one group that emerged from Reggio Emilia in central Italy), others militant Catholics (a faction came out of the Trento student movement). Small groups soon began to organise violent acts in cities such as Milan, Turin and Genoa.

These were fringe groups, but they had a past. Rossana Rossanda, communist and journalist, would later admit that they were part of the 'family album' of the left.[107] Violent language and tactics had been part of the movement for years – and the so-called 'Servizi d'ordine' (Groups of Order) used by the student movement and far-left organisations were adept in using force to get their way and 'control' demonstrations. These groups were also skilled in resisting attacks from neo-fascists and taking on the police on the streets.

The cult of class violence often came together in a heady mix alongside myths linked to Che Guevara, the Spanish/Basque Resistance, and Latin American groups like the Tupamaros, as well as experiences in Germany, Northern Ireland, China, Palestine and elsewhere. While many people flirted with the armed struggle, far smaller numbers took up arms. A key factor in this choice was the violence of the state itself, and interpretations of events such as those in Piazza Fontana as inspired or directly carried out by or – at the very least – covered up by the state or parts of the state machine. Many also looked back to the anti-fascist Resistance for inspiration, calling themselves 'new partisans'. Some former partisans became linked to these new movements, although the connections made by the self-styled *brigatisti* (members of the Red Brigades) were often fanciful.

'Strike one in order to educate one hundred' (the Red Brigades)

'That day four of us decided to take part. I drove the van. We waited until 6, but Macchiarini didn't turn up. We left ... The next day – 3 March 1972 – we came back at the same time – around 5 p.m. – and parked the van about 10 metres from his car.'
Alberto Franceschini, Red Brigades[108]

In the end, their target turned up. They beat him up a little and threw him into their van, and drove off. Idalgo Macchiarini, the victim, was 'afraid, he was quiet'. Then they took a photograph, complete with two guns and a card strung around their victim's neck on which the following slogan was written:

Red Brigades [complete with star]
Strike quickly and escape!
Nobody will remain unpunished!
Strike one in order to educate 100!
All power to the proletariat in arms

Part of the slogan came from Mao. Later, one of the *brigatisti* involved told his version of the story: 'We wanted to make people see that Macchiarini would be the first of a long list. Everyone – bosses and under-bosses – needed to feel that they were possible targets. They needed to be afraid to go out, and to see every worker as an enemy who was to be respected and feared.'[109]

The photograph became famous. Macchiarini did indeed look terrified. He had two guns pointed at him, after all, and one was pressed into his cheek. The slogan-card was tied around his neck. He was then released. But who was he? And why was he a target? Idalgo Macchiarini worked for the Siemens company in Milan where he was a lower manager. This was the first kidnapping (and the first of what became known as 'quick kidnappings') by an organisation that called itself the Red Brigades, a tiny group that had decided to go underground and use violence as a tactic. Some of the *brigatisti* had worked or were still employed in the Siemens factory, and therefore knew Macchiarini. Many on the extra-parliamentary left applauded the kidnapping. One group wrote that 'this action can be seen as a consistent element of a general willingness on the part of the masses to pursue class war, including through violence'. Another claimed that 'these are actions with a class-based, proletarian quality'.[110]

On 12 February 1973 in Turin, members of the Red Brigades captured one of the leaders of the neo-fascist trade union – a man called Bruno Labate – and shaved his head, before releasing him after a few hours. As with Macchiarini, the group had waited for him outside his house and pushed him into a van. He was interrogated and left tied to a pole in front of the factory gates at the vast FIAT Mirafiori factory. It was 1.30 p.m., and the shift was changing. Many workers were impressed. It was said that when Labate asked for help, some workers replied that he should have been killed. A leaflet was distributed by the Red Brigades that accused CISNAL of dividing the working class, organising blacklegs, and spying on other workers. The leaflet finished with a rhetorical flourish: 'We want to liberate our city … ARMED STRUGGLE FOR COMMUNISM'.

In December 1973 a FIAT administrator (Ettore Armerio) was kidnapped and held for eight days. This was no longer a 'quick-kidnapping'. The Red Brigade militants felt more confident, both of their own ability to carry out these 'actions' and, they claimed, of the support they enjoyed amongst parts of the workforce. With time, the Red Brigades would intensify their tactics – using political assassination and further kidnappings (or a combination of the two). More victims would follow.

The media was fascinated by these activities, and the Red Brigades were adept at using this for their own ends. They invented pithy slogans and symbols to communicate their message, although their comuniqués and documents were increasingly long and opaque. Photographs were issued for immediate use in the press. These were techniques that were also used by professional advertisers.[111]

In April 1974 the BR turned their attention to the state itself –
seizing a magistrate called Mario Sossi in Genoa. Sossi had overseen the prosecution of a previous left-wing group. He was an
obvious target, but his kidnapping further raised the stakes. Now,
specific demands were made – the release of prisoners from that
previous prosecution. After Sossi was given a 'death sentence' by
the Red Brigades, eight prisoners were set free and allowed to
apply for a passport. It appeared that the Red Brigades had the
upper hand, and the state seemed to be retreating. On 23 April,
Sossi was released unharmed. It was a propaganda victory for
the Red Brigades. In June they carried out their first assassinations – of two neo-fascists in Padua. Later trials confirmed the
role of five Red Brigade members in this attack – which, they
claimed, was aimed at gathering material from the offices of the
Movimento Sociale Italiano. The Red Brigades, for the first time,
claimed responsibility for these murders.

The state soon fought back. Special anti-terrorist units were
formed – and a tough general took charge of the state's strategy.
His name was Carlo Alberto Dalla Chiesa and he had cut his
teeth during the Resistance and in anti-Mafia struggles in Sicily.
Attempts were made to infiltrate the militant groups and 'supergrass' evidence was encouraged. Soon this new strategy was showing signs of success. In September 1974 two of the leaders of the
Red Brigades – Renato Curcio and Alberto Franceschini – were
arrested near Turin thanks to a tip-off. Curcio would soon escape
in a dramatic jail-break led (from the outside) by his partner (in
life, and in the Red Brigades), Margherita Cagol. Both Cagol and
Curcio had been part of the student movement in Trento in the
1960s. In 1975 Cagol was killed in a shoot-out (although some
claimed she had been shot after being captured) at an isolated
farm in the north of the country.

In January 1976 Curcio was rearrested in Milan. The trial process in Turin of the leaders of the Red Brigades began in a climate of violence and intimidation. The authorities were unable to
appoint a jury because of fears over reprisals, while the accused
refused to recognise the court, or accept appointed state lawyers
for their defence, and threatened those who did play this role

with violence. Without a lawyer for the accused, no trial could move forward. The first lawyer who took on this role was Fulvio Croce – president of the lawyers' association in Turin and a veteran of the anti-fascist Resistance. In April 1977 Croce was murdered outside his office. The Red Brigades claimed responsibility. However, despite this background, the trials were eventually held and heavy sentences were handed down. Curcio remained in prison for the next twenty-two years.

The arrest and trial of Curcio did not lead to the end of the Red Brigades, as militants on the outside continued to assassinate a series of people, and aimed to strike at what they termed 'the heart of the state'. The most dramatic moment in the history of the Red Brigades, and one of the most intense in post-war Italy, involved another kidnapping, more than six years after the 'quick kidnapping' of Idalgo Macchiarini in Milan. The Red Brigades had come a long way since that first 'action' in 1972. This time their target would be a household name in Italy, a man who had been Prime Minister.

Fifty-Five Days in Rome

On 16 March 1978 one of Italy's most powerful politicians, the Christian Democratic grandee Aldo Moro, was captured in broad daylight in the centre of Rome. Five of Moro's bodyguards were shot dead and the politician was taken alive. This was to be the Red Brigades' most audacious and celebrated act. Moro was kept in a tiny cell-like room in an apartment (almost certainly in Rome itself) and later interrogated by a self-appointed 'people's court'. The verdict of the 'court' was shocking: Moro was sentenced to death.

For fifty-five days the police and secret services failed to locate his whereabouts. There are numerous explanations for this lack of success, including strong suspicions that some people from within the state machine were aware of Moro's location. The Red Brigades – true to their media strategy – issued a series of communiqués. There was also a fake, forged message, which led to a farcical search for Moro in a frozen lake. Rome was paralysed, with roadblocks everywhere. The eyes of the world were on Italy. Moro was an international figure. Politicians were divided over strategy. Some – the Christian Democrats and the Communist Party – called for a hard line (effectively condemning Moro to death). Others – most notably the Socialist Party – argued for negotiation, and there were talks with the kidnappers through intermediaries.

While in captivity, Moro was given pen and paper. He then wrote numerous letters – to his family, to politicians and friends – as well as a lengthy 'testament'. The Red Brigades censored and used these letters for their own ends. Some were sent to their intended destination, others were not. Moro's tone became increasingly desperate and angry as time went on. His appeals to his party to save him led those on the outside to argue that he was being forced to write certain things, or had gone mad. He was, it was said, 'no longer Moro'.[112] These explosive letters (and their author's fate after the fifty-five days) would inspire a large body of conspiracy theories and counter-stories in the years that followed.

After fifty-five days, despite numerous appeals for clemency (including one from the Pope himself), the Red Brigades carried out their promised death sentence. In a challenge to the authority and competence of the state, Moro was shot (in an underground car park) and his body dumped in the back of a red Renault 4 in the centre of Rome, not far from the central offices of both the Communist Party and the Christian Democrats. Italians watched in shock on television as the car boot was opened to reveal Moro's curled-up body, crushed into the boot of the car.

'The Moro case' soon became one of Italy's great mysteries. Every detail was worked over and discussed. Numerous trials have failed to provide clarity. Had Moro been killed (or allowed to die) for wider political reasons beyond those linked to the aims of the Red Brigades? Most importantly, was his death 'convenient' because of his desire to do an imminent deal with the Communist Party? Arguments also focused on the supposed disappearance of Moro's briefcases. Conspiracy theorists were given

a lot of material to work with, including a series of strange coinci-
dences. During Moro's kidnapping a group of people – including
the future Prime Minister and European Commissioner Romano
Prodi – held a séance. They then claimed to have heard the word
'Gradoli'. One of the Red Brigades' hideouts in Rome was in
Via Gradoli – and it was 'discovered' thanks to a water leak that
appeared to have been caused on purpose.

Two Funerals, One Body

Aldo Moro was given a state funeral on 13 May 1978, but his family refused to participate. They blamed the state for the failure to
liberate him. In this decision the family were also adhering to the
wishes of Moro himself who, in a letter written in captivity to his
great friend, the politician Benigno Zaccagnini, had said that 'due
to an obvious sense of incompatibility, I request that State authorities and politicians do not participate at my funeral. I want there
to be just those who really loved me and who therefore deserve
to accompany me [to the grave] with their prayers.' The family
ended their own letter with a stark promise. 'Our family will stay
silent and asks for silence. History will pass judgement on the life
and death of Aldo Moro.'[113] Moro had been buried three days
earlier, on 10 May, in a tiny cemetery outside the capital.

Despite this, the state funeral went ahead in Rome in the vast
spaces of the Basilica di San Giovanni in Laterano, with the Pope
and the entire Christian Democratic leadership in attendance, and
even a coffin, but no body. The Pope was carried into the Church
on a chair. Footage from that body-less funeral was later used in
Pierluigi Bellocchio's powerful film about the Moro kidnapping,
Buongiorno Notte. In that film Bellocchio imagines a scenario in
which Moro escapes and is saved. This alternative ending served
to reinforce the national trauma of what had really happened.[114]

Moro's murder was a turning point for the Red Brigades
although it appeared, at the time, as their greatest triumph. The
brigatisti had seemed to be all-powerful and almost impregnable.
After all, hadn't they kidnapped, held and shot dead a powerful

politician in the centre of Italy's capital city, and got away with it? But hindsight was to show that the decision to execute Moro was a serious political error. The Red Brigades would shoot and injure or kill more people in the period after 1978, but the movement itself – such as it was – became increasingly detached from its self-styled 'armed wing'. A sense of omnipotence had increasingly cut off the men and women of the Red Brigades from the real world. It was clear that they had been blinded by ideology.

The defeat of what – on the left – became known as the 'armed struggle' was down to a combination of factors. The decline of the Red Brigades' movement itself emptied the 'sea' in which the 'terrorist' 'fish' could thrive, to use Mao Zedong's metaphor. ('The guerrilla must move amongst the people as a fish swims in the sea.') Meanwhile, the state adopted a dual strategy of repression and big incentives for those who turned state's evidence. Once the wall of silence had been broken, militants were quickly rounded up. Most then spent years in prison. A slow detachment from the movement took place behind bars – and only a tiny few remained entirely unrepentant. Prison reforms in the 1980s encouraged forms of reintegration into society on release. Other militants escaped into exile. Various levels of 'detachment' were given legal status in order to encourage this process.[115] The struggle against the 'armed struggle' also involved state violence and repression. In March 1980 five members of the Red Brigades were shot dead in Genoa by *carabinieri* during a raid on their flat-hideout. Years later the photos from that raid were released. They showed a blood-splattered apartment and a string of bodies in the tiny corridor. Most of the dead had not had time to get dressed.

The armed struggle also contributed to its own downfall. Targets became increasingly difficult to explain to the wider movement. In the 1970s those assassinated included magistrates who had bravely investigated neo-fascist activity (such as Emilio Alessandrini, murdered in Milan in 1979), academic economists and even a factory worker. Guido Rossa was a migrant from the Veneto region who moved to Genoa (via Turin) to work in a large metalwork factory in the 1960s. Married with a daughter in her teens, Rossa was a communist and active in the union movement.

In October 1978 he came across a man trying to hide Red Brigade leaflets in a drinks dispenser in his factory, and he went to the *carabinieri*. In January 1979, as he got into his FIAT 850 to go to work, he was shot in the legs. One of the group then returned to the car and fired at Rossa's heart. He had just turned forty-five and he died wearing his worker's overalls. A photograph showed him slumped over the wheel of his car. Huge numbers turned up for his funeral, and many were carrying red flags.[116]

A number of journalists, many of them on the left, were also murdered or shot in the legs. Why were these kinds of people being murdered or attacked? In the earlier period, many of the actions of these groups had seemed to enjoy some level of popularity and were even seen as 'cool' – as with the kidnapping of judges and factory supervisors or the humiliation of fascists. But as the blood spilt became greater, and closer to home, this sense of belonging to a wider struggle dissipated.

By the early 1980s the armed struggle was effectively over, although there would be sporadic killings over the next twenty years – especially with regards to those who were trying to reform labour laws. Most former terrorists served their time and were released from prison. Many wrote books and some were fully integrated back into society. The victims of the 'years of lead' were largely forgotten in this process, as attention focused for many years on the perpetrators and their motivations. This focus shifted in the 2000s, when a series of publications and debates began to discuss the role and life histories and experiences of the victims and their families.

Two books in particular stand out from this period – both written by the children of people killed during the 1970s. Mario Calabresi's book *Spingendo la notte più in là* (2007) was a study of his father Luigi Calabresi, the police officer who had arrested Giuseppe Pinelli and who was shot outside his house in 1972 in Milan in what was one of the first political assassinations in Italy of the 1970s.[117] Calabresi's book was a lyrical, intimate and painful account of his father's death, the campaign that led up to it, and the aftermath. It was also a call to (peaceful) arms. Why had the victims of violence been forgotten?

The other key text was also by a child of a victim. Walter Tobagi had been a brilliant journalist and writer who had been shot dead by self-styled young left-wing terrorists – again in Milan – in 1980. Tobagi's death was something of a mystery, and his killers served short sentences as they turned state's evidence. Benedetta Tobagi's book – *Come mi batte forte il tuo cuore* – published in 2009, is an extraordinary account of her own father's murder and the trials that followed.[118] Taken together, these texts began to overturn the focus of the media on those who had committed violence. New paradigms of memory emerged.[119]

'Black' Terrorists

Those who took up arms were not just from the left. Neo-fascist 'terrorists' also proliferated right across Italy in the 1960s and 1970s. Of some 4,384 officially registered acts of violence in Italy between 1969 and 1975, the vast majority (some 83 per cent) were attributed to the neo-fascist right.[120] Unlike the Red Brigades, neo-fascists were involved in placing bombs that were part of a 'strategy of tension'. Right-wing militants also carried out politically inspired assassinations – of judges and others – as well as more random and opportunistic beatings and killings of leftist militants. Certain parts of cities were often under the control of right-wing militants, and they dressed in a specific way to distinguish themselves from left-wing militants. They also punished those who 'betrayed' them, often in prison.

A myriad of groups and groupings emerged and disappeared at regular intervals in the post-war period – *Avanguardia Nazionale, Fronte Nazionale, Ordine Nuovo* and others. Neo-fascists were successful in attracting young people to their cause, and creating a counter-culture that stretched from J. R. R. Tolkein across to certain forms of music and with links to sport and fandom. An entire new generation was attracted to neo-fascism and its ideas were developed to keep up with the times. The choice to adhere to neo-fascism was often marked by seemingly minor personal events. Gianfranco Fini, future leader of the Movimento Sociale

Italiano, later said that his militancy on the neo-fascist right first developed after he was prevented from seeing John Wayne's film *The Green Berets* in a cinema in Rome by a left-wing protest. Others joined because of their family background, or the part of the city they grew up in – major cities became divided into mainly black or red zones – or thanks to the passions unleashed by the spiral of violence that engulfed Rome, Milan and elsewhere in the 1970s.

Some of these militants took up arms. Valerio Fioravanti had been a child TV star in a popular family drama called *The Benvenuti Family* in the late 1960s. He was radicalised in Rome thanks to the militancy of his brother Cristiano and some of the events he witnessed in the 1970s. Towards the end of that decade a small group was formed by the Fioravanti brothers and others. Its first activities were attacks on 'left-wing' targets. The group also collected guns and money through violent robberies and called themselves, for a time, the NAR (*Nuclei Armati Rivoluzionari*). One of their most controversial early 'actions' was an armed raid on a left-wing radio station in Rome, guilty of having insulted, in their eyes, some neo-fascist 'martyrs'. When the armed NAR militants arrived at the station they came across a small group of women preparing for a feminist transmission. The raid ended tragically with the throwing of Molotov cocktails into the studio (which, unsurprisingly, caught fire) and the shooting of some of the women in the legs.

Soon the NAR began to up the ante looking towards the state for enemies. In June 1980 a magistrate, Mario Amato, who had investigated neo-fascist terrorism, was shot in the head and killed in broad daylight while he was waiting for a bus. Photographs of his dead body were made more poignant by the holes he had worn in his shoes. The killer escaped on a motorbike. Amato had not been issued with an armoured car because, it was said, they didn't operate before 9 a.m. He had been followed numerous times in previous months to check on his daily routine. When Valerio Fioravanti heard of the 'success' of this murder, he allegedly 'purchased champagne, mussels and oysters' for a celebratory dinner. Then the NAR issued a leaflet: 'Today 23-6-1980 …

we have carried out the death sentence against ... Mario Amato. Today he ended his squalid life full of lead. Others will also pay.'[121]

The NAR killed a number of policemen and other people who got in their way, such as gunshop owners. They issued rhetorical and overblown claims of responsibility and copied many of the techniques used by the Red Brigades. They also began to murder rivals within the neo-fascist right itself. The group was finally stopped in its tracks by chance in February 1981, when a shootout with *carabinieri* near an arms dump in a canal in Padua left two officers dead and Valerio Fioravanti severely injured. His partner (in life, and in the NAR) Francesca Mambro called a doctor, which saved his life but also led to his arrest.

Cristiano Fioravanti was arrested in April 1981 after escaping from the shootout by the canal. He gave evidence against his fellow terrorists, benefiting from a deal that saw him do less than a year in prison. His 'betrayal', therefore, also involved his own older brother Valerio, who was given eight life sentences and served twenty-six years in prison. A journalist later wrote that the brothers 'had become like Cain and Abel'.[122] Valerio wanted to kill his brother, but he was never given the opportunity to do so. They would meet at various trials, but 'they didn't even look at each other'.[123] A number of the other members of the group were killed in clashes with the police. Many experts and others claim that the NAR and other neo-fascist groups were protected by parts of the state and the secret services, and also used to carry out crimes that were seen as politically important or part of the 'strategy of tension'.

As the 'years of lead' drew to an end, the 'strategy of tension' continued to cause death and suffering. The worst massacre of all took place in August 1980, in Bologna, a 'red' city governed by the Communist Party. The target was the city's train station.

Bologna: 2 August 1980

'A vision of the apocalypse.'

A witness to the aftermath of the Bologna station bomb, 1980[124]

It was 10.25 in the morning on 2 August 1980 and the station waiting room was packed with people waiting for trains to take them on holiday. Suddenly a bomb exploded, ripping apart the waiting area and bringing down part of the station. Eighty people were killed (their ages ranged from three to eighty) and 200 injured, including a number who were inside trains stopped in the station. Many assumed that Bologna had been chosen because of its long associations with the left and the Italian Communist Party. 'Red Bologna' was a symbol, and not just for the Italian people. The city reacted in a robust way to this outrage. A municipal bus driver, Agide Melloni, drove back and forth throughout the day transporting the dead to the mortuary, using his usual city bus. He continued to drive that same bus in Bologna for years after the tragedy. In the aftermath of the bombing, free taxis were also provided for all those who needed to move around Bologna.

In the case of Bologna – unusually in terms of the 'massacres' of the 1970s and 1980s – a final judicial sentence was reached. Valerio Fioravanti, Francesca Mambro and another member of the NAR – Luigi Ciavardini – were convicted in 1995 of having placed the station bomb in 1980. They have always denied that they took part in this specific action, and opinion remains divided as to their guilt. Moreover, if there were people who had ordered the massacre from above, they have not been discovered and therefore never been put on trial. Others were sentenced for having set false trails or organised cover-ups. The Bologna bombing remained the worst terrorist attack in Europe in terms of loss of life until the Madrid train bombings of 2004. On the main plaque in the station the phrase 'A fascist massacre' is used with reference to 1980.

Today, a large crack in the wall, a stopped clock and a hole in the ground are all part of the memory of the 'Bologna bomb', alongside numerous plaques. Melloni's bus (Bus 37) has become one of the symbols of the collective response to the bomb, and it is currently preserved in a museum.[125] Every year since 1980 a large demonstration has been staged on the anniversary of the massacre. This has usually been organised by the Association of the Families of the Victims, which has been tireless in its search for truth and justice and its quest to keep the memory of the victims alive. The

Association has its own offices in the city and one wall there is covered with clocks that have been presented to them over the years. These are not working clocks: they are all stopped at one time: 10.25 a.m. Bologna's station itself also has one of its clocks permanently stopped at 10.25, in memory of the victims of 2 August 1980.

Revolution, Reform and Blood

The 1960s and 1970s were a time of crisis and blood but also of radical and innovative protest and structural reform. It was a time of ferment in all areas of life. Italy's schools, mental hospitals, prisons and even its families were transformed. But the forces working against democratic change were strong and left a legacy of death and destruction. The inability to provide justice for the victims of the 'strategy of tension' and other forms of political violence weighed heavily on the Republic and threatened to undermine the entire legitimacy of the political system. The role of the state itself in some of these crimes remains one of the great open questions of the post-war period. It was a time of hope but also of divided memories and anger. Democracy survived, but connections to the political class itself were fatally weakened. Italy had modernised its institutions and legal system, but these changes had not come without a very significant cost.

4

The 1980s and 1990s: From Boom to Collapse and Beyond

1980: The End

The 1980s began with an event that marked an ending. In October 1980 a number of people marched through the centre of Turin carrying placards and chanting slogans (although most of the demonstration was held in near-silence). These people were not on strike, or demanding concessions from the employers. They were asking for an *end* to strikes and a return to work. A dispute called at FIAT (after an announcement of mass sackings by the company) had been met by an unprecedented counter-demonstration of those who 'wanted to work' – mainly white-collar FIAT employees. Their slogans were about 'opening the factory gates' and against 'violent pickets'. It became known as the 'March of the 40,000' (although most estimates put the actual numbers as far lower) and was heavily criticised at the time, but its significance was to endure.

The year 1980 is often seen as the end of the wave of workers' struggles that started in the early 1960s (well before the peak of 1969). However, the wave had already slowed well before then: 1980 was the moment when this 'end' became clear. The revolution had not happened – FIAT was still in control of its own factories – but workers did have houses, children at school, pensions, cars. Capitalism was still in place, and globalisation

was spreading. Meanwhile, FIAT no longer needed a giant Italian-based factory like Mirafiori in Turin, and further plants began to open across the globe as the company diversified. Soon, Italy would de-industrialise. Its short-lived and tumultuous second industrial revolution was over. Fordism, Italian-style, was finished.

In 1979 FIAT employed the film director Hugh Hudson to make an advert that depicted an entire car being created almost without human intervention – to the tune of Mozart's *The Marriage of Figaro* (the words were slightly modified, as in the line '*fortunatissimo family car*'). Completed cars drove in unison on the company's famous banked roof at the Lingotto factory and onto a car carrier for transport and sale. It was a celebration of the end of the working class. The final slogan was prophetic: 'FIAT Strada: Handbuilt by Robots'. During filming in Turin, Hudson remembered that 'There was a strike, and we got locked in the factory.' FIAT knew what was coming. Society's task in Italy (above all in industrial cities like Turin and Milan) was how to manage the gradual end of an entire class of people – factory workers. In plant after plant the sirens stopped, and gates closed forever.

A post-industrial phase had begun. For some places this also led to a deep-rooted crisis of identity. As Giuseppe Turani wrote (about Milan), 'it was a great industrial centre, with a strong working class and a strong ruling class. Both were proud of their work and their own missions [but it was now] a city in which nobody really produces anything (not bolts, not saucepans, not bicycles and certainly not cars) ... they produce thoughts, opinions, shows, legal cases, advertising, finance ... a city of talents, different from a city of thousands of blue-collar workers'.[1] In 1981 the pioneering photographer Gabriele Basilico published a beautiful series of images of Milan's factories – most of which were already closed, and many of which would soon be demolished or turned into housing, supermarkets or universities.[2] It wasn't just the industrial working class that was on the way out, but also the places – the 'cathedrals of work' – where that class had operated.

After the Factory

In general, this was a managed and largely orderly retreat, but the end of the factory system left deep gaps in cities. Extensive spaces were abandoned. What would fill them? For a time new foreign immigrants into Italy found some sort of physical shelter in these former 'palaces of work'. These previously vibrant buildings often became dark, forbidding and dangerous places. Some were simply demolished, making way for housing projects or out-of-town hypermarkets, or mixed developments such as in the vast Bicocca area in Milan that was once home to the Pirelli factory complex. Bicocca became a shopping centre (Bicocca Village) and multiplex with an added university campus and sleek housing for the middle classes.

FIAT's Lingotto factory was emblematic of the transformation from the industrial to the post-industrial. The jewel in the crown of the original FIAT-Agnelli empire, with its rooftop race track and spiral road up to the top, this vast factory stopped producing cars in the late 1970s after sixty or so years. It then became a glittering shopping centre with an art gallery in a glass bubble on the roof, designed by Renzo Piano. When Gianni Agnelli, the last link to the industrial age and a key member of Italy's 'royal' industrialist family, died in 2003, his body was placed on show on the Lingotto roof in the art gallery.[3]

With the end of the industrial era, the very rhythms of Italy changed. From a 9 to 5 society, governed by shifts and clocks, the dividing lines between work and non-work became harder and harder to define. Vast numbers of people were self-employed. Many were in a 'precarious' position, with short-term contracts and flexible working practices. The blue uniforms of the working class disappeared from the streets. Smoke no longer billowed from chimneys. Not surprisingly, the union movement went into decline, and struggled to adapt to a new 'flexible' working landscape.

Alongside the rapid decline of the working class (and the final disappearance of the peasantry) the mass parties of the post-war era entered unwittingly into a deep, organic crisis. They were empty shells, held together by out-of-date structures and lacking in new ideas or any sense of renewal. Many of their leaders had been in power for decades. Their power seemed invincible and eternal, and they saw nothing wrong in the way that things worked (or didn't).

Politics in the 1980s: The 'Moral Question' and Partitocracy

In 1981 the then leader of the Italian Communist Party, Enrico Berlinguer, gave an explosive interview to the centre-left daily newspaper *La Repubblica*. 'Political parties today are above all mechanisms of power and clientelism,' he argued. He also claimed that the parties were out of touch, and he went further. The parties, he said, 'manage interests ... some of which are criminal'. Where once these had been mass organisations, 'they no longer organise the people ... they are federations which group factions together ... each one of which has a "boss" and a "vice-boss".' Berlinguer's conclusion was stark: 'The parties have occupied the State and all of its institutions [and] local organisations, insurance boards, banks ... cultural institutions, hospitals, universities, public television and some of the major newspapers.' Berlinguer made it clear, however, that he saw the Communists and their history as outside of this analysis. The Communists were different, and it was Communist *history* that had created this difference. 'We were in prison with the workers, we were on the mountains with the partisans, we were in the poor neighbourhoods with the unemployed, with women, with the marginalised working class, with the young; we have led certain cities, regions – which we have governed with honesty.' 'The moral question,' Berlinguer argued, 'is at the centre of Italy's problems.'[4]

The parties needed to change, and quickly. They were in danger of becoming obsolete. But Berlinguer's warnings were not heeded. The Cold War was still being fought. Nobody saw the collapse of the Soviet Empire coming. For most politicians and those connected to the system, it was business as usual. Berlinguer was the first politician from within the system to attack the partitocracy and highlight 'the moral question'.

By the 1980s Italy had become a country ruled by parties – a *partitocracy*. Political organisations had penetrated deep into the state at every level. By the 1980s, many of these organisations were mass parties only in name. They continued to have newspapers, offices and hold festivals, but the active memberships of the 1950s and 1960s and 1970s were fading fast. Party memberships now functioned largely as transmission belts for resources down from the state and local government, and votes up from 'the people'. There was little that was virtuous or democratic about this circle of power. Factions argued not over ideology or even policy, but rather about the distribution of funds.

The system had become, in many places, a precise network of corruption and power – where bribes and favours oiled the wheels. Privileges piled up. Some even went as far as to dub Italy a *kleptocracy* – a place where robbery was institutionalised. Theft was the way things worked, the raison d'être of politics itself.[5] Later, this political elite would be rebranded (negatively) as 'The Caste'. Mediators were crucial – the politicians themselves, lawyers, speculators, deal-makers, those with information, unions, administrators, architects, journalists. Many of these groups were protected by out-of-date corporate structures and guild-like regulations, which reproduced privilege. Major building projects and 'big events' were particularly vulnerable to corrupt practices and rake-offs. Post-disaster funding was also seen as rich pickings.

There were small signs that the system was beginning to break down. In the 1980s scandals brought down a local centre-left administration in Turin and hit the Socialist Party in the northern region of Liguria. Links were uncovered between organised crime and politicians. Clientelism and corruption were national issues, linked to forms of 'recommendation' (*raccomandazione*) that influenced job markets. This term referred to various ways in which people were put forward for jobs and positions of influence, outside of official and open channels. Phone calls and private conversations helped those who were 'recommended' to move to the front of the queue. It was difficult to obtain a post (in both public and private sectors) without the door in some way being held open by somebody with power. When investigators began to take on this system in the 1990s, they often found thousands of letters from ordinary people in the offices of politicians, neatly filed away. This was a way of doing things that affected people in deep and long-lasting ways – and could even force them to emigrate. As 'Rita' put it:

> If you stay in Italy, the only way to get a job is through *raccomandazione*. When you go for a job, everyone tells you that you need a *raccomandazione*. If you ... try to get work without a *raccomandazione* then you are a fool because you either make it your life's goal to go against the system, or you end up living at home with your parents until you are 50.[6]

Some have argued that most Italians were quite happy for this system to continue. 'The consensus,' according to the magistrate Vito Marino Caferra, 'for that system came via a vast range of clients linked to the partitocracy and to the direct beneficiaries of corruption, but also from a larger group of people who practised other forms of illegal exchange (even if these could not be prosecuted under the law) which were widespread within civil society.'[7]

In the same year as the 'march of the 40,000' the novelist Italo Calvino published a bitter article. It was entitled 'Once upon a Time there was a Country which was Ruled by Illegality'.[8] 'It wasn't as if there weren't any laws,' Calvino wrote, 'but the system needed high levels of money to keep it going, and the only way it could obtain this was by illegally requesting funds from those who had them, in exchange for favours. And those who provided this money had probably become rich through favours exchanged previously. So, this was a circular economic system which had a certain sense of harmony.' Calvino explained how, in this imaginary country (which sounded very much like the Italy of 1980), almost everybody thought such a system was normal, and even justifiable. Laws (and their application) appeared to many as simply ways of regulating internal struggles amongst the élite. Only 'the honest people' occasionally disturbed the 'complete happiness' of this country's citizens. But who were 'the honest'? They lived in a kind of 'counter-society', where they had managed to survive in its 'gaps'. This, for Calvino, was Italy. A society where the honest lived like petty thieves, and vice versa. In hindsight, Calvino's depiction of Italy would come to be seen as both prophetic and realistic.

Berlinguer had certainly been right on one point. The parties had lost touch with social reality. They were working for themselves and to maintain their own entrenchment in power. This detachment reached its peak in the 1980s and 1990s, when parties seemed only interested in their own factions and organisation. Take, for example, this description of Christian Democratic politics in the early 1990s:

> The compromise on Forlani's [a major Christian Democratic figure] candidacy had naturally been reached with De Mita's [another major Christian Democrat] consent, as he had decided to avoid a clash ... but the compromise provoked discontent and dissension in the ranks of the left faction. The most satisfied faction was that of the former dorotei [a former faction within the Christian Democrats], now confident of being able to take over many positions of power in and outside of the party. If former doroteo [i.e. ex-member of the former Christian Democratic faction] Vincenzo Scotti [another powerful Christian Democrat] had hopes until the last minute of becoming party secretary by presenting himself in the improbable role of mediator, another former doroteo Antonio Gava, knew he would not succeed, if for no other reason than that his control of an extremely high number of party cardholders would, many feared, give him excessive power.[9]

Only an insider could follow these debates. We don't need to understand the ins and outs of Christian Democratic politics at that time to see how the party was, by now, entirely absorbed by its own party-focused struggles – with little reference to what was going on in the outside world. Tactical manoeuvres around power and resources had become detached from everyday life. When the storm came, it would sweep away much of this party machine in a very short time. As the political scientist Mario Caciagli concluded in 1991, 'the DC is unwilling to make basic decisions about the country's most urgent and dramatic issues'.[10] This failure would soon prove fatal not just for the Christian Democrats, but for the entire party system.

Berlinguer was a Communist with a strong sense of public morality. As Patrick McCarthy argued, 'Convinced that the decision to become a Communist was a moral choice that shaped one's entire existence, Berlinguer saw the PCI as a community based on an ethic of self-sacrifice. The solution to the economic crisis ... lay in these values, which inspired the policy of austerity.'[11] Berlinguer was opposed to what he described as 'squandering and waste, the priority given to special interests, unbridled individualism, the folly of consumerism', as he argued in a book called *Austerity: A Chance to Transform Italy*.[12]

But he was fighting against the tide, in every sense, including amongst his own supporters. It was clear by the 1980s that Berlinguer's party was part of the problem, not of the solution. Communist elected officials had become integral to power structures at a local and national level. With notable exceptions, they were vital to Italy's rule of parties – the *partitocrazia*. He had laid down an alternative path, but his advice was not to be followed. Moreover, although Berlinguer's 1981 interview was a call to arms, his own policies during his political life had contributed to the 'continuous bargaining process among the principal anti-fascist political parties' and to party-based and clientelistic structures for institutional power sharing.[13] Berlinguer was also out of touch in another, crucial sense. Most Italians did not see austerity as a chance to transform their country, or themselves. Consumerism and mass culture had become central to their outlook and way of seeing the world. They had no connection to the values Berlinguer was extolling.

In June 1984 Enrico Berlinguer died a dramatic, public death: a militant death. He had a stroke while giving a speech on stage, in a piazza in Padua, and struggled on in full view of the crowd. Later in his hotel he fell into a coma. His demise soon afterwards led to an outpouring of grief – he had been one of the most loved of all Italian politicians. This tragedy contributed to an impressive electoral result for the Communist Party in the European elections of that year – when it won more than 11.5 million votes (some 33 per cent of the electorate) – beating, for the first time, the Christian Democrats.

Berlinguer's funeral in Rome drew an even bigger crowd (some estimates say that one and half million turned out) than Togliatti's in 1964. Togliatti had finally been laid to rest in Rome's vast, sprawling Verano cemetery, within a sort of collective grave (constructed in 1972) that resembled a committee meeting of the dead, with simple tombs in a semi-circle. Togliatti's gravestone there is slightly taller than the others, as if he is presiding over a meeting, even in death. Every member of the so-called *Direzione* (a special kind of permanent executive that met from time to time) of the party (and its successors) still has a right to be buried there. Berlinguer's grave, however, is to be found in another cemetery in Rome (with just his surname on the stone).

The end of the Cold War, and the near-simultaneous self-destruction of the Italian Communist Party itself, were just around the corner. Berlinguer would remain as a potent memory of a past that was gone, never to return, 'the symbol', as Phil Cooke and Gianluca Fantoni have argued, 'of virtually everything that used to be right and is now wrong in Italy'.[14] But, at the same time, his 'moral' message would be stripped of any real content, and endlessly re-used as a rhetorical device for a critique of all politicians and of politics itself – as a catch-all anti-political set of slogans.

Berlinguer had understood and exposed the disintegration of the party system (without applying that critique to his own party). But his set of values were disconnected from the cultural and economic consensus in the country at large. Italian society had changed dramatically. The industrial working class was on the way out, and systems of information and cultural exchange had been revolutionised. This could be seen most powerfully in the case of television. To understand this transformation, we need to visit a small place near Rome, in June 1981, the same year as Berlinguer's interview.

The Boy in the Well: Alfredino Rampi
and Italian Television – 1981

In June 1981 a boy was playing close to his home in a place called Vermicino, outside Rome. It was early evening. Then he disappeared. His parents looked for him everywhere and called the emergency services. Soon, firefighters, police and others arrived at the scene. Someone heard cries.

The boy had fallen down a deep (and recently dug) well close to building works linked to the construction of a new house. Vermicino wasn't even a real place at all – just a collection of buildings. The boy's name was Alfredo (or *Alfredino* – little Alfredo) Rampi and he was just six years old. The well was 80 metres deep, with water at the bottom. It was a dark, rocky and muddy cavity, and very narrow. The first attempts to save Alfredino were close to farcical. A wooden plank was dropped into the well and got stuck, causing problems for the subsequent operation. Then a microphone was passed on a line down to the little boy. By measuring the wire the men and women at the scene found that he was stuck 36 metres down, his arms pinned to his sides against the wall of the well.

It had been blisteringly hot during the day, outside the well. Alfredino suffered from heart problems. His cardiologist would also be a constant presence over the following days. There were disagreements about how to save the boy. Small men were winched down to him to assess the solution, as were cave climbers. The rescue operation was risky, especially for those who were sent down into the well. There could easily have been other deaths.

An appeal was made on local television for a crane. This caught the attention of a national television journalist and their TV cameras turned up. The Rampi rescue operation became a live, rolling news event (something that was very unusual at the time) on national television. Amidst the chaos, Alfredino's parents stood by, desperate for their boy to be saved. As the nation became engrossed with the emotion and drama of the situation, Sandro Pertini, President of Italy, made the trip from Rome. He would stay at the site for some fifteen hours.

The solution – it was decided – was to dig another tunnel parallel to the well, then cut across, and pick him up from below. But the new tunnel was too close to the original one. Vibrations from the drill probably caused Alfredino to fall even deeper down the well. When the team finally got through, they found the boy was below them, not above. At that point, someone had to go down in the dark space, tied up, and try to pull Alfredino to safety. Two or three heroes stepped up, and they nearly succeeded in dragging him out, but Alfredino was covered in slippery mud and none of the equipment worked.

Time went on, Alfredino became weaker and weaker, his voice fading. The 'rescue' operation was a mess. Frantic arguments took place over the best way to save Rampi. Nobody really seemed to be in charge. Another microphone was dropped down to hear the boy's weak voice (and his piercing cries were shared with millions of Italians). Alfredino seemed to be losing consciousness. Television commentators discussed the rescue operation in immense detail. The camera rolled on.

The nation was transfixed. Some 20 million stayed up to watch late into the night. Thousands of ordinary people also descended on Vermicino – some estimated that 10,000 or so were there by the end. Money was made. Street traders turned up to serve the onlookers who made their way to the site. Traffic jams snaked around the surrounding roads.

When it became clear that Alfredino was not going to make it, the television broadcast was cut. The longest Italian live transmission in history was finally over. The fixed camera had, by then, been transmitting to the whole of Italy for some sixty hours. In Rome, the presenter Giancarlo Santalmassi tried to understand what had happened: 'we wanted to see something linked to life and we have witnessed something linked to death'.[15] The writer Giovanni Arpino wrote that watching the images was like 'being slapped hour after hour'.[16] Alfredino Rampi's death had burned itself into the national consciousness. It became a spectacle. The stats were noteworthy. On 12 June – a Friday – there were 28.6 million Italians watching at 8.45 p.m., and 30 million at 11.00 p.m. Some 16 million were still there between 1 and 2 a.m. This was close to a record audience. Only the World Cup final (with Italy, and Sandro Pertini again) held in Spain a year later, in July 1982, would see a bigger audience. And, as Massimo Gamba points out, this audience was in many ways different – more significant, 'spread over a period which went way beyond 90 minutes'.[17] Gamba also reports that televisions were placed in the streets, and that some broke down, having been on for such a long time. For the journalist Andrea Pomella, 'Alfredino changed everything. It was not only television that changed, but people as well. The mass media discovered that horror … could be a kind of spectacle. Alfredino's cries for his mum transmitted through the microphone got through to every house. A television linked to suffering emitted its first wail.'[18]

Some felt a sense of shame at the spectacle and the role of the television spectator in creating it. In the Communist Party's daily L'Unità, Alfredo Reichlin asked: 'Should we also have been stuck in front of our TVs for hours and hours?' Reichlin didn't reply to his own question. A Catholic journalist later said that 'it was a despicable episode, a terrible dark moment in the history of our television'.[19] It would take a further thirty-one days to recover Alfredino's body. On 11 July specialised miners were finally able to bring the boy out of his tomb. A large crowd turned out for his funeral in Rome on 15 July. President Pertini was also there.

As with so many other Italian tragedies, the aftermath was one of innumerable discussions, debates, false versions, trials, myths and suspected cover-ups. Today, a simple stone cross and a photo of Alfredo stand at the place where he died. There is also a statue of him close to the local parish church. Walter Veltroni later called Rampi's fate 'part of the emotional experience of the entire nation'.[20]

The house that was being built was illegal, as was the fatal well itself. Nobody knew exactly how or why Alfredino had fallen in, and numerous conspiracy theories would emerge over the days and months to come, including the claim that the little boy had been pushed. A manslaughter trial relating to the building and protection of the well was held in 1984. But all those on trial were eventually cleared, or were unable to stand trial because of ill health. A further inquest was then held into claims that Alfredino had been murdered, but this led nowhere.

One positive outcome did emerge from the Vermicino disaster – the formation of a national civil protection force able to take charge in moments of this kind. This was no comfort, however, to the parents of Alfredino, or to the millions who had witnessed the tragedy in their own homes. Later, the Vermicino tragedy would be re-evoked in a novel by the visionary writer Giuseppe Genna, *Dies Irae*.[21]

Television itself did not learn the lessons of Vermicino – or perhaps (in a perverse way) it did. Four years later, in May 1985, the cameras were at a football game in the Heysel stadium in Brussels. It was a big game, a European Cup final, between two well-supported and famous clubs – Juventus and Liverpool. A combination of dreadful organisation and fan disorder led to tragedy as thirty-nine fans (thirty-five of them Italian) were crushed to death inside the stadium before the game. Incredibly, the match itself went ahead, and was transmitted live, with full commentary, in many countries around the world, including Italy. This led to endless discussions. The lap of honour of the Juventus players after the game was seen as in bad taste. The show had to go on, whatever the consequences. Everything, it seemed, had to be televised.[22]

In retrospect, Vermicino is often seen as a kind of turning point, a moment when the voyeuristic aspects of television took over and got a grip on the Italian imagination. It is often argued that Italy's relationship with television took a turn for the worse after Vermicino. The television transmission also threw up other, horrible, aspects of this kind of 'programme'. Many watching criticised Alfredino's mother for changing her dress and eating an ice cream. She did not adhere to traditional ideals expected of a distressed mother, at least as framed through the TV camera. 'Facts' were not filtered through journalism or interpretation, but fed directly into people's homes.

The power of television was also a challenge for the central cultural, social and political institution in Italy – the Catholic Church. How was the Church adapting to modernisation and a consumerist society?

Secularisation and the Church

'They believe in God, but they don't go and visit him at home.'

Francesco Alberoni[23]

'Italian Catholicism has responded very imaginatively and effectively to the challenges posed by the forces of change ... and adapted accordingly ... the Italian Church has ... seen off liberalism, Fascism and Communism. It remains to be seen how it will fare in the longer term under a "regime" of global, consumerist capitalism, whose unrestrained individualism has been identified ... as probably the most insidious of all the enemies of Catholicism.'

John Pollard[24]

The familiar story of the twentieth and twenty-first centuries told by historians (and others) about Italy is one of increasing secularisation, as the Church lost power over its followers and society as a whole. This story is backed by statistics that show fewer people attending mass and declaring themselves to be Catholics. But things were never quite so simple, on the ground. Saints' days and festivals remained extremely popular, new Catholic organisations were created, and the Catholic world still had its tentacles in every nook and cranny of everyday life – from finance to education to culture to the press.

The official Catholic response to 1968 was innovative. In that year an organisation known as *Comunione e Liberazione* was created in Milan. This was an attempt to take on the radical students in their own territory – within the universities and schools – but also to create a new vehicle for the transmission of Catholic ideas. This cultural and political grouping would become highly influential. 'CL' – as it was often known – carved out a powerful space for itself within educational institutions and in the political and business world. CL power reached to the upper echelons of political power, and was greatest in Milan and Lombardy, Italy's richest zone, where it was expressed for some time through the President of the Lombard Region and CL militant, Roberto Formigoni, who remained in power for eighteen years. As the historian John Pollard has written, 'The influence of *Comunione e Liberazione* cannot be underestimated: it has two well-read journals ... [it controlled] manufacturing and service industries and social welfare organisations valued at £2bn worldwide; and its political arm ... exerted much influence.'[25]

The Vatican has become much less interested in Italy and Italian politics since the 1980s. Since 1978, only non-Italian Popes have been elected – a Pole (1978–2005), a German (2005–13), and an Argentinian (2013–). The revision of the 1929 Lateran Pacts between Church and State in 1984 removed the stipulation that Roman Catholicism is the 'sole religion of the state'. With the end of the Cold War, Italian politics became much less central to the Church's world view (that battle had clearly been won) than it had been in the past. There was no longer any presumed direct threat to the Church from within Italy itself. As a global organisation – perhaps the most global organisation of all – the Church began to look elsewhere for resources and opportunities to exert political influence. No sitting Pope had even ventured outside the Vatican between 1870 and 1929. In 1962 Pope John XXIII was the first Pope to leave Lazio since 1870 and Pope Paul VI was the first Pope to take a plane – in 1964. Since 1978, however, Popes have always been on the move. John Paul II travelled 1.2 million kilometres during his time as Pope.

Meanwhile, the Italian state continued to help fund the Vatican. An Italian law passed in 1985 (following the aforementioned negotiations over the Lateran Pacts) allowed taxpayers to choose to donate a small part of their taxes to 'good causes'. With the lira this was fixed as eight out of every 1,000 lire, and it has remained as eight out of every 1,000 euros. Possible 'good causes' – at that stage – included the Catholic Church and other religions. In 1989,

41 per cent of all Italians filling out tax returns chose to give this money to the Catholic Church (a figure which represented over 80 per cent of those who made a choice). Immense amounts of money were involved – in the twenty-first century the overall figure began to reach over one billion euros. It was clear that the Church continued to enjoy a lucrative relationship with the Italian state.

In other areas, as well, there were no obvious signs of secularisation or an increased separation of Church and State. The 1929 Lateran Pacts had provided for obligatory religious teaching in all schools – apart from elementary or primary schools. In 1984 this was extended further to all kinds of school, but it was now possible to opt out. Yet in the real world few parents/children took this route. In 1986 an estimated 93 per cent of children still took religious classes (with figures in the high 80 per cents for *licei* or upper schools). As I write, there are still over 25,000 teachers of religion working in Italian schools, financed by the state.

Bettino Craxi: Modern Politics, Money and Corruption

'The modernisation of this country is ongoing, and for me this is an irreversible process.'
        Bettino Craxi, Speech to Milan's Stock Exchange, 1985[26]

One key politician presided over much of the 1980s, prefiguring and moulding a new post-political and post-mass politics. His name was Bettino Craxi, and this period is often known as the 'Craxi era'. On 4 July 1983, Bettino Craxi became President of the Council of Ministers, the first Socialist to hold that post in Italian history. Craxi's political strategy had been clear for years – he wanted to 'modernise' and de-radicalise his party. The replacement of the party's hammer and sickle symbol with a red carnation was a clear sign of change in this direction – away from the party's Marxist past and towards the centre ground.

The acknowledged model for Craxi was François Mitterrand, elected as President of France in 1981. Craxi was post-ideological and post-left, and he understood the power of television as the medium for transmitting his message, as well as the importance of personalising politics around a strong leader. For the cultural historian Stephen Gundle, 'Craxi was the first politician [in Italy] to develop a profile based on personality ... he was the object among supporters of a personality cult of sorts that extended even to his wife and family.'[27] Craxi cared little for the mass parties of his youth, and even less for the trade unions. He struck up strong political and personal alliances with businessmen including his great friend Silvio Berlusconi – a thrusting media and housing magnate. These two men would often help each other out in the 1980s and 1990s.

Craxi had done his time moving through the party's traditional structures. The Socialist Party had its roots in the workers' and reformist movements of the late nineteenth century, and had been crushed under fascism before returning to the political scene. Craxi worked as a young man for the Socialists in the working-class (and Communist) citadel of Sesto San Giovanni outside Milan – known, at that time, as the 'Stalingrad of Italy'. He had also been on the Central Committee of the party from the late 1950s onwards. But he increasingly saw these bodies as outdated and out of touch with a changing Italy. His power base was in Milan, a city with a strong Socialist tradition but also one that was undergoing rapid change from an industrial to a post-industrial city. In 1968 Craxi was elected to Parliament for the first time. Tall, imposing, balding, bespectacled and decisive, Craxi appeared as a man who could act independently of his party if the situation required it, or even take on the might of the United States. He was by no means a great speaker in any traditional sense – his pauses often seemed longer than his actual sentences – but Craxi created a kind of 'personal party'.[28] A cult of personality soon developed around him.

He was an ideal leader for a new phase in Italian politics and society. In 1976 he had made his first major move at a national level – taking over the Socialist Party at a congress held at the Midas hotel in Rome (the name was just a coincidence). He would not relinquish control until the corruption scandals of the 1990s.

For Craxi, the party was a means to an end. He was interested in power. Craxi's political thought was hybrid and difficult to pin down. He professed to be an admirer of the socialist philosopher Pierre-Joseph Proudhon, and was a collector of Garibaldian statues, books, paintings and other relics. But his strengths lay in his pragmatism, in his mastery of the political machinations of the Roman scene and the influence afforded to him by his economic and media links in Milan.

Yet while he often appeared to be 'new' and almost anti-political, Craxi's governments were not exactly a clean break with the past. His second administration from August 1986 included the near-eternal Christian Democrat Giulio Andreotti as Interior Minister, Antonio Gava from Naples (often suspected of links to Napoli's Camorra crime syndicate) as Minister for Industry, and veteran Christian Democrat Carlo Donat Cattin at the Ministry of Tourism. However, despite this conservative 'team', Craxi also revelled in a post-industrial image, gathering around him designers and fashionistas such as Valentino. He held the 1989 congress of his party in a cavernous revamped former factory space in Milan – and his keynote speech was transmitted on an enormous triangular screen to a crowd of enthusiastic and often glamorous supporters.

His popularity was associated with Italy's 1980s boom, which was based on the success of the 'Made in Italy' brand, high-quality export goods, a rise in financial capital, tourism and the birth of powerful global companies in the fashion and design sectors. This was a boom with its capital in Milan, and one of Craxi's slogans was 'Milan at the centre of Italy's progress'. Milan had reinvented itself in a few short years as a capital of glamour. It was a time when, as one journalist wrote, 'even the masses and housewives bought "24 ore" [the Italian version of the *Financial Times*] to check the share prices as they shot up ... when Craxi came from Palazzo Chigi [the residence of the Prime Minister in Rome] to Palazzo degli Affari [the Italian stock exchange in Milan] to receive applause'.[29]

Craxi made changes in key areas. Whereas political power had traditionally been concentrated in Rome in Republican Italy (and before), Craxi kept his main residence in Milan – a move that marked the political-economic nexus of alliances he had forged in the 1970s and 1980s. When in Rome he stayed in a hotel. On Mondays, Craxi would lunch in the traditional Milanese restaurant in Milan, *Al Materal*. It was there, it was said, at a simple table, over *ossobuco alla milanese* and wine, that he would conduct the important business of the week.

After a post-war period marked by crises and a kind of revolving-door system that led to numerous governments from within the same coalition, Craxi stayed in power for over one thousand days (at that time, a record). He thus provided – at least on the surface – both stability and continuity. The phrase used at the time was 'governability'. The 1980s were dominated, politically, by what became known as *Il Pentapartito* – the five-party coalition. The five parties included three minor organisations, the Liberals, Social Democrats and Republicans – all of which were tiny entities – and two major parties, the Socialists and Christian Democrats. This was a stable coalition, despite nine governments in ten years. Very little changed over that time in terms of personnel, and the key political figures were Craxi for the Socialists and Ciriaco De Mita for the Christian Democrats. Craxi was also willing to take on the still-powerful trade union movement – and in doing so (over indexed wage rises) he was backed by a majority of the Italian people in a referendum in June 1985 – another sign of the changes that had first been seen with the 'March of the 40,000' in Turin in 1980.

Craxi found solid backing amongst those tired of the militancy and turmoil of the 1960s and 1970s. Many families were now experiencing real prosperity for the first time. He appealed to voters across the spectrum, including those from the right. As the historian Giulio Sapelli has pointed out, 'In an inquiry among the membership of the MSI [the neo-fascist party] in 1989, we find that 35.7 per cent of members interviewed respected Bettino Craxi "more than all the others".'[30] This post-political appeal would set the scene for Italy's next generation of politicians. But Craxi's role as a pioneer had a dark side. For Sapelli, Craxi's secretaryship represented 'a move towards an autocratic ... clientelism with an abundance of resources acquired by the savage extension of the illegal control of the markets'.[31]

Craxi presided over a sizeable increase in Italy's public debt. His legacy would be more debt for all, and decades of austerity. Moreover, Craxi built up extensive networks of corruption and illegal political financing while in power. Secret bank accounts were opened and filled with billions of lire. Further controversy was created thanks to his close links with Silvio Berlusconi, which led to widely discussed political deals around media regulation. So, while Craxi talked the language of transformation and of institutional reform and presented himself as outside of the political system, he was deeply embedded within it. His use of power was similar to that of the Christian Democrats who had preceded him, without the checks and balances of a mass party and numerous factions. This combination of power and patronage led to grotesque moments where the public and the private were not so much blurred, but completely dissolved into each other. As the historian Paul Ginsborg relates, 'When Bettino Craxi ... went to China on an official state visit in November 1986, he took with him a personal entourage of 52 members, including his children and their respective partners.'[32] Craxi's key non-political ally was a man who had made his first fortune as a 'brick king' in Milan. The two men's fates would be intimately connected in the 1980s and 1990s.

The Salesman: The Many Lives of Silvio Berlusconi

'A City for Number Ones'. That was the slogan that screamed out from the posters. The advertising campaign was for new flats, in a vast complex on the edge of the city of Milan. It was an ambitious project – covering more than 700,000 square metres. The architects would later also redesign the San Siro football stadium in the city. In the early 1970s, in Milan, nobody took much notice of what was happening in that previously rural area, close to the city's main airport at that time. But this building project was to change the city, and Italy, forever. The profits from this complex made the Edilnord company that built those flats a fortune.

The main businessman behind the venture was in his mid-thirties at the time, and he had already made some money from construction. His name was Silvio Berlusconi and he was born in a working-class neighbourhood of Isola in Milan in 1936. His father worked in a small bank and he studied law at Milan University. His thesis was significant in terms of what would later come to pass – it was a study of advertising contracts.[33] Much of the rest of Berlusconi's life is surrounded by myth – so much so that it is often difficult to separate fact from fiction. Did he work as a singer on a cruise ship? Which football team did he support? How exactly did he make his first fortune? All of these questions are part of the controversy around every aspect of Berlusconi's personal and business life.

Milano 2 (begun in 1970 and completed in 1979) was different in so many ways to other forms of housing in the city – and in Italy. The traffic was separated from the housing blocks by complex sets of walkways and there was an artificial lake. Milano 2 had everything – six schools, a sports club, its own television station. In a city with tiny amounts of green space, Milano 2 had abundant parks. But the complex was not anti-car: far from it. Every flat had a garage. Here, you were meant to have at least one car. The neighbourhood was distinct, but not self-sufficient. It was perfectly tuned to a new lifestyle and aspirant, consumerist population. Large fences cut off the neighbourhood from the rest of Milan.[34] It was urban but designed to be without the problems of the actual city, described as 'clean, orderly and safe' – a little piece of the United States in Milan – an 'enclave'. The three-sided apartment blocks all looked on to parkland, and away from the rest of the urban environment. Milano 2 was self-referential. Its community was not that of the city it was named after. It was claimed that there were 'no class differences' in Milano 2. Another of the slogans that sold these flats was 'Silence is Priceless. Here is the Paradise of Silence.'

The times they were a-changing in Milan in general. A new
post-industrial epoch was beginning, which would be known –
appropriately – by an advertising slogan: *Milano da Bere* (Milan
is Good to Drink). Milan, the richest city in Italy, was becoming a place of money, work and glamour. Soon, Berlusconi built
Milano 3 in another Milanese suburb. Another feature was added
to the flats in Milano 3 – moving walls. Families could, in theory,
shift the internal geography of their living space around to meet
changing circumstances.

Berlusconi's wealth and power grew. In 1974 he purchased a
striking palazzo – Villa San Martino – with 145 rooms and extensive grounds (covering some 90 acres) outside Milan near a town
called Arcore. Like almost every aspect of Berlusconi's life and
career, this property deal was not without controversy. In August
1970 the owner of the villa, Camillo Casati Stamp di Soncino, had
killed himself after murdering his wife and her lover. The only heir
to the villa was the couple's daughter, just nineteen at the time.
According to Italian law, she was not able to assume control of
the property. The villa was sold to Berlusconi through a lawyer
and intermediary, Cesare Previti, for what was seen as a price well
below market level. Berlusconi didn't actually complete the payment until 1980. Previti became one of Berlusconi's most loyal
collaborators. Later, Berlusconi commissioned a famous architect to build an impressive mausoleum in the grounds, a place
he showed to dignitaries on foreign visits. The mausoleum was
above all built to house Berlusconi's future dead body, but places
were also reserved for his most faithful friends and collaborators.
He showed world leaders around it, including Mikhail Gorbachev.
Arcore would also be the venue, in the 2000s, for his 'bunga bunga'
parties or 'elegant dinners', as Berlusconi called them.

Even as the flats inside were being sold, Berlusconi was constructing a myth about Milano 2. He had built the neighbourhood
'from nothing', he said. And in the years after its construction,
Berlusconi would often make reference to the 'Milano 2' model
and its success. When earthquakes hit, Prime Minister Berlusconi
often proposed that the reconstruction be along the lines of his
'model neighbourhood' from the 1970s. With time, more of this

northern part of Milan and its environs would come under his control – with Milano 2 itself, and the prestigious Mondadori publishing house close by in stunning building designed by the Brazilian architect Oscar Niemeyer.

In 1990 Berlusconi took over as President of Mondadori after a protracted legal and financial struggle. The other pretender to the ownership of this company, the industrialist and rival media magnate Carlo De Benedetti, complained, and the case went to arbitration. Berlusconi lost the first case, but it went to appeal. The newspapers and magazines owned by the group were divided up. The Rome-based centre-left daily *La Repubblica* and the weekly magazine *L'Espresso* went to De Benedetti, while Berlusconi kept another weekly magazine, *Panorama*, as well as the publishing wing and a TV station.

All that Money . . .

Berlusconi's beginnings as a successful businessman – as with almost all other aspects of his personal and public life – are contested. Even while Milano 2 was being built, the first accusations were being aired publicly. In 1976 the journalist Giorgio Bocca wrote that 'Someone called Berlusconi built Milano 2, that is he opened a building site which cost 500 million lire a day to keep going. Who gave him this money? ... Perhaps Mr Berlusconi could tell us the story of his life? We would love to know more.'[35] In Nanni Moretti's film *The Cayman* (2006) a Berlusconi-type figure is covered with cash that falls from the ceiling in an enormous suitcase, during a semi-dream sequence. 'All that money, fallen from the sky, but where does it come from?' asks the protagonist of the film, soon afterwards.[36]

Berlusconi's entire life (which stands at the heart of his image as a successful entrepreneur and later politician – a 'self-made man') is debated – his business achievements themselves, his political career, his relationships with women. Parallel versions of 'the truth' about him have been carried forward over time. Berlusconi himself has often provided alternative descriptions of his own past and his own history. The mythical character of Berlusconi's life is a key aspect of his appeal.

Is there any evidence of a connection between Berlusconi and the Mafia? In the late 1970s there were a spate of kidnappings in Italy (including many in Milan). The victims were often industrialists or their relatives, and ransoms were often paid. In this period, it seems, Berlusconi might have been subject to threats of kidnapping, of him or of his children. Berlusconi then 'employed' a man called Vittorio Magnano as 'horse-keeper' on his Arcore estate (from 1974 to 1976). Was this to provide protection, or to keep an eye on Berlusconi, or both? Some analysts read this move as a sign of some sort of agreement with Cosa Nostra.[37] We also know that Berlusconi kept a gun in the 1970s, as can be seen in a famous photograph from that time. It would, of course, have been surprising if a businessman and politician with the resources and power of Berlusconi had not attracted the attention of the Mafia. As to where the money really came from, we cannot be sure. To cite Mafia expert Federico Varese, 'Despite the best efforts of prosecutors, it has proved impossible to trace the origins of 94 billion lire that made its way into Berlusconi's coffers between 1978 and 1985.'[38] Berlusconi has always denied any wrongdoing.

His Aerialness: Berlusconi and Television

One thing was missing from Milano 2: there were no TV aerials. In the rest of the city, ever since television had been introduced into Italy in the mid-1950s, roofs had been covered with forests of TV antennae. Surely Berlusconi had not forgotten the most important consumer durable of all – a television? But, once again, Milano 2 was ahead of the game. All the houses had a cable TV system, built into their apartments. This system would form the basis for Berlusconi's second and most important business venture. He began transmitting something called *Telemilano* – first to the residents of Milano 2.

In 1975 the RAI state television service was reformed. Direct government control over state television was replaced with a parliamentary commission whose make-up and forms of election changed over time. In theory, more independent news channels were set up. Overall political control remained, but different parties or tendencies now had 'their' own channel. Broadly speaking, the Christian Democrats dominated RAI 1, the Socialists were given RAI 2 (not bad, for a relatively small party), and the Communists had RAI 3, which was set up in 1978. In theory, the 1975 reforms were to de-centralise media power and take some of the politics out of the management of state television.[39] But this is not what ensued. These reforms did not produce autonomy. It would also be difficult to say that they increased the quality of programming, or the value for money for Italian licence-fee payers.

State control over Italian television remained total until the 1970s. In that decade, however, this monopoly was challenged by local channels, which began to transmit in provincial cities and elsewhere. Their diet of programmes was low budget, and usually focused on local news, sport and mild sexual titillation. It was clear that there was demand, from below – from the public itself – for something different to the dull fare available on state television, and for content that was more in tune with the society that Italy had become by the 1970s.

The RAI's monopoly was overthrown, legally, by a judgement from Italy's Constitutional Court in July 1976. Private television was now legal (as long as it was 'local', a term that was hotly contested). Italy would never be the same again. Legal battles over the reach and operations of 'local' TV continued right through the 1970s and into the 1980s. By law, only state television could transmit nationally. But Berlusconi decided to take on the media establishment. He made a direct challenge to this situation by creating 'national' networks, which he achieved through video-cassettes that were shown at the same time across the country. This would form the first step towards his vast media empire of the 1980s and 1990s. His channels became *Canale 5* (which grew directly from *Telemilano* in Milano 2), *Italia 1* (which Berlusconi bought from the publisher Rusconi in 1982), and *Rete 4* (controlled by Berlusconi after 1984). In 1984 the legal battle over national and local transmission came to a head when three separate judges ruled that these networks should be closed. Berlusconi's 'national' networks were deemed to be illegal. These much-loved and – by that time – popular channels were threatened with a blackout.

It was at this point that the political system came to Berlusconi's rescue. Prime Minister Bettino Craxi – who was, as we have seen, a close friend and political ally of Berlusconi – forced through an 'urgent and necessary' decree (passed with a confidence vote) that allowed these channels to continue transmitting nationally. Craxi's decree (which was transformed into law) was extremely controversial. It was a law designed to protect a specific business interest – that of Silvio Berlusconi. Five Christian Democrat ministers resigned in protest. All of them were from the left of the party. There were also problems with the constitutional nature of the decree.

Thanks to Craxi's decree, Berlusconi was able to construct a media empire that dwarfed that of all other competitors in Italy. He would go on to gain control of significant parts of the publishing industry (books, magazines, newspapers) and – crucially – a big stake in advertising production and sales. Italy's staid media landscape was revolutionised. Huge amounts of money were made – much of it by Berlusconi and his companies. By 1990 his company (then known as Fininvest) controlled half of Italy's national TV channels. There were to be further political favours for Berlusconi's television networks. A new law regulating the entire TV system – called the 'Mammi Law' after the Minister of Telecommunications at the time, Oscar Mammi – was passed in July 1990. But this simply reproduced or 'photographed' the existing situation at the time – as such, it cannot be called a reform.[40]

Berlusconi surrounded himself with a close-knit group of business collaborators (some of whom he had known since school). Two famous photographs seemed to encapsulate Berlusconi's hold over this inner circle. In one celebrated image, Berlusconi and his entourage (a group of middle-aged and older men) are pictured about to go for a run. They were all on holiday together, in Bermuda. It was 1995. Nothing particularly strange there, you might think. But the men were all wearing exactly the same outfit – white T-shirt, white socks – and they were all preparing to run in a line behind

Berlusconi himself. Another, similar, image (from 1991) showed another group (this time mixed) sitting at a table, on a luxury yacht. Once again, they were all dressed in the same way – this time with red and black (AC Milan's colours) striped shirts. Berlusconi, this time, was in the middle – smiling his famous smile.[41]

Neo-Television

There were three key courses in the Berlusconian TV diet. One was made up of soap operas (*Dallas* was his most obvious early success) and films bought as a package. The second key feature was football and chat about football. Thirdly, there were game shows with intense levels of in-programme advertising. News was absent (it would later become central) and there was no attempt at any kind of high culture or educational programming. Berlusconi's TV was garish, loud, fast-paced and exciting. It was in your face. It sold you things, openly.

There can be little doubt that many Italians – almost certainly the majority of those who watched a lot of television in the 1970s and 1980s and 1990s – enjoyed the material being pumped out by Berlusconi's channels. It was a key part of their lives. When Italians were given a chance to break up Berlusconi's media empire through a referendum in 1995, they refused to do so by a big majority – 15.3 million to 11.6 million. Berlusconi did not invent consumerism, or individualism. He did, however, play a key role in shaping the ways these trends took hold in Italian society and culture. By 1999 Italians were watching around four hours of TV every day.[42]

Before Berlusconi, Italian television was funded through two means – firstly, a licence payable by all TV owners called '*il canone*'. This was one of the most evaded 'taxes' in the Italian Republic, but it still brought in considerable funds. Secondly, state television also had advertising, although this was heavily controlled in the early period of the medium's history. Berlusconi's stations, however, did not have a licence fee. He relied entirely on advertising.

The cultural critic Umberto Eco invented the term 'neo-television' in 1983.[43] As ever, the work of Eco was extremely influential. He drew a contrast between what he called 'Paleo-Television', which he said 'was produced in Rome or Milan for everyone. It spoke of the appointment of ministers and it saw to it that the public learnt about harmless things, even if that meant telling it [the public] lies.'[44] In the 1970s and 1980s this all changed. As Eco argued, 'With the multiplication of channels, privatisation and the arrival of new electronic devilries, we are now living in the era of Neo-Television.'[45] But what was 'neo-television'? For Eco, 'whereas Paleo-TV talked about the external world, or pretended to, Neo-TV talks about itself and about the contact that it established with its own public'.[46]

Until the arrival of private television, as we have seen, the RAI was a state monopoly. The shift of audience in the 1970s was stunning. From a monopoly, with all the audience, the RAI managed to lose half its viewers by 1982. This dramatic transformation obviously affected advertising revenues. Only a third of this revenue was going to the RAI by 1983. Most Italians clearly didn't want to watch the state channels any more (now that they had a choice, at last) and advertisers didn't think that the advertising on RAI channels would sell their products. They looked elsewhere. No wonder viewers were angry when the judges threatened to remove these channels from the airwaves. Berlusconi and other private channels had taken half the viewers and two-thirds of the money in a few short years. For the RAI, it was a disaster. They had to adapt, and quickly. One strategy was simply to copy the formats and programmes aired on private TV. Neo-television was no longer a competitor, it was the norm.

From Scandal to Triumph: The 1982 World Cup and the 'Footbalisation' of Italy

'[Enzo] Bearzot [Italy's manager in 1982] succeeded where Camillo Benso conte di Cavour and Vittorio Emanuele II and Garibaldi all failed.'

Franco Ferrarotti and Oliviero Beha, *All'ultimo stadio*, 1983[47]

Nobody believed they could do it. As the 1980s began, Italian football, was, to put it mildly, in a state of crisis. A national betting and match-fixing scandal (known as *Totonero*) had shocked fans and the public in 1980. Players were arrested in dressing rooms and taken to prison, there were criminal trials and long sporting bans were handed out. Violence in the stadiums was rife. The national team performed poorly in the 1980 European Championships (held in Italy). Italy's *Gli Azzurri* (*The Blues*) thus went to Spain for the World Cup in 1982 under a cloud. One of their most promising players – the striker Paolo Rossi – had just returned from a ban linked to that scandal. Rossi has always denied playing any role in match-fixing.

Low expectations were fully confirmed in the early part of the tournament. Italy were not just bad, they were terrible. The team scraped through the group stage with a mere three points from the same number of games, thanks to a 1-1 draw with Cameroon that, it was later claimed, might have been fixed.[48] Italy's players and staff have always rejected such claims. Expectations were of a hasty exit in the next stage of the tournament, and the post-mortems were already being prepared as journalists sharpened their pens.

Then, suddenly, everything changed. Italy beat Maradona's Argentina, and then – incredibly – knocked out the favourites Brazil in a match of high drama. Rossi became an instant national hero with a hat-trick. Poland were dispatched in the semi-final with ease. By now, the *Azzurri* were unstoppable. Despite a missed penalty in the first half, Italy beat old rivals West Germany 3-1 in the final, with goals from Rossi (again, he took the golden boot), Marco Tardelli and Alessandro Altobelli. The cup was theirs, and was lifted by forty-year-old goalkeeper Dino Zoff. Four matches had transformed the fortunes of the team.

Football, as is well known, has the capacity to focus the attention of disparate communities – at the same time, in the same place, in terms of the same event. It utilises a form of universal language that is easy to learn and allows for chat about football before, during and after games. The year 1982 was also far enough away from the Second World War and fascism to create distance from that regime. This was a tournament watched above all by a generation born after the war. The players themselves were nearly all part of the post-war generation.

But why was 1982 so powerful in terms of national mobilisation and national identity? The 1982 'event' contained a series of stories that could be told and retold, while other elements of the 'expedition' could be conveniently forgotten, or simply used to reinforce the mythical elements of the tale. The characters and stories were all there – and they could be visualised. A key factor in 1982's impact was the way that this game was experienced in a pre-Internet era. Italians consumed the World Cup tournament almost entirely through their own private televisions, in the domestic sphere. There were a few big screens set up in 1982 but millions of Italians stayed in, or went round to friends. The 1982 final achieved a 95 per cent audience share. This remains a record, and one that will never be beaten, given changes to the media system. Only a stubborn 5 per cent watched the other channels, it is said. There really would never be an event like it in Italy, before or since.

Thus, on that hot day in July, something like 36 million Italians across the country, from Sicily to Piedmont, watched the same game, with identical commentary, without mobile phones or twitter. Italian migrants across the world joined them – from Toronto to Sydney to New York to Buenos Aires. Football's ability to unify an entire country – and a diaspora – was exacerbated by the social and technological context of the time, the peak-time nature of the tournament and the success of the national team.

Nando Martellini was the only commentator – a reassuring presence who knew exactly what he was doing. When the referee raised the ball above his head to signal full-time Martellini announced the famous phrase *'Campioni del mondo, Campioni del mondo, Campioni del mondo'*. This was not just a clear use of a classic advertising technique – repetition – but a reminder that this was Italy's third World Cup. Emotions were unleashed through a unique, singular and unrepeatable visual and aural experience. For the final, a TV producer in Genoa had the brilliant idea of placing a camera in an ordinary family living room. The room was packed, with people of all ages, and a mix of men and women. They held horns and grasped flags to their chests. When the first goal went in, they went completely crazy. A huge emotional release was then associated with Marco Tardelli's powerful cross-shot, which left Germany's goalkeeper motionless – and made it 2-0 to Italy. Tardelli set off running, arms out wide and mouth open. This moment became known as 'Tardelli's scream', a clip repeated so often it emblazoned itself on the minds of millions – many of them also screaming, back home, in their living rooms. Further celebrations followed goal number three, and full-time. Once the game was over, people hit the streets.

A spontaneous open-air party followed that, in popular memory (and sometimes in reality), went on for days. Not everybody went to work the next day. Impromptu tables were set up and food and drink were passed around. The symbols of the nation were exhibited without shame or fear and streets were 'retaken' (albeit briefly) despite the dark years of 'lead', of political violence, when many had been scared to go out. This party had some ritualised elements to it – the random driving of cars, full of people hanging out of windows, the hooting of horns. Fountains became swimming pools (it was hot). Fake 'death' notices were issued for Germany. But there were some new elements to the celebrations. Many emigrants remember 1982 as the first time they felt that they counted in the countries to which they had emigrated. The party in Toronto, for example, was notable for its size and length.[49]

In Italy, journalists noticed the proliferation of Italian flags – something that had been rare and had polarised Italians in the political struggles of the 1960s and 1970s. As Luciano Curino wrote in La Stampa, 'there have never been so many flags on the streets. Many still had the Savoy symbol, and had clearly been found at the bottom of cupboards after some forty years or so.' The Savoy symbol – a 'shield' with white cross on a red background and a blue border – was right in the middle of the Italian flag until 1946. There was a sense that these dusty (and pre-Republican) flags had become acceptable again, with the 1982 victory. Children were dressed in Italian colours, and buildings were painted in the same way. A sense of community was created. To cite Curino again, 'This is a night where everyone speaks informally and there are continual hugs and the repetition of the phrase: "we are champions of the world".' And this sense of community went beyond those who were football fans, including 'those who know nothing about football'.[50]

Italy's Grandfather

Paolo Rossi was the hero on the pitch, but the victory was identified above all with someone who was neither a player, a manager, nor a sports journalist. That man was the President of Italy, Sandro Pertini, who only saw one game in the flesh in Spain (the final) and only then decided to attend at the last minute. Before the final, Pertini had stayed in Rome, but photos of him watching games on television were released to the press. Pertini had learnt the lesson of the Alfredino Rampi story from a year before, where hours of live television coverage had ended in tragedy. This time, he would minimise the risks involved.

Pertini's image as a man of the people and someone special was already well in place by the time the 1982 World Cup began. As Silvio Lanaro has written, Pertini was 'never over-the-top, but always aware of the part he was playing'. He 'placed himself above politics in a natural way which everyone saw as sincere. He was a man of spartan tastes and a studied form of straightforward emotions. [It was said that] he wouldn't move a finger if the TV cameras were not there to record things. He often went out into the streets, and liked appearing in crowds, and he celebrated like a kid when Italy won the 1982 World Cup.'[51]

Pertini flew out to Spain on the morning of the final. He took a DC9 – an Italian military plane. Pertini was very clear that he and he alone would represent Italy during the final. He arrived in Madrid to be met by King Juan Carlos himself at the airport. But what was it about Pertini's actions in 1982 that impressed them on to the Italian national consciousness? First, there was the figure of the man himself. Pertini was tiny, bespectacled, ageing. He usually smoked a pipe, and wore a suit, like many men of his generation. He looked like an ordinary 'grandfather', but he was the President of Italy, the head of state, the President of all the Italians, as he himself had put it at the time of his election.

Pertini, for example, refused to move into the Quirinale Palace, preferring a 'modest' flat in the centre of Rome. No trappings of power for him. Pertini became a kind of lay Pope. He also insisted in being driven around by his wife in a small FIAT 500 (he couldn't drive). There were stories that he often tried to throw off his bodyguards, and he was straight-talking when it came to corruption, the Mafia, politics and everyday life.

Pertini had become President at an extremely difficult time for Italy – in the midst of the 'years of lead' linked to political violence and a deep economic (and political) crisis. He became known as the 'Funerals President' for his constant presence at the funerals of those killed due to this violence. He was also fond of taking the part of 'the people' against the state (and politicians) at certain times, as with his emotional denunciation of state inefficiencies after a traumatic earthquake in the Neapolitan area in 1980, or his speeches attacking political corruption.

During the match, Pertini behaved like a fan – just like the millions across Italy, celebrating in the same way, at the same time, with him. Pertini, however, was in front of the cameras. Most fans were also watching him watching the game. The key difference was that Pertini was there, sitting next to the King of Spain. In that moment, the Italians and Pertini (and the players on the pitch) were fused as one – the identification was total. When Altobelli raised his hands after the third goal that put Italy 3-0 up, Pertini also raised his hands in exactly the same way.

The perfect, final touch to all this was an ordinary card game with some of the players and the manager on the plane back to Italy, with the World Cup trophy sitting on the table. On the Monday morning, the day after the game, the DC9 returned to Rome – this time with Pertini, the entire team, and the World Cup. Pertini was the first to disembark from the plane in the capital. Modestly, it is said, he did not want to carry the cup. But he was identified with the victory – the first person the crowds saw in Rome. The return was perfectly stage-managed. There were thousands of fans inside Ciampino Airport and hundreds

of thousands on the roads leading to it. Pertini, it is said, successfully argued that the team (and himself) should return to Rome
by car instead of helicopter. This was a stark contrast with the
fallout after the 1970 World Cup, when the players and manager
had been forced to hide in a hanger to escape the wrath of the
fans, or the aftermath of the catastrophic 1966 tournament when
the players were pelted with rotten tomatoes in Genoa airport.

Did Pertini's past history matter in all this, as is often claimed?
Was this, in some way, an *anti-fascist* World Cup? Pertini's life
story appears to encapsulate, on its own, Italy's 'short twentieth
century'. He was a veteran of the First World War and had been a
key leader of the anti-Fascist Resistance. He took part in the deci-
sion-making that had led to the execution by partisans of Benito
Mussolini near Lake Como in April 1945 and the beginning of
the final insurrection in Milan that liberated the city before the
Allies arrived. Pertini's brother Eugenio had been executed in
Flossenburg concentration camp by the Nazis on 25 April 1945 –
Italy's official day of liberation.

One of the effects, however, of Pertini's powerful association with the 1982 World Cup victory was that his radical past
was pushed into the background. He became universal, safe and
almost cuddly. The Pertini myth remains powerful, turning up
in politicians' speeches and advertisements at regular intervals.[52]
Everyone could agree on how good they felt about Pertini in
1982. More generally, 1982 remains one of the most powerful collective moments of national identification from Italy's post-war
period. Its power has strengthened over time, even for those who
have no direct memories of that event.

God in Naples: Maradona, 1984–91

In June 1984, 70,000 people paid 1,000 lire each to gather in a
vast concrete bowl. It was a football stadium, but there wasn't
a match on. Instead, a small man with thick curly hair, wearing
a tracksuit and a Napoli scarf, emerged from the tunnel. He was
cheered to the rafters as he did a few tricks with the ball for the

adoring crowd. The place was Naples and the stadium the Stadio San Paolo. SSC Napoli had been founded in 1926, and they had never won the Serie A title. Maradona took time to settle in with the team, but in 1987 he led Napoli to their first *scudetto*. The city erupted in days of celebrations, and Maradona became a god-like figure. Southern pride was lording it – for once – over the richer and perenially successful clubs from the northern cities. Napoli went on to win a second title in 1990 as well as various other trophies during Maradona's tenure.

In 1990 Italy hosted the World Cup, and the *Azzurri* found themselves playing Argentina in the semi-final – and in Naples. It was a dramatic game, which went to penalties. In the build-up, Maradona himself had played on the possibility that the Neapolitan crowd might favour him – their hero – over their 'Fatherland'. He told a journalist that 'For 364 days a year you are treated like dirt, and then they ask you to support them.' Italy messed up their penalties, and the winning kick was left to Maradona himself – who didn't miss. Fans at the final in Rome between Argentina and West Germany booed and whistled as the Argentinian national anthem was played, and West Germany won. Maradona was already a hate figure for many fans and non-fans in the north of the country, but after 1990 he was a marked man.

Quite quickly, after the World Cup, the Argentinian's time in the city turned sour. He was investigated for tax evasion, tested positive for cocaine use, and fled Italy in March 1991. Meanwhile, photos emerged of Maradona cavorting with leading Camorra figures, including one of him sitting in an empty and luxurious bright red shell-shaped bathtub with two well-known bosses – who appeared to be fans by the look of their 'Maradona' haircuts.[53] Accusations were made by supergrass witnesses that Napoli had thrown the 1988 championship, when they had lost four of their last five games and Milan took the title. None of this was ever proven in a court of law.

The tax authorities tried to get Maradona to pay back what they said he owed them (34 million euros), but with little success. Every time he returned to Italy, they would take something

off him – his earrings and Rolex watches, for example, or his fee
for appearing on *Celebrity Come Dancing*. The Camorra photos
and stories and accusations of tax evasion and match-fixing did
little to diminish the love felt by Napoli fans for Maradona, and
the historic impact of his seven years at the club in the 1980s and
1990s. Yet they did reveal, once again, the intimate connection
between sport, society and politics in Italy.

Maxiprocesso: The Mafia on Trial

Despite the seemingly immoveable nature of her political class,
the Italian state was not a monolith. At the same time as Craxi
was concentrating political power in Rome, other sectors of
the Italian state achieved surprising success in the war against
organised crime, especially in the South. This struggle led to an
exceptional event in the 1980s, a collective trial of Mafia bosses
and their associates and it took place in the very heart of Mafia
power – Palermo, in Sicily.

In February 1986 an exceptional trial began in Palermo. It was
held inside a prison, in a special court building surrounded by
separate barred and locked cell-rooms that became known as the
'aula bunker' (the bunker room). The trial would last until the end
of 1987 – and the numbers alone tell the story of a moment that
would change Italian history. Over 450 people were put on trial in
that special 'courtroom'. This figure also explains the name given
to this event – the *maxiprocesso* – the maxi-trial.

This number also tells us something else. This was not a
trial directed at certain individuals (although it was also that)
but at a criminal organisation – and possibly the most powerful and oldest criminal organisation of all – the Mafia. This
unprecedented judicial event had been made possible by the
courageous work of a group of magistrates, and the testimony
of supergrasses (or *pentiti*). With the *maxiprocesso*, it was clear
that the state's supergrass strategy had paid off. By getting leading mafiosi to turn state's evidence, the magistrates had been
able to understand and document the workings of an elaborate,

secret organisation – and to use these testimonies to bring that organisation down.

Tommaso Buscetta, a flamboyant *mafioso* from a humble background (he had sixteen siblings), was the key figure. His lengthy confessions laid bare the workings of what was known as 'Cosa Nostra'. Buscetta was arrested in Brazil in 1984 and his decision to talk to the magistrates was to change Italy, and Sicily, forever. It has been argued that Buscetta 'has so deeply revolutionised the state of knowledge about the mafia that mafia studies can be divided into pre- and post-Buscetta'.[54] His testimony 'revealed the nature of the controlling body, the *commissione* or Cupola, the internal structure of the individual *cosca* and the ritual used for the initiation into the mafia'.[55] Eleven members of Buscetta's family were killed by the Mafia in revenge for his 'betrayal', both before and after he started to speak to magistrates. For example, two of his sons were kidnapped and murdered in September 1982 and later that year his son-in-law was also killed. The carnage continued right through 1984. The Mafia does not forgive, or forget.

In the dramatic setting of the aula-bunker, and with TV cameras rolling, a succession of *mafiosi* testified, one by one, in front of the judges. Buscetta was sometimes protected, in the courtroom itself, by a bullet-proof set of screens. He wasn't seen as safe even inside the bunker-room. The defendants and accusers knew each other – and were often related by blood or through criminal association (an alternative kind of 'family'). Threats were not empty, especially when they came from mass murderers. There were also surreal moments. The leading *mafioso* Michele Greco – who was known as 'The Pope' – blamed cinema for the bad name of the Mafia. He said that if people had seen '*Moses* instead of *The Godfather*' everything would have been fine.

There was another context for the *maxiprocesso* beyond legal and judicial changes, and the emergence of supergrass testimonies. In the late 1970s and early 1980s hundreds of people had been killed in what became known as '*la mattanza*' – the massacre, the butchery – a power struggle within the Sicilian Mafia that spread to other parts of Italy. This was a slaughter carried out by death squads, and it only ended with a victory by a group-family who were dubbed the Corleonesi. The head of this faction was Totò Riina, and he became the so-called boss of bosses.

Riina's methods were brutal, and he made many enemies. Bodies were discovered every day. Between 1981 and 1993 at least 500 people were killed in Palermo alone, 1,200 in Catania, 500 in Agrigento. An estimated 2,000 people were killed in Reggio Calabria over the same period. For the journalist and Mafia expert Enrico Deaglio 'what took place was not a "Mafia war" but a new kind of "civil war". The rest of Italy tended to ignore these events, without understanding how this increase in violence would lead inevitably to a change in the nation itself.'[56] Riina would avoid capture until January 1993. He wasn't at the maxi-trial but his shadow hung over the whole legal process.

At the maxi-trial, the *mafiosi* usually proclaimed their innocence, and often referred to themselves in the third person. Their defence often made an appeal to a self-projection or mythical reality as 'good fathers' or 'simple peasants'. Often, these *mafiosi* also spoke directly to the presiding judge from their cages, which encircled the bunker courtroom. These were men who rarely spoke in public, and seldom 'appeared' at all, but were now testifying in front of TV cameras and to the whole of Italy. They often spoke in a kind of 'code', sending messages and threats back and forth.

There were insults, and constant protests. Many of the leading *mafiosi* continued to claim that there was no such thing as the Mafia at all. This wasn't just a trial about a series of crimes, it also worked at a metaphysical level. *Mafiosi* were not just proclaiming their innocence, but the non-existence of an entire criminal organisation – a collective innocence. The myth of the 'noble mafia', which helped (and came from) the people, was often repeated in the trial, and not just by the *mafiosi* themselves, but also by former *mafiosi* and supergrasses who claimed that the 'mafia is no longer what it was'.

Legal change was also important in the run-up to the *maxi-processo*. It had taken far too long, but a law had at last been passed in 1982 that defined what the Mafia was, and saw 'association' with the organisation as a crime. This law was pushed through in just ten days (and was never voted on by the parliamentary chamber, but passed in commission – an emergency procedure allowed for by the constitution) after the Mafia murder of a Communist politician – Pio La Torre – in Palermo in April 1982.[57] Buscetta told the magistrates about the organisation's initiation rites, its rules and regulations, its complicated management of gender and class, and its routine use of horrific acts of violence. A total of 366 arrest requests had been issued in Palermo in September 1984, following these revelations.

The trial itself lasted nearly two years. The judges took thirty-one days to decide after the courtroom part of the process was over. It took ninety minutes for Judge Alfonso Giordano, President of the Court, to read out the verdicts. Heavy jail terms were handed down – amounting to a total of 2,265 years in prison, while 114 people were cleared. Some 200 lawyers took part. Enrico Deaglio later wrote that the *maxiprocesso* trial was 'the Mafia's Nuremberg'.[58] For John Dickie, 'After 130 years, the Italian state had finally declared the Sicilian mafia to be an organised and deadly challenge to its own right to rule: it was the worst defeat in the entire history of the world's most famous criminal association.'[59]

Two magistrates were the driving force behind the maxi-trial, and the investigations leading up to it. Giovanni Falcone and Paolo Borsellino were both born in Palermo, the former in 1939, the latter in 1940 – and both in a neighbourhood known as La Kalsa. The two men had known each other as children. They studied law (a degree that takes at least five years to complete) at Palermo University before becoming magistrates. Borsellino was a brilliant student. He was said to be the youngest magistrate in Italy when he entered service soon after graduating.

In the 1980s the two men began to work together on anti-Mafia investigations in the city. After the murder of magistrate Rocco Chinnici in 1983 by a car bomb that also killed three other people, they became a key part of the so-called 'pool' of anti-Mafia investigators who prepared the maxi-trial. Falcone was a man vaguely from the left (he had voted for the Communists on at least one occasion) while Borsellino had been active politically within the far right as a student. Neither were members of political parties.

In 1986 Falcone married the magistrate Francesca Morvillo (in a semi-secret ceremony with only four witnesses, held at midnight) after divorcing his previous wife. Borsellino was married with three children. Both had experienced the loss of colleagues to Mafia assassinations. They lived their lives under constant armed guard, twenty-four hours a day. They were aware that they were living on borrowed time.[60]

Given Italy's three levels of justice, and the fact that previous verdicts had been quashed by higher courts, it was crucial that the maxi-trial convictions were rendered definitive by the appeals and High Court. In January 1992 this happened. The battle led by magistrates in Palermo had come to fruition. It was now clearly possible for the state to take on and (partly) defeat the Mafia. But for the Mafia, once the sentences were confirmed, it was payback time. They didn't want their leaders in prison, where they struggled to control their organisations. It was no longer enough for the Mafia to infiltrate and mould the state's institutions to its own ends. Now it would be open warfare, against the state.

Hiding in Plain Sight

Not all leading *mafiosi*, as we have seen, had been present during the *maxiprocesso*. They were 'in hiding', something which, for some of the more powerful ones, could go on for years, even though these men were still, usually, in Sicily itself. Leading *mafiosi* 'on the run' lived relatively normal lives – their children went to school, they had operations in hospital. To avoid bugging, Mafia boss Bernardo Provenzano decided to use tiny handwritten notes – known as *pizzini* – which were easy to hide, written in a kind of code, and left little trace – to communicate with the outside world and his organisation. Tip-offs from informers within the police and *carabinieri* usually meant that these 'on-the-run' *mafiosi* could move from hideout to hideout in time to avoid capture. Most remained close to their home territories for their period as fugitives. In this way, leading *mafiosi* such as bosses Riina and Provenzano avoided capture for decades, identifiable only by worn, out-of-date photos of their younger selves. They would not be captured, finally, until Riina was caught in 1993 (in Palermo, after being on the run for twenty-three years) and Provenzano in 2006 (after a record-breaking forty-three years avoiding capture). Provenzano was picked up close to his home town of Corleone. Both men had been in Sicily for most of their period as fugitives from justice. It was where they felt most safe, and with reason. Their long lives hiding in plain sight were a sign of how powerful the Mafia felt within its own territory.

The End of the Cold War and its Impact on Italy

'Say something left-wing. Anything. Say something.'

Nanni Moretti[61]

Despite rising public debt, the post-industrial boom was ongoing, and political stability seemed guaranteed by the *pentapartito*, five-party coalition. Italy's political class appeared stable as the end of the 1980s appeared on the horizon. The Cold War settlement was still very much in place, and there were few obvious signs of any cracks in the edifice of the major parties and opposition groupings. Then, very quickly, almost without warning, the Soviet empire began to fall apart. All the certainties of the past crumbled, and in an unexpected way. Nobody was prepared for what was to follow. The first momentous event domestically was the rapid demise of Italian communism.

On 12 November 1989, a few days after the fall of the Berlin Wall, Achille Occhetto, the moustachioed fifty-three-year-old leader of the Italian Communist Party, gave a speech in La Bolognina, a zone in the city of Bologna. Occhetto was said to be in tears. The date of the speech was not chosen by chance – it was the celebration of a mythical local event, the 'Battle of Porta Lame', involving partisans during the Second World War. His audience that day included former partisans from that clash. He had decided to begin a process that became known as 'the breakthrough' or 'the turning' – 'la svolta' – in a phrase which harked back to Palmiro Togliatti's famous and controversial political compromise in 1944, 'la svolta di Salerno', when Togliatti had accepted a broad coalition as a way of defeating fascism. It is said that Occhetto made the decision to begin la svolta on his own, after a conversation with his driver, a former partisan. The entire speech that day lasted less than six minutes.

The choice of place was important. Bolognina was where the Communist Party was not just a presence; it was considered almost a religion. Occhetto's speech was a short one, but it would transform the Italian left, and lead to the quick dismantling of the structures and traditions that had made the Communist Party the largest of its kind in the Western world, and an international model for many. Twenty years later in 2009, looking back, after a lifetime spent as a communist – inside and outside of the party – Lucio Magri tried to work out 'when did the end of the PCI begin'?[62] Was it in 1979 (Afghanistan)? Or in 1984 (the death of Berlinguer)? Or in 1989, with la svolta?

In the period that followed la svolta, the party's language changed. As Patrick McCarthy later pointed out, 'From autumn 1989 to spring 1991 the PCI turned inward and talked mostly to itself.'[63] Occhetto's speech shocked many in the party, leading eventually to the first split in its history.[64] He made an explicit link between the partisan struggle and the developments being led at that time by Mikhail Gorbachev in the Soviet Union. 'You [he told the partisans] won the war and if you want these victories to survive, we need to make great changes and not just defend things.' 'We need to move forward,' he added, 'with the same courage you showed at the time, during the Resistance.' He was promising socialism, but with a human face.

It was an astonishing and theatrical moment. Many in the party were firmly opposed to change of this kind. They were proud of their past, their history, and their brand of communism. It was what made them 'communists'. In fact, in many ways, this was what they were most proud of. To paraphrase an interviewee in Svetlana Alexievich's book about Soviet and post-Soviet Russia, Second-Hand Time, the only thing these militants 'couldn't do

THE 1980S AND 1990S

without was the past'.[65] The Communist Party had taken a long time to finally 'break' with Moscow – and perhaps it was not until 1981 that the final shift took place, with the military takeover in Poland in that year. Even after 1981, however, links with the Soviet model – whatever that model meant by then – remained. It was perhaps not surprising that Occhetto's call was seen by many in the party as a betrayal of their identity – as an acceptance of the accusations that had been levelled against them for so long. Giuliano Pajetta, one of the old guard, said that 'I am not ashamed of this name nor of our history, and I don't want to change because of what they [the Communists of the East] have done. If they change the name what will they create, a third Socialist Party?' Opposition to *la svolta* came from major and distinguished figures in the party. Pajetta would die soon afterwards, and was buried to the sounds of the Internationale. He never saw the outcomes that arose almost inevitably from Occhetto's speech.

A debate exploded within the party, much of which was linked to symbols – the hammer and sickle, the name, communism itself, whatever that meant. Should these be changed, and, if so, into what? Nanni Moretti made a powerful documentary chronicling these heartfelt and often emotional debates. Its title was ironic, but also accurate – *La Cosa* (*The Thing*).[66] Enormous passions were unleashed. What was the Communist Party, what had it been, and what should it become? The Partito Comunista Italiano meant a lot to people. It had been central to their lives, their identities. Now it risked extinction (or self-extinction).

This was also a discussion about history, identity and tradition. What did it mean to be 'a Communist' if the Soviet world had disintegrated? How could a party with such a history and culture modernise and win power? Militants whistled and heckled some of the party leaders in the street. Much of this was highly emotional and charged. People were in tears. As the anthropologist David Kertzer wrote, 'The battle over the *svolta* was waged to a great extent as a battle over symbols and fought to a considerable extent through ritual. Ritual provided the primary means through which the party leaders were able to tap the passions of the members and sympathisers.'[67]

Things moved fast. Occhetto called for a new 'consitituent phase' and the creation of a new 'political force' with a different name. Despite opposition, it was also clear that a majority of the party were on Occhetto's side. A special congress was called for March 1990. Three motions were put to the vote – Occhetto's, a compromise motion, and one that was explicitly opposed to *la svolta*. Some 67 per cent eventually voted for the leadership motion (a big victory, but not a massive one in a party such as this) – a decision that sealed the fate of the Italian Communist Party. The Partito Comunista Italiano was no more. A small minority left the party altogether to form a new organisation that still called itself 'Communist'.

True to Occhetto's word and his mandate, the leadership decided on a new name and symbol. On 10 October 1990 Occhetto was photographed holding up a large piece of card with a tree on it. The new name was the rather unwieldy Partito Democratico della Sinistra or PdS (Democratic Party of the Left), and the symbol was a large oak (later, people would also refer to the party as 'the oak'). There was also a little bit of a compromise here, because in the trunk of the oak there was a smaller symbol – the hammer and sickle and the letters PCI. An unseemly lawsuit followed over the ownership of the old PCI symbol – the hammer and sickle itself. A break had been made with the past, but it was not a complete one. Occhetto and others were clearly worried about voters deserting them, and they were right to be so concerned. Yet another congress was now called – the last ever of the Italian Communist Party – and the PCI's twentieth.[68] This time Occhetto's speech lasted two hours (not everything had changed) and he called for nothing less than the creation of a 'new Italy'.

On 3 February 1991 the Italian Communist Party was formally dissolved. The party split as a minority group of militants and intellectuals left to form a new party (which they claimed was really still the old PCI) – Rifondazione Comunista (RC). Others from outside of the party also joined up with this new grouping, which kept the Communist name and some of the old symbols. For a time, the umbrella grouping of Rifondazione Comunista enjoyed considerable success, before slipping off the electoral radar. Communism had an afterlife, but not a particularly long one. Both of these parties would undergo numerous transformations, name changes, splits and reunifications over the next twenty-five years, under a variety of symbols and alliances.

One accusation made against Occhetto – at the time, and since – was that he had simply dismantled structures that had been built up through nearly seventy years of organisation and militancy. Many felt that a wealth of experience and cultural and political work was being discarded, with nothing to replace it. Even Norberto Bobbio, a distinguished socialist reformist, was sceptical. 'The haste,' he wrote, 'with which they have been throwing their old cargo overboard seems suspect to me.'[69] Certainly, the era of mass political parties was at an end, and that included the most mass party of all – the Communist Party.

Many still wanted to see themselves as communists in the wake of *la svolta*, and Rifondazione Comunista did well in elections in the 1990s and 2000s, but these numbers soon dwindled. By 2008, there would be no deputies at all elected under a hammer-and-sickle symbol. A relative silence also started to fall about the Communist Party and its role in post-war Italy. Even historians largely ignored the subject, unless it was to denounce the party as wedded to Stalin. For years, the Italian Communist Party had been a model of innovation and cultural policy for many. Now, both its past and present seemed no longer even worthy of study. Anti-communism survived communism itself – it also had an 'after-life' – but it too was destined to fade. Although there was a time lag, the end of the Cold War effectively heralded the end of those fault lines – communist and anti-communist, fascist and anti-fascist – that had patterned the First Republic.

Enormous quantities of ink had been spent, during the Cold War, in the examination of the minutiae of the changing relationship between the Italian Communist Party and the Soviet Union. Every shift in position seemed extraordinarily important. However, the rapid collapse of the USSR after 1989 and the break-up of the Communist Party into various parts and new organisations made this issue appear, in hindsight, as far less decisive. By the end of the 1990s, the question or spectre of the USSR had disappeared almost entirely from the centre stage of Italian politics.

Identities changed. Some argued that ideology itself was being replaced by other forms of political mobilisation – linked to territory, ethnicity, anti-politics. Post-fascism and post-communism became fashionable terms. Many politicians were 'ex' something or other – ex-communists, ex-fascists, ex-Christian Democrats. A series of technical governments and 'big coalitions' emerged. All this seemed to herald a kind of post-democracy. In Colin Crouch's words, 'elections ... exist and can change governments [but] the mass of citizens plays a passive, quiescent, even apathetic part'.[70] Without mass parties, and in the Internet age, the collective mobilisations of the past had changed and fragmented.

The end of the Cold War did not just affect Italy's political system. It also dissolved borders and opened up countries that had been sealed off for nearly fifty years. In Italy's case, the first, dramatic outcome of this process was seen in Albania.

New Invasions: Italy's Borders and the End of the Cold War

After the Cold War ended, it was Italy's east coast that became the subject of debate and conflict. A new (and seemingly vast) potential immigrant population took to the stage after the end of the Enver Hoxha dictatorship. Thousands of Albanians clambered onto ships and headed across the Adriatic. In March 1991, after democratic elections were held for the first time, a number of them tried to get to Italy. Most of those in this first wave were given refugee status and distributed across the country. A few months later, in August, more Albanians attempted the crossing, but a number from this so-called 'second wave' were turned back. In this short time the Albanians were redefined as 'economic migrants'. While the first group had been seen as desperate victims, those that followed were seen as dangerous invaders.

In August 1991 one notable boat landing led to a stand-off that dominated the news agenda headlines for days. The ship – called the *Vlora* – was carrying an incredible 21,000 people. The journalist Enrico Deaglio later described it as being like a 'gigantic bunch of grapes which moved across the sea'.[71] This enormous and overcrowded vessel became the symbol of this moment of crisis. A photograph of the ship was later used for anti-immigrant propaganda with the simple word *Basta!* (*Enough*) as well as by the provocative advertising guru Oliviero Toscani in an advert for Benetton. This image 'was reissued and replayed in countless magazine articles and television documentaries on migration ... the "Albanian emergency" was encamped on the front pages of all Italian newspapers'.[72]

The film director Gianni Amelio was inspired by these events to make his film, *Lamerica* (1994). In it two Italian businessmen looking to make a quick buck are caught up in the post-Communist chaos in Albania. They meet an Italian soldier who had remained in the country after the Second World War. The film is continually interspersed with images from Italian television, which certainly played a role in the depiction inside Albania of Italy as a land of plenty. In the final, epic, scene of his film, Amelio recreates the voyage of the *Vlora*. One of the Italian businessmen has ended up on board, as has the Italian former soldier, who thinks he is going to *Lamerica*, not Italy. The film ends with close-ups of the faces of the migrants, full of hope about their journey. But we, the spectator, know what really awaits them. Amelio put Albanians on screen, but of course he was also talking about Italians and their own history of emigration – those who really went to *Lamerica*. The Albanians revived bad memories for Italians. As migrants they were a reminder of poverty and a past that was still a little too close for comfort.[73]

The captain of the real ship was a forty-year-old man called Halim Milaqi. Later he recalled how people simply invaded the *Vlora* in the port town of Durazzo in Albania after he had unloaded his cargo of sugar. A man held a screwdriver to his side and told him to start the ship. As they embarked, there were cheers. It was a moment of liberation. Some of those on the ship were armed. People ate some of the sugar left in the ship's cargo. There was very little drinking water. Most of those on board just had the clothes on their back, and some were in flip-flops, or swimming costumes. There were also army deserters in full uniform. The *Vlora* arrived at the port of Bari (the first intended destination had been Brindisi) at 10 a.m. on 8 August 1991. Many of those who should have been dealing with a situation of this kind were on holiday at the time (including the city's Prefect and its Chief of Police). The ship's radar was broken.

The *Vlora* was directed to the part of the port that was furthest away from the city. Other migrants arrived in other boats right down the coast, but it was the *Vlora*, not surprisingly, that captured the attention of the media. The Albanians were chanting a football chant: *Italia, Italia*. It was chaos. Nobody knew what to do. Military vessels surrounded the ship. All attempts to stop the *Vlora* entering the port were in vain. At one point the captain said he didn't have a reverse gear. Conditions on board were appalling, and some people hadn't had any water for twenty-four hours. Milaqi also remembered that some passengers wanted to return immediately to Albania, but his ship was seized by the authorities. The orders issued from Rome were to keep people on board, but this was impossible.

Some passengers threw themselves into the sea on arrival, others climbed down ropes to reach the shore. A number headed straight for the city. The heat was suffocating, and there was very little shade. The police began to use truncheons to move the crowd back. There was no plan for numbers on this scale, so the authorities came up with a place to 'put' the Albanians – the old football stadium (called the Stadium of Victory). City buses were used to move people from the port to the stadium over a six-day period. But, inside the stadium, things soon took a turn for the worse. Some tried to escape, and the gates to the stadium were closed. A tiny baby (just 980 grams) was born prematurely inside the stadium. The husband of her nineteen-year-old mother had already been deported.

Stadium of Victory

The Stadium of Victory had been built under fascism, and was still covered in fascist slogans. The construction of the stadium had been announced in 1928 with these words: 'In memory for future generations not only of the sacrifice of the Fallen, but also the great Victory brought by our army and enhanced by Fascism'. History was coming back to haunt Italy. *La Stampa* drew obvious parallels as it republished articles from the 1930s describing the 'triumphant' invasion of Albania just before Italy officially entered the Second World War.

The stadium was not inaugurated until 1934, despite being still unfinished, in the presence of Benito Mussolini. It was built in what was in part open countryside, but connected to the sea (which was close by) by a straight 'monumental' road. In 1943 it was hit by two Allied bombs and during the war the Allies seized it for their own use. It was not until 1945 that Bari football club played there again. Some 300 million lire was spent on the stadium in 1978. Bari played 945 games there between 1934 and 1990, when it was replaced for the World Cup with Renzo Piano's beautiful but absurd new structure.

As the journalist Luigi Quaranta remembered, looking back at the events of 1991 from 2011: 'And so the eight horrible days of a state of siege around the stadium began, where the more violent and determined groups effectively kept the others as hostages. And there were numerous families and children. Because the stadium was closed the problem of water and food for the five to six thousand people inside became an urgent one.'[74] Bottles of water were thrown in from the outside, or dropped from helicopters, something that was both dangerous and made embarrassing TV for the authorities. The whole 'event' now became something of a media circus. Some young and bare-chested Albanians covered their faces, and took on the police and *carabinieri*. Tear gas was fired. Prime Minister Giulio Andreotti was caught by surprise – he was on holiday in the posh mountain resort of Cortina, and the Italian President Francesco Cossiga was also enjoying a break in Courmayeur. The Italian state had gone on holiday, or so it appeared.

Some locals tried to do their best – such as the Christian Democratic mayor of the city at the time – Enrico Dalfino – who organised food and drink for the children locked inside the stadium, but the general impression was one of confusion. Groups of Albanians were loaded onto planes and deported, others were removed by sea, while a number escaped into Italy itself. Many were told lies – that they were being taken to other Italian cities – just as they were about to be deported. As the numbers were reduced, the authorities tried straightforward bribery – 50,000 lire for all those who decided to go home. President Cossiga turned up in a dark mood, calling the administration 'cretins' and attacking Mayor Dalfino.

Very quickly, the mainstream press changed its language. From 'refugees' the Albanians became seen as 'extremists'. The tone hardened. This was now an 'emergency', with Albanians depicted as 'desperate' people who were 'invading' Italy. The 'dreams' of the migrants had turned into an 'inferno', an 'exodus' from the 'chaos' of their own country. They were also depicted as ignorant innocents, who had no idea of reality: 'They only know the Marxist-Leninist version of Italian and Albanian history given to them by the regimes of Hoxha and Alia,' wrote Sergio Romano in *La Stampa*.[75] Incredibly, there were no victims, either during the crossing or in the stadium. Alarmist language infected both the left and right. *L'Unità*, the Communist Party daily, wrote of 'Another flood of refugees'. Activity around this coastline soon calmed down – and this demonstrated that it was not Italy's geographic borders themselves that were 'porous'. Rather, it was geo-political developments and shifting frontiers, as well as globalisation, that created changing flows of potential labour and refugees back and forth across continents and seas.

Berlusconi and Football

Silvio Berlusconi once said that he was 'condemned to win'. During his rise to fame and fortune, he constructed an image for himself as a consummate victor. And nowhere was this image more influential and powerful than in the world of football. By the 1980s, football was Italy's most popular spectator sport. Cycling had been left well behind and millions tuned into football games and highlights and chat shows on television. Italy's 1982 World Cup victory had helped Serie A become the richest and most powerful league in the world. A succession of glamorous foreign stars arrived in that decade in the lead-up to the country's hosting of the World Cup itself in 1990 – an event that also led to massive investment in the country's football infrastructure, including a range of new or revamped stadiums.

It was during this decade that Berlusconi first 'entered the field' and became president of one of Italy's most historic and well-supported teams – AC Milan. He thus both contributed to and profited from the 'footbalisation' that reached down into all aspects of Italian society. Football was not just a sport, it was something that patterned lives, conversations and politics. AC Milan was a great club in a deep crisis. They had suffered two relegations in three seasons, one thanks to a shocking corruption scandal – *Totonero* – which saw players arrested in dressing rooms for match-fixing, and once because they were simply very bad on the pitch.

In 1986 Berlusconi purchased AC Milan. It had often been said that he was originally a fan of their great rivals – Inter Milan – but if he had been, he soon made a rapid conversion to the red and black side of the city. He announced his arrival with a typical flourish, landing by helicopter on the training ground during a pre-season break. Indro Montanelli, the conservative journalist who became one of Berlusconi's great enemies, was sceptical: 'The red and black fans are partying after hearing the news that Berlusconi has decided to buy their club. They are convinced that in a flash he will create a championship-winning, cup-winning team … and maybe they are right. There is just one danger. The new president might want to also be the technical director, the manager, the masseur, the captain and the striker. And all this could be acceptable. But there will be one other condition; he would also like to be the referee.'[76]

Berlusconi's footballing strategy was revolutionary. He would transform the Milan team on and off the pitch, bringing his entrepreneurial methods to bear on the company and using his televisual and advertising acumen to change football itself. As he said at the time, he wanted to 'Milanise Milan ... to import into the company those business-type methods and initiatives which would make the team represent our city'.[77] On the pitch, Berlusconi wanted a new kind of football. He employed a little-known manager with no Serie A experience – Arrigo Sacchi. He also looked abroad for new talent – bringing in the Dutch trio of Ruud Gullit, Frank Rijkaard and Marco Van Basten. Sacchi revolutionised tactical traditions, employing a high-pressing game and introducing an attack-at-all-costs mentality. *Catenaccio* – the defensive style and way of understanding football associated with Italy – was consigned to history. AC Milan swept all before them, winning Serie A in 1988, 1992, 1993, 1994, 1996, 1999, 2004 and 2011, but above all taking the European Cup/Champions League in 1989, 1990, 1994, 2003 and 2007. Fans flocked back to a restructured San Siro stadium (revamped for the World Cup in *Italia 90*) where season ticket holders peaked at 70,000 or so a year.

These victories and the manner with which they were achieved were closely associated with Berlusconi. He invested in the club – spending millions on top players – and attended games in the VIP section. He also, as Montanelli predicted, commented on tactics, the transfer market and individual performances. He took credit when the team won, and blamed someone else when they didn't. In a country where 26 million people declared that they were football fans, he could exploit the power of football. He also understood the universal value of sporting language – and he would later use this kind of language in his political campaigns and as a form of communication. Football gave Berlusconi visibility and authority. It also fused seamlessly with his media control and spread. Neo-calcio – a new form of the game designed above all for consumption via the screen, in the home, and through a series of programmes many of which were not strictly to do with the game at all – worked alongside and within the world of neo-television. By the early 1990s Berlusconi was a man of immense influence – through his media, sporting, advertising and construction interests. He had a network of powerful political allies and was a role model for many. Berlusconi had always been ahead of his time, able to understand and profit from the changes that were taking place all around him. But, like everyone else, he had no inkling about the remarkable events that were soon to overwhelm Italy. Suddenly, and quite unexpectedly, everything was about to change.

5

The Second Republic

Tangentopoli and *Clean Hands*: The Scandal and
Investigation that Ended the First Republic. 1992–3

'There seems no reason why the Clean Hands investigation
should not go on forever.'

Patrick McCarthy[1]

'A democracy that was bought and sold.'

Antonio Di Pietro[2]

Corruption scandals had come and gone during the first Italian
Republic. In the 1960s, for example, the 'banana scandal' saw
bribes handed over by banana importers. Petrol companies
dominated the scandals of the 1970s and 1980s, alongside air-
line companies (such as the American giant Lockheed). These
cases led directly to legislation for the public financing of
political parties (1974) – one of the most unpopular laws in
the history of the Republic. Further scandals were connected
to the provision of supplies to public companies, such as the
'golden prisons' scandal (expensive prison construction) and
'golden blankets' scandal (overpriced blankets for night trains).
The investigations were usually short-lived and left the system
itself intact.

This time it would be different. A corruption investigation and
a scandal would now overturn an entire political system. The first
act of the scandal took place in a sprawling municipal old people's

home, in Milan. This complex was known locally as *La Baggina* but its official name was the Pio Albergo Trivulzio. The institution was a hangover from Milan's glorious reformist past (it was built in 1910 and had roots that went back to the eighteenth century) and was owned by the local council. To be president of the Baggina was to hold the reins of a formidable set of resources and clientelistic contacts. Mario Chiesa, the president in 1992, had risen up the ranks of the city's powerful Socialist Party. He was one of the new guard in the party, on the fast track to power, and he was enjoying himself. Archive film showed him taking Bettino Craxi – his political boss – around the home and joking about the services on offer. Chiesa also lined his pockets and financed his party through illegal means. He would routinely ask suppliers to the old people's home to give him rake-offs on their contracts, in cash. This was common practice.

On 17 February 1992 a businessman who had been 'asked' to pay a bribe in this way (seven million lire, about £2,500 at the time) decided not to do so, and went to the police. He was wired up, and sent back to complete the deal. Chiesa, however, realised that something was wrong, and tried to flush the cash down the toilet. He was arrested and sent to the city's crumbling prison, San Vittore. Soon, he would name names. Like a deck of cards, the whole system came tumbling down. *Tangentopoli* ('Bribesville'), a name given to the scandal by the journalist Piero Colaprico, had begun.[3]

General elections were scheduled for 5 April 1992, just as the Chiesa case was beginning to hit the news. Bettino Craxi (leader of the Socialist Party) tried to employ the 'bad apple' theory, calling Chiesa a 'rascal' live on television. But the damage had been done, and things would soon get worse. All the major 'old' parties lost millions of votes in that election. The Christian Democratic vote fell below 30 per cent for the first time. Meanwhile, the newly formed Partito Democratico della Sinistra or PdS (the former Communist Party) won a mere 16.1 per cent of the vote (a fall of 10 per cent from five years earlier). This was a significant decline. Nearly four million voters had abandoned the party. Rifondazione Comunista – who had split over '*la svolta*' – got a sizeable 5.6 per cent. Italy's rigid party system was breaking up. New forces were making themselves heard. Some 3.3 million voters opted for the Lega Nord (the Northern League, who only stood in the north and centre of the country). In 1987 – the last general election – the Lega had barely registered. Mario Chiesa's confessions were a crack in a system that was, in any case, beginning to collapse.

Magistrates in Milan, using new powers granted them under recent judicial reforms, and forming themselves into a 'pool' as with the anti-Mafia magistrates in Palermo, began to unravel a network of corruption. The investigation was named 'Clean Hands'. Political kickbacks were linked to the construction of Milan's new 'yellow' Metro line, and to stadiums built for the 1990 World Cup. Politicians and businessmen were lined up to appear in the law courts and offices in Milan's imposing, fascist-built, Justice Palace in the centre of the city. It was clear that, by confessing, they would get off relatively lightly. Most chose to do so. Soon, the investigations had reached right to the top. Political support for the investigations came in from the Lega Nord, and opinion polls showed mass backing for the magistrates. A Lega Nord Deputy underlined his thirst for justice by displaying a noose in Parliament. In Perry Anderson's words, the Lega was 'the battering ram that weakened the struts of the traditional party system in Italy'.[4]

Many, many arrests and trials were to follow. Most of Italy's politicians would be seen in the dock, and often these trials were transmitted live on television. It was a procession, and the star of the show was a public prosecutor, a man from the South, whose manner was aggressive and whose grasp of Italian was not always perfect – Antonio Di Pietro. For a time, he was the most popular man in Italy. Some politicians stood up for themselves. They claimed that they had taken bribes, yes, but 'for the party' and to pay for the 'high costs of politics'. This very rarely turned out to be true (many had also amassed private fortunes). Moreover, it didn't wash with the public, who made little distinction between different 'forms' of corruption.

The very fact that this 'defence' was used showed how distant the political class was from public opinion. Bettino Craxi – one of the key figures in the whole *Tangentopoli* story – later said that everyone had paid something, and every party had received money, with no exceptions. The Chiesa arrest was the beginning of an almost endless number of legal procedures, investigations and trials. In 1993 Prime Minister Giuliano Amato (another Socialist) tried to close Clean Hands down, but the public was not ready to accept this 'political' road towards what was called 're-pacification'. There was a large appetite for justice. Some compared the televised trials to witch trials.

In September 1993 a man called Duilio Poggiolini was arrested in Switzerland – he had gone on the run. Few Italians had heard of him, but he was a powerful figure in the Italian health ministry and on various linked European and global institutions. He played a key role in the choice of drugs to be used within Italy's vast health service, and their price-fixing. The investigators found a surprising series of valuable items in Poggiolini's house in Naples – and he was soon dubbed the King Midas of the Health Service by the press. As one journalist wrote at the time, there were 'jewels, ancient forms of money, gold bars and diamonds ... when the *carabinieri* opened a safe, alongside a magistrate and a lawyer, they were stunned. Inside was a treasure-trove like that from *One Thousand and One Nights* ... or as described in stories about pirates'.[5] Attention soon centred on Poggiolini's wife, Pierr di Maria, who was also given a new ironic title in the media (in English) *Lady Poggiolini*. Much of the fortune seemed to belong to her, and some of it, it was claimed, was hidden in a pouffe. Both 'Lady Poggiolini' and Duilio Poggiolini spent months in prison, and confessed to taking bribes over an extensive period. After his wife's death in 2007, Poggiolini was later discovered – in 2015 – to be living in a poor-quality old people's home in Rome.

Clean Hands and *Tangentopoli* coincided with the rise of a new force in Italian politics, a social movement that attacked the political system itself and provided cheer-leaders for the anti-corruption magistrates. This movement was poised to take advantage of the political collapse brought about by the scandal.

Il Senatur: The Rise of Umberto Bossi and the Lega Nord

'Lombardy is a nation, Italy is only a state.'

Umberto Bossi, 1985[6]

The Lega Nord was officially founded in a notary's studio in December 1989 by nine men. One of them was Umberto Bossi, who had been born in a small town called Cassano Magnago in 1941. This administrative act brought together a number of small local 'leagues', including those from the rich, productive regions of Lombardy and the Veneto. Bossi's family was working class, and much of his past has remained somewhat mysterious. He had supposedly worked as a 'doctor', but there are no signs that he was ever qualified in medicine. He had also been a member of the Communist Party in the 1970s. Gianfranco Miglio (the early theoretician of the movement) once said of Bossi that 'he reads nothing. He has never read anything at all.'[7]

The journalist Sergio Romano described Bossi as 'charisma in search of something to do'.[8] Others have seen Bossi as having a 'strongly demagogic personality'.[9] A tall man with unfashionable glasses and unruly hair, Bossi spoke in a raucous roar, or rather, he shouted. He 'adopted the spoken language of everyday life'.[10] His oratory was rude and gendered and he famously gave an interview on a beach in an ordinary white vest.[11] Bossi was always scruffy. His jackets weren't tailor-made – instead they were almost deliberately ill-fitting. His hair looked like he had cut it himself. Not for him a villa in Sardinia or holidays in Antigua. Bossi took his holidays in a relatively nondescript mountain village in Italy. He didn't seem to care what he looked like and carefully cultivated his image as a man of the people. He appeared be 'a part of the social context to which his supporters belonged.'[12] Bossi was first elected to the Senate in 1987 (leading to his nickname, *Il Senatur*, a play on words linked to northern dialects and their use of the letter 'u'), proof that the movement had impressive concentrations of votes in some of its heartlands – the small-business-dominated provinces of Varese and Bergamo to the north and east of Milan.

Bossi was certainly nothing like any of the mainstream politicians from the First Republic, except perhaps some of those who
had been in the neo-fascist party. He claimed that the Lega had a
'hard-on' to show how tough they were. Some even came up with
the term 'hardonism' to define the Lega's way of doing things.
Bossi also once said that there were '300,000 martyrs' ready to
give their lives for the cause of federalism.[13] And, in a period when
he fell out with Berlusconi, he called the TV magnate – memorably – *BerlusKaiser*. Bossi was frequently racist, xenophobic, sexist
and homophobic. He was also extremely rude about the sacred
symbols of the Italian nation. In July 1997 he said during a meeting in nearby Como that 'when I see the Tricolor flag I get angry.
I use the Tricolor to wipe my arse.' And in September of the same
year, in response to an Italian flag flown from a window during a
Lega demonstration in Venice, Bossi advised the woman holding
the flag to 'put it ... in the toilet'. These phrases led to investigations into Bossi for the crime of 'Insults against the Flag'. In
one of these cases he was given a sixteen-month suspended prison
sentence many years later. But a change to the law in 2006 led to
this sentence being reduced to a small fine.

The Lega had made impressive electoral inroads in the north
before *Tangentopoli*. In 1991, for example, it topped the polls in
the industrial city of Brescia, ahead of the Christian Democrats
and former Communists. But it was the corruption scandals of
1992–4 that really opened up opportunities for the movement.
In addition, biting austerity policies introduced by successive
governments in the 1990s angered northern working-class voters.
Everything the Lega had been saying about the political class –
that it was corrupt, out of date, and ripping off northern Italy –
appeared to be confirmed. A Lega mayor was elected in Milan
in 1993, and Lega lists also performed well in regional elections.
There were even signs of a breakthrough beyond the north. The
Lega's anti-system message resonated with many voters.

Suddenly, with the Lega, Italy had a 'Northern Question'.
For so long, it had been the 'Southern Question' that had been
discussed and analysed. The Lega acknowledged the existence
of a Southern problem, but argued that instead of the North

subsidising the South, the North should be set free. This was not a national issue. It was the nation itself that was the issue. Lega propaganda also attempted to connect the nation it called Padania to other independence struggles – such as those in Scotland, Palestine and Catalonia.

In its early years, the other main enemies of the Lega were southern Italians (often referred to with the insulting term 'terroni') and 'the South' in general. The South, for the Lega, was a nebulous entity, and it was often merged with the state and politics *tout court*. Lega propaganda railed against 'Rome the big thief' (a city that the Lega promised it would 'not forgive') for collecting high taxes but providing nothing for the hard-working North. Bossi and the other *leghisti* used direct, blunt language – some of it violent. These voices and this anger would dominate the end of Italy's First Republic.

Tangentopoli and other corruption scandals provided rich material for Lega campaigns. The Lega was going to war – and for a long time it remained a permanent protest movement (or at least it claimed to be such), even when it was in government. The Lega was often known as '*il carroccio*' (a medieval mounted battle standard) after one of its references to past northern military struggles. Just as the main parties were ditching their symbols – the hammer and sickle, the crossed shield – along came the Lega with a whole new set to fit a new generation. The Lega's symbols were those of a warrior from the twelfth century – Alberto Da Giussano – who had supposedly defeated the Holy Roman Emperor, Frederick Barbarossa, at a place called Legnano. This was a powerful founding myth. Da Giussano was depicted in his armour, sword in the air. Journalists flocked towards this new movement with its shocking way of doing politics. The Lega was aided by 'the free publicity provided by the media's reporting of Umberto Bossi's outrageous style of campaigning'.[14]

Lega slogans – often used on posters – carried a clear message. Pictures of potential immigrants with the word '*Basta!*' ('Stop!'), or of Muslims praying with the phrase 'Fuori dalle balle' ('Get Them Out'). Other slogans attacked Traveller communities. 'Racial discourse became widespread via the media presence of the Lega Nord.'[15] This was years before the infamous 'Breaking Point' poster produced by the Leave campaign during the Brexit referendum campaign in the United Kingdom. Lega slogans screamed a sense of injustice: 'IL NORD PAGA PER TUTTI' ('THE NORTH IS PAYING FOR EVERYONE'), and it announced clearly that enough was enough: 'BASTA TASSE A ROMA (NO MORE TAXES FOR ROME!)'.

It was clear that by the mid-1990s the Lega was a strong political force. After taking 8.7 per cent of the national vote in 1992 (and 17.9 per cent in the North), in the 1996 election the Lega plundered a stunning 29 per cent of the vote in the Veneto and 26 per cent in Lombardy. The Lega was a social movement, which attracted those opposed to globalisation and Europeanisation (it was anti-EU and anti-euro). Lega propaganda also promised law and order and a crackdown on corruption. It called for tax cuts and occasionally asked its followers to stop paying taxes altogether (a tax strike). *Tangentopoli* provided the perfect backdrop for Lega propaganda, with politicians, tax officials, businessmen and state employees caught feeding off the system and justifying the high costs of the political system. Lega cries of 'Basta!' found a deep resonance as the political personalities from the First Republic were put on trial.

The Manager: Carlo 'il bello'

He didn't look anything like a criminal, yet Carlo Sama was a key figure in the *Tangentopoli* investigations and trials. He played a central role in the sensational Enimont trial (which began in October 1993 and lasted six months, with fifty-one hearings and 117 witnesses – including two former Prime Ministers and seven other ministers who were called to testify). It was during this trial that the mechanisms linked to the illegal distribution of public and private funds to the political parties were laid bare.

A top-level businessman and 'manager', Sama calmly told the court about the exact amounts he had paid to political parties and

who had received the money. Beautifully turned out and coif-
fured (he was known as 'Carlo il bello' – 'Carlo the good-looking
one'), he seemed to see the distribution of money to politicians
as just another part of his job. In many ways, this was true. In
1988 the state-run energy giant ENI had fused with the equally
big Montedison company. What emerged was a massive chemical conglomerate. All political parties were paid off to sweeten
the deal. This gigantic set of kickbacks was given a name by the
press – the *superbribe*.

Sama's matter-of-fact tone was deeply revealing about the normality of corruption in the First Republic. Those involved didn't
even see what they were doing as a crime, or wrong in any way.
This was the way things were done. Some politicians, such as the
Liberal Party leader of the time, Renato Altissimo, attempted
to defend themselves by saying that 'they hadn't asked' for the
money but that they had nonetheless 'thanked' Sama for his political contribution. Many of those arrested during *Tangentopoli*
had broken the law on the financing of political parties (a relatively minor offence). Parties were publicly funded, but this had
done little to slow down the flow of corruption. Even a new anti-
corruption movement such as the Lega Nord had been paid off –
getting their own slice of the pie. Umberto Bossi defended the
bribe, even though he claimed he knew nothing about it. He said
it was a lifeline for a young movement in need of funding.[16]

Trial by Television: The Cusani Trial

Tangentopoli quickly became part of the 'society of spectacle'.
Many of its key moments were played out on television, above
all through certain trials. As the journalist Pino Corrias stated in
his magnificent four-part TV documentary on *Tangentopoli*, 'For
months, every day ... the collapse of the First Republic was shown
on television, a collapse that was told every day in the courtroom
during the Cusani trial, and which the Italians watched live.'[17]
The key televisual moment of the scandal (which was, in reality,
a complicated set of investigations) was the trial of Sergio Cusani

(also known as the Enimont Trial), a former left militant who had become a kind of middleman for the party system and various public bodies – as well as a high-level financial advisor.

Costly bribes had been paid to favour the break-up of two big companies, after a failed merger. Cusani (like Carlo 'il bello') had been given the task of paying off the parties, one by one. He was a mediator – a crucial role in post-war Italy. A series of politicians were called to testify. Some of them had been central figures in the First Republic. In many cases their power would soon be slipping away. Cusani spent four years in prison. Unlike almost all of the politicians who were found guilty, he served his time.

Tangentopoli attracted big audiences. Presenters and reporters took up fixed spots outside the law courts and the prisons in Milan, and some became famous on the back of their time on screen during *Tangentopoli*. Ironically, perhaps, it was the Fininvest journalists (working for Berlusconi) who were able to make the most of the spectacular features of the scandals. The chit-chat between anchor-man and arch-Berlusconi loyalist Emilio Fede in the studio and timid reporter Paolo Brosio on the street outside the law courts was highly entertaining and dramatic. *Tangentopoli* was good for advertising revenue. It was another example of the 'TV of pain' that enjoyed such a high level of popularity in that period – another long-term product of little Alfredino Rampi's death in the well in 1981.

The Functionary: Severino Citaristi

Tangentopoli was a very bad time for those who held posts that had never garnered much interest amongst the public – the treasurers of the major political parties. It was difficult not to feel a little sorry for the ageing and frail treasurer of the Christian Democrats, Severino Citaristi, who nobody had really heard of before the scandal broke. His was a classic case of being in the wrong place at the wrong time. Citaristi became involved in over seventy different investigations. It had been his job to collect and cash the bribes. But now he was testifying live on television. He ended up with a long prison sentence and a huge fine to pay. Yet, given his age, he managed to avoid jail. In any case, Citaristi was not the main target of the investigations – he was the monkey, not the organ-grinder.

Much more damaging overall was the court testimony of the Christian Democratic bigwig Arnaldo Forlani on 17 February 1993. Forlani (unlike Craxi) claimed he had no prior knowledge of any wrongdoing and said that Citaristi had 'a bad memory' (to much laughter in the courtroom). He issued a blanket denial that many saw as ridiculous and unlikely to be true: 'I have never been involved with political funding. I did not know that some contributions had been received in ways that violated the law governing party funding. I found this out by reading the papers.' The political class that had governed Italy for so long still didn't get it. They had convinced themselves that the system was somehow a logical and justifiable one, cutting themselves off from the real world and creating what would later be called a privileged 'caste'. As he was harangued by Antonio Di Pietro – whose basic Italian was both brutal and direct – Forlani's nerves were betrayed by a fleck of white spittle that dribbled out of his mouth. It was a psycho-drama, being played out live on television, in front of national audiences.

Tangentopoli both helped to cause and marked the end of the First Republic. A series of politicians and parties had taken regular kickbacks (and paid them out) and they had been happy to do so. They had queued up to get their share, which they had seen as being due to them by right. But it wasn't their money. A corrupt system was exposed, for all to see. *Tangentopoli* soon spread from Milan to other cities. Between 1992 and 1994 some 12,000 people were placed under investigation across Italy and at least 5,000 people were arrested.

The trauma of *Tangentopoli* was accompanied by suicides (at least ten of them) and mysterious deaths. On 23 July 1993 Raul Gardini shot himself in the head. His body was found in his bedroom in the beautiful Palazzo Belgioioso right in the centre of Milan. He was still wearing his dressing gown and was found by his butler. Gardini had got up, eaten his breakfast, and read the newspapers. He left a note for his three children and his wife. It contained just one word: 'Grazie'. Gardini felt that his arrest was imminent. He was a central figure in the Enimont investigations. Gardini was a powerful businessman in the chemical industry, a public figure in Italian life and a striking and charismatic man. And like many other industrialists and businessmen, he had paid off the political parties to obtain favours and, quite simply, because this was how things worked.

On 20 July 1993 Gabriele Cagliari committed suicide in San Vittore prison by pulling a plastic bag over his head in the shower. He was sixty-seven years old. Some commentators later claimed that he had been murdered. Cagliari was another very powerful man. At the time of his arrest he was president of the vast state-run electro-chemical-petrol multinational company ENI. He had been in San Vittore for four months. Cagliari had written a letter home to his family complaining about his treatment: 'For these magistrates,' he wrote, 'we are not allowed a future, a life ... I am convinced that these magistrates see prison as an instrument of their work, a form of psychological torture ... they are taking us on a road towards authoritarianism. I don't want to go there.' The letter remained unsent before his death.[18]

Decade of Austerity

Tangentopoli's political crisis coincided with high levels of austerity. High public spending was no longer possible nor acceptable in a post-Cold War world. Communism was no longer a threat. The largesse of Italy's welfare state, with its generous 'baby pensions' (awarded to some state employees after just twenty years of service), was no longer sustainable. Italy was not a front-line state in a war (against communism) any more. It was on its own. Moreover, the post-industrial boom of the 1980s had proved to be short-lived. Italy had high levels of public debt and creaking state services. As politicians resigned en masse, and parties wobbled, Italy turned to post-political, technical and emergency governments. Drastic cuts were announced. Italy, it was said, needed to get its finances under control to meet the requirements of the Maastricht Treaty.

Giuliano Amato, a Socialist and economist, presided over the first of these austerity administrations, between June 1992 and April 1993. Taxes were increased and, in an extraordinary move, money was taken directly from millions of private bank and post-office accounts and transferred to the state. Amato did a deal with the trade unions, but many workers were unhappy, and violence returned to the streets of Italy. In October 1992 a Catholic trade union leader was struck in the face by metal screws as he spoke to a crowd of angry workers in Milan.

Amato's government was followed in April 1993 by an admin-istration led by a man who had not been elected to Parliament – Carlo Azeglio Ciampi, President of the Bank of Italy. Having a non-parliamentarian as head of the administration (allowed for by the constitution, but rare) would become increasingly common in the years to come. Ciampi wanted to have former Communist ministers in his cabinet (for the first time since 1947), but dra-matic events in Parliament caused a crisis almost before his gov-ernment had started work.

On 29 April deputies were asked to vote on six motions to authorise investigations into Bettino Craxi arising from *Tangentopoli*. A majority refused to do so in four of the cases put before them. This was also the occasion of Craxi's last speech to Parliament. He had already resigned as Secretary of the Socialist Party – in February 1993 (after his first *avviso di garanzia* – a warning that he was under investigation). In his speech Craxi quoted himself from a previous speech to Parliament made in July 1992. He more or less confessed to breaking the law, saying that:

> everyone is aware that a good part of political funding is irregular or illegal. The parties have newspapers, carry out campaigning, run associations and possess different and often extensive structures ... and they often collect funds in irregular and illegal ways. If a good part of this is to be considered as a purely criminal activity, then a great part of the system itself is criminal.[19]

But Craxi denied any corruption for personal gain. He defended his political record ('I have stood in ten electoral campaigns') with vigour and attacked the magistrates for their investigations and tactics. He also accused others of hypocrisy. Craxi's speech ended with a long citation from a letter left by the Socialist deputy Sergio Moroni, who had shot himself in the mouth after being placed under investigation for corruption involving waste collection and the railway system. Moroni was suffering from kidney cancer at the time. He complained in the letter about the media coverage of *Tangentopoli*. 'I do not believe,' he wrote, 'that our country will be able to build the future it deserves by creating a pogrom-like atmosphere towards the political class.'[20] In protest at Parliament's decision regarding Craxi's legal issues, the former Communist ministers resigned from Ciampi's government. They had only just been sworn in. It was an inauspicious start.

Raining Coins

After Craxi was 'cleared' by his parliamentary colleagues, there were press reports of a party in the Hotel Raphael in central Rome – where Craxi had stayed during his periods in the capital since the 1970s – with Silvio Berlusconi in attendance. On 30 April 1993 Craxi walked out of the hotel, as he had done so many times before. But this time it was different. There were no adoring fans. Instead, an angry crowd was there to greet him. They threw coins and lighters, and held out banknotes saying '*Prenditi anche queste*' ('Take this as well'). Others invoked 'prison' for the former Prime Minister. Some were more judgemental: 'Shame on you'. It was said to be 'raining coins'. *La Stampa* wrote that there was a '*clima da anni di piombo*' ('a climate like that during the years of lead' – the period of political violence in the 1970s).[21]

Six months later, at the end of October 1993, under pressure from public opinion and from the magistrates, Parliament voted to abolish parliamentary immunity altogether for investigations into deputies and senators. This immunity had been part of the

1948 constitution and had been designed to protect parliamentarians against excessive judicial interference. A parliamentary vote would now only be required before arrests and to authorise phone-taps. Bettino Craxi continued to receive *'avvisi di garanzia'* (notifications that he was under investigation) – the final total was twenty-six. He stood down as a candidate in the next elections, held early (again) in 1994. This meant he could now be arrested at any time. As a result, he decided to flee the country, becoming officially a fugitive from justice. It was an astonishing fall from grace for the man who had held the office of Prime Minister for over a thousand days during the 1980s and whose face had been all over election posters as recently as 1992.

The authorities tried to take away Craxi's passport (in reality he had two passports), but he had already departed. On 21 March 1994 Craxi was driven to the airport in the company of his son, Bobo. He then took a private jet from Ciampino Airport in Rome for Tunisia, where he had a holiday home (in a place called Hammamet) and political connections. It was said that he had hired the plane from his friend, the mineral-water businessman and fascist sympathiser Giuseppe Ciarrapico. Craxi's wife Anna was already in Tunisia. Bettino Craxi would never return to Italy. In January 2000 he died in Tunisia and was buried there. His tomb, in white marble, carries the epigraph *'La mia libertà equivale alla mia vita'* ('My freedom is the same as my life').

Presidents and Power

During the First Republic, while the major parties were strong, the President of Italy remained more than a figurehead. But in a crisis, and as the party system began to wane and collapse in the 1980s and 1990s, the head of state suddenly became central, and rather powerful. Those powers that had appeared as largely symbolic now appeared decisive. Snap elections – outside of the normal five-year cycle – became common, and emergency governments almost the norm. These were administrations made up largely of 'experts' as opposed to politicians, and tasked with specific short-term aims such as the passing of emergency budgets. All of this was overseen by various Presidents, starting with Francesco Cossiga (President from 1985 to 1992) and followed by Oscar Luigi Scalfaro (1992–9), Carlo Azeglio Ciampi (1999–2006) and Giorgio Napolitano (2006–13).

Moreover, all laws required presidential approval. In the past, this had usually been little more than a rubber stamp. Luigi Einaudi, President from 1948 to 1955, refused to sign a mere four of the 3,000 laws he was presented with during his term of office. But as the First Republic came to a shuddering halt extensive negotiations over laws (and the appointment of ministers) began to become the norm. Institutional conflicts flared up between various sectors of the state. The Italian President has always been the representative of the nation – the fatherland – and its figurehead. But Italy's crisis of the nation state in the 1980s and 1990s and the rise of the Lega led to an increase in 'constitutional patriotism'. The centrepiece of this form of patriotism was identified by many Italians as the President of the Republic.

Presidents started to try to appear above (and against) the political system, as the system itself disintegrated. Francesco Cossiga had been as integral to the power of the Christian Democrats as it was possible to imagine. But in the early 1990s he suddenly started attacking the parties and became known as '*Il picconatore*' ('The demolisher'). In 1991 he said that 'we can no longer mess about now. It's time to demolish things ... I have undermined the system so much that it cannot survive and must be changed.' At the time these seemed little more than the ravings of someone detached from reality. However, again in hindsight, Cossiga's populist popularity at the time was illuminating, prefiguring a shift to personality over party.

'Their faces are like their arses': Satire and *Cuore*

Tangentopoli also led to a boom in satire. A new satirical newspaper called *Cuore* (*Heart*) enjoyed its greatest period of popularity as the scandals struck Italy.²² A kind of political *Private Eye*, *Cuore* was famous for its headlines: 'They have formed the same government as before, we will use the same headline "Their faces are like their arses" – again'. Another popular joke was about the clocks going back (something known as 'Legal time' in Italian). The headline was 'Legal time has begun. The Socialists are panicking'. *Cuore* built on a solid satirical tradition that had started way back before fascism, and been continued by the sophisticated newspaper parodies of magazines such as *Il Male* and other publications. Beginning in the pages of the Communist daily *L'Unità* before going it alone for a while, *Cuore* encapsulated a desire to speak truth to power, at last, and ridicule those who had ruled Italy for so long.

And it was not just about the headlines. Other regular columns were all the rage – such as a readers' vote on 'What is it that makes life worth living?' (most of the winners were usually to do with sexual acts) and others such as 'The ugliest churches in Italy' (a critique of the devastating effects of post-modernist architecture in Italy). *Mai più senza* ('I have to have this') was dedicated to useless consumerist items, whilst another rubric satirised the trend for the use of absurd names for shops in Italy, often with inappropriate English words, such as *Occhial House* (a real optician, in Milan), or a shop called *Sexy Wig* (in Rome). *Cuore* also featured serious satire and journalism, but it was its strong sense of fun and silliness that marked it out from the rest of the left-leaning press at the time, with its depressing tendency to take itself very seriously indeed. *Cuore* festivals aped those of the former Communist Party, but were far more creative. Yet *Cuore*'s success was short-lived. After the end of the First Republic, reality began to outpace satire itself. The jokes in *Cuore* had worn thin.

Other new satirical forms – on television as well as in the newsstands – accompanied the spectacular collapse of the First Republic. *Blob* – a daily evening slot that knitted together clips from various television channels in a brilliant and inventive way – was a big success. Politicians became more vulnerable, and satire was politicised and bolder. Previously, most television satire was safe and conservative, and politicians would often appear alongside their 'satirists'. Comedians dressed as politicians would exchange lame 'risqué' jokes with presenters and showgirls. Those who attacked the ruling political class, such as the comedian Beppe Grillo, who compared Socialists to 'thieves' on TV in 1986, were banished from state television.

Now more cutting and dangerous programmes began to emerge. *Avanzi!*, broadcast between 1991 and 1993, was a mix of satire and surreal comedy, where impressions of politicians and others had much more of an edge (particularly those invented by brother and sister Corrado and Sabrina Guzzanti, some of which were based on real people, while others were 'types' taken from Italian society). Politicians were no longer safe from public ridicule and hatred. Numerous shows also fed off the corruption crisis, making their shock-jock presenters (like the eccentric Gianfranco Funari) famous almost overnight. News outlets covered the scandals as rolling news, with constant updates of arrests and rumours of further developments, which were often leaked to journalists by magistrates.

Illustrious Corpses

As Italy's political class disintegrated, the Mafia extracted its revenge on those who had betrayed its trust, or had placed its men behind bars. In March 1992 Salvo Lima, a powerful Christian Democratic politician and a mediator between the party and the Mafia in Sicily, was being driven to Palermo. Suddenly, a gunman blew out the tyres on the car. Lima knew what was coming next. He ran. But these were professionals. Two shots finished him off, before the killers sped off on a motorbike. Lima had failed, in the eyes of the Mafia, to overturn the results of the maxi-trials. His bloodstained body, badly covered in a sheet, surrounded by bored-looking uniformed cops, was also a warning to Rome. Giulio Andreotti was in the front row at Lima's funeral. He knew that the signs coming from Palermo were not good ones for his own political prospects.

Giovanni Falcone and Paolo Borsellino were aware that they were marked men. The Mafia was gunning for those who had inspired the *maxiprocesso*. Their first target was Falcone – and the date is etched in the history of Italy – 23 May 1992. Falcone was fifty-three years old. The preparations for the attack were elaborate. A skateboard was used to place some 500 kilos of explosives underneath the motorway that runs from Palermo's airport to the city itself. Falcone had earlier flown in with his wife, the magistrate Francesca Morvillo. They were due to go on holiday.

Unusually for a man with such high levels of police protection, Falcone decided that he would drive. Some 400 metres away, up on the hills, stood seven men who would carry out the explosion. They chain-smoked as they waited for Falcone's entourage. Fifty-one cigarette stubs were later discovered at the scene. These stubs would provide DNA traces to identify those who set off the explosives. An extensive hole was blown in the motorway by the bomb, which killed three bodyguards instantly. Falcone and his wife, whose car crashed into the crater left by the blast, died soon afterwards, in hospital. If Falcone had been sitting in the back, he might have survived the blast. The film director Paolo Sorrentino later recreated the bomb attack in his semi-fictional biopic based around the life of Giulio Andreotti – *Il Divo*. The mangled remains of one of the cars were preserved as a reminder of the tragedy. Many of Sicily's citizens refused to accept this murder. A social movement was born, and it took to the streets. Sheets were held up outside windows as a sign of protest.[23]

One of the widows from the so-called Capaci massacre (named after the site of the bomb attack) was called Rosaria Schifani (wife of Vito). Rosaria made a passionate speech at her husband's funeral, fighting back the tears. She started reading a text, but then diverted from her script, speaking 'in the name of those who have given their life for the state' and then adding, with a sigh, 'the state!' Rosaria then spoke directly to the 'men of the Mafia' 'because some of them are in here ... they are certainly not Christians'. 'Even you,' she continued 'can be pardoned for your sins. I forgive you, but you should go down on your knees ...

but they won't change.'[24] In Rome, Parliament was pushed into electing an outside candidate for the Presidency, just two days after Falcone's death. The new head of state was a conservative Christian Democrat called Oscar Luigi Scalfaro – and he would be inflexible in his defence of the state and legality during his time in office.[25]

Falcone's death was not the end of the horror. His murder was only the beginning of a full-scale Mafia war against the state. Next on the Mafia's hit-list was Paolo Borsellino – close friend and collaborator of Falcone. Borsellino would also be killed by a bomb, but this time the murder would take place in the city of Palermo. Borsellino often visited his mother, and it was there that the Mafia struck. A massive car bomb was prepared and parked outside her house. As Borsellino arrived on 19 July 1992 in Via d'Amelio, there was a huge explosion. Another five bodyguards (one of whom was a woman) died alongside Borsellino himself. Borsellino's death, added to that of Falcone, shocked Italy to the core. Just fifty-seven days separated the murders. When Rome's politicians turned up for the funeral of Borsellino's bodyguards in Palermo, the mourners tried to attack them, breaking through police cordons. Italy's new head of state – Scalfaro – and its police chief looked terrified as they were saved from the crowds, who chanted 'Fuori la mafia dallo stato' ('Get the Mafia out of the state'). Italy had reached breaking point.

In the years that followed, numerous roads and squares all over Italy were dedicated to Falcone and Borsellino. A celebrated photo of the two men, taken by Tony Gentile a few months before their murders, on 27 March 1992, became 'one of the most widespread vehicles of public memory for the two heroic magistrates' and was used during demonstrations and on T-shirts and protest 'sheets'.[26] The image is powerful because of its context. As Gentile himself says, 'What makes the photo moving is the understanding between the two, the bond of trust that unites them, the laugh that reveals their great friendship. They are like two great friends meeting in a bar. Borsellino's face radiates serenity. Neither seems weighed down by his role. And, above all, there is the fact that both were killed by the Mafia within two months of one another.'²⁷ The photo has become 'one of the most iconic photographs in Italian history', which symbolises 'an act of resurrection of the dead judges'.²⁸

Italy had failed to protect those who had served the state. But the Mafia were not finished yet. The war against the state showed no signs of slowing down. In May 1993 the Mafia moved to a new level. Its attack was now against Italy itself. On 27 May a bomb exploded in the centre of Florence, close to the celebrated Uffizi art gallery, one of the most visited museums in the world. Five people were killed, including a fifty-day-old baby. Two months later, further blasts hit Milan and Rome, destroying a museum and damaging two churches, and killing another five people in the northern city (three firefighters, a traffic policeman and an immigrant who was sleeping on a park bench). The Mafia was using its military power to destabilise the country and spread terror. One of its key demands was linked to its many members who were now locked up.

It is claimed that the state (or sections of it) negotiated with the Mafia in this period. This alleged series of discussions is sometimes called '*La Trattativa*' ('The Negotiation'). The agreement supposedly reached between these two parties is the subject of much controversy. But if these scandalous talks did take place, then the key issue on the table was to do with those bosses who had ended up behind bars.

Mafiosi in Prison

In the wake of the Falcone massacre in May 1992, and to try and break the link between leading *mafiosi* and their organisations in the outside world, prison rules were tightened still further. This led to a temporary set of measures known generically as the '41-bis', and subject to parliamentary scrutiny. The 41-bis rules applied to certain *mafiosi* and others. They cut down on family visits (adding a plastic screen between the relatives and the prisoner) and created a situation of relative isolation and lack of contact with other prisoners, lawyers and outsiders. This change of regime is graphically represented in the first series of the TV version of Roberto Saviano's *Gomorra*. Camorra boss Don Pietro Savastano moves from Naples' old-style Poggioreale prison, where he is able to phone to the outside world and send messages through his family to the organisation in the city, to a more modern 41-bis regime where he begins to lose touch with his foot soldiers in Naples itself.

Some argue that the controversial so-called 'discussions' between the state and the Mafia, which are said to have taken place between 1992 and 1993, focused on the application of the 41-bis measures. The Mafia hated the 41-bis rules and did all they could to get them to be relaxed. In this period in 1993 those held under this regime fell from over a thousand to fewer than five hundred. This is sometimes seen as evidence that the state made direct concessions to the Mafia in exchange for the end of the bombing campaign. The Minister of Justice who ordered the relaxation of 41-bis measures was called Giovanni Conso. As John Dickie writes, he 'offered the explanation that this act of clemency was a purely personal initiative, aimed at sending out an accommodating signal'.[29] Over the years, this set of measures was renewed on various occasions and subject to other reforms in 2002. The thought that concessions were made to the Mafia in this way, what Dickie dubs 'negotiating by bomb', is one that haunts the history of this period.

Lawyers took the 41-bis measures to the European Parliament – forming an alliance with human rights organisations. The Mafia also went public with a series of protests. In July 2002 Mafia boss Leoluca Bagarella (who was being held under the 41-bis regime) read out a 'statement' during a trial. 'I am speaking in the name of all those prisoners held in L'Aquila prison under the 41-bis regime. We are tired of being used, humiliated and treated as pawns in political games.'[30] Bagarella rarely spoke in public, so his words were significant. After ten minutes, the judge stopped him and ordered that the text of his speech be seized by police.

The Mafia also used other spaces to publicise their cause. During a football match between Palermo and Ascoli in

Palermo's *La Favorita* stadium on 22 December 2002, a strange 7-metre-long banner appeared on the terraces. It read 'Uniti contro il 41 bis: Berlusconi dimentica la Sicilia' ('United against the 41 bis: Berlusconi is forgetting about Sicily). This was a clear message to the then Prime Minister Silvio Berlusconi, and it was one that came directly from the Mafia itself. It later transpired that Mafia bosses from the Brancaccio zone of the city had taken the banner to the stadium. In February 2003, Italy's President Carlo Azeglio Ciampi visited the Fondazione Sciascia in the town of Racalmuto where Leonardo Sciascia, the great Italian writer and intellectual, had been born in 1921. He was faced with a written protest on the wall of the Fondazione: 'Uniti contro il 41 bis'.

Did these protests work? There has been a long debate around this issue. Some argue that the relative relaxation of some of the prison rules and the transition of certain bosses to a more relaxed environment is evidence of a conspiracy between the state and the Mafia, or even an 'agreement' between organised criminals and political elites. Many experts claim that the 41-bis has worked, and should be kept in place. Yet we should not forget that Falcone was a key figure in the setting up of national coordinated anti-Mafia structures based on those which had worked so well in Palermo. These organisations were to 'utterly transform the fight against the mafias'.[31] Falcone's sacrifice had not been in vain.

Neo-Post-Fascism

As the Cold War ended, so did the political limbo of the neo-fascists, who had operated mainly within a party called the Movimento Sociale Italiano (MSI). The MSI had been kept out of the corridors of national power since 1945. A brief flirtation with a centre-right alliance in 1960 had ended in violence, and had not been attempted again, and the neo-fascists were still seen as beyond the pale in the 1980s. In 1987 Bettino Craxi had shocked many by simply holding a meeting with the neo-fascist politician

Gianfranco Fini. The 1990s would see the neo-fascists play a central part in both central and local government. From political outcasts they would end up holding the reins of power. This process became known as the *sdoganamento* – the 'bringing back into the fold' – of the neo-fascists.

Fini understood that the end of communism also had repercussions for the right, whose anti-communism had been a key part of its identity. He attempted to renew his own party ranks – adopting a new name less linked to historic aspects of fascism (Alleanza Nazionale) and shifting the party away from direct support for the legacy of the Mussolini years – above all over the shameful anti-Semitic laws of 1938.[32] In 1995 Fini would lead his party into their own *svolta* during a congress in a place called Fiuggi in central Italy. The Fiuggi congress wound up the Movimento Sociale Italiano officially in favour of Alleanza Nazionale and 'recognised' anti-fascism as a 'value'. A small splinter group broke away but remained on the margins of national politics. Post-fascism was now a reality. *Tangentopoli* represented an opportunity for the MSI, which had been largely outside of the system and had relatively 'clean hands' compared to many other mainstream parties. Along with the Lega, the MSI and later Alleanza Nazionale were the most fervent supporters of the anti-corruption magistrates.

It was, however, clear that the move away from explicit fascism had not been linear or straightforward. Many militants and elected representatives from the Movimento Sociale Italiano/Alleanza Nazionale held onto their neo-fascist (or simply fascist) views and refused to alter judgements concerning Mussolini or his twenty-year period of dictatorship, the *ventennio*. In fact, once in power they often pushed for commemorations linked to the Fascist period to be revived and intervened over street names and monuments linked to Mussolini's regime. This rehabilitation of Italy's Fascist past was aided by the words and actions of some Communist and post-Communist politicians, who urged Italians to try to understand the 'young boys' who had fought for Mussolini. It seems that many wanted to move on from the anti-fascist consensus that had been at the heart of the 1948 Constitution. Even the supposedly moderate Fini had described Mussolini as 'the greatest statesman of the twentieth century' (although he later said he had changed his mind). Moreover, the anti-political features that had marked the MSI out when it had been excluded from the system now began to disappear. Once in power these supposedly 'pure' politicians acted very much like all the rest. Their hands did not remain 'clean' for very long.

The Second Republic, the *Mattarellum* and the End of the Christian Democrats

As *Tangentopoli* raged on, with endless trials, resignations and arrests, early elections were called for 1994. They would be the first elections of the so-called Second Republic. In some ways, this was merely a label to apply to a sense of change, as the old parties disappeared and new leaders and movements emerged. But the term Second Republic was also an accurate reflection of structural changes to the constitution and the political structure of Italy, such as drastic reforms to the electoral system.

Unlikely figures emerged as reformers in this period. Mario Segni, a moderate, fresh-faced Christian Democratic politician (and son of a former President of the Republic), had inspired a campaign to change Italy's electoral system of proportional representation. In June 1991 – before the *Tangentopoli* scandals that began in 1992 – nearly 27 million Italians turned out to vote on a measure that removed preference votes. In the previous electoral system, voters could indicate preferences for large numbers of candidates as well as opting for a political party. Preference votes had been a part of corrupt voting conventions for some time – combinations of preferences would be agreed to check people had voted the right way. The major parties all called for the status quo to be maintained in the referendum and Bettino Craxi famously advised voters to 'go to the seaside' instead of voting. The scale of the rejection of his advice (a massive 62.5 per cent of Italians voted, and over 95 per cent chose to get rid of preferences) was

a sign of things to come. In the spring of 1993 – in the middle
of *Tangentopoli* itself – a further referendum got rid of the PR
system for the Upper House. For a time, on the back of these referendum campaigns, Segni was flavour of the month and a possible candidate for Prime Minister, although he quickly faded from
political prominence.

Parliament was now obliged to come up with a new electoral
law. What they decided was something of a mess – and would only
be used in three subsequent general elections. It became known –
thanks to the Italian political scientist Giovanni Sartori – as the
Mattarellum. This epithet referred to the Italian politician and
future President of Italy Sergio Mattarella – who helped to put
together the law – but was also a play on words referring to the
Italian term for 'crazy' – *matto*.

The law was indeed a little crazy. Three-quarters of seats would
now be decided on a first-past-the-post system similar to that of
the United Kingdom. The other 25 per cent were to be assigned
through a fiendishly complicated set of different PR systems.
Only nerdy psephologists really understood, for example, the
'd'Hondt method' used for some of the Senate seats. In any case,
the PR 'section' of the vote provided a safety net for powerful
politicians if they lost their seats. Heaven forbid that some important politicians might fail to be elected. Italians now had three
ballot papers – two for the Lower House and one for the Upper
House. Some were as large as pillowcases. It took time for the
law to bed in – constituencies had never been a part of the Italian
system. The idea (in theory) was to create a system that would
allow for different coalitions and parties to win elections and govern, with direct links between elected politicians and a defined
electorate. The new system, it was argued, would 'unblock' the
structures of the First Republic. It would be difficult, however, to
define the law as a success.

One effect of this new electoral system was to force parties
and groupings into pre-electoral alliance pacts. Previously, alliances would be formed after the election (although these coalitions often remained the same for years). Now, they needed to
be agreed before voters went to the polls. The left moved quickly

to adapt to this change and, as the campaign for the 1994 elections, with this new system, began, it looked very much like the so-called Alleanza dei Progressisti or Progressive Alliance, formed by Achille Occhetto (who now led the former Communist Party) and encompassing a series of centre-left and left-wing parties and groups, would sweep to victory.

Meanwhile, the Christian Democrats were in disarray. The party had already split, as Mario Segni and other modernisers left to form a separate centre-left grouping. Under immense pressure, Mino Martinazzoli, leader of the Christian Democrats in 1993–4, followed the Communist Party in changing his party's name. He chose a name from the past – the Partito Popolare Italiano or PPI – a reference to Italy's first moderate Catholic political grouping, formed in 1919. The PPI stood on a centre-left platform. The party that had governed Italy for the entire post-war period had rapidly disappeared and split into different parts, under pressure from *Tangentopoli*.

An important group of Christian Democratic politicians moved off to the centre-right, forming yet another new party. Other Christian Democratis chose a series of paths, from left to the far right. The unity imposed by the Cold War, which had kept such a disparate group of people together for so long, was gone. The idea of one overarching Catholic party seemed out of date. It was an historic moment and incredibly, nobody really noticed. The Christian Democrats went down with barely a whimper. With their collapse and re-branding and the imminent disappearance of the Socialists, who were now without Craxi as figurehead, there seemed little doubt that Occhetto and his Progressive Alliance were guaranteed an easy victory in 1994. But then, almost from nowhere, another figure stepped into the void. He would define himself as a 'man of destiny'.

Taking the Field: Berlusconi Enters Politics, 1993–4

'Italy is the country I love.'

Silvio Berlusconi, 1994

Silvio Berlusconi's first direct entry into politics took place in November 1993, when he held a press conference in Rome. He surprised everyone on that occasion by backing the neo-fascist but seemingly moderate politician Gianfranco Fini as Mayor of Rome (run-off elections were about to be held for that post). Berlusconi declared that 'if he was Roman, he would vote for ... Fini'. Many still saw the neo-fascist party as politically untouchable and journalists at Berlusconi's faithful weekly magazine, *Panorama*, went on strike in protest. When a foreign journalist at the press conference pointed to the crimes of fascism, Berlusconi stated that Fini had been 'born in 1952', that fascism 'ended fifty years ago', and that his work in the media over twenty years or so proved that he was 'outside of these kinds of ideologies'. He said that the journalist should be ashamed of himself.

It was clear that Berlusconi was ready to build alliances that overcame those from the past, and he had little patience for prevailing political orthodoxies. His performance at the press conference was also a sign of things to come, as he denounced communism as an ideology that had been 'rejected by history' and had led to 'poverty, terror and death'. Communism had barely survived the end of the Cold War, but anti-communism was alive and kicking. It was to become clear, just a couple of months later, that Berlusconi was already preparing his official entry into Italian political life.

On 26 January 1994 the moment came. VHS copies of a speech were sent to all the main television stations, who dutifully played them at peak time. Berlusconi was adept, right from the start, at controlling the news agenda. This event would become known as the '*Discesa in campo*' – the 'taking to the field'. Berlusconi was in a suit, sitting behind a desk inside what appeared to be an office, but was in fact a TV studio designed to look like an office. He had not read French Situationist Guy Debord, as far as we know, but he certainly understood the power of what Debord called the 'society of the spectacle'. Carefully placed pictures of his family were in shot, as were some books.

His statement was brief, and he read from an autocue, although he held some pieces of paper in his hand. The paper was blank. He spoke in short sentences, in clear and 'non-political' phrases.

Some of his language was that of the football world. Much of the statement was about himself. He – Silvio Berlusconi – following Craxi, and Bossi – was moving Italy towards a new phase of personalised politics, without mass parties, through television, and closely linked – in his case – to his own private businesses. He had decided to 'take the field' and to 'take an interest in public affairs' because he 'didn't want to live in an illiberal country':

> Italy is the country I love ... Here I have learned about my profession as a businessman, from my father and from life itself. Here I have acquired my passion for liberty ... In order to carry out this new life choice, I have today resigned from every institutional position in the business group of which I was the founder. I am therefore giving up my role as a publisher and an entrepreneur in order to put my experience and my dedication at the service of a battle in which I deeply believe . . .[33]

Berlusconi also warned Italians about the dangers they faced. 'If the political system is to work, it is essential that a "pole of Liberty" emerges in opposition to the left-wing cartel, a pole which is capable of attracting to it the best of an Italy which is honest, reasonable, modern ... we believe in individuals, in families, in business, in competition, in economic growth, in efficiency, in the free market and in solidarity, which is the offshoot of justice and freedom.'[34]

The 'taking of the field' was met with an outburst of hilarity. But it was soon clear that this was an extremely serious political project, which had been in gestation for some time. Some claimed that Craxi himself had provided Berlusconi with advice. Soon, a new political party was formed – but it wasn't a party like any of the others. It would fight the 1994 elections, in alliance with other forces.

Forza Italia

In just a few months, Berlusconi and some of his business associates (above all Marcello Dell'Utri and others from the advertising group *Publitalia*) created the possibility for a series of *'micro-comitati elettorali locali'* ('small local electoral committees'). These were known officially as clubs. It was easy to set up a club. 'Anyone who wants to respond to Berlusconi's appeal simply needs to fill out a form and send it via fax to the National Centre in Milan in order to pre-constitute a club.'[35] By the time the election was fought, a few months later, an incredible 13,000 clubs had been 'pre-constituted' across Italy. The real number of active clubs, however, was closer to 2,000.[36]

Why did Berlusconi 'take the field'? Did he feel the need to sacrifice himself for the good of the country? Was communism a real threat to the freedom of Italians? Or, was there something else really going on? Did Berlusconi feel lost without the political protection Craxi had provided for most of the 1980s? Did he enter politics – as a very rich man indeed – to save his companies and provide himself with institutional power? Was his narcissistic personality unable to resist the possibility of becoming Prime Minister, as the established parties departed the scene?

Forza Italia was never a democratic entity. It was and always has been both a personal and a business organisation (some called it a business party) inextricably linked to Berlusconi the man and Berlusconi the businessman. Sometimes, there would be talk of primaries or internal elections, but these never materialised. Berlusconi brooked no dissent, and many people within his alliance left or were thrown out after minor or major disagreements. There was a high turnover in terms of spokespeople and candidates. But one figure remained constant – that of Berlusconi himself. This 'light' and new organisation won 8 million votes in the elections of 27–28 March 1994. An incredible 90 per cent of those elected on the Forza Italia platform had never set foot in Parliament before. Berlusconi was a populist – the first to come to power in Europe after 1945 – promising to create a million jobs and cut taxes. But he also used weapons provided from history – above all anti-communism.

To keep the left out – who had looked certain victors – Berlusconi had forged a rapid two-prong electoral deal with the Lega Nord (in the north of the country) and Alleanza Nazionale, the post-fascist grouping that had replaced the Movimento Sociale Italiano, elsewhere. Berlusconi had identified an alliance to the right as having the potential for success. Fini's moderate strategy and repositioning of the post-fascists, was, for a time, a big success for both. A patchwork Lega-AN-FI government was created soon afterwards. Berlusconi became Prime Minister of Italy. Many Italians were amazed, or in shock. Foreign commentators were equally stupefied. Some 76 per cent of those elected overall had not been there in the last Parliament.

During election campaigns (then, and ever since then) Berlusconi called on all the big guns at his disposal. Popular programmes would come to a halt 'spontaneously' and well-liked presenters would declare their voting intentions – always during prime time. The legendary comedian and presenter Raimondo Vianello, for example, explicitly declared that he would vote for Berlusconi and Forza Italia. 'Finally, I know who to vote for,' he told his fellow presenter in a fake ad-libbed dialogue. The veteran presenter Mike Bongiorno did the same live on TV, telling his viewers and fans that Fininvest (Berlusconi's company) had 'never sacked anyone' and that 'Berlusconi fulfils his promises'. The Christian Democratic Party itself (or what remained of it) would have been wiped out if it hadn't been for the 25 per cent of deputies elected under a PR system. A mere 4.2 million Italians chose to vote for the newly formed Partito Popolare Italiano, the official replacement for the Christian Democrats. A total of 7.4 million Christian Democratic votes had disappeared in the two years since the 1992 elections. It was an epic decline.

A Political Earthquake

The year 1994 signalled the end of mass party politics in Italy. It was the first election since 1945 without the Christian Democrats or the Communist Party on the ballot paper, and the Socialists had been wiped out by the 'Clean Hands' investigations. For many, this was a new system entirely – a Second Republic. The general elections of 1994 saw a myriad of new groupings on the ballot papers. These elections were also held under the new mixed system – the *Mattarellum* – with 75 per cent of candidates elected in first-past-the-post constituencies. The turnout was 86.1 per cent. The old electoral system – a very generous and open form of proportional representation – had been abolished, as we have seen, thanks to a referendum held in 1993. This combination of factors led to some shock results. In the constituency of Mirafiori Sud in Turin – historically a quintessentially working-class area – the voters chose (by just 352 votes) an unknown psychiatrist called Alessandro Meluzzi – standing for Berlusconi's Forza Italia – against the left-wing candidate, the trade unionist and former communist Sergio Chiamparino (who would recover politically to become a future mayor of the city). It was a symbolic moment. The workers – the FIAT workers, in Turin of all places – had opted for Berlusconi over the remains of the Communist Party. Meluzzi himself was also a former communist, as were a number of other candidates in Berlusconi's new grouping. And results in Milan confirmed trends across the north – the centre-right won every single seat there – including those in the 'red belt' around the city. In the so-called 'Stalingrad of Italy' – the former factory-suburb of Sesto San Giovanni to the north of Milan – the left also lost to a Forza Italia candidate.

An historic phase was over – that of the mass parties and their partitocracy that had flourished during the Cold War 'settlement'. Nobody knew or predicted it at the time, but a new double-decade (*ventennio*) was about to begin – the Berlusconi era. Berlusconi also performed extremely well in Sicily. In the centre of Palermo an experienced neo-fascist candidate, Guido Lo Porto, easily defeated the heroic anti-Mafia magistrate Antonino Caponnetto.

Yet the hybrid electoral system had thrown up some quirks. Only the defection of two Catholic senators allowed Berlusconi to win an initial vote of confidence. He was forced to rely on decrees in order to do anything at all. Moreover, Berlusconi's political alliance (or, to be more precise, his two separate alliances – one in the North and one in the South) was fragile. He had made an electoral pact with the Lega Nord in the north of the country and post-fascists in much of the rest of Italy. There was no common programme. Instability was built into the government from the start.

Berlusconi in Power: Act 1

'I would like to remind you, if I may, that you are not the state.'
Umberto Bossi to Silvio Berlusconi in Parliament, 1994[37]

Berlusconi's first few months were exhilarating, despite protests and dismay on the left and, to some extent, internationally, as well as from within Italy's institutions. He appointed the first non-Christian Democratic Interior Minister – Roberto Maroni, of the Lega Nord. Yet there were also continuities with the past. Berlusconi's first cabinet was hardly new. It contained two former Liberals, both of whom had served in governments under Craxi, while seven members had come directly from the Christian Democrats, and four had been in the neo-fascist Movimento Sociale Italiano. On 18 May 1994 Berlusconi's AC Milan team crushed Barcelona in the Champions League final, 4–0. At around the same time, Berlusconi won a crucial vote in the Senate. It was a moment that symbolised the all-compassing nature of his media and sporting empire. It also underlined how these different sectors were part of a colossal and personal 'conflict of interests', undermining the very basis of the democratic state itself.

But soon things started to unravel. The Clean Hands investigations were continuing and now they were beginning to circle around Berlusconi's Fininvest empire. Reaction from the Berlusconi camp was immediate. This was a 'politically inspired investigation', they said, designed to sabotage a democratically elected government. Two Fininvest managers ended up in prison. It wasn't looking good for Berlusconi's new government, especially with the climate surrounding investigations and arrests at that time. His election also revived interest in a strange, semi-secret Masonic association known as the P2. The P2 scandal had unravelled in the 1980s when lists were released of its powerful

members. Berlusconi had been a member – no. 1816, to be precise. Duilio Poggiolini – the King Midas of the Health Service
arrested in Switzerland during *Tangentopoli* – was also a member.
Some saw the P2's secret plans for 'democratic revival' in Italy as
being implemented by Berlusconi himself.

Berlusconi had wanted to appoint one of his own lawyers –
Cesare Previti, the intermediary in the strange purchase of his lavish villa – as Minister of Justice, but the President of Italy, Oscar
Luigi Scalfaro, resisted this move. Previti was made Minister of
Defence instead. Over twenty years later, in 2006, Previti would be
convicted of corrupting a magistrate. A further conviction would
follow in 2007 for similar crimes. It was the end of Previti's political career, although he only spent a few days in prison despite a
six-year sentence.

Berlusconi's new government was quickly caught up in a
titanic struggle with parts of the judiciary. On 13 July 1994,
on the eve of Italy's participation in the World Cup semi-final
in the United States (a very good time to bury bad news), the
Berlusconi government issued a decree. Governments in Italy
can draw up decrees without going to a parliamentary vote. After
sixty days, if not converted into law, these decrees lapse. The text
was a frontal attack on the methods used by the Clean Hands
judges. The so-called 'Biondi decree', which was signed by the
Italian President on 14 July, was designed to impact directly on
the work of the magistrates. It revoked the power of arrest for
a series of crimes, above all those involving public officials and
corruption.

The magistrates had already carried out hundreds of arrests,
and many of those taken in had confessed and named other names
while in jail, which then led to further arrests and confessions. This
was proving to be an effective judicial strategy. But Berlusconi's
government was attempting to stop these arrests – and just at a
moment when the magistrates appeared to be getting close to
his own business empire. The decree caused a storm, despite an
Italian victory in the World Cup semi-final and impending final
(a terrible game, which ended 0-0 and which Italy lost on penalties to Brazil, a game most remembered for Roberto Baggio's

penalty miss). Alfredo Biondi was the Justice Minister who gave his name to the decree. He had been a Liberal Party politician and had allied himself to Berlusconi in 1993.

In a dramatic protest, the entire magistrates 'pool' from Milan's Clean Hands investigation appeared live on television. They were all standing up, in a group. Di Pietro himself looked dishevelled and unshaven. He read out a collective statement. The magistrates criticised the decree and asked to be moved to other work. It was an open challenge to Berlusconi's government. Meanwhile, prisoners began to be released under the decree. The first was one of the most famous – or infamous – of those picked up during *Tangentopoli*, the former Health Minister Francesco De Lorenzo, whose arrest had been splashed on the front pages of the newspapers and had made national news. An angry crowd met his exit. A total of 2,764 prisoners were immediately released. Some argued that the decree was unconstitutional, as it treated similar crimes in very different ways.

Meanwhile, the decree was given a damaging label by journalists – the 'thief-saving decree'. Looking back, the 'thief-saving' decree appears to be the first of a series of 'personal' laws that Berlusconi would pass or try to pass during his time in government – a strategy that would continue (with breaks) until well into the twenty-first century. The man who had come to power thanks to the space left by *Tangentopoli* was now trying to close the investigation down – as it got close to his own interests and businesses.

Both of Berlusconi's main political allies – Alleanza Nazionale and the Lega Nord – soon realised that the decree was highly unpopular (although they had initially agreed to it) and said that they would withdraw from the coalition in protest (and thus bring down the government). Roberto Maroni (Interior Minister) of the Lega threatened to resign if the decree was confirmed. Crowds gathered outside Milan's courthouse, chanting 'Maroni, Maroni, arrest Berlusconi'. Maroni said that he had not even read the text of the decree, and that he had 'trusted' Biondi with the text.

Meanwhile, others blamed Berlusconi's lawyer, Cesare Previti. Almost immediately, Berlusconi began to back down – he had little choice. First he said that the decree could be changed. Parliament then spoke. The vote was negative. A total of 418 deputies voted against, with just thirty-three in favour. The decree was withdrawn on 19 July. It was a significant victory for the magistrates and the Clean Hands investigation. They felt empowered. Surely nothing could stop them now. At the end of that month Silvio Berlusconi's brother and business partner, Paolo, was arrested on charges of bribing bank officials. He had first been arrested on 11 February 1994 and denied any wrongdoing – but he later admitted paying bribes.[38] The net was closing in on the Prime Minister of Italy. If Silvio Berlusconi had gone into politics to save his companies from judicial investigation, it wasn't going to plan.

In November 1994 the Italian Socialist Party dissolved itself, more than 112 years after its foundation in Genoa (two 'new' organisations emerged from its ruins).[39] It was an inglorious end to what had been, for much of the twentieth century, a dignified history as a reformist and – occasionally – revolutionary organisation. PSI members had played a key part in the fight against fascism, but the party's time in power with the Christian Democrats had proved fatal. As a relatively small party with access to state resources, the PSI was particularly vulnerable to corrupt systems and clientelistic temptations. Many former socialists ended up as part of Berlusconi's coalition or moved directly into Forza Italia.

Naples: 'The Prime Minister is under Investigation'

On 22 November 1994 Berlusconi was due to chair an international meeting in Naples to discuss 'the fight against organised crime'. The timing could not have been worse, or better, depending on your point of view. Somebody had leaked a story to Italy's leading quality newspaper, *Il Corriere della Sera*. The headline that day was: 'Milan: Berlusconi is under Investigation'. The article continued like this: 'The judges have applied the final blow ... The Prime Minister has been registered as a person under investigation, for corruption, in alliance with his brother Paolo and

Salvatore Sciascia, a manager responsible for tax affairs in the Fininvest group. Both men were arrested last summer ... a deal was made with various officials from the Tax Police.'[40] Two journalists had somehow got hold of a photocopy of the official notification. The article was released in a way that did maximum political damage to Berlusconi – and on a global scale. Berlusconi would need to come in to be questioned. It was one hell of a scoop. No other papers reported the news.

Berlusconi immediately claimed that his businesses had been a victim of extortion from the tax officials. And, in any case, he added, the sum was so pitiful that in the context of his empire it was an amount that would pass by 'in thirty seconds'. He clicked his fingers to make this point. In his defence, he went straight to his favourite audience – the TV-watching public at home. Standing in front of the Italian flag and an Old Master painting, he claimed to have 'never corrupted anyone' and that he was sure that it would all end in nothing. In a political meeting he went much further. This, he said, is a 'Republic of the Judges'; he also compared magistrates to 'executioners'. Just a few months earlier, Berlusconi had been in talks with the head of that Republic, Antonio Di Pietro, over his possible appointment as Minister of Justice. How quickly things had changed.

War with the Judiciary

A war with the judiciary was now in full swing, just months after Berlusconi's triumphant victory in the 1994 elections (a victory whose way had been paved by *Tangentopoli* itself). The legal process relating to the November 1994 tax case was only completed in 2000, when the High Court cleared everyone involved. In the first trial, Berlusconi had initially been found guilty. On appeal, he was cleared on one count while three counts had fallen by the wayside due to the statute of limitations. This pattern would be repeated on a number of occasions in subsequent years. Political discussion of legal cases often related to the pre-trial phase, while few bothered to follow in much detail the interminable proceedings that took place in court. There would then be a flurry of interest as the sentences came in. Only legal experts could really follow the whole history of the process. 'Guilty' and 'innocent' often became categories detached from the legal realities of actual cases and decisions. Italy's three-tiered justice system, with automatic appeals, meant that a definitive sentence was only achieved once the High Court had looked at the case. Legal processes took years to complete, and the political ramifications of these trials were often out of step with the actual proceedings and legal outcomes.

Right from the beginning of his time in power, the affairs of Berlusconi's media empire and those of the government were fatally intertwined. As soon as the magistrates got close to Berlusconi the businessman, they were – at the same time – getting near to Berlusconi the politician. An insurmountable 'conflict of interests' stood at the heart of the Italian political system, despite Berlusconi's promises about 'blind trusts' or the selling of his companies. Many of the companies were also handed over (symbolically) to close family members. These two 'sides' to Berlusconi's public life were never divided in any clear way. In fact, Berlusconi made his business success into a key part of his appeal as a politician.

In December 1994 a seven-hour interrogation of Berlusconi took place in Milan. Later, he went on television to 'explain' what had happened, this time in front of a Canaletto painting and sitting behind a desk. Berlusconi's idea of democracy was plebiscitary, not parliamentary. He believed in speaking directly to 'the people', usually via the television screen. He saw Parliament as, essentially, a 'waste of time', as he once said, although he used it to pass numerous 'personal laws' in his own favour. He had little sense of the state, or of public or collective good.

Meanwhile, opinion-makers and others were unleashed on Berlusconi's television channels to criticise the magistrates, often with the use of violent language. The counter-attack also came from within the institutions themselves. Official inspectors were sent to Milan by the Justice Minister to look into the methods used by the Clean Hands team. Personal attacks were made, especially on Antonio Di Pietro. Numerous 'dossiers' did the rounds. Di Pietro himself was placed under investigation in Brescia for various relatively minor charges, and his own personal and lengthy legal odyssey began.

The Fall of Berlusconi's First Government: December 1994

The political fallout of the Berlusconi tax case in 1994 was immense. The Lega Nord (who had set themselves up, initially, as strong supporters of Clean Hands) pulled out of the coalition. Berlusconi and his allies called this decision a 'betrayal', 'electoral theft' and a 'great overturning' of the electoral result. Sometimes they even compared what had happened to a coup. Bossi told Berlusconi in Parliament (in a mocking way, aping the media magnate's use of the phrase 'if I may') 'Let me remind you, if I may, that you are not the State.' On 22 December 1994, Berlusconi was forced to resign as Prime Minister. He had lost his majority. Berlusconi learnt a lesson that day – he needed the Lega just as much as they needed him – both to win and to govern. He would later form a solid alliance with the Lega that would lead to a series of election victories after 2001.

But Berlusconi's swift decline was not just linked to the Clean Hands investigations. Opposition to him in the country was strong, as was a sense of disgust among many about the presence of former or post-neo-fascists at the heart of government. As mayors and councillors from Alleanza Nazionale were elected all over Italy, and its ministers served in office, anti-fascist values experienced a resurgence. On Liberation Day – 25 April 1994 – a powerful anti-fascist demonstration marched in the rain through the centre of Milan. This forest of umbrellas was an impressive display of the survival of anti-fascism. When Umberto Bossi tried to join the march, he was met with whistles and insults. Attempts to reform labour laws were also met with massive demonstrations in November 1994 in Rome, when an estimated one and a half million turned out to protest.

Interregnum: 1995–6

Berlusconi's first government lasted just nine months. He would then remain in opposition until 2001. In 1995 a different majority was formed without a new election (backed by the Lega) under the leadership of Lamberto Dini, who had been Berlusconi's Finance Minister. This was a centrist and partly 'technical' government, containing experts as well as politicians. It was also 'post-democratic', made up in the main of experts from outside of the main political parties. Forza Italia and Alleanza Nazionale went to the opposition benches, bitterly complaining that the winners of the election had seen their power usurped. Early elections were called (again) for 1996 – these would be the third set of general elections in four years. Berlusconi's first government had been a disaster on all fronts. But he licked his wounds, mobilised his TV channels and media outlets, and was soon back for more.

Antonio Di Pietro resigned as a magistrate in December 1994, ostensibly to fight his own legal battles that were being held in Brescia, close to Milan. Berlusconi expressed 'regret' for Di Pietro's decision (the magistrate was still extremely popular) and there were demonstrations in his favour. In the end, Di Pietro was cleared of all charges in a series of trials in Brescia. He would later, like Berlusconi, 'enter the field' and go into politics, but with much less impact on the system. His departure from the Clean Hands investigations marked the beginning of the end for the *Tangentopoli* scandals. But magistrates elsewhere were still investigating crimes that went right up to the upper echelons of the Italian state.

Trial of the Century: 'Beelzebub' in the Dock

It wasn't just the *mafiosi* themselves who appeared before judges in the 1980s and 1990s. Their alleged supporters and allies were also brought to trial. In some cases this went to the top of the political tree. In the wake of *Tangentopoli*, the so-called 'trial of the century' took place in Palermo in the mid-1990s (1995–9). In the dock was Giulio Andreotti – seven times Prime Minister – a man who for almost the entire post-war period (and especially since the 1970s) had been the incarnation of Christian Democratic power. Unlike Craxi, Andreotti had voted for his own 'authorisation' to proceed to trial in Parliament. He played the role of statesman during the lengthy trial (there were a hundred hearings or so) and frequently attended proceedings – speaking for some twelve hours over the course of the whole process. At the end of the trial, he shook hands with the magistrates. Sixty supergrasses were called and some 500 witnesses in total testified.

The accusation was that Andreotti had forged close links (a 'criminal pact') with the Sicilian Mafia over an extensive period (from at least 1968 onwards, the prosecutors claimed) to achieve and consolidate his political power.[41] Salvo Lima was said to be his political link to the Mafia and was described as 'one of the politicians who received most support from Cosa Nostra'. Magistrates argued that Andreotti held meetings met with Mafia bosses. Sensationally, they presented evidence that Andreotti met Totò Riina himself on a specific date – 20 September 1987 – and the two men had kissed. This 'kiss' was something that resonated with public opinion. And if Andreotti had been close to the Mafia – close enough to kiss its leaders – then so had the Italian state itself. The detail in the accusations was impressive – but based almost entirely (as was inevitable) on supergrass evidence. The Mafia doesn't have archives.

On 23 October 1999 – following a momentous and dramatic trial – Andreotti was cleared. The supergrass evidence had not been believed. On appeal (in Italy both prosecution and defence have an automatic right to appeal) things became more complicated. The appeal judges absolved Andreotti of any crimes committed after 1980. Before then, however, they said that he had been involved in 'concrete collaboration' with leading *mafiosi*. Yet that earlier period was covered by the statute of limitations. This meant that Andreotti could not be convicted of crimes before 1980. It was an ambiguous decision, and a convenient one. Andreotti was neither innocent nor guilty, although it was and is often claimed that he was 'cleared'. A leading politician – possibly the most powerful man in Italy for much of the post-war period – had been closely linked to a murderous criminal organisation.[42] But he walked free from the courtroom and continued to appear on television and make speeches in Parliament almost right up to his death in 2013 at the age of ninety-four. The enigma of Andreotti, so brilliantly portrayed by Toni Servillo in Paolo Sorrentino's masterpiece *Il Divo*, remained intact. Had there been a 'double state'? A public democracy and a private machine that ordered murders and handed out favours in return for votes? Andreotti encapsulated the darkness at the heart of Italy's democratic system.

Padania and the Lega Nord

In the 1990s many Lega Nord militants believed that they were doing nothing less than constructing a new nation – which they called *Padania*. The party-movement set up an alternative Parliament of the North for a time (in Mantova) and created its own semi-official set of bodyguards (dressed in green), as well as an anthem, a flag and a history (plus a football team, a cycle race and a beauty contest). Lega voters were often working class, and from the provinces as opposed to the big cities. At a Lega Congress held in Milan in 1993 a ten-point programme was agreed. One of these points was a contestation of the nation of Italy itself: 'The Italian Union is a free association of the Federal Republic of the North, and the Federal Republic of Etruria and the Federal Republic of the South.' Much of this was clearly absurd. But Padania had also been identified by experts as an economic entity before the Lega rose to power. Much of the North – with its small to medium-sized family firms, flexible specialisation and industrial traditions – provided a post-Fordist model widely studied by economists and social scientists. Padania was a new 'nation' that inspired high levels of emotional attachment, and a hard, economic and cultural and social reality linked to concepts of 'hard work', and a desire for freedom from 'politics' and 'the state'.

Ritualistic Lega events included their annual meetings in Pontida (after 1990), a wide valley in the Province of Bergamo, one of the Lega's heartlands. Close by, in an abbey, a series of northern cities had joined together in 1167 to fight Emperor Barbarossa and the Holy Roman Empire. Padania, the Lega claimed, also had a history. Peak Padania came in September 1996, when the Lega organised a semi-mystical gathering that began at the source of the Po River. Umberto Bossi called that river 'the Po God'. He collected some water from the source of the Po in a special glass phial and poured it out during a big gathering in Venice, when declarations of 'independence' were made. This was one of the phrases used: 'We, the people of Padania, solemnly proclaim: Padania is an independent and sovereign federal Republic. We offer each other ... our lives and our sacred honour ... we affirm our right and our desire to assume the full powers of the state, to collect all tax, to vote for all laws and to sign all treaties.' An Italian flag was lowered and a Padanian one raised. Part of the journey to Venice had been made by boat. In the same year Lega mayors refused to swear obedience to the Italian state.

Some saw this as folklore, as part of a political game aimed at putting pressure on the Italian state to concede more powers to the region. Others viewed it as something much more serious – no less than an attempt to subvert the Italian state and nation and its constitution, which stated clearly that Italy was 'one and indivisible'. If all this was an elaborate piece of theatre, or a farce, then some of Bossi's followers would misinterpret his message.

On 9 May 1997, seven months after the 'declaration of independence' in Venice, a group of eight men drove in a lorry from Padua to Venice, where they boarded a car ferry. They then forced the ferry (at gunpoint) to drop them at Venice's main square – Piazza San Marco. Inside the lorry was a kind of self-made fake tank (which looked real, and would later be dubbed the 'tanko') with a Venetian flag. The men had supplies. From there some of them proceeded to take control of the city's biggest bell tower – knocking down the doors and climbing the stairs. Two of the men remained in the square with their fake 'tank' (no vehicles are, of course, normally allowed into Venice itself). It was around 1 a.m.[43]

Once inside the tower, the men flew the flag of Venice and issued a statement: 'Attention. The Veneto *serenissimo* government has occupied the San Marco bell tower. Long live San Marco, long live *la Serenissima* [a name often used for the Venetian Republic]'.[44] The 200th anniversary of the end of the Republic in 1797 was just a few days away. Negotiations took place. A TV antenna appeared on the tower. But this revolution lasted less than a day. At 8.40 a.m. the tower was freed by a special group of trained *carabinieri* using tear gas – and all the men were arrested. One of the group ended up in hospital. Dramatic pictures showed the *carabinieri* teams climbing the tower and capturing the 'tanko'.

The Lega Nord denied any connection to the action. But they later campaigned for the men (who included a builder, two electricians, a worker, a teacher, an 'expert' in UFOs who had managed to introduce messages into state TV broadcasts and a tailor) during the lengthy legal processes that followed, which were not finally completed until 2011. The fake tank was later proudly exhibited in public after money was donated to buy it back at a public auction by supporters of the men.[45]

Tangentopoli: A Judicial Revolution?

'The repression of criminals has the typical effects of the predator, namely improving the ability of the prey. We caught only the slowest prey, leaving free those who ran fastest.' Piercamillo Davigo, magistrate[46]

Tangentopoli felt – at the time – very much like a revolution. Powerful politicians were arrested almost daily. Many abandoned their political careers altogether. It was an exciting time. The powerful were being put on trial and humiliated, and sent to prison with their belongings in plastic bags. The main political parties all collapsed. In 1987 the election had been a traditional, post-war struggle between the Christian Democrats, the Communists and the Socialists. By 1992 the Communist Party had left the scene, and by 1994 the Christian Democratic Party was itself divided into a series of groupings and had been renamed. In 1996 none of these parties would even be on the ballot paper. Milan's magistrates appeared to have the power to wipe out an entire political class. The disintegration or transformation of the major mass parties was so swift that people struggled to make sense of it all. Party offices, newspapers and cultural associations were closed down. In the case of the minor parties, who had often exercised power way beyond their actual support, this process was extremely rapid. Ballot papers expanded to include a bewildering array of new parties and formations.

Yet, as time went on, *Tangentopoli* began to look more like a blip than a revolution. The crushing defeat in June 1993 of the anti-corruption candidate Nando Dalla Chiesa – son of a *carabiniere* general killed by the Mafia in Sicily in 1982 – by a Lega Nord candidate, in the run-off for Mayor of Milan, marked the end of the 'revolutionary' phase of *Tangentopoli*. Many people applauded as politicians were arrested, but they were less interested in reforms to tax systems or attempts to unpick systems of corruption that went deeper into everyday personal and business life. *Tangentopoli* – as a series of successive scandals showed – dealt with the symptoms of a rotten structure, but not the causes, or indeed the system itself. Moreover, *Tangentopoli* was an incomplete 'revolution' even on its own terms. Many of the old Christian Democratic oligarchs survived the end of the party itself (and often these were the very worst sections from that party), often (but not always) recycling their careers within Forza Italia or the post-fascist Alleanza Nazionale.

The powers given to investigating magistrates in Italy by the 1948 Constitution and the 1989 judicial reforms were used to (mainly) positive ends in the period 1992–4. But many innocent people were also caught up in a witch-hunt whipped up by a vampiric media. Italy is a country where judicial rights before trial are minimal – phone taps are ritually leaked and published in newspapers and magazines, TV programmes discuss in detail the guilt or otherwise of suspects, all and sundry are called to debate the merits of judicial investigations. During *Tangentopoli* the Milan judges made 'liberal' use of preventative detention – usually to force confessions that then incriminated others. Investigative magistrates are appointed via public competition in Italy, which has allowed a judiciary not restricted by social class to emerge from within civil society. Investigating magistrates cannot be sacked or taken off trials except in special and rare circumstances. They are promoted more or less automatically and are responsible solely to a semi-autonomous body known as the Higher Council of the Magistrates. Sometimes this autonomy led to judicial mistakes or worse. The idea that the judges would eventually bring Silvio Berlusconi down prevented the left from seriously tackling the massive conflicts of interest that marked his position as political leader and media magnate rolled into one.

Counter-Attack: *Tangentopoli* as Conspiracy

Politicians did not take these investigations lying down. They counter-attacked. Some accused the magistrates of a political conspiracy. The legend of the *'toghe rosse'* (the 'red tunics', as worn by magistrates) – supposedly communist-inspired magistrates – was born. A linked accusation was that the investigations were one-directional. Bettino Craxi produced a 'dossier' that accused the Italian Communist Party of taking money illegally from the Soviet Union over a period of decades. Other criticisms of the magistrates focused on the widespread role of preventative arrests and the media 'witch-hunts' that accompanied the process and led to confessions. Judges were over-anxious, it was claimed, to use handcuffs and throw people in prison.

Media reporting was over the top. During *Tangentopoli*, it seemed, people had to prove they were innocent. It was assumed that they were guilty. It should be noted here that those arrested or placed under investigation were by no means only from the Christian Democratic Party, or the Socialists. Many were communists or former communists. Was the Communist Party (or its heirs with new names) still different, as Enrico Berlinguer had argued? Not in Milan, where a number of party functionaries were arrested during the *Tangentopoli* scandals of 1992–3.

Berlinguer's warnings about the 'moral question' had not been heeded, even in his own party. For example, the judges in Milan wrote this in 1996 in a sentence relating to corruption around the construction of a new Metro line: 'in terms of the Milanese [Communist] Federation, the entire party ... was directly involved in the systems created around the Metro construction, from at least 1987 onwards ... From 1987 to 1992 the PCI-PDS received 18.75% of the total bribes paid linked to the Metro – at least 3 billion lire.'[47]

Moreover, magistrates soon began to enter politics themselves, on both sides of the divide, riding the wave of their popularity during the investigations. Tiziana Parenti, who had investigated alleged corruption in left-leaning cooperatives (and was therefore no 'red tunic'), became a candidate for Berlusconi's Forza Italia. She stood next to him on stage in some of the early party rallies. Parenti had been a communist in her youth, and was a part of the Clean Hands pool. She was elected to Parliament in 1994 but in 1998 she moved towards the centre and eventually to the (tiny) Socialist Party – a dead end in every sense. Her political fame was short-lived.[48]

In the midst of the scandals new kinds of political chat-shows, transmitted live every evening, began to garner large audiences. Key programmes in this period were Gad Lerner's *Milano Italia* and Michele Santoro's *Samarcanda*. These shows were a combination of genres. They contained examples of reportage and serious journalism, but they often included live transmissions from 'the piazza' (usually angry 'normal' people somewhere outside in a square). In the studio there would be a mix of politicians and journalists (often shouting at each other, or talking to 'the piazza') together with a presenter-led comment. These programmes were transmitted for hours, and made their presenters into stars. It was a model that seemed fresh and exciting at the time. But it would be repeated time and again, ad nauseam, for years to come.

Clean Hands did not just investigate or arrest politicians. Tax officials were questioned, unveiling a system of favours and bribes in the tax collection system. When the trials came around, many of those who had received money found it difficult to understand whether their actions were wrong in any way. The system of corruption was so 'normal', so well-oiled, that they failed to see what the fuss was all about. This led to some near-comical scenes in court, with puffed-up officials defending their actions against all-comers. A sense of impunity had clearly held sway, for years, or perhaps forever, inside some of Italy's institutions. But *Tangentopoli*, especially as time went on, increasingly divided Italians. Craxi was a villain for many – a hate-figure – but for others he became a scapegoat and a martyr – a tragic hero. Other scandals followed at regular intervals. A political class had been removed (although many still seemed to be very much around) – but corruption appeared to be endemic. In some ways it even seemed to be getting worse. During *Tangentopoli* everything had seemed so straightforward. All politicians were thieves. All the magistrates were heroes. As time passed, these divisions seemed far less clear-cut.

We will return to politics later with the 1996 elections, but with the end of the Cold War it was not just politics that was being transformed. Italy's problematic relationship with her own past was also opening up, and this created the possibility for new approaches to memory and history. Nothing was certain anymore, and values such as anti-fascism were called into question. The trial of a former Nazi in Rome would provide dramatic evidence of how deeply rooted Italy's divided memories really were.

Five Too Many? The Priebke Trials and Italian Memory

In the late 1980s and early 1990s a young academic called Esteban Buch started digging around into the presence of numerous former Nazis in a German mountain 'colony' in Argentina known as San Carlos de Bariloche. He came across a tall, distinguished man called Erich Priebke. Probing further, he found that Priebke was a former Nazi officer who had been in Italy for part of the Second World War and he linked him to the notorious Fosse Ardeatine massacre in Rome in 1944. In 1991 Buch published a book about Bariloche (in Spanish), but nobody picked up on the story until a US ABC TV crew went out to Bariloche in May 1994. The team came across the volume in a second-hand bookshop and then went hunting for documents in various archives. It is said that they also found Priebke's name in the phone book. He was clearly hiding in plain sight. Bizarre conspiracy theories even claim that Hitler himself settled in Bariloche after the war.

Then came the most dramatic moment of all, on camera. The reporter Sam Donaldson walked up to Priebke (who was dressed in a natty hat and elegant jacket) in the street and asked him, in English, whether he had been part of the Gestapo in Rome. Priebke – rather surprisingly – replied in the affirmative. He also said that those killed in the Nazi wartime massacre in Rome had been 'mostly terrorists' and added that he 'didn't shoot anybody'. He had, he said, 'followed orders'. Priebke then drove off (his parting shot to the journalist was 'You are not a gentleman'), but a whole new phase of his life was only just beginning. The interview was shown on Italian television the very next day and the authorities moved swiftly into action (after years of inaction). Priebke was kept under house arrest in Argentina and the Italian state became interested in the case. A seventeen-month legal battle followed over his extradition to Italy. On 21 November 1995 Priebke arrived in Rome. The Second World War was about to jog Italy's collective memory once again – right in the centre of Italy's capital city. The events that followed would reopen old wounds and inspire historical research.

Fosse Ardeatine

On 23 March 1944 a column of 156 police troops from the Bolzen regiment (attached to the German army) were marching through the centre of occupied Rome. At around 3.50 p.m. a bomb exploded in the narrow street of Via Rasella killing thirty of them (three more were to die later) as well as at least two Italian civilians. The bomb had been set off by an official armed partisan unit.

The troops responded by firing indiscriminately into the houses
on the street and rounding up residents in Via Rasella.

The next day, in a planned reprisal, 335 people were taken to
the Fosse Ardeatine caves just outside the city by the German
occupiers and shot over a period of four and a half hours. Only
three had already been condemned to death (for partisan activity), while 154 were under investigation by the German military police and seventy-five were in custody purely because
they were Jewish. Other victims were taken from Regina Coeli
(Rome's prison) or selected from those picked up around Via
Rasella. The following day, 25 March, a German army poster
appeared across Rome and in newspapers. It accused 'criminal
elements' of planting the bomb and added that 'The German
Command ... has ordered that for every German killed ten
communist-Badoglian criminals will be shot. This order has
already been carried out.'[49]

Ever since that bomb exploded in Via Rasella, these facts themselves have been in dispute. In various arenas of public opinion –
the press, the courts, the streets, political parties and historical
journals – these facts have been raked over, debated and restated.
Constant accusations of conspiracies, mendacity and cover-ups
have dominated these disputes. There is no need here to enter into
this debate in detail, as other historians have already spent time in
the accurate reconstruction of what actually happened in March
1944 in Rome. What remains of great interest are the historical
and political debates surrounding these facts and these controversial events. The debates are not confined to Rome or to Via
Rasella and the Ardeatine Caves, but take in big questions of participation, the Resistance, consensus, memory and responsibility.
Today a national memorial stands at the site of the massacre, and
an annual celebration is held where the names of the 335 victims
are read out.

The historical debate over Via Rasella and the massacre and
the bomb needs to be seen within the context of ongoing discussions that began almost immediately after Liberation. Since 1945
two competing myths had dominated debate over the Resistance,
and until the late 1980s the political overtones of the dispute

dominated the need for real historical enquiry and openness. In short, the 'need' to support the Resistance myth born out of the anti-fascist tradition overrode the desire to look more carefully (on the left) into the real support for and impact of the Resistance. In this version of events, the Resistance was a mass movement that stretched from Abruzzo upwards and those who opposed (or took no part in) the armed struggle were mainly dismissed as fascists or collaborators. The alternative myth, given historical weight by the historian Renzo De Felice in the 1970s, was of a Resistance supported only by a tiny, ideologically committed minority. The majority took no part in the movement and this 'grey zone' (made up in part of those who had given their 'consensus' to Mussolini) stood by, waiting for the war to end. If we translate these myths to Via Rasella, we get two classic (and very different) versions of events. In the first, Via Rasella was a heroic act of war carried out, yes, by a necessarily small group but with the (active and passive) support of vast sectors of the urban population.

For the other myth, Via Rasella was a pointless and vanguardist terrorist attack that achieved nothing and led to the deaths of 335 innocent victims in the Ardeatine Caves. Most Romans, supporters of this version believe, were opposed to this type of action, and convinced of Rome's special 'open city' status and the imminent departure of the Germans. Many continued to believe that the partisans could have handed themselves in and avoided the massacre.

Neither of these versions captures the complexity and trauma of the Resistance, nor the specific circumstances surrounding Via Rasella. Many Romans were terrified (and angered) by the attacks on German troops, but many supported the Resistance (in myriad ways) and helped the opposition organisations. As with all the German massacres during the war, the blame and the responsibility have been laid, obviously, at the door of the German army itself. But Via Rasella shows that many people (including the Italian Fascists, but also large sectors of the ordinary population) blamed the partisans for 'causing trouble' and inviting revenge attacks. The specific features of Via Rasella should not prevent these debates being placed within the series of studies of divided memory that began to appear in Italy in the 1990s.[50]

The whole Via Rasella-Fosse Ardeatine controversy may well have faded into the same foggy memory as many other similar moments of bloodshed if it were not for the surprising events surrounding the discovery, arrest and trials of Priebke, fifty years on. Priebke's role in the massacre was important. He had been ordered to prepare the list of victims and personally took part in the slaughter, as did many officers and ordinary soldiers. As events unfolded in the 1990s, Priebke's activities in 1944 and (above all) his trial became central to the debates over memory and history. The presence of Priebke became the key to satisfying the thirst for justice felt by many families of the victims and the Jewish community after the 'escape' of Herbert Kappler, the high-ranking German officer who organised the massacre, from an Italian hospital bed in 1977 to West Germany. Kappler had been held in a military prison for most of the post-war period.[51] The lack of any kind of real repentance by Priebke himself probably added to the exaggeration of his role.

A Nazi on Trial: Rome, 1996

'The Fosse Ardeatine has become an open wound in the memory and feelings of Rome. One has only to scratch the surface of memory and the stories gush out.'

Alessandro Portelli[52]

'The Priebke trial ... brought so many things back to memory ... brought it all back to life.'

Adriana Montezemolo[53]

Priebke's first trial in 1996 was held in front of the military tribunal of Rome and, right from the beginning, the judges responsible for the case revealed themselves as under-prepared to preside over a case of this importance. They were surprised by the big public attendance at the hearings and the extensive coverage in the

Team/Alinari

Demonstration in favour of divorce, early 1970s. The slogan on the woman's shirt reads 'Nobody will force you to divorce if you don't want to' and 'For the rich there will always be the Sacra Rota [the Vatican body, also known as the Roman Rota, with the power to annul marriages].'

Austerity, circa 1973.
A petrol-pump
attendant waits for a
petrol ban to end.

The singer Mina, 1962.

Clashes between police and demonstrators during a general strike, Via Larga (central Milan), 19 November 1969. A policeman would die during these clashes.

Demonstration, Milan, 1 May 1964. The first banner reads 'Houses for immigrants'; the second reads 'Stop deaths in the workplace'.

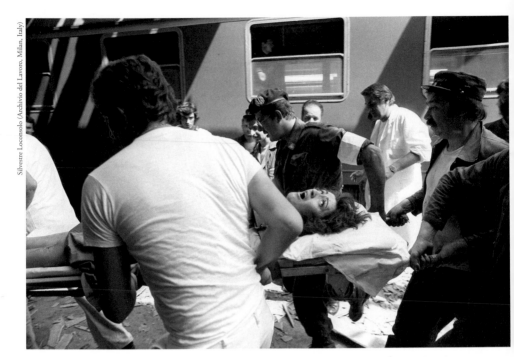

An injured victim, Marina Gamberini, being carried away after the Bologna station bomb, 2 August 1980. Gamberini survived.

First Red Brigade kidnapping, 1972. Idalgo Macchiarini has a gun pointing into his cheek. The poster reads: 'Strike and escape! Nobody will go unpunished! Hit one in order to educate one hundred! Power to the armed proletariat!'

Photo taken by the Red Brigades of their hostage Aldo Moro, 1978. The headline reads 'Has Moro been killed?'

The clean-up operation after the Seveso chemical leak, 1976.

Celebrations in Naples for Napoli's Serie A Championship victory in 1990. One of the other banners reads 'Vote Communist'.

Bettino Craxi, 1984.

Umberto Bossi, 1990s. The poster behind him says: 'Defend all Italians. We will vote for the Lega. North–Centre–South'.

Magistrate Antonio Di Pietro in the courtroom, early 1990s.

The Vlora arrives in port, Bari, August 1991. Some Albanians are swimming in the water.

Egyptian immigrant making pizza, Rome, 2000.

Palermo, 2000: anti-Mafia protest near a tree (outside Giovanni Falcone's house) which became a focus for protestors. The sheet says 'They were not killed. Their ideas walk on our legs'.

Silvio Berlusconi and Colonel Mu'ammer Gaddafi, Ciampino airport, Rome, 2009. Berlusconi was Prime Minister at the time.

Italian (and foreign) press. The trial was dominated by technical and military-legal issues that left those looking for 'justice' both confused and angry. For example, much time was spent in discussions over Priebke's responsibility in the death of the so-called 'extra five' victims who died in the Ardeatine Caves. This debate tended to legitimate the whole idea of vendetta massacres in war and reduce the case to a technical one centred on the personal (not moral) 'errors' of Priebke as list-holder. There were surreal moments. Priebke admitted to having holidayed, twice, in Italy after the war. He had visited Rome as recently as 1980. He clearly felt that he was in no danger despite his past. It was like a bad parody of the film *Marathon Man* ('Is it safe?'). It was said that he had even been back to Via Rasella (and some accounts claim he was recognised there). It wasn't safe. But Priebke had felt as though it was.

In themselves, the Priebke trial and re-trial did not add more than a few details to the whole story of the Fosse Ardeatine. But the trials themselves became part of that experience, especially the debates in the press. The testimonies of witnesses and family members were moving and powerful. Long-suppressed rage and pain came to the surface again. Right-wing newspapers and the distinguished Italian journalist Indro Montanelli all ran campaigns either against the partisan role in the whole sequence of events or, as in Montanelli's case, in direct support of Priebke as a 'fellow soldier'. Neo-fascists daubed walls with graffiti calling for Priebke's release, and for the arrest (instead) of the man who had set off the bomb in 1944 – Rosario Bentivegna – who was still alive and living in Rome.

The role of the families and Jewish community during the hearings was constant and revealed how deeply the massacres had affected the fabric of certain parts of Rome and its peoples. The most explosive moment came with the first verdict of the court in July 1996. On hearing that Priebke was guilty but 'not punishable due to his good behaviour since the massacre' and the fact that he was 'following orders', a large crowd blocked the exit to the courtroom for hours. Many demonstrators were from Rome's Jewish community. The first Priebke verdict was traumatic – especially for the families of the victims. But those protesting were not only from that generation. Young people, born years after the war, were also there – and they too were angry (and well-informed).

Italy's Justice Minister was forced to re-arrest Priebke on a technicality and a re-trial changed the original decision. The legal process then dragged on until 1998, when Priebke was given a life sentence – to be served under house arrest, in Rome. The oral historian Alessandro Portelli was moved by the case and the divisions it re-evoked to write a masterpiece, *The Order Has Been Carried Out*. As he wrote, 'Time was suspended on March 24, 1944, and stood still until the Priebke trial set it in motion again.'[54] Italy's past was being opened up – and the presence of neo-fascists in central government for the first time, as well as in many local administrations, led to a series of 'memory wars' in the 1990s and 2000s.

Priebke's trial also led directly to the discovery of what became known as the 'cupboard of shame'. A magistrate looking for documents relating to the case came across a large cupboard with its doors turned towards the wall and closed. On further investigation the cupboard turned out to contain numerous documents relating to massacres and other crimes carried out during the period of Nazi occupation of Italy.[55] They had been 'archived' by a military magistrate way back in 1960 – and hidden away. The time had 'not been ripe' for major legal proceedings against ex-Nazis (and Italian Fascists). That was a period of the Cold War, and West Germany had been an ally. Now, however, investigations could be re-opened. The 'cupboard of shame' provided material for numerous (less high-profile) trials across Italy with regards to ageing Nazis from the wartime occupation. Justice was done – in some cases – but most of the protagonists on both sides were now dead.[56]

After the Trials: Priebke's Final Years in Rome and his Death

Priebke, who showed no remorse for his actions, wrote his autobiography under house arrest. In 2007 he was given permission to work in a legal office (at the age of eighty-three), but photographs of him out in Rome on a scooter caused offence and quickly led to a revocation of this order. Priebke duly remained in Rome until his death in October 2013, at the age of one hundred. But the controversy that had marked his later life continued to follow him to his grave. Argentina refused his wish to be buried there, and Germany didn't want him either. So where was he to be buried? As with the body of Mussolini between 1945 and 1957, Priebke's corpse is now buried at a secret location. Clashes had broken out at his first funeral service in Albano Laziale near Rome, and led to its cancellation. Eight people were later put on trial for public order offences linked to the events of that day. His lawyer has since confirmed that Priebke is buried in an unmarked grave in 'A small cemetery run by the Interior Ministry'.[57]

Pure Climber: The Marco Pantani Story

Cycling had been losing ground in popularity to football and motor sports in Italy since the 1960s. Then, out of nowhere, in the mid to late 1990s, a cyclist emerged who seemed to reignite latent passions for this sport. His name was Marco Pantani, and he had grown up in the sleepy seaside resort of Cesenatico in central Italy.

Pantani was a pure climber, slight and frail, but beautiful to watch as he sped up mountains, leaving all the others in his wake. In 1998 he won the Giro d'Italia and the Tour de France in the same year, a feat only previously matched – for Italy – by the great Fausto Coppi. All of Italy stopped to watch him on television, waiting for the moment when 'the pirate' would throw off his bandana and attack the other cyclists. Audiences were massive. Some referred to 'Pantanimania'. In 1999 Pantani seemed unbeatable, and was on the verge of a second Giro in a row. But then disaster struck. Pantani was forced to leave the race 'for health reasons' after a test. There wasn't yet a test that could detect EPO, a synthetic substance that increased red blood cells and helped performance. The authorities were forced to use indirect measures linked to levels of red blood cells in Pantani's body to send out a warning. The leader was gone, with the race seemingly in the bag. It was headline news.

Pantani pleaded his innocence, but many assumed he had been taking EPO – which was widespread in the sport at the time. The whole affair had a detrimental effect on Pantani's psyche, and he was never the same cyclist, or man, again, despite a series of short-lived comebacks. In February 2004 the police were called to a holiday residence in Rimini. Inside one of the rooms they found a dead body, partially clothed. It was Pantani. Magistrates concluded that he had died from a cocaine overdose, and drug dealers were prosecuted (but later cleared) for their connection to this tragic event. But that was not the end of the story. Rumours continued to circulate that the 1999 ban had been orchestrated, perhaps by criminal organisations. In 2014 the media reported that magistrates had reopened the case following claims that Pantani might have been murdered. They found no evidence to justify criminal proceedings. Pantani's story has inspired books, documentaries and films, and across Italy there are monuments and memorials in his name. Every year, the Giro has a Pantani climb in his honour.

1996: The Anti-Berlusconi

From the ashes of *Tangentopoli*, the centre-left attempted to construct a new identity, reaching beyond its declining working-class base. This strategy bore electoral fruit in 1996. Romano Prodi was the complete antithesis of Silvio Berlusconi. He was almost deliberately non-charismatic, a politician right down to his bootstraps, and an institutional figure. But the men were also different in many other ways. Prodi, for example, preferred the unfashionable sport of cycling to football. He cared little about his appearance, and his love life was of no interest whatsoever. He was, in short, quite boring – almost anti-populist. Yet Italians liked him, he was reassuring and didn't promise what he couldn't deliver. He was the only leader to regularly beat Berlusconi in general elections.

In 1996, following Berlusconi's disastrous first experience as Prime Minister in 1994–5, Prodi won a majority. He had negotiated a deal with Rifondazione Comunista over standing down in selected seats. Prodi presided over a broad centre-left coalition. It had also given itself a new name – The Olive Tree. Added legitimacy had been provided by a new system of primaries set up to select the centre-left candidate. In October 2005, 4.3 million people voted in the first primary, and 3.2 million chose Prodi. This system would become the norm (on the centre-left) and was extended to local areas as with the selection of candidates for city mayors.

Prodi's first government (1996–8) was radical in comparison with what had gone before (and what would come afterwards). A Green politician was appointed Minister for the Environment, for example. Economically, however, Prodi was conservative, accelerating the privatisation of Italy's state assets and raising extra taxes (including a special one-off 'Euro-Tax' – which, in hindsight, inspired very little protest) to help the country stay within the limits required for the single European currency. Prodi had very close ties with the EU and would go on to become President of the European Commission between 1999 and 2004. He was a firm believer in the European project and he took much of Italy with him, at least for a time.

However, in October 1998, Rifondazione Comunista announced that it was leaving the alliance. This led to the end of Prodi's first time in power. The actual issue that provoked RC's departure seemed somewhat marginal at the time (limits on the number of working hours) and probably masked a power game within the centre-left. This self-inflicted division allowed Berlusconi to map a road back to power. The comedian Giacomo Poretti of the popular threesome *Aldo, Giovanni e Giacomo* would later develop a tragi-comic character based on the masochistic tendencies of the Italian left. He was called Tafazzi and he spent much of his time hitting himself in his own genitals (held in a jockstrap) with a plastic bottle. Some used the term *Tafazzismo* to describe the Italian left in general. Unity across the left (and disunity on the centre-right) had led to the centre-left victory in

1996. Disunity on the centre-left in 2001 gave Berlusconi (who in the meantime had made peace with the Lega Nord) an easy victory.

It was surprising that, despite their five years in power between 1996 and 2001, the centre-left never drew up any legislation to deal with the conflict of interests that had paralysed Berlusconi's first government in 1994–5. Perhaps it was thought that Berlusconi could be controlled, and even (cynically) that anti-Berlusconism was a useful tool to mobilise voters. If that was the case, it was a tragic political error. The fallout from the division of the left would drag on right up to the formation of the Partito Democratico (Democratic Party) in 2007. But by then, the appeal of any party or movement with an explicit link to communism had faded considerably. After Prodi, centre-left governments limped on towards the next elections – in 2001. Meanwhile, the Partito Democratico della Sinistra (Democratic Party of the Left) had changed its name to the Democratici della Sinistra (Left Democrats) – but nothing much else changed. Prodi was no longer the leader of the Olive Tree coalition, and his successors proved no match for Berlusconi, Bossi and Fini.

The Euro, European Integration and Italy

The road towards a single currency and European integration at a political level always included Italy, which was nonetheless a difficult and unstable partner in the run-up to the birth of the euro. Altiero Spinelli, who we met earlier as author of the *Manifesto of Ventotene* during the war in the Fascist camp, was a key player in Italy's move towards European integration and in the drafting of various historic treaties in the 1980s.[58] In 1984 he described himself as 'the midwife who helped Parliament to give birth to this baby [the draft treaty on European Union]'. 'Now,' he added, extending the metaphor, 'we need to help it to live.'

Yet, despite the centrality of Europe and the European ideal in Italy, in purely political terms, Brussels has tended to count less than Rome in terms of power, influence and prestige. Italians have served as President of the European Commission on just two occasions, with Franco Maria Malfatti (1970–2) and Romano Prodi (1999–2004). Malfatti's resignation to seek domestic political power was symptomatic of the peripheral nature of European politics in Rome, and perhaps it was only with Prodi (and Mario Monti, who went from the European Commission to become Prime Minister of Italy in 2011) that Europe as a political entity was taken seriously by the Italian political elites.

Italy's relationship with Europe in a broader sense was always contradictory. European integration was popular domestically but most Italian politicians who got themselves elected in Strasbourg very rarely attended debates and many saw the job as an expenses gravy train. All indications showed that in the post-war period Italians were strongly pro-European, and supporters of further integration. But it also appeared true that the 'Europeanism' of Italians was somewhat nebulous – and not really linked to support for specific policies, institutions, or ideas. The undoubted 'pro-Europeanism' in Italy should also be seen in the light of the deep and historic detachment and even hatred of many Italians towards their own state and political system. Europe wasn't Italy, and this helped to make it popular.

On 1 January 2002 – just after midnight – many Italians celebrated the New Year by walking to their local cash-point machine and taking out some shiny new euro notes. Set-piece celebrations marked the moment. The lira was no more. It wasn't particularly missed, in itself. But prices soon appeared to double on most items (this may or may not have actually been the case, but it certainly felt that way). Italy had struggled to meet the economic parameters for the euro. Swingeing domestic cuts were required and implemented in the 1990s – as well as tax increases – in order for Italy to meet the requirements set down by the Maastricht Treaty of 1992. This was unpopular at home, but the blame tended to be transferred to domestic elites rather than Europe.

Over time, the euro would become a convenient scapegoat for many of Italy's economic woes. Romano Prodi, the architect of Italy's entry into the Eurozone, was kicked upstairs to become President of the European Commission in 1999 (a position he would hold until 2004). He had been rewarded for his efforts in pulling his country into the single European currency. But by whatever measure you care to choose, there is little doubt that, today, the attachment of Italians to 'Europe' is in decline, and this is a European-wide trend. Italians continued to look and move to other areas of Europe in order to find work and study, but these high levels of mobility and cultural openness were increasingly detached from identification with the institutions and policies of the EU itself.

New Italians?

'There was a constant increase of different kinds of figures – like migrants – who had needs which were met at times by a sense of welcome, and at other times by blind hostility.'

Alessandro Portelli[59]

'There is no such thing as a black Italian. Balotelli, you are African.'

Football chant directed at the footballer
Mario Balotelli, 2009 and passim[60]

Italy had never been an entirely mono-cultural or mono-ethnic country, but foreign immigrants were relatively rare in the post-war period. There were pockets of refugees from some of the former Italian colonies – Somalia in particular – who settled in Italy, especially in the 1970s, and some economic migrants here and there. But the numbers involved were tiny and stable outside of some localised areas, and these communities were absorbed without too many difficulties. These groups rarely impinged on national debates or became part of political narratives. They barely registered.

This all changed in the 1980s, 1990s and 2000s. As Italians became richer, they abandoned the 'dirty' sector of the job market. Italy now wanted cleaners, waiters and home helps, but also factory workers and agricultural labourers. An ageing population and smaller families, coupled with different work patterns, created needs for large numbers of home-based carers for the elderly and the young. This left economic space, and provided a market, for significant foreign immigration – for the first time. After years of sending its own population abroad (although this movement continued), Italy was now a receiving country. By 2013 there were at least 3 million migrants employed within Italy's labour market (out of an estimated overall total of some 5.3 million, around 540,000 of whom, it was said, were 'undocumented'). Some 670,000 or so migrant children were studying in Italian schools, and over 210,000 immigrants had started small businesses.[61]

In the 1990s, Italy was entirely unprepared – culturally, legally and socially – for the arrival of foreign workers. Laws regulating population movements were outdated and, in many cases, totally absurd. Every city had a 'foreigners office', run by the police, that issued 'Permits to stay' giving immigrants certain rights, and these permits had to be renewed at regular intervals. With the mass migration of the 1980s and 1990s, these offices simply could not cope with the numbers. Moreover, with entry into the European Union, and free labour rules, a two-tier system was in place. Residents of the EU still had to apply for their 'permit to stay', but they had faster queues to stand in and were treated relatively humanely. The same could not be said of non-EU foreign migrants, who often had to wake up at dawn to stand behind crash barriers in lengthy queues on the street. To add insult to injury the Migrants Office was often only open in the mornings. Many migrants ended up in the illegal, 'black' economy, which had always played a significant role in Italian economic life.

This two-tier system also applied to language and labelling. '*Extra-comunitari*' was a term that soon began to appear in the press and official reports. Technically, it applied to all those from outside the European Union (with its shifting borders), but this term was mainly used for black migrants, or, later, so-called 'white-blacks' from Eastern Europe (Albanians, and then Romanians, Bulgarians and Poles) – and rarely if ever for Swiss or American citizens. Language and its meanings shifted as the EU itself changed. Many mainstream terms were, quite simply, racist. For many years, for example, quality newspapers and politicians referred to a so-called group they dubbed the '*vù cumpra*'. This was meant to describe black street-sellers with poor Italian – 'you want to buy'. It took years before this racist phrase was phased out of journalism and political discourse.

The first waves of migrants were exotic, and caused little discussion. But a second wave in the mid-to-late 1990s rapidly became a hot political topic with increasing tensions and fears. Specific urban areas became quickly identified in the media with immigration and crime (usually without much evidence that they were dangerous in any way). There were violent incidents. Racism inside football grounds became commonplace. Confusion also reigned over exactly what racism was. There had been no real debate in Italy over these issues. Language was infused with stereotypical phrases and terms. Italy's colonial past was rarely discussed, but its cultural legacy was clearly a presence. Italians felt threatened by migrants – especially black migrants. There was a high demand for 'security', with frequent calls to the police or *carabinieri* regarding groups of migrants who had in fact committed no crime.

Immigrants were recruited to a range of jobs, and they also formed their own businesses. Many worked in the low-pay, cash-in-hand sector in jobs involving cleaning, washing and child-care, but whole categories of migrant work were created that replaced those traditionally carried out by Italian families – such as care for the elderly and sick. Others were easy prey for rapacious inter-mediaries and organised crime in agriculture (especially in the South), where conditions were often appalling, or the fake goods industry. Building sites, once again, as in the 1950s and 1960s, were key entry points for immigrant workers.

Initially, the immigrant arrival was often stigmatised in the media as an emergency. People were found sleeping rough in abandoned factories, or railway carriages. Newspapers called these places 'hotels of fear'. The creaking welfare state struggled to deal with these new arrivals. Special laws and decrees were passed, often in a panic – and rarely with a sense of strategy. Conflicts quickly emerged, and politicians became involved.

The Lega stoked the fires whenever it could.[62] This was also a moment when the stereotype of the 'good Italian' came under pressure. Racism became a feature of Italian society. Identities were tested and stretched. The victory of a black Italian woman – Denny Mendez – in the Miss Italia TV beauty show in 1996 caused widespread debate.

Sport, Racism and Migration

Sport was an important area for immigration, integration and racism. Black Italian sports stars began to emerge in the 1990s. Carlton Myers was a spectacular basketball player who had been born in London to a Caribbean father and Italian mother and who moved to Italy at the age of nine. He became a star for teams based in Pesaro and Bologna, and once scored eighty-seven points in a game. With the national team he took the squad to European gold. This led to a unique honour for a black Italian, as he was chosen to carry the national flag at the opening ceremony of the 2000 Sydney Olympics. Fiona May (Italian by marriage) and Andrew Howe in athletics were other early examples of black Italian sports stars.

Meanwhile, a series of black Italian football players began to emerge. Fabio Liverani, a highly technical midfielder, was the first black player (born in Rome – he had an Italian father and a Somali mother) to play for Italy, and went on to have a long career in Serie A. He was also the first black Italian manager of a Serie A team (Genoa, where he lasted for a mere seven games).

The Murder of Abdellah Doumi

'Where were the other people who could have saved that young Moroccan? How many people looked on and didn't try and help? That left bank of the Po is always busy. Are these passive spectators also complicit in what happened?'

Don Ciotti[63]

In the 1990s specific urban zones and other areas often became flashpoints for conflict with foreign migrants – who were frequently treated as a public-order 'problem' in themselves – thanks to their mere presence on the streets. One such zone was the so-called Murazzi area on the banks of the Po River in Turin.

The whole issue of violence in that area on the banks of the Po River exploded on the eve of the first round of the city's mayoral elections in April 1997. One night more than fifty young men, armed with iron bars, stones, bottles and toy guns, and dressed in bomber jackets and balaclavas, went on the rampage. Foreign immigrants were forced to flee from the group and one man, a disc jockey, was beaten around the head. The gang, many of whom were linked to far-right groups, then continued their violence in the city centre, smashing a number of cars. On the night of 19 July 1997 (at 5 a.m.) a twenty-six-year-old Moroccan man drowned in the Po. His name was Abdellah Doumi. The young man had been chased by at least ten young Italians (some of whom wore motorbike helmets) and, whilst in the water, bottles, rocks, wooden boxes and even a vacuum cleaner had been thrown at him. One of the gang had then shouted to Doumi to 'Go, go, swim to the other side.'[64] Those allegedly responsible were arrested almost immediately – twenty-four-year-old Piero Iavarone and three of his friends. A week later three hundred immigrants demonstrated near the point where Doumi died, calling for justice for the drowned man. At their first trial Iavarone and the other three were convicted of murder and sentenced to twenty-two years in prison. After a long campaign in their favour, this sentence was reduced on appeal.

The explanations for this event were manifold. Some saw the violence as a political act, others as the natural consequence of 'high' immigration. Before long, the Doumi murder was almost entirely forgotten.

Controlling the Migrants

How did foreign immigrants arrive in Italy? Some came by boat, others by plane or train and some by car or coach. Many arrived illegally, but amnesties led to some form of legal status being achieved, although this could also be lost at the stroke of a pen. There were mixed marriages. Refugee status was relatively rare. Over time, a complicated legal and security infrastructure was constructed to allow the Italian state to try to classify and punish 'illegal' immigrants. Hapless local Foreigners' Offices were soon flanked by other institutions, rules and regulations. This system included a network of newly constructed immigrant detention centres, known euphemistically as Centres for Temporary Permanance (set up in 1998) – later rebranded as Centres for Identification and Expulsion. These custodial structures were holding centres for immigrants who had committed no actual crime, but were in a legal limbo (although later merely being an illegal immigrant was made into a criminal offence). Conditions inside were often dreadful. Numerous immigrants also ended up in the prison system. A series of measures were passed relating to migration.

The Bossi-Fini law of 2002 seemed to tighten controls around illegal migration – but this measure did the opposite of what it said it would. The law led to an increase in undocumented migration and migrants and to greater exploitation of new arrivals in the workforce and elsewhere. The political message of being 'tough on migration' was transmitted to the electorate, while employers could continue to recruit cheap labour. This duplicity was a constant feature of the management of migration in this period in Italy and elsewhere. Free movement in the EU also had an impact, changing the provenance of migration with time as more countries were admitted.

Meanwhile, thousands attempted to make it to the borders of Italy (and thus of the European Union itself) by boat – from the Albanian coast initially and later across the Mediterranean from Africa and elsewhere. For a time Italy's navy was employed to 'reject' this movement (and this tactic led quickly to tragedy), but soon a kind of compromise was reached. Potential immigrants would be escorted to Italy, identified and processed. Many, however, didn't make it. This movement became part of an industry, making money for people smugglers and some of those who exploited migrants on arrival. Criminal associations tapped into the way that funds could be raked off from state assistance designed for the new arrivals.

Italy wouldn't concede the vote to non-EU migrants – for any form of election. This deprived the migrant community of any access to power and political representation. They struggled to make their voices heard. Even those born in Italy were unable to obtain citizenship until they were eighteen. Proposals were brought forward to change this state of affairs at various times, but they failed to make progress in Parliament. No party or movement wanted to be seen as soft on immigration or crime.

In certain parts of Italy entire sectors saw immigrants employed in jobs previously held by Italians. Around Brescia, for example, many of the still-functioning factories were staffed almost entirely by black workers, while many Sikhs specialised in the production of one of Italy's most famous products – Grana Padano cheese. In the area around Pessina Cremonese in the north of the country Sikh men worked through the night to create this cheese.

In the early 2000s, as I was returning from a mountain walk in the Trentino area of the country, I came across two Romanian men who had taken over the care of the local cows for the summer, living in a mountain shack that had been long abandoned. Sub-cultures and communities of immigrants set up their own informal networks involving travel and support. Coaches moved back and forth across Europe and beyond. Phone centres and computer cafés allowed migrants to contact their families at home. Satellite dishes sprang up on the outside of housing blocks to create access to foreign television networks.

Below the surface, away from the rhetoric and the political marketplace, complicated and contradictory forms of integration did take place. Immigrant children attended Italian schools. Some immigrants became public figures. Second and third generations of (former) immigrants grew up entirely in Italy – creating as they did so new forms of hybrid culture, language and social connections. New immigrant chains were part of this process, as they had been in the early twentieth century and in the 1950s and 1960s with internal migration.

But was Italy a fundamentally racist country? Political movements openly fanned the flames of racism. Clearly, many of these immigrants were 'needed but not wanted', as the American sociologist Aristide Zolberg has argued, or 'useful invaders' in the words of the Italian sociologist Maurizio Ambrosini. Italians were 'reluctant importers' of immigrants.[65] There were opportunities for these new arrivals across the Italian economy, but their activities in social, political and cultural spaces were highly restricted. By excluding immigrants from political representation, Italy was happy to collect taxes and profit from their labour, but gave them no chance to express their desires in a democratic way.

Some have described these populations as 'non-people', lacking in basic rights and without any access to political power, but still present within society and above all in the social, agricultural, service and industrial sectors.[66] They were both invisible and highly 'visible', in selected ways, at the same time. So, as Ambrosini argues, despite the obvious fact that Italy is now a multi-ethnic country 'In their cultural representations, Italians tend to deny this reality.'[67] Politics refuses to deal openly with economic and social realities. The outcome for migrants and Italians and migrant Italians is a toxic combination of confusion, fear, segregation, exclusion and embedded racism. Nowhere was this more obvious than with Muslims in Italy and the constant debates and tensions over the building and use of mosques.

Mosques and Islam in Italy

Mosques (or potential mosques) were often the focal point of discussions and protests around multiculturalism and conflict in Italy (as they were elsewhere in the world). In the early period of foreign immigration, a few new mosques were built with little controversy. They hardly registered. But soon, as immigration became a hot issue and anti-immigrant parties began to campaign around racist themes (often but not always masked as 'security' or 'cultural' issues), the building and use of mosques became more difficult and politicised.

In Milan, a small mosque was built in Segrate just outside the city in 1988. It aroused little comment. But since then, every proposal to build a new mosque closer to the city centre to serve Milan's Muslim population has been blocked and has often led to demonstrations and protests. For many years many of Milan's Muslims used a nondescript former garage in the northern part of the city – in a road called Viale Jenner – for their prayers. This structure was too small for the numbers using it, and so people would often spill out onto the street. There were constant complaints from local residents, usually about the use of public space and noise. In the end, this 'centre' was partly closed.[68] Plans were put in place for a new mosque, but these were gridlocked by political hostility, local 'protest committees' and 'bureaucratic procedures'. Controversies over mosques were not confined to Lombardy, but also occurred in numerous other places across Italy. All this was, of course, wrapped up in an international context patterned by the events of 11 September 2001 in New York.

Oriana Fallaci's 'The Rage and the Pride'

The ominous date of 11 September 2001 was a turning point in terms of Italy's current difficult relationship with Islam. On 15 September – just four days after the attacks on the Twin Towers in New York – the celebrated Italian journalist Oriana Fallaci published a long, rambling and polemical article-letter (running to over 10,000 words) in Italy's most mainstream quality newspaper, *Il Corriere della Sera*. In it, she described the 'dangers of Islam' in violent terms. A prolific, popular writer with a high public profile – and a fearless interviewer of those in power around the world – Fallaci had been silent for more than a decade. She was in her flat in New York when the attacks took place. A subsequent book (first published in December 2001) based on this article became a runaway best-seller – shifting millions of copies across the world. In Italy alone this book had gone through thirty-six editions by 2004 with sales of over a million copies. Fallaci had always been on the left, and her transformation to a symbol of the 'struggle' against 'Islam' was an unlikely one. A number of other books on the same theme – all of them big sellers – would appear over subsequent years.

In introducing Fallaci's sensational piece in the *Corriere della Sera* the paper's editor Ferruccio De Bortoli described her as 'our most celebrated writer [she no longer used the word journalist]'.[69] De Bortoli predicted – rightly – that her words would create extensive debate. Fallaci signed off by saying that 'I have said what I wanted to say. I was forced to by my pride and my rage. I was allowed to by my clear conscience and my age. But now I need to get back to work. In short – I want to be left alone.' This sentence gave her long piece its overall title, 'The Rage and the Pride'. But she did not keep her word. The 'door' was well and truly open. Fallaci would return to the subject of Islam frequently after 2001.

Who was Oriana Fallaci? A partisan during the Second World War, she was probably the most prominent and widely read Italian journalist of the 1960s and 1970s. Her speciality had been in reportage and exclusive interviews – as a kind of high-level foreign correspondent – but she had also published a series of highly successful novels and autobiographical essays. Her position as a woman in a very male world – that of the war reporter – made her an object of admiration for her female readers. While interviewing the Ayatollah Khomeni, for example, she took off the chador she had been asked to wear. Fallaci had a long relationship with a celebrated Greek opponent of the military junta – Alexandros Panagoulis – and had risked her life during her time as a correspondent, most notably in Mexico in 1968, when she was shot while reporting.[70]

But what did Fallaci actually argue in that infamous article-letter and series of subsequent books? As the cultural historian Charles Burdett has pointed out, 'According to the vision set out by [Fallaci] Islam – as a religion and as a civilisation – represents an unmoving body of thought and belief which structures human identity in such a way that it is relentlessly hostile to the West ... [for Fallaci] fundamentalism is not a separate reality, divorced from the central current of Islam, but the expression of the inner form of the Muslim world'.[71]

Fallaci, who had not lived permanently in Italy for years, went further than this with regard to foreign migrants. She drew an explicit link between what she saw as radical Islam, terrorism and population movements. Fallaci claimed, for example, that 'By now there are tens of thousands of Osama Bin Ladens, and they are not to be found only in Afghanistan or in other Arab countries. They are everywhere, and the most aggressive of them are in the West. They are in our cities, our streets, our universities.'

Fallaci's descriptions of foreign immigration to Italy were almost deliberately offensive. She seemed to rely on her experiences in Florence when she wrote that:

> the one-time capital of art and culture and beauty ... now has arrogant guests – Albanians ... Tunisians, Algerians, Nigerians – who fervently support the drugs trade and prostitution which strangely does not seem to be prohibited by the Koran. These people are close to the Uffizi gallery ... in front of the National Library, near the entrances to museums. They can be seen on the Ponte Vecchio where every so often they knife or shoot each other ... on the steps of the San Lorenzo church they get drunk ... what hypocrites ... and insult women ... And if anyone protests ... 'Racist, racist' is the reply... And this happens in other cities, like Turin ... that city which created Italy and now no longer seems to be an Italian city at all. It feels like Algiers, Dacca, Nairobi, Damascus, Beirut.[72]

This was the level of 'journalism' employed by Fallaci concerning migrants to Italy. Her invective had a vast influence right across Italy and beyond. She claimed that all Muslims were opposed to 'Western civilisation', underlined what she saw as the superiority of Italian culture and the West in general, and lumped together a series of historical figures from the Arab world – such as Yasser Arafat and Gaddafi (many of whom she had known personally during her time as an intrepid investigative journalist). Moreover,

she depicted immigrants as invaders and potential terrorists who
wanted to destroy the worlds they were coming to.

Anybody who opposed this view was dismissed as a
'do-gooder' (*buonista*) or a 'so-called expert'. It was a violent and
extreme point of view, but now it was mainstream. Fallaci's books
became the most best-selling non-fiction publications in Italian
history. Her supporters praised her 'politically incorrect' courage
in speaking out. For many on the left, however, her polemics were
a betrayal of her own past. There was considerable opposition
in the academic world, and beyond, to Fallaci's one-sided and
misinformed view of immigrants and Muslims. Others unpicked
the links she made between the values of the Resistance and the
Risorgimento and her 'rage and pride'.

Fallaci rejected the view that there was something called 'moderate Islam'. 'There are millions and millions of fanatics,' she
wrote, 'the real protagonist of this war is not him [Bin Laden].
It is not even the country that gave birth to him or which gives
him hospitality. It is the mountain. That mountain which for one
thousand and four hundred years has not moved, which does not
emerge from the depths of its blindness, does not open its doors
to the gains achieved by civilisation, that does not want to know
about liberty and justice and democracy and progress.' Mosques
were something to be opposed, in Italy. They were homes to 'terrorists or aspiring terrorists'.

Fallaci seemed increasingly unhinged, but she was taken very
seriously indeed. In 2006, in *the New Yorker*, she expressed
dismay at a mosque planned for a place called Colle Val d'Elsa
not far from Siena. Her words were (once again) intentionally
inflammatory:

If I'm alive ... I will go to my friends in Carrara – you know,
where there is the marble. They are all anarchists. With them,
I take the explosives. I make you *juuump* in the air. I blow it
up! With the anarchists of Carrara. I *do not want* to see this
mosque – it's very near my house in Tuscany. I do not want
to see a twenty-four-metre minaret in the landscape of Giotto.

When I cannot even wear a cross or carry a Bible in *their* country! So I BLOW IT UP!'[73]

Umberto Eco replied to Fallaci's original long piece in *Il Corriere della Sera* with an article of his own in *La Repubblica*. He did not mention Fallaci by name but denounced cultural chauvinism and called for tolerance. 'We are a pluralistic society because we permit mosques to be built in our own home, and we cannot give this up just because in Kabul they put evangelical Christians in jail,' he wrote. 'If we did, we would become Taliban ourselves.' Eco reminded those who believed that Western civilisation was superior that 'Hitler – who burned books and criticised "degenerate" art and had those he saw as part of "inferior" races killed – was also part of Western culture.'[74]

Suddenly, the 'dangers of Islam' were front-page news. Centre-right and far-right groupings took up Fallaci's war cry. In this context, eccentric figures emerged who were quickly adopted by the media. Magdi Allam was a Muslim based in Italy. He later converted to Catholicism, renaming himself Magdi Cristiano Allam. In 2008 he published a book entitled *Thank You, Jesus*. He was a constant presence on Italian television around this time and was employed as a high-level journalist on quality newspapers such as *La Repubblica* and *Il Corriere della Sera*. Allam was at times critical of Fallaci's catch-all condemnation of Islam, but he became known above all for views that seemed in line with some of those of 'The Rage and the Pride'. He described mosques, for example, as 'centres of indoctrination' and potential 'recruiting grounds for terroristic activity'. These debates and tensions continued well into the twenty-first century, and were played out not just at an intellectual level, but on the streets and squares of Italy's cities and towns.[75]

Violence and crime in Italy were often framed in ethnic terms – as part of a kind of immigrant-induced 'emergency'. On 13 February 2010 a fight in Via Padova in Milan led to the death of a young Egyptian man. A small riot followed in the area, with some smashed windows, mostly, it seems, involving young immigrants. The reaction from the press and the political system was instant, with references to the ethnic mix of the area and reporting of shocked reactions of (white) Italians. In the face of this media reporting, Milan's centre-right administration soon passed local by-laws that placed restrictions on local immigrant-run businesses in terms of activities and opening hours. But a positive reaction to the facts of Via Padova also came from below, with attempts to understand and value the ethnic and cultural mix of the area, and the setting-up of a successful festival which presented a different side of the city from that of a hostile 'casbah' as depicted in some of the press and on local television stations.

Italy, Islam and the Catholic Church

A series of powerful new social and cultural challenges faced the Church in the 1990s and 2000s. The most important of these was the arrival in Italy of significant numbers of non-Catholics. Italy faced what John Pollard has called 'a new, and uneasy, religious pluralism'.[76] Muslims were by no means a majority of the immigrants who settled or worked for a time in Italy in this period, but they did become a significant minority. Reliable statistics are still difficult to come by, but it appears that Muslims made up 2 per cent of the total population of Italy by 2005. However, the differences in available figures are significant, with a range from 1 to 1.5 million.[77]

Islam is now the second-biggest religion in the country. What does this mean for Italy, for these Muslims and for the Catholic Church? As Charles Burdett has argued, 'It is perhaps no exaggeration to say that Italy's relationship with Islam, and by extension with the Islamic world, represents one of the most important cultural and societal questions currently facing the country.'[78] Italy as a whole struggled to understand and adapt to the presence of Muslims right across the country, especially in the phase where immigration took on mass proportions and after the 9/11 attacks in New York.

How did the Church react to mass immigration and the presence of a sizeable Muslim community? On the one hand,

Catholic (and other religious) organisations and charities were at the forefront of work with immigrants on the ground. Catholic immigrants often revived churches and were a strong presence. There were strong differences over this kind of policy, however, within the Church's hierarchy. Bishop Biffi of Bologna, for example, has criticised the Church (in which he was a powerful figure) for a so-called 'politics of acceptance or welcome' towards Muslims. But in other ways, the Church set itself up as part of the 'war between civilisations' that marked the twenty-first century, in particular under Pope Benedict XVI (2005–13). His successor Pope Francis has proposed a different way of seeing the role of the Church, with calls for integration and public displays of solidarity with immigrants. In March 2016 the Pope kissed and washed the feet of twelve immigrants, some of them Muslims, in a refugee centre north of Rome. He then said that 'Muslims, Hindus, Catholics … Evangelicals [are] all brothers and children of the same God … We want to live together in peace.'[79]

Crucifixes

The continuing power of the Church could also be seen in the physical presence of its symbols.[80] The existence in some (but not all) public buildings of the crucifix goes right back to measures passed at the time when the nation of Italy was born. Fascist measures in the 1920s then stated that crucifixes should be part of the 'furnishings' of schools, alongside a portrait of the King. Italy's constitution incorporated the Lateran Pacts in 1948, and this meant that a crucifix continued to be displayed in many Italian schoolrooms, often behind the teacher on the wall at the front of the class, and this was extended in the 1960s to the new middle-school system, when the text was slightly changed to include a photograph of the President of the Republic, and not the defunct King. And it was not just schools that were involved. Courtrooms also sometimes (but not always) contained crucifixes.

In November 2009 the European Court of Human Rights in Strasbourg declared that the presence of the crucifix in Italian schools was not legitimate.[81] This judgement followed a long battle by an Italian citizen of Finnish origin, Soile Lautsi (whose children went to school in Italy), who appealed to both the Italian Constitution and the European Convention in her campaign, which had begun way back in 2002. The legal struggle continued, with complicated decisions that involved numerous judges and courts. Some of these judgements looked to describe the crucifix as a more universal cultural symbol, and not a religious one.

The judgement that came down from Strasbourg was met with outrage in Italy, and in the Vatican. Even the centre-left politician and former Communist Pierluigi Bersani was critical. He stated that 'good sense has fallen victim to the law. I think that an ancient tradition like the crucifix cannot be offensive to anyone.'[82] Lega Nord politicians were particularly vehement in their opposition, and one called (perhaps provocatively) for a crucifix to be added to the Italian flag itself. The Lega saw the crucifix as part of its new 'battle against Islam'. Italy appealed against the 2009 sentence, and it was overturned in 2011. The crucifixes remain in place. Italy was technically a secular country, and Catholicism was not – officially – the state religion. But this secular status was often unclear and muddied.

Cult: Padre Pio

Padre Pio, a Capuchin friar from the deep south of Italy – San Giovanni Rotondo in the Province of Foggia in Apulia – claimed to have been 'given' the stigmata in 1918. He quickly became a celebrated figure and people flocked to hear him preach. For many years the official Church argued over what to do with Padre Pio, and his increasingly powerful cult. There were attempts to move the friar away from his power base and home town in the South, which were resisted. But later Padre Pio was given special treatment, and allowed to continue with mass in Latin while Italian

was being introduced in the rest of the country's church services. His miracles and 'stigmata' were given official blessing and
long queues of people would wait to confess their sins to Padre
Pio himself.

Despite controversy within and outside of the Church, the cult
of Padre Pio grew and grew, especially in the post-war period. The
historian Sergio Luzzatto wrote that 'Padre Pio would become
the most venerated saint in twenty-first-century Italy, more
popular that St Anthony of Padua and St Francis of Assisi, more
popular even than the Virgin Mary or Jesus of Nazareth.'[83] As
money came in via devout pilgrims who made the long trip down
to San Giovanni Rotondo, a sparkling new hospital, confirming
Padre Pio's image as a man of the people, was built in the 1950s.
Padre Pio was not just a very holy man. He was also a benefactor
in the eyes of many. Luzzatto's powerful book pointed out that
there was also a dark side to the cult, including strong links to fascism and mysterious deliveries of carbolic acid, which might have
provided another explanation for that 'stigmata'.

Padre Pio died in 1968. But his cult blossomed. Millions of
Italians and others continued to make pilgrimages down to his
home town and church in San Giovanni Rotondo. In the early
1990s the celebrated Genovese architect, Renzo Piano, designed
an imposing new space to accommodate these pilgrims, and
construction took place over a thirteen-year period before the
new church was finally opened in 2004. It has seating for over
6,500 people, while another 30,000 or so can stand outside in the
piazza. Padre Pio was fast-tracked to sainthood, being beatified
in 1999 and canonised in 2002. He was now (officially) Saint Pio,
but many of his followers continue to call him by his original
title. His 'humble' reputation seemed to jar with that grand title.
Many of his fans carry images of him in their wallets or fixed to
their cars. His white beard, balding pate, friar's robes and bandages or gloves to cover his stigmata are unmistakeable. There are
also statues to him in and around thousands of churches across
Italy. Various Popes made visits down to the South to bask in his
glory. Padre Pio is big, big business. Over 160 hotels operate in

the small town of San Giovanni Rotondo alone. Some claimed that Padre Pio was the biggest religious draw in Italy (and the world) after Rome.

Catholicism and the way people related to it changed over time, and Padre Pio's cult, and the business around it, was a key symbol of this transformation. The big attraction in the Church itself in San Giovanni Rotondo after 1968 became Padre Pio's body. As one website put it: 'Here you can admire the body of the Saint, stored in a glass box, with his face covered in a mask which reproduces his features perfectly. His clothes are original ones, including the socks and gloves that Saint Pio used to protect his stigmata and which he kept inside his monk's cell.' In addition, visitors could visit the monk's humble dwelling containing 'a kneeler on which Saint Pio passed hours praying and suffering and the sofa where he would lie down when he was overcome with pain'. A wax museum in the town reproduced scenes from Padre Pio's life and the former friar also had his own digital TV channel (which mostly showed static shots of mass). The Church claimed that nearly eight million people visited San Giovanni Rotondo in 2009.

How did such a cult not only survive, but flourish, in the supposedly secular world of twentieth- and twenty-first-century Italy, where divorce was rife, Church attendance figures were plummeting and there was a crisis in terms of recruiting priests? Did the cult tell us something about the way that the relationship between Italians and the Church had changed and developed, but nevertheless remained powerful and deep-rooted? In 2016 Padre Pio's remains were brought to St Peter's in Rome for a week to celebrate the extraordinary Jubilee of Mercy planned for that year. Massive queues of people waited for hours to view the body. Many took selfies when they finally reached the saint, in a glass case, next to the Croatian Friar Saint Leopold Mandic (who had lived most of his life in Padua).[84] Pope Francis had apparently made a personal request to facilitate the transfer. Padre Pio and Pope Francis were, for many Catholics, the face of the Church in the twenty-first century.

6

Italy in the Twenty-First Century: Crisis, Post-Democracy and the Triumph of Populism

'A man with an entirely personal version of the truth, so that whatever he says is true ... He tells lies, but he believes them.'

Indro Montanelli on Silvio Berlusconi[1]

'Fiction is better than reality.'

Silvio Berlusconi[2]

'All of Italy's political life has rotated around Silvio Berlusconi: all eyes turn to him, all thoughts, hopes and fears.'

Maurizio Viroli[3]

Peak Berlusconi: 2001–6

Berlusconi's 2001 victory – which would lead to a stable and lasting government – was also about hard political choices. In 1994 his victorious alliance had been more of a fragmentary pact than a real set of agreements. He was looking at that point to bring together a regionalist party and a nationalist party and he had no experience of government, and neither did Bossi or Fini. Berlusconi had never even worked within and around the structures of Parliament. This would change in the long period before Berlusconi had another chance at power – in 2001. By then, he had been part of the political system for seven years, and his alliances had a solid foundation. Centre-right coalitions had governed at local and regional levels. They were ready, and Berlusconi was not willing to let 1994 happen again.

In 2001 his opponents on the centre-left were weakened by that damaging split to the left in 1998 – which had brought down the first Prodi government. Rifondazione Comunista stood alone in the Upper House, while a 'non-belligerence' pact was agreed for other parts of the election. The centre-left's leader by then was a good-looking but ineffectual politician called Francesco Rutelli. Berlusconi outmanoeuvred his opponents, taking centre stage throughout the campaign and making full use of his media power, despite new access rules. In April 2001 he had millions of copies of a magazine containing his 'life story' (redubbed 'An Italian Story') sent to every house in Italy. As the vote came closer, Berlusconi pulled another rabbit out of the hat – something he would repeat in subsequent campaigns.

On 8 May 2001, live on prime-time television, the presenter Bruno Vespa allowed Berlusconi to present what he called a 'Contract with the Italians'. This unprecedented access to direct political communication with a TV-watching public (on a publicly funded channel) was a sign of things to come. A fawning Vespa would occasionally venture some mild criticism, but he knew which way the wind was blowing. The 'Contract' was also displayed on a larger sheet of paper that Berlusconi had brought with him for the occasion (Ed Miliband's ill-fated 2015 stone tablet was a pale imitation). It began as follows:

'Contract between Silvio Berlusconi born in Milan 29 September 1936 leader of Forza Italia and the House of Liberties, who acts in agreement with all the allies in the coalition, and Italian citizens. It is understood and stipulated as follows . . .' Five promises were made: tax cuts (with precise figures); a crack-down on crime; pension rises; the creation of 1.5 million jobs (an old favourite from 1994, with an extra 500,000 added for good measure); and, finally, public investment for a ten-year Major Works Plan including 'roads, motorways, underground lines, trains, waterways and flood defence'. This was designed as a 'real' but (fake) contract. Berlusconi promised that if four of the five promises were not met after five years in power, he would retire from the political scene. 'The Contract', the document concluded, 'will become valid and operative on 13 May 2001 with the vote of the Italian electorate.'

Berlusconi was permitted to read out the whole contract (on special 'formal' paper) live on television, with Vespa hovering behind him (in a light outfit, so as not to compete with his master's usual smart dark suit). Vespa played the triple role of sidekick, straight-man and 'notary'. There was even a special wooden desk for the signing (as in 1994's 'taking of the field'). The studio had been completely transformed for this media event. Berlusconi then signed the document with a flourish. He ad-libbed that his victory was 'certain'.

The contract was not fulfilled. Some argue that none of the five promises was met.[4] Unsurprisingly, this did not prevent Berlusconi standing in the 2006 and 2008 elections. It was a dazzling and audacious piece of political theatre – a personal appeal direct to 'the people'. The centre-left had nothing to remotely compete with this level of political marketing. It could be argued that they had never understood the power of television. Five days later the Italians went to the polls.

Berlusconi's confidence was confirmed on 13 May 2001. It was a stunning victory. His coalition won 18.4 million votes, while Rutelli's soft left alliance managed just 13 million. The 1.9 million votes for Rifondazione Comunista gained them just a handful of seats.[5] Berlusconi had a comfortable majority in both houses. There would be no repeat of 1994. As the Berlusconi era was born, many began to look back to the First Republic with nostalgia, even longing. At least the Christian Democrats had displayed a 'sense of the state', it was said. Yes, the old system had been corrupt and dishonest, but it hadn't *celebrated* its corruption and dishonesty. The vulgarity and kitsch of the Berlusconi era was hard to bear.[6]

After 2001, Berlusconi had a stable government majority and he set out to govern for the entire length of an administration, something that no post-war Italian Prime Minister had managed to do. Power in the First Republic had been centralised, but not excessively personalised before the 1980s. Berlusconi remained in post for over 1,400 days – beating the record of his friend Bettino Craxi, his only predecessor to govern for a solid amount of time without a break. Berlusconi would be Prime Minister for eight out of the next ten years (2001–6 and 2008–11) – and for a grand total of over 3,300 days in power (including 1994). Only two other men have governed for longer overall since Italy was unified in the nineteenth century – Benito Mussolini (who didn't have to bother too much with elections) and Giovanni Giolitti.

Berlusconi's first big international commitment in 2001 as Prime Minister was to be held in Genoa – where the G8 summit was due to take place.

Genoa, 2001: Days of Rage, Days of Violence, Days of Death

The summit started with a party, and a concert by Manu Chao. Despite all the build-up, the warnings, the elaborate rules put in place about security and the fenced-off 'red zone', the G8 meeting in the port city of Genoa between 19 and 21 July 2001 seemed to be passing off without too much trouble. Protesters had planned numerous counter-demonstrations and other events to coincide with the summit, and stringent security measures were set up across the city. On 20 July, very quickly, things took a turn for the worse. Repeated police charges across the city and assaults on demonstrators, who often had their hands held up in a sign of passivity, were preceded by attacks on banks and 'symbols' of capitalism by masked individuals who were quickly identified in the media as something called the 'black block'. Strangely, the 'black block' met with very little police resistance as they roamed through the city on 20 July. The rest of the two remaining days of the Genoa summit was a litany of violence and high tension.

At about 5.30 p.m. on 20 July (after an entire day of clashes) a twenty-three-year-old man called Carlo Giuliani was shot dead as he moved towards a *carabinieri* van with a fire extinguisher in his hands in a square called Piazza Alimonda. The fatal shot was allegedly fired by a raw *carabiniere* conscript called Mario Placanica. The *carabinieri* vehicle drove over Giuliani in its hurry to escape. The investigation that followed cleared Placanica of any blame, as it was argued that his shot had struck a flying stone before hitting Giuliani – and that in any case he had acted in 'self-defence'. No trial was ever held. These official versions were contested – and continue to be so – by the family and the defence. Piazza Alimonda was unofficially renamed after Carlo Giuliani.[7]

A later report argued that 'democracy had been temporarily suspended' in Genoa. During the period of the demonstrations, an unofficial holding station was set up in a barracks in a place called Bolzaneto, at the edge of the city. Here, many of those arrested were held for extended periods. They were also left untreated despite serious injuries. Fascist songs were played to them on mobile phones and they were subjected to psychological and physical abuse. Many were foreigners who spoke no Italian.

Bolzaneto was a place of physical and mental torture. Nobody was permitted to see a lawyer. A British woman was insulted and asked to stand for more than an hour against the wall, with her broken wrist in a plaster. A young German woman sat in the cell for hours, crying, her mouth bleeding from where her teeth had been knocked out. On the way to the bathroom, the 'prisoners' saw a room with a sheet blocking the door, from which came occasional screams. Some prisoners had their hair cut off. Democracy and legality returned only when those in Bolzaneto were sent to normal prisons, where they were given access to a lawyer and proper medical care.

The final act of this catastrophic series of events took place in and outside a school building known as the Scuola Diaz, named after one of Italy's military heroes from the First World War. The school was being used as a dormitory for demonstrators – who had often come from abroad. On 21 July a number of demonstrators were settling down for the night. Many had been traumatised by the violence they had seen on the streets. At around midnight, hundreds of armed and helmeted police and *carabinieri* (more than 500 in total were involved) suddenly forced their way into the building. They savagely beat a British journalist, Mark Covell, on the street outside as they made their way in.

Inside, there was carnage. Defenceless men and women were attacked and ninety-three arrests were made. Many ended up in hospital. The walls and floors of the school were covered in blood. A procession of stretchers took the injured into ambulances. Later, film footage showed senior policemen planting Molotov cocktails and black T-shirts inside the building. All of the ninety-three demonstrators were cleared. No proper public inquiry was ever held. Brave magistrates continued their investigations in the face of official cover-ups and hostility. Some officials were found guilty for the violence in the school and in the Bolzaneto holding station – and selected demonstrators were prosecuted for events on the streets earlier. Genoa's violence and its aftermath were harrowing for many of those who were there, and marked an inauspicious beginning for Berlusconi's centre-right coalition.[8]

Berlusconi in Power: *Ad Personam*

'Berlusconi's regime is surely a degeneration of democracy into the power of a demagogue.'

Maurizio Viroli[9]

'All citizens have equal social dignity and are equal before the law.'

Italian Constitution, 1948, Article 3[10]

Berlusconi did not seek political power to become rich. He was already very wealthy when he stood as a candidate. *Forbes* magazine, in 2003, estimated that he was worth some $5.9 billion by that time – and was the forty-fifth richest person in the world. As Perry Anderson put it, 'He reversed the typical path from office to profit by amassing a fortune before achieving office, which he then used not so much to increase his wealth as to protect it, and himself, from multiple criminal charges for the ways he acquired it.'[11] Nor did Berlusconi see himself as someone with a grand design for Italy. He didn't like 'communism', whatever that meant in 2001, but he was no ideological free marketeer or privatiser. Given the choice between pushing through an unpopular reform and abandoning it, he would usually choose the latter course of action, unless the reform had a direct impact on his own personal interests. His (defunct) 'Contract' with the Italians had a vaguely Keynesian look to it – public investment, tax cuts, pension rises. Romano Prodi and the emergency technical governments (1993–4 and after 2011) privatised more than Berlusconi's administrations.

Berlusconi used power to make himself more powerful, and enjoyed the glamour of the extra fame and access he achieved. He embraced what some called his 'conflict of interests'. He saw no conflict, only a series of opportunities. He managed to present his conflict of interests as a positive – a campaigning asset. He was 'too rich' to be bribed. His companies employed 'thousands of Italians'. He had 'sacrificed' a successful business career for the good of Italy. As Umberto Eco wrote, he established 'the identification of the party, the country, and the state with a series of business interests'. Eco added that Berlusconi had established the idea of a 'convergence of interests … persuading the country to accept the idea that his personal interests coincide with those of the national community'.[12] Thus began a phase of the personal use of the state and government.

Berlusconi's time in power after 2001 was marked by a series of attempts to use the state and Parliament to influence his own businesses, judicial status, and further solidify his political power. Laws and measures were dubbed 'ad personam' or 'personal' laws in the press because of the way they seemed designed to help Berlusconi himself, his companies, and his friends, and in a variety of ways.

Some affected Berlusconi's own legal problems – such as measures relating to illegal accounting (in 2001 he was involved in five ongoing trials relating to this crime) or international searches by the tax and police authorities (which threatened his offshore holdings and interests). Others were a more direct attack on the judiciary, such as attempts to move trials to more

THE ARCHIPELAGO

accommodating areas and away from what he saw as his judicial enemies (above all in Milan). A few aided Berlusconi's sporting-business interests (such as the so-called 'save-football' decree of 2002, which allowed football clubs to take years to pay taxes they owed). Crucially, the statute of limitations was reduced for trials, directly leading to some of Berlusconi's own trials not making it to the end in time.

As well as these beautifully designed bits of 'personal' legislation, Berlusconi also tried – on two occasions – for the jackpot. He wanted to make himself, and other top institutional figures, *immune from prosecution* for all but the most heinous of crimes. Berlusconi justified these measures as an attempt to defuse the ongoing war between himself and the judiciary – which he claimed was politically motivated. However, for many, it was obvious he was trying – through a series of laws – to make himself above the law.

The first attempt at obtaining immunity became known, rather grandly, as the *Lodo Schifani* (2003). It proposed to suspend trials for the five most powerful institutional figures in the Italian state while they held those posts. Berlusconi, of course, held one of these positions. This was the key part of the text: 'The President of the Republic, The President of the Senate, The President of the House of Deputies, The President of the Council of Ministers [and] The President of the Constitutional Court cannot be subject to criminal trials for any crime relating to the period before they took on these roles or during the time they are in office.' Luckily for Italy, the Italian Constitution is a robust document. It states clearly, for example, that 'the law is equal for all'. It also includes a clause that makes investigation of a reported crime obligatory – to prevent political favours on the part of the judiciary. Berlusconi's 'immunity' measures were thrown out by the Constitutional Court.

In 2008, soon after yet another election victory, Berlusconi tried again. This time, only four people (or institutional posts, to be more accurate) were to be made 'immune' from trials. This was what that law proposed (it became known this time as the

Lodo Alfano): '1. Except for cases linked to Articles 90 and 96 in the Constitution, criminal processes for the individuals who hold the posts of The President of the Republic, The President of the Council of Ministers, The President of the Senate and the President of the House of Deputies, are suspended from the time they take up these posts until the time that they leave. This suspension also applies to criminal processes relating to facts before the individuals took on these posts.' Berlusconi and his lawyers thought they had a good chance of getting this modified measure through the Constitutional Court. They had tried to avoid the pitfalls of the 2003 'Lodo', and they put pressure on the judges involved (two were even invited to dinner in Berlusconi's villa in Arcore). But they were wrong, again. The Constitutional Court stood firm.

Nonetheless, politically and culturally, it was quite worrying to say the least that these absurd and unprecedented laws were both voted through Parliament and signed by Italy's President. Very few of those within Berlusconi's own alliance – including the Lega – disobeyed his orders. He had constructed a business or personal party, and he had almost complete control of this organisation and its allies, and therefore of Parliament itself. Berlusconi used the *Lodo Alfano* for three separate trials, before the Constitutional Court pronounced its verdict. Berlusconi's Parliament seemed, at times, like a personal fiefdom.

Less obvious 'personal' laws and clauses aiding Berlusconi were often hidden away in bigger laws, or in the budget, such as help for media companies or incentives to buy digital boxes (sold by Berlusconi's brother, Paolo). Many of these texts or clauses were drawn up by Berlusconi's lawyers – some of whom had been rewarded for their work with parliamentary seats. In general, Berlusconi saw Parliament as useful only when it could be used to his own advantage. He was rarely in the chamber, and said that he saw the whole institution as a 'waste of time'.

Most of these measures led to protests in the press and on the streets – as well as in Parliament. But, equally, the centre-right often complained bitterly when decisions went against them – thus undermining the legitimacy of both the constitution and the Constitutional Court. Berlusconi had little time for parliamentary or representative democracy. He appealed directly to 'the people'. The state was there to serve his personal interests. The political scientist Giovanni Sartori described Berlusconi's regime as a 'sultanate, the worst of all courts'[13] in reaction to the 2008 immunity vote.

Taking his cue from Sartori, the historian Maurizio Viroli wrote a devastating account of Berlusconi's time in power. It was entitled *The Liberty of Servants*. He saw Berlusconi's power circle as a court: 'a form of power characterised by the fact that one man is placed above and at the center of a relatively large number of individuals – his courtiers – who depend on him to gain and preserve wealth, status and reputation'.[14] Berlusconi could employ what Viroli called the 'old trick of seducing the populace by telling it that it is omnipotent and that no one must attempt to limit the people's power'. Viroli concluded that 'where a court has formed, the liberty of the citizen cannot exist'.[15] At least thirty-five 'personal laws' were passed (although not all ended up as law) between 1994 and 2011. Berlusconi surrounded himself with a mixed bag of former Christian Democrats, ex-Socialists, former Communists, regionalists, former Fascists as well as employees from his companies, his lawyers and many others. On reflection, it was surprising that this coalition of forces survived for so long, and there was a high turnover amongst the allies. Any signs of betrayal were heavily punished.

In the foreign sphere, as befits a Sultan, Berlusconi loved to strut his stuff with other powerful men. He got on particularly well with Vladimir Putin and George W. Bush and, it seems, with Tony Blair. Angela Merkel couldn't stand him, however, and he memorably insulted the entire European Parliament during an embarrassing outburst in July 2003. Berlusconi's idea of foreign policy was almost entirely related to a sense of spectacle. On 6 April 2009 a powerful earthquake hit the small, beautiful student town of L'Aquila in the Abruzzo region. A total of 309 people (including an unborn baby) were killed. Eight students died as a student hostel (which had already been identified as 'at risk' in the case of an earthquake) collapsed. Silvio Berlusconi immediately grasped the opportunity to put himself in the limelight.

First, he decided to move Sardinia's planned G8 summit (millions had already been spent to host the world's leaders on an island called La Maddalena) to L'Aquila itself. The structures built for the summit on the Sardinian island were never opened. This wasn't because Berlusconi cared deeply about L'Aquila, but because he knew that the ruins of that town provided a more powerful backdrop for photo opportunities with Barack Obama and others. Then, Berlusconi proceeded to identify himself with the reconstruction effort in L'Aquila. He made numerous trips to the town, and equally numerous promises.[16]

More generally, Berlusconi saw the state as a resource through which he could reinforce or shore up his own power. When things became shaky, he bought people – with promises of institutional power. Of course, this type of spoils system had always been around. With Berlusconi, it became more obvious and even an acceptable part of the way things worked. He knew that his appeal to his supporters was closely linked to his power as a multi-billionaire and TV magnate, and he was also able to make or break careers in a variety of spheres and institutions. For Berlusconi a press conference was not actually a place where journalists were allowed to ask him questions. It was, instead, yet another opportunity for him to put on a show. Occasionally, a journalist would stand up to him. But Berlusconi's reaction would usually be to humiliate that brave individual.

Other tactics were more sinister – the character assassination or denigration of individuals, including magistrates, in newspapers, magazines or on television, or the use of 'dossiers' to smear them. Parliamentary Commissions – which had often been used to investigate in detail key features of Italian life, such as the Mafia or political violence – were now being employed for what appeared to be purely political motives. One was set up to look into a supposed scandal involving a telecom contract that was linked to the centre-left, another into past dealings with the Soviet Union by Italian Communists.

Opposing Berlusconi

Silvio Berlusconi's entry into politics and his time in power led to opposition from a variety of forces inside and outside of Italian society. Often, this opposition was from within the institutions themselves – teachers, students, magistrates – but it was also to be found in the wider world, and globally. Women organised in large numbers to defend their rights against Berlusconi's hostility. Anti-Berlusconi forces criticised his conflicts of interest and use of 'personal laws', his manipulation of democracy and his personal life. Protests against fascism played a key role in the early period – with the anti-fascist demonstrations in Milan on 25 April 1994 standing out as a high point.

Some of these movements were ephemeral, albeit spectacular. In January 2001, as Berlusconi was in control of central government with what seemed like a stable coalition, a series of small and spontaneous groups came together to form what became known as the *Girotondi* movement. The beginning was a 'March of the Professors' led by the historian Paul Ginsborg and the geologist Francesco Pardi in Florence. Later, in Rome, people 'held hands' in protest in front of the city's law courts. This holding of hands gave the *Girotondi* ['ring o'roses'] a name. The film-maker Nanni Moretti became involved, criticising the tepid nature of the official centre-left opposition to Berlusconi. In September 2002 an enormous gathering was organised in Rome – some say that around a million people were there. Paolo Ceri has called this 'the largest autonomously assembled demonstration in the history of the Republic'.[17] Many of these groups continued to organise locally and set up discussion groups – but the national movement faded and fragmented after 2002. Further social movements against Berlusconi would rise and fall in subsequent years, but none would come close to the national reach and power of those seen that year.

Opposition to Berlusconi's government strengthened during Italy's intervention in the Iraq War. Most Italians were opposed to the conflict and this movement was symbolised by the forests of rainbow peace flags that appeared all over the country. Constant demonstrations were held during the time of the invasion and afterwards. On 12 November 2003, Italy suffered its worst loss of life in a military incident since the Second World War. A suicide attack on a Multinational Specialised Unit in Nasiriyah in Iraq caused twenty-eight deaths. The victims included twelve Italian *carabinieri*, five Italian soldiers, two Italian civilians and nine Iraqi civilians. Elaborate funerals took place for the Italian victims in Rome, and 12 November was later designated as 'A Day of Memory in favour of Military and Civil Victims engaged on International Missions'. Streets and other spaces across Italy have been renamed in honour of the victims, although this memory is – as with so many other memories in Italy – contested, politicised and divided.

The Second War with the Judiciary

Opposition also continued from within the institutions themselves, and within the state. In January 2002, at the inauguration of the 'legal year' in Milan, the powerful magistrate Francesco Saverio Borrelli – who had been deeply involved in the 'Clean Hands' investigations that had led to the end of the First Republic – spoke out in front of his colleagues. Borrelli attacked proposed reforms to the judiciary: 'The reforms which have been announced, or rather used as threats with punitive intent towards a judiciary which can certainly make improvements in terms of efficiency, but is also clearly independent, have little to do with actual efficiency … there has been an attempt to … place obstacles in front of investigations … including an orchestrated and angry media campaign.' Borrelli concluded with a phrase that would be taken up by many, and which originated during the First World War. We must 'Resist, Resist, Resist', he said. The battle lines had been drawn. Berlusconi's allies and ministers walked out of the speech in protest.

Borrelli's call to 'resist' marked the beginning of a new phase in the long-running battle between Silvio Berlusconi as politician-businessman and the judiciary – a struggle that had begun in 1994 and which has raged for more than twenty years. Entire books have been written about tiny aspects of this 'war', which gripped Italy (and, to some extent, the rest of the world). Thousands of days were spent analysing trials, evidence, the statute of limitations, witness statements, bank accounts, budgets and accounts, phone calls. Lawyers (Berlusconi employed a whole team) became rich on the back of these endless trials and procedures.

Ironically, the longer the trials lasted, the better – for Berlusconi. Italy's statute of limitations was a key factor in this 'war'. Trials – depending on the crime involved – were time-limited. If you could drag the process out for long enough, you could avoid conviction (although judges might still outline how you had committed crimes, you could not be found *guilty* of those crimes). This was also a battle between institutions. Berlusconi would often argue that he couldn't attend trials or hearings because of institutional commitments (a useful way of using up time, depending on how that time was counted). There were lengthy clashes about these 'absent notes' and statute of limitations time limits.

Sometimes, trials went right down to the wire. Occasionally, however, it was clear that the judges were relatively happy for time to run out. In this way, they were freed from the political ramifications of their decisions. On occasions this was explicitly stated by judges and magistrates. Berlusconi, his associates, his political allies and his media outlets made frequent attacks on the judiciary – either personally or as an institution. Sometimes, this took the form of personal attacks. Dossiers were used (as with Di Pietro) and smears employed. The extraordinary nature of this series of legal-political events was heightened, of course, by the fact that for much of this time Berlusconi was also Prime Minister and head of one of the most powerful media conglomerates in Europe, as well as president of a leading football team, AC Milan. Every legal move was also a political one.

In power, Berlusconi passed laws that directly affected not just his private business interests, but also the entire judicial process. Despite these numerous trials and accusations, he would not be found guilty in terms of Italian law (at all three levels of justice) until 2013, when a conviction for tax evasion was confirmed by the highest court. In all the other cases, time either ran out (in some cases, by a matter of days) or he was cleared. Where time ran out (the trial took too long for any verdict to be valid), this was sometimes because the statute of limitations (the time limit itself) had been lowered by laws passed under one of Berlusconi's governments. Media campaigns against magistrates, witnesses or lawyers also contributed to a climate in which it seemed easier to fudge the issue than come down on one side or another.

These investigations and trials were public events, which dragged on for years and led to almost constant comment in the press and on television (right across the world). Very quickly, two sets of opinions emerged. One side claimed that Berlusconi was 'unfit for office' and should resign, and that he had only avoided guilty verdicts through his ability to employ expensive lawyers and his political influence. Others, including Berlusconi himself, saw this whole series of trials and investigations as a politically inspired conspiracy. This was a war without quarter, fought out in the media, in Parliament and in the courtroom.

Meanwhile, Berlusconi used all the other weapons at his disposal to avoid conviction. His TV channels pumped out propaganda on an almost daily basis attacking individual judges and the judiciary in general. Personal smears and 'dossiers' were used against particular magistrates. On one occasion a Berlusconi magazine published a 'reportage' concerning a magistrate who was presented as an oddball because he sat on a park bench and wore – shock horror! – purple socks.

It was difficult for many commentators and ordinary voters to understand why Berlusconi hadn't resigned in the face of scandal and judicial protest. Italy's complicated three-tier prosecution process also helped him. On occasion he was initially found guilty at a lower judicial level, only to be cleared on appeal or by the Cassation Court (Italy's final tier of justice). On other occasions judges baulked at the political implications of a guilty verdict, and preferred the fudge allowed by the statute of limitations. Here, the judges could effectively pass judgement on Berlusconi in their written rulings, whilst allowing him – as an elected Prime

Minister – to go free. Sometimes, the evidence simply wasn't strong enough. But, in the end, he could escape no longer. His relative political decline was also judicial.

There were other long-term effects of this 'war with the judiciary' – which did not begin or end with Berlusconi. Many lost faith in the entire legal system (and the frequent errors and excesses of the system played a part here). Judicial proceedings were politicised. Accusations of conspiracy stuck, and were used by all sides. Berlusconi also treated the legal process as a show, within which he could intervene as and when he pleased. The courtroom was another potential stage. As many had warned way back in 1993, this situation was in part the inevitable outcome of the unresolved conflict of interests created by the election of Silvio Berlusconi as Prime Minister. He used his political power to boost and defend his business interests. When the centre-left was in charge, however, from 1996 until 2001, they did little or nothing to resolve this issue. An anti-Berlusconi industry emerged – which sold books and newspapers. It was almost as if the left needed Berlusconi to hold itself together.

Censorship and Media Power

State television – or some sectors of it – also attempted resistance in the face of Berlusconi's onslaught and his extensive media power. This led to one of the most notorious acts of Berlusconi in government. On 17 April 2002 he held a press conference in Bulgaria (where he was on an official trip). He cited three TV personalities by name – all of whom worked for the RAI television service – and said that all three had 'used public television, paid for by everyone, in a criminal manner'. Berlusconi called for the three men to be sacked, or at the very least censored.

Who were the three men in question? One was a legendary figure from Italian television and print journalism – Enzo Biagi – who had, at that time, a daily five-minute spot on RAI 1 (the most watched channel) just after the news (peak time – it attracted eight million viewers). A popular figure, Biagi was hardly a radical, although he had been a partisan in the war. But Biagi had a high sense of ethics. He would not bow to the needs of the new powerful forces in Italian society. Daniele Luttazzi, on the other hand, was a quick-fire comedian who had taken a big risk. In March 2001 (during the election campaign) he mentioned the unmentionable. Live on his *Satirycon* TV show on RAI 2, he delved into the alleged links between Berlusconi and the Mafia. The format was an interview with the investigative journalist Marco Travaglio. The response was immediate. As Alexander Stille wrote, 'to judge by the reaction of the political world one might have thought that Italy had been attacked by a foreign power or that a major political figure had been assassinated'.[18] Panic set in amongst RAI executives, and Berlusconi's friend and associate Marcello Dell'Utri (who would later be convicted of association with the Mafia) was given a 'right to reply'.

The 'third man', Michele Santoro, was an ex-Maoist and a presenter of magazine programmes that mixed journalism and political debate with a high dosage of rhetoric. He also dipped into the alleged Mafia-Berlusconi relationship in March 2001. This time Berlusconi was so furious he decided to call up during a live programme and was put on air. None of these three interventions had made much impact electorally, judging from the actual results in 2001.

Berlusconi had waited a year or so before taking his revenge on the three TV presenters/journalists. His pronouncement became known as the 'Bulgarian edict'. All three men were suspended from the RAI. By this time, new people were in charge. Berlusconi had managed to 'occupy' the RAI state television service – although political interference in state media was hardly new to Italy. Biagi and Santoro only came back to the fold in 2007.

Explaining Berlusconi

'Don't you understand, if something isn't on television, it doesn't exist.'

Silvio Berlusconi[19]

But what was Berlusconism? How can we explain this rise to power and lengthy period of electoral success? Some saw Berlusconi, or 'Berlusconism', in a much wider context, going back to the beginning of Italy itself as a nation in the nineteenth century.[20] They understood his appeal as playing off wider trends in Italian history – low levels of state legitimation, a lack of respect for the law, a tendency to follow leaders rather than policies or ethical programmes. Was Berlusconi the product of his time – television, consumerism, individualism? Or was he the product of *Italy itself*? Did Berlusconism come before Berlusconi, and would it outlast him? Had he transformed Italy, or simply reflected already existing trends and contexts? Perhaps the real answer lay somewhere in the middle. Berlusconi(sm) needs to be seen in the context of post-industrial Italy, where private television and football became key cultural vectors. But its core message of every man and woman (or family) for themselves against the state, politics and the rule of law was a more deep-rooted one.

The Berlusconi age saw him win three general elections (1994, 2001, 2008) and lose three (one extremely narrowly) (1996, 2006, 2013). He was kicked out of office twice after being elected – in 1994 (when his majority fell apart) and in 2011 (in the wake of an impending financial crisis). Both times he claimed that 'the people' had been betrayed, and that what had happened was a kind of coup. Many times he was written off, described as being 'finished' politically. But he almost always came back from the dead. The final blow appeared to be that definitive legal judgement for tax evasion in 2013 which, combined with a new law linked to politicians and their criminal records, meant that he was excluded from Parliament. Yet this wasn't necessarily fatal, politically.

Matteo Renzi, for example, was Prime Minister without being elected (and sitting in Parliament) from 2013 to 2016. But Berlusconi's exclusion coincided with a split in his party and the sense that significant parts of his electorate were now looking elsewhere. A lengthy endgame developed, where negotiations (explicit or otherwise) took place over Berlusconi's 'exit-strategy'. This was in part judicial, and in part political. The Berlusconi era was over, but its legacy remained powerful. As with Margaret

Thatcher in the United Kingdom, many drew clear parallels between Berlusconi and all those who came after him – on all sides of the political spectrum. Politics had become irredeemably personalised and 'anti-political'. Berlusconi's contempt for 'the public' and truth and consistency became part of the system. His post-fact and narcissistic, non-party strategy became a winning formula for many others. Thus, we moved seamlessly into the era of Renzi, Salvini and others – not to mention Trump and Grillo. Numerous 'little Berlusconis' tried their luck.

2006: Another Scandal and another World Cup

Peak Berlusconi ended in 2006. Romano Prodi had returned from the European Commission, and the centre-left was (formally) united again, back in the wide Olive Tree grouping and a complicated and fragmented alliance called L'Unione. One of the last acts of Berlusconi in government had been to pass a new electoral law. In a break with tradition, this was done without cross-party consensus. It was defined by its own creator as an 'obscenity' or a 'pig's dinner' – *una porcata*. This term led to the law becoming known as '*Il Porcellum*', a combination of the phrase used for the previous law (*Il Mattarellum*) and the word '*porcata*'.

Italy's short-lived experiment with first-past-the-post was over (for now). The 'Porcellum' was presented as a return to proportional representation, but it took power from the voters and handed even more of it to party leaders. Blocked lists and the removal of preferences meant that almost all of those who would be elected were effectively selected by party leaders *before* the vote. To have any chance of governing, parties and movements had to form an electoral coalition – and indicate a 'Head of Coalition'. Winning lists were to be given extra seats – in theory – to allow them to govern. It was fiendishly complicated. The reform set down a 4 per cent threshold before a party gained any seats. The total votes for each coalition being the sum of the votes of those coalition parties that had won at least 4 per cent of the national votes. In the Senate, however, majority bonuses were assigned to the winning list in each region, as opposed to nationally. An extra unpredictable factor was introduced by the granting of votes and seats to Italians living abroad.

The law was extremely unpopular but, as it favoured the major parties, very difficult to change. There were lengthy debates between the parties over changes to the law in the years that followed, but Italy went to the polls in 2008 and 2013 with the same system. A referendum in June 2009 to abrogate parts of the law failed to attract the necessary numbers of voters to make any difference. A further attempt to change the law by referendum was thrown out by the Constitutional Court in 2012.

Everyone had predicted that Berlusconi would lose in 2006. All the polls pointed that way. However, Berlusconi ran his electoral campaign by occupying the television screens, once again. In one TV debate with Prodi he promised, as the credits rolled, to abolish a hated local housing tax. The Italian people had seen it all before, but it still seemed to work. The first election using the 'Porcellum', in 2006, was Italy's 'Florida moment'. The election was decided by a mere 26,000 votes and by votes that came in from Italian residents abroad. There were numerous accusations of electoral fraud (on both sides) and Berlusconi refused to concede defeat. The system had created a broad centre-left coalition with a tiny majority in the Senate, making it almost impossible for them to govern. If just a couple of deputies changed sides, then Prodi's time in power would be over, almost before it began.

From *Calciopoli* to Triumph

Many Italians were mesmerised in the summer of 2006 not by the political drama in Rome, but by a football scandal that shocked the nation. An investigation into illegal betting rings in Naples uncovered myriad links between top clubs, referees, agents and players. Wheeler-dealers at the top of the football ladder appeared to be able to influence games and fix the transfer market. The sporting justice authorities quickly decided that Juventus – the biggest, most successful, most powerful, most loved and most hated club in Italy – was at the centre of the system, and relegated it to Serie B for one season as a result. Some 10 million Juve fans were in shock. But 16 million non-Juve fans were exhilarated.

Juventus was also stripped of two championships (including the one they had just 'won', in 2006), a verdict they (the club and many of the fans) refuse to accept to this day. Judicial proceedings were much slower and more complicated, and were only finally completed in 2015, with accusations against Luciano Moggi, the former sporting director of Juventus, and others falling under the statute of limitations. However, in the ruling written by the judges, Moggi was described as 'the brains behind an illegal system which affected games in the 2004–2005 Championship (and not only then)'. Moggi, they added, had been at the head of a 'criminal organisation', which 'had an extensive structure and roots in various institutions'.[21] The outcome of the trials was a classic Italian judicial compromise. Moggi stayed out of jail (while banned from football for life) but the judgement concerning his alleged crimes was clear.

The so-called '*Calciopoli*' scandal darkened Italy's name abroad, and marked a decline in the country's footballing fortunes in terms of its domestic leagues (it probably also cost the country the chance to host a European championship). But the scandal also divided Italian football fans into opposing camps, who carried forward 'alternative' sets of 'facts'. Some saw the scandals as the final unmasking of a system of power centred around an all-powerful and successful club. Others (Juventus fans, in the main) viewed the entire process as a conspiracy against their team organised by jealous and bitter rivals. *Juventini* tended to refer to the scandal as '*Farsopoli*' and the club itself still counts its championship victories as including the two trophies that had been officially taken away.

In 1982 Italy had emerged from a damaging football scandal to win the World Cup. Could history repeat itself? In the run-up to the 2006 tournament in Germany, the squad and the manager were under fire. The captain Fabio Cannavaro was criticised for seeming to defend Moggi, and some demanded his resignation, while the manager Marcello Lippi was attacked for the alleged role of his son Davide – a football agent – in the scandal (he was later cleared of any wrongdoing).

The team thus went to Germany with the press on their back and extremely low expectations. But, as in 1982, the scandal and the pressure it created seemed to unite the players. Italy moved forward inexorably, with a solid defence, an almost unbeatable goalkeeper (Gianluigi Buffon), and the occasional moment of genius from 'the architect' – midfielder Andrea Pirlo. A favourable draw saw Italy play Australia in the first knock-out round, when a generous penalty was converted with aplomb by Francesco Totti in injury-time at the end of the match. Italy were already down to ten men, but they had won. Australians are still angry about that penalty.

After beating Ukraine easily in the quarter-finals, Italy faced hosts Germany in Dortmund. It was a pulsating match but neither team had scored with just a minute of extra time to go. Penalties appeared inevitable. Then Pirlo stroked a no-look pass through to the unexpected Italian hero – Fabio Grosso – who hit it first time into the corner. Grosso set off on a celebration that appeared almost as a parody of Marco Tardelli's scream in 1982. Seconds later Italy scored again, with a beautiful team goal through Alessandro Del Piero. The final would be against France, in Berlin.

Italy were not the better team, but France couldn't break through after two early goals left the game poised at 1-1. Then, with twenty minutes left in extra-time, Zinedine Zidane suddenly stopped, turned around and head-butted Italian defender Marco Materazzi in the chest. The referee had not seen the incident, but according to the official report the fourth official told him what had happened. Zidane – France's best player, and their lead penalty-taker – was sent off. It was his last act as a professional football player. Controversy followed over what exactly Materazzi had said to Zidane. In all probability, it was an insult to do with Zidane's sister. Materazzi later published a book called *Che cosa ho detto veramente a Zidane* (*What I Really Said to Zidane*), which contained 249 possible phrases.[22] The final meandered towards penalties. Italy – untrue to previous form – scored all of theirs. France hit the bar with one. Italy had won their fourth World Cup and their captain Cannavaro was named player of the tournament. The calls for his resignation had been forgotten. National celebrations naturally followed that unexpected success – a triumph built on teamwork. But the party was not that of 1982.

For one thing, the match was on two different networks, and a minority of spectators chose Sky over the RAI coverage. Many immigrants in Italy also had satellite TV to choose from. So there were at least two sets of commentators (and summarisers) involved. Moreover, thousands of big screens were put up all over Italy in 2006. In many ways, the match was watched as if it was 'just' another league match – as if the fans were in a stadium. This made it similar to a big Serie A game – whereas, in 1982, it had clearly been a different type of event, experienced above all within the domestic space. The 2006 experience was diluted and its memory was inevitably destined to fade into those of club-level Champions League or Serie A victories, whose celebrations were becoming increasingly ritualised and instantly forgettable as a result – a brief outburst of joy, followed by a swift return to normality.

It was also important that neither Prime Minister Romano Prodi nor the President at the time, Giorgio Napolitano, attempted to make political capital from the victory. The 2006 World Cup victory had no Pertini. Perhaps it was just as well, however, that Berlusconi was no longer in charge. We can only imagine how he would have tried to exploit the triumph. The next two World Cups (2010, 2014) were ignominious failures for Italy, and seemed to confirm a trend of increasing disaffection with the national team. Catastrope followed in 2017 as Italy failed to even quality for the World Cup after losing 1-0 to Sweden over a two-legged play-off. The last time a World Cup had not included Italy was in 1958. The success in 2006 did not exactly cancel out the trauma of *Calciopoli*, but it certainly helped. In any case, in terms of domestic football, things soon returned to normal. Juventus were promoted straight back to Serie A, and by 2017 had won a record six more championships (in a row) and were playing in a sparkling new stadium that was the envy of all the other clubs in Italy. If *Calciopoli* was a revolution, it was an extremely short-lived one.

Late Berlusconi

Romano Prodi's government limped on until 2008, surviving a series of close votes. Its weakness and ineptitude were reflected in its high numbers of ministers, deputy ministers and under-ministers – over one hundred people in total at some points. But in January 2008 a small number of senators changed sides and voted against the government. New elections were called for April 2008 – with the same 'obscene' electoral system as in 2006. Later, one of the senators who had switched coalitions claimed that he had been paid (by Berlusconi) to do so. Magistrates opened inquiries into the allegations that senators had been treated as if they were footballers in the transfer market. Berlusconi denied the charges. One former Senator – Sergio De Gregorio – has confessed to this crime (he said he had received three million euros) and has already been convicted. After a guilty verdict in the lower court for Berlusconi and a journalist called Valter Lavitola, in April 2017 the appeal court declared that the trial process had fallen under the statute of limitations – too much time had passed since the events themeselves. The judges, however, also stated that corruption 'had taken place'.[23]

In 2007 – amongst much pomp and ceremony – the Partito Democratico (Democratic Party) was formed from the ashes of the Partito Democratico della Sinistra (Democratic Party of the Left), the Democratici di Sinistra (Left Democrats), centrist Catholic groupings of various kinds, the Olive Tree and L'Unione (The Union). As the Democratic Party, the centre-left had officially dropped any reference to the 'left' in its name. The model for many was Tony Blair's New Labour, or at least the way that Blairism had been translated into Italy – shorn of associations with the Iraq War but very much still linked to a promotion of style over substance.

The 2008 campaign of the Partito Democratico was led by Walter Veltroni, who resigned as Mayor of Rome in order to head a coalition that excluded the far left but included Antonio Di Pietro's small and personalised anti-corruption movement. The decision not to form alliances to the left (part of the rationale behind the formation of the PD), nor even to mention Berlusconi during the campaign, proved to be a mistake. Berlusconi won the election easily despite his coalition losing nearly two million votes. He even had a solid majority in the Senate. The centre-right coalition also had a new name by this time, as Alleanza Nazionale had begun to fuse with Forza Italia into one organisation – the so-called Il Popolo della Libertà (The People of Freedom) in 2007–8. This fusion would be completed in 2009, after the election.

Yet Berlusconi's increasingly authoritarian attitude to his allies and the financial crisis – which hit Italy hard – began to have an effect from the very beginning. His seemingly solid majority suffered a major blow in the summer of 2010 when Gianfranco Fini formed a new parliamentary group called Futuro e Libertà, which could initially count on thirty-three deputies. In November 2010 ministers and vice-ministers from this group left the government. Fini and his group criticised what they saw as the dictatorial aspects of Berlusconi's government as well as highlighting the ongoing issue of conflicts of interest and 'personal laws'. Fini came very close to bringing down the Berlusconi government in December 2010, when the Prime Minister survived a confidence vote by just three votes. The split left Berlusconi with a tiny majority, although his government struggled on until November 2011 as the economic and debt crisis deepened. Late Berlusconi was increasingly desperate, and beset by a series of corruption and sex scandals.[24]

Bunga Bunga Republic: Berlusconi and Sex Scandals

Berlusconi's first public problems in this area came as close to home as it is possible to get. The signs had been there. In January

2007 Berlusconi's long-suffering second wife, Veronica Lario, mother of three of Berlusconi's five children, wrote a letter to *La Repubblica*, probably the most anti-Berlusconian of all the Italian daily papers. She was responding to reports that Berlusconi had told another woman that 'if I wasn't married, I would marry you straight away'. Lario asked for a public apology, 'not having received one privately'.[25] Quickly, Berlusconi did say sorry. But he had been warned, and he didn't appear to take heed of Lario's comments.

In April 2009 Berlusconi made a surprise appearance at the eighteenth birthday party of a young woman near Naples. Her name was Noemi Letizia and she apparently referred to Berlusconi by a nickname – 'Papi' (Daddy). Noemi told journalists that she had met Berlusconi. The exact nature of their relationship was not made clear. But the effects of that party and the accompanying photos were cataclysmic for Berlusconi. For Veronica Lario, it was the final straw. She decided to divorce him. She released a statement: 'I am closing the curtain ... on my married life.' 'I can't,' she added, 'be with a man who hangs out with underage women.'[26] Divorce did not come cheap for Berlusconi. Three women judges initially decided that he had to pay three million euros a month to Lario. But a bitter legal process dragged on for years, well after the actual divorce had taken place. All of this was, of course, played out in the media.

Rubygate

Worse was to follow. At around 11.30 p.m. on 27 May 2010, Berlusconi asked his senior bodyguard to dial a cellphone number in Milan. He was worried, desperate even, to prevent a scandal. But by making that phone call, Berlusconi paved the way to the deepest crisis in a political career spanning some seventeen years. The phone call in question was to the cellphone of a man high up in the running of the central police station in Milan, and it set in motion a series of events that were to lead (probably) to a unique event: a Prime Minister of a democratic country going on trial for, amongst other things, 'exploitation of underage prostitution'. As with most of the scandals linked to the Berlusconi era, the facts themselves are contested, and the legal processes that followed were interminable and confusing. Moreover, Berlusconi has never been given a final conviction for any alleged crime linked to these events. To understand why that phone call was made, what it contained and its consequences, we need to start in February 2010.

In that month, it seems, Berlusconi had been introduced to a seventeen-year-old Moroccan woman called Karima El Mahroug. Her 'stage name' was Ruby Rubacuori – 'Ruby the Heart-Stealer'. 'Ruby' had come over to Sicily with her family sometime in 2003, when she was just nine. By 2010 her Italian was fluent. After running away from home, for a time she worked as a *cubista* (someone who dances on a raised 'cube' in a night-club) and a belly-dancer. Her dream was to move into the world of television and advertising, industries centred around Silvio Berlusconi's vast media empire in Milan. In February 2010 Ruby was invited to the Prime Minister's lavish villa in Arcore. There, she met Berlusconi in person and, it is alleged, was given thousands of euros in cash. What else went on between them is a matter of some dispute. Over the next few months she was to spend a lot of time with him. According to mobile phone records, these meetings took place on 14, 21, 27 and 28 February, and then on 9 March, followed by 4, 5 24, 25, 26 April, and 1 and 2 May 2010. According to investigating magistrates, she received 'money and gifts' after these visits.

The crisis on 27 May was sparked by the fact that Ruby had been called in for questioning by police, after a friend had accused her of theft. Berlusconi was clearly worried, and he wanted Ruby out of that police station, as soon as possible, and on his own terms. To do this he adopted an absurd story, claiming that 'Ruby Rubacuori' was, in fact, the granddaughter of Hosni Mubarak – at that time President of Egypt. Berlusconi allegedly told the police that an international diplomatic incident might ensue if Ruby was not released. The story told by Berlusconi seemed to do the trick. Nobody bothered to check whether Ruby was even Egyptian.

Berlusconi insisted that Ruby be handed over to another 'friend' called Nicole Minetti (twenty-five at the time). In March, Minetti, previously a dental hygienist, had been controversially elected as a Regional Councillor in Lombardy on a centre-right list, despite no previous political experience. So Ruby, the fake granddaughter of Mubarak, was to be handed over to Minetti, the 'fake' politician, for safekeeping. Once outside the police station, the two went their separate ways. Ruby ended up at the house of a Brazilian prostitute. According to the magistrates investigating the case, Berlusconi had abused his political power to obtain Ruby's release from the police station. Berlusconi denied the charges, claiming that he had acted in good faith.

For a time, nobody got word of the weird events of that night, but Milan's magistrates were on the case. They tapped phones and began to collect evidence. Houses were searched across the city and a series of people called in for interview. Meanwhile, Berlusconi began to realise that he had made a terrible mistake. He had given a group of magistrates material that they could use to bring him down, once and for all. Was this the final act in a war that had been raging since 1994?

In October 2010 the story broke in the Italian press, and then the magistrates announced that they were placing Berlusconi and others under investigation for 'the exploitation of underage prostitution' and 'abuse of office'. A 380-page document was sent to Parliament (and published in the press) calling for the right to search some properties owned by Berlusconi. It contained phone-tap material (not all of it, it must be said, directly relevant to the case), as well as a detailed account of the events of 27–28 May. Berlusconi's supporters in Parliament rallied round their leader. They claimed that Berlusconi had, at the time, *really believed* that Ruby was Mubarak's granddaughter. A vote in Parliament tried to block the investigation. A total of 316 Italian parliamentarians dutifully voted in favour of their leader. Their discipline was total. One journalist quipped that the Italian Parliament had voted to decide that Ruby was indeed Mubarak's granddaughter. Back in May 2002 Berlusconi's friend and business partner Fedele Confalonieri (who at that time described himself in English as 'Chairman of Mediaset') had written a letter to the *London Review of Books*. In it, he took issue with Perry Anderson's analysis of Berlusconi's supposed links to the Mafia. 'In terms of social stigma,' he wrote, 'such a slur is comparable to being charged with sexual abuse of a minor.' Was this a Freudian slip, or a premonition?[27]

On Sunday 13 February 2011 (a year after Silvio and Ruby first met) more than a million Italians, the majority of them women, took to the streets of Italy to demand Berlusconi's resignation. Their slogan was a simple one, taken from the title of one of Primo Levi's novels: *'If Not Now, When?'* The theme song of the movement was Patti Smith's 'People Have the Power'. This vast demonstration (which took place in some 231 Italian cities, as well as in New York, London, Paris and Brussels) was organised without official political backing, and by a variety of groups including the 'purple-people' movement, a youth, web-based network that had been campaigning for some time against Silvio Berlusconi and the political 'caste' governing Italy.

Details emerged of so-called 'bunga bunga' parties in Berlusconi's villa in Arcore. Berlusconi had taken this epithet from another of his soon-to-be-ousted and once-powerful political male friends – Colonel Gaddafi. For the magistrates, these were events where young women were paraded in front of ageing, powerful men. For Berlusconi, they were 'elegant dinners'.[28] The world's press feasted on this scandal. Berlusconi was convicted after a first trial, but cleared on appeal of all charges. The political damage remained, though. Rubygate returned to haunt Berlusconi. Allegations emerged that witnesses during the first trial had been paid off in return for their silence. Berlusconi's legal odyssey showed no signs of slowing down.

The sweeping victory of the centre-left in Milan in May 2011 was a clear sign that he was losing his grip on those places that had supported him through thick and thin. Thousands celebrated the 'liberation' of the city in Milan's central Piazza del Duomo. And all this in Berlusconi's home town, where he had his TV stations and his advertising and publishing houses, and where his football team had just won the Italian championship.

Endgame: Post-Berlusconi?

On 12 November 2011 Berlusconi's fourth government fell amidst financial turmoil linked to the euro crisis. There was no election: Berlusconi was simply replaced in government by an entirely unelected set of 'technicians' or 'Professors' as they became known. Three days earlier Mario Monti had been made a life Senator by President Giorgio Napolitano. Monti was a well-known EU insider (he had spent around ten years in Brussels as a European Commissioner) and respected economist. A plan was in place. Pressure had been brought to bear on Italy from within the European Union – above all from France and Germany. At a press conference on 24 October, Angela Merkel and Nicolas Sarkozy laughed knowingly when the subject of Berlusconi was raised in a question. The writing was on the wall.

There was little appetite for a return to the lira in Italy, but no real love for the euro either. After the 2008 crash, Italy's debt had been under heavy global pressure. Anti-European rhetoric had taken hold in political narratives on the populist right in the 2000s (through Berlusconi and the Lega Nord, who would go as far as to call the euro a 'crime against humanity') and would be a key part of the appeal of anti-political movements in the twenty-first century.[29] Berlusconi attempted to associate the centre-left with price rises and the economic crisis – which he often tried to blame on the euro.

Il cavaliere's exit was met with a street party in Rome, including a choir that sang the Italian national anthem. Many were overjoyed, especially long-term opponents of Berlusconi. *La Repubblica*, which had made anti-Berlusconism into something of its raison d'être over the years, published a special 'Atlas' entitled *The Years of Berlusconi*. It ran to 256 pages and cost €4.90. A bargain. Even they called Berlusconi a 'Revolutionary who changed Italy', although this change, they argued, had not been for the better.[30]

Berlusconi had been treading water ever since the 2008 financial crisis, despite his victory in the elections of that year. He had continued to lose segments of his coalition in the period since

2008, as some of his former allies lost patience with his inability to deal with the debt, and an obsession with personalised politics. Gianfranco Fini, meanwhile, faded quickly away – a minor scandal linked to a house in Monte Carlo was the final blow to his career. The major scandals affecting Berlusconi also played a part in his downfall. Personal laws were no longer working. The Berlusconi project had unravelled.

Professors in Power

Mario Monti's government set about implementing EU-inspired austerity policies. It began with dire warnings of imminent disaster. Monti said that the government might not even be able to pay the wages of state employees for much longer. There was talk of a Greek-style bailout, or of a dramatic exit from the euro. The government was streamlined – with just thirteen members. Monti himself took on responsibility for the economy and others doubled up their roles. Post-democracy seemed to be much more than a passing phase. Monti's government did not increase the popularity of the European Union within Italy. During the austerity period of 2010–12 some polls showed trust in the EU within Italy falling by some 20 per cent.[31]

An impressive majority waved through Monti in the Senate and Lower House (where the vote in favour was 556 deputies to just 65). The Berlusconi era was over, or so it seemed, especially since his loyal allies the Lega Nord had previously split away and gone into opposition. Meanwhile, the crisis continued as Italy's economy flat-lined, with no signs of even a minimal recovery on the horizon. The initial popularity of Monti's government soon faded. Labour laws were liberalised, leading to a dramatic battle with the trade unions. Financial markets and Eurocrats were satisfied, but not many Italians were convinced.

7

Italy Today

New Emigrants: Italians on the Move

Despite Italy's official status as a receiving country, and constant debates over immigration, emigration from Italy continued well into the twenty-first century. Many professions were closed off to younger Italians, who were forced to look elsewhere, or accept precarious or unpaid work as they waited for gaps to appear in a restricted market. In 2014 there were 13,623 'Ordinari' (the equivalent of professors in a British university) in Italy. Only six were under forty years old. The average age of 'researchers' (the lowest rung on the academic ladder) was forty-six.[1] This pressure – the existence of a kind of gerontocracy – led to a so-called 'brain drain', a trend that, every so often, would result in hand-wringing and brow-furrowing articles in Italian newspapers. Italy's increasingly two-paced labour market, with an older group of 'guaranteed' employees on secure contracts, and a mass of younger people on the outside, was a strong push factor for emigration.

By 2015, at least 200,000 Italians were living in London (although the real figure was almost certainly higher than this). A third of these emigrants were between eighteen and thirty-four years old. The 2008 crisis was a key factor in the acceleration of these movements.

As the migration expert Russell King has pointed out, writing about what he calls the 'lure of London', 'evidence for a true brain drain effect comes from the simple statistic that there are eight times more recent Italian graduates living abroad than there are foreign graduates living in Italy'.[2] When these migrants were interviewed, most mentioned the 'crisis', and complained that there was no space for them back in Italy.

For Arianna, who was in her twenties, 'There is a socio-political situation in Italy that I really don't like ... Italy is an old society folded in on itself ... There is no investment in young people and you can see this from the politics.'[3] Italian migrants also tended to see Italy as a non-meritocracy, where favours and patronage were the only ways towards a proper job opportunity. As King argues, 'profound disenchantments with the way Italian society and the job market are organised lead to a kind of "rejection" of Italy and, amongst some of the interviewees, almost a "disidentification" with the country of their birth, upbringing and education'.[4] So this was not just a question of economic migration. It was something more deep-rooted, reflecting an emotional and political frustration with the home country, and the way it worked (or works). Whether or not the Italians in London were really a new generation, this was certainly true of how they saw themselves.[5]

Luca Vullo, an Italian film director working in London, compared current Italian migration to that of the post-war years. 'We did not experience a World War, but our country is falling to pieces and people cannot withstand it anymore.'[6] Vullo made a film called *Influx* about Italians in London.[7] He summed up the contradictions of Italian life in London when he said that 'life here is a jungle ... yet it is a fair jungle, whereas Italy, unless you have the right connections, is a jungle with no chance of success'.[8]

The processes involved in this new migration also meant that there was little contact with the historic, older migrants who had arrived in previous moments. 'The old and new migrations are detached from each other and they rarely have the chance to meet and communicate.'[9] The new migrants are often bilingual or have a good knowledge of English, and are far better educated than those who had come before them. Moreover, social media and transport connections meant that it was far easier to maintain links with the home country and family than in a previous era. New Italian migrants agree, however, about their negative assessment of Italy – and this created a kind of group identity.[10] This research was carried out, of course, before the Brexit vote of June 2016.

Five Star Movement

Meanwhile, back in Italy, new forms of populism were emerging to challenge those propagated for years by Berlusconi and the Lega. Italy's political map was about to be redrawn by a movement led by a comedian and an Internet guru.

Beppe Grillo (born in 1948 in Genoa) had been a popular, lively TV comedian in the 1980s. His material in the main had not been particularly topical. He had then, it is said, been 'excluded' from public TV networks in 1986 after making jokes at the expense of powerful politicians, including one gag where he referred to the Socialist Party (indirectly) as 'thieves'. Grillo went on the road, pulling in the crowds for his increasingly messianic show. He was a volcanic and tireless comedian with a mop of shaggy greying hair. His shows were one long – and funny – outburst of anger – and his ire was directed, increasingly, against society, politics and the economic system. At one point in the early 2000s, Grillo would end his show by smashing up a series of computers with a huge sledgehammer on stage. 'I believed in you,' he would say, as he hugged a monitor, pretending to cry, and then he would invite a member of the audience up on stage to deliver the final blows. During his routine he would say that 'behind the Internet there are always the same people ... there is nothing'.[11]

But as the 2000s wore on Grillo quickly embraced the Internet and social media, writing a highly popular blog (launched in 2005) that began to attract millions of readers every week.[12] In alliance with a savvy hi-tech guru, Gianroberto Casaleggio, Grillo decided to utilise the Internet as an alternative source of 'information' but also – and increasingly – as a mobilising tool for a new movement. He developed a form of 'digital populism'.[13] Umbrella themes brought in supporters (many of them very young) from left and right. Five Star propaganda highlighted the corruption of the political class and the privileges afforded to politicians (such as ludicrously generous pension-type payments), environmental issues as well as anti-corporate and pro-consumer campaigns. New people entered politics from within civil society. They promised to do things differently, that they would not participate in the political game, and that they would be 'honest' and 'clean' if elected. Many identified neither with the left or the right. A high number were relatively young, and well educated. Was this a new political (or anti-political) class in the making?

In 2009 the Movimento 5 Stelle (Five Star Movement) was formed (it originally had a more left-sounding name – the Movement of National Liberation – but this was dropped). It was launched with what Grillo called a 'non-statute' and an elaborate programme with over 120 points. Electoral success was quick to follow. In the meantime, Italy was falling apart, still governed by a moribund Berlusconi government, paralysed by corruption scandals on an almost daily basis, sliding into a deep recession and financial crisis. Not surprisingly, many people stopped voting altogether, or began to abandon the major parties.

Crucial to the rise of the M5S (as it was often called) was the success of a book written by two distinguished journalists, Sergio Rizzo and Gian Antonio Stella, that detailed the grotesque waste perpetuated by the 'political class'. Its title was eloquent: *La Casta* (*The Caste*; 2007). This book was 'the spark whch lit the fire. It provided a powerful frame which directed the anger of the Italians towards an immobile political system.'[14] It sold 1.2 million copies in 2007 alone. Italians were particularly angry about the special kind of pension arrangements that politicians had awarded themselves. It only took five years in Parliament to qualify for generous payouts. Politicians could also 'add up' these payments if they were elected to different bodies. After the controversy created by the revelations in *La Casta*, which used forensic journalistic techniques to lay bare political corruption and privilege, successive measures attempted to reform this system – although these met with legal and political opposition. Before and after their election, representatives of the Five Star Movement rejected all such privileges. The Movement called itself a 'free association of citizens'. It was 'not a political party' and it wouldn't become one. It also 'recognised that all citizens should govern'.

Grillo's M5S provided the context for democratic Internet-based forums and local meet-ups that quickly morphed into votes on a wide scale. In 2012 the movement took off dramatically. In local elections in May an unknown Five Star representative was elected Mayor of Parma, one of Italy's richest cities, which until the late 1990s had been a centre-left stronghold, and had been governed (badly and dishonestly) by Silvio Berlusconi's party for more than a decade. It was a landslide against the centre-left candidate – with thirty-nine-year-old Federico Pizzarotti winning over 60 per cent of the vote. Pizzarotti had only been active in politics since 2009. In regional elections in Sicily the Five Star Movement gained more votes than any other party and elected fifteen regional councillors. In typical exuberant fashion, Grillo had swum across the Straits of Messina (three kilometres) to launch his campaign – a Mussolinian gesture that showed how adept he was at manipulating the media he professed to hate.

The 2013 national elections were another formidable demonstration of how far the movement had come in such a short time. Only the votes from Italians abroad prevented the M5S from becoming the biggest party. A total of 8.8 million Italians voted for the M5S. It was a result – without allies – to be compared with Berlusconi's in 1994. Some 648 of the 945 elected representatives in the previous Parliament stood for re-election, but only 344 were returned to office. All the deputies and senators elected in the M5S lists were new to Parliament. Many of the M5S representatives were in their twenties and thirties. Most were completely unknown to the media and the voters, and had little or no political experience.

Grillo refused all overtures to ally with the Democratic Party and kept his deputies in opposition. From outside Parliament (his conviction in 1988 for causing death by dangerous driving disqualified him, in any case, from being a candidate) Grillo ruled the movement with an iron fist. Any dissent was met with almost immediate expulsion – in decisions that were supposedly decided by what was grandly called 'the Internet', but which amounted to a relatively small amount of people voting online.

Very quickly, there were signs that the more radical elements of the M5S were being ditched as Grillo pushed an anti-euro, anti-EU and anti-immigrant line. An alliance with Nigel Farage's UKIP in the European Parliament sent out a clear message. Grillo and Casaleggio appeared to be firmly in control of the 'loose' organisation they had created. These shifts moved in parallel with clear signs that many centre-right voters who had had enough of Berlusconi or Alleanza Nazionale or the Lega were moving over to the M5S. There is also no doubt that some abandoned the centre-left – perhaps temporarily to wait and see whether the M5S would deliver.

There was a high turnover within the M5S in terms of candidates and militants. In Parma, Mayor Pizzarotti and some of his councillors left the movement in October 2016 after a succession of run-ins with Grillo. The councillors complained about the way the organisation was run, with what they called ' "Confirmative" votes where the only choice is to agree with what has already been decided; political leaders who proclaim that they are in charge; party leaders nominated from on high; dynasties like those found amongst the worst families of employers'.[15] They added that 'we haven't changed, our values and our desire to change things haven't changed'. Pizzarotti easily beat the official M5S candidate in the successive mayoral elections in 2017, and, standing as an independent, was re-elected for a second term.

Victory in mayoral elections in Livorno in June 2014 showed once again that the M5S could win in left-wing heartlands, challenging what remained of the Communist Party traditions. Grillo took anti-political politics to the limits. The character and non-political origins of M5S's candidates were seen as extremely important, as was transparency over their income, expenses and further access to privileges enjoyed by other sections of the 'political class'. The M5S was against lots of things – the euro, immigration – but what was it actually for? Was it ultra-democratic, or a form of autocracy, where 'the net' became a fetishistic replacement for 'the masses' or 'the people'? Grillo and his followers tended to criticise all 'mainstream media' as 'publicly funded' and part of the system.

The M5S had certainly hit on a winning formula (in the short term), building on widespread anger at immigration, the ongoing crisis and EU institutions including the euro. Italy's debt crisis had led to austerity policies, youth unemployment was extremely high, and pensions were squeezed. The results of 2013 showed the extent and power of the populist wave in Italy. Monti's new political party was marginalised – winning just 9 per cent of the vote. Grillo was selling an illusion – like Berlusconi before him – but it was a new form of illusion. Italy's main problems, Grillo claims, are political – corruption and the power of 'the caste' (which is also, they argue, to be found in the media, the trade unions, the judiciary and other sectors of public life). If we can change those in power, they argue, we can resolve everything. But Grillo has little concrete to say on the economy, on the public debt, or on immigration apart from easy slogans, such as 'immediate expulsion for all illegal immigrants'. His programme is an anti-programmne.

If everyone was 'honest' and 'new', Grillo seems to be saying, then everything would be all right. We are 'pure', say the Grillini, we are 'clean', we are not 'them'. But if history has shown us anything since *Tangentopoli*, it is the fact that being 'honest' or not are pointless categories. Of course, not all politicians are the same. But every Italian movement and party that has proclaimed itself to be honest and clean has ended up in the courts. This is a process that began to happen to some of those within Grillo's movement as well – especially elected officials. The M5S approach is to concentrate on the symptoms, not the causes of Italy's problems.

None of this seemed to prevent the electoral march of the Grillini. In June 2016 another semi-unknown M5S candidate won a mayoral electoral runoff – this time in the biggest and probably most difficult city to govern in Italy – Rome. Virginia Raggi had only been a local councillor since 2013. She more than doubled the result of the centre-left candidate, winning 67 per cent of the vote and 770,000 votes. Rome had been beset by extensive corruption scandals for years, culminating in the exposure of extensive links between organised crime and the political class. Grillo's propaganda, blogs and tweets often focused on an anti-immigrant message – in part in response to the aggressive racist politics of the Lega Nord, which had been revived by a new leadership (Matteo Salvini) and identified with Marine Le Pen in France and Euroscepticism. In June 2015 Grillo tweeted a call for direct elections 'before the city [Rome] drowns in rats, rubbish and illegal immigrants'.

In 2016 – following the shooting of a man in Milan who had carried out a terrorist attack in Berlin – Grillo blogged calls for the expulsion of illegal immigrants and the temporary suspension of the Schengen Agreement. He wrote that 'Italy is becoming a breeding ground for terrorists, which we cannot either find or capture, and who, thanks to Schengen, can move freely around Europe. We need to act now.' In 2017 Grillo opposed new citizenship law proposals for immigrants born in Italy.

Rome's new mayor, Virginia Raggi, was thirty-seven years old on election and had worked as a lawyer – training in the legal studio of one of Berlusconi's lawyers and closest friends, Cesare Previti. Raggi's administration started by ruling out a Rome bid for the Olympics (a generally popular 'No'). But there were soon problems with some of her officials and legal issues began to emerge. Arrests and investigations followed, and she was officially accused of lying to anti-corruption officials. In December 2016 experts expressed disquiet at a 'contract' signed by M5S candidates that guaranteed they would resign from office if convicted or even if merely placed under investigation. The contract also tied the hands of M5S administrations in terms of alliances and votes.[16] However, the most problematic part of the contract was the promise to impose a 'fine' if elected candidates 'damaged the image' of the movement. It also seemed that Grillo could insist on a resignation. M5S spokespeople supported the move, claiming that they were fed up with elected officials defecting to mainstream parties. The early death of Casaleggio at the age of sixty-one in April 2016 robbed the movement of one of its most important figures, but other young candidates soon appeared on the scene – and Casaleggio's son Davide took over part of the mantle left by his father.

Grillo and his movement railed against the entire political system, and he did his homework. He documented absurd levels of state contributions for non-existent political newspapers, for example, and he attacked both left and right, almost equally. Berlusconi was 'a psycho-dwarf', while Pierluigi Bersani (leader of the centre-left Democratic Party in 2013) was a 'zombie' and 'Gargamella' (a character from the Smurfs cartoons). Mario Monti was 'rigor Montis'. Grillo's language was violent and straightforward, and he organised 'Fuck-off days' of protest against the governing parties (and in fact against all parties). He also criticised big business and called for more shareholder democracy.

Grillo's followers, as far as we know, tend to be young and idealistic. Most of his candidates have little or no political experience. The 2013 Parliament as a result was the 'newest' since 1994. Rigorous standards are expected of them. Many if not all have grown up with the Internet and use it almost exclusively to communicate and obtain information and news. Grillo's party is postmodern and post-political, yet rigidly controlled and hierarchical.

The Rise and Fall and Rise of the Lega and the Future of Italy

Over time the Lega Nord changed tack on many of its claims and policies. It zig-zagged between more secessionist positions (where it called for radical federalism or even the separation of North and South into two different states) and a more moderate stance (especially in a governing coalition with Berlusconi after 2001). Federalist reforms passed by Romano Prodi's centre-left government in 2001 were confirmed in a referendum (where 16.8 million Italians voted and 64 per cent backed the reforms). But those proposed by Berlusconi's government (including the Lega) fell to defeat in a similar referendum in 2006 (this time 26 million

voters turned out, and 61 per cent voted No to the reforms). Only
Lombardy and the Veneto voted Yes. This was a bitter blow for
the Lega. Its decentralist ideas and policies (including the devolu-
tion of educational and police powers) had become confused with
other constitutional reforms while the vote also became a referendum about Berlusconi himself. In any case, Italy's constitution
had been built to last – and many preferred it that way.

There was a sense that the Lega was able to turn on and off its
claims for an independent Padania in line with political context.
In power, the movement became more moderate – and increasingly part of the system. Some accused it of 'Romanisation' – the
ultimate sin for Lega politicians. The Lega had four ministers in
the 2001 cabinet formed by Berlusconi. They proved to be a faithful ally of Berlusconi's Forza Italia in and out of government and
that first 'betrayal' of 1994–5 soon was forgotten. A life-threaten-
ing stroke undermined Bossi's leadership capacities in 2004. He
remained active in politics and powerful within his own movement, but the real leader of the Lega became Roberto Maroni – a
quieter, much more effective politician, but with nothing like the
charisma or power of Bossi in the 1980s and 1990s.

It could be argued that the Lega and Bossi got too close to
power – nationally and locally – and in doing so betrayed many
of their populist roots. Corruption scandals in the twenty-first
century would lay bare just how far this process had gone.
Only twenty years after *Tangentopoli*, a political scandal hit the
very party that had demonstrated most fervently in favour of
the magistrates and 'Clean Hands' in the 1990s. The movement
whose militants had happily displayed a noose in Parliament in
its call for politicians to be swept from power now found itself
in the dock. Umberto Bossi, members of his family and leading
members of the Lega were accused of corruption and of spending money destined for political campaigning for their personal
pleasure. In 2012 the scandal hit the newspapers. Headline writers had a field day. *La Stampa*, for example, led with this: 'From
Rome the Thief to Padania the Thief'.[17]

The investigative newspaper *Il fatto quotidiano* wrote that
'We risk using a euphemism in calling what has happened an

earthquake.'[18] Umberto Bossi soon resigned as Federal Secretary (although he was soon reappointed as 'Federal President' – nobody was quite clear about the difference between these two posts) followed by his son Renzo Bossi, who had been elected as a Regional Councillor. The details that emerged from time to time about the Bossi family were amusing and shocking at the same time. Renzo, for example, had failed his final school exams three times before passing at the fourth attempt. The press became interested in the fact that he appeared to have passed a degree in Albania without attending any classes. He later claimed that he knew nothing of this qualification. Journalists responded with titles such as 'Bossi's son. He didn't know he had graduated'.[19] Bossi's other son Riccardo (who denied charges against him, which went to appeal) was convicted by a lower court of illegal use of public funds in 2016, a conviction confirmed by the Court of Appeal.

The Lega treasurer Roberto Belsito was arrested and charged with a variety of financial crimes, and various trials were ongoing in 2017. Beyond the legal outcomes, the affair did immense damage to the Lega and its reputation. However, few Italians were surprised. Political corruption had continued apace despite *Tangentopoli*, with every party, movement and organisation being involved at some point or another, as well as numerous business people and private individuals. There were so many of them that the public suffered from 'scandal fatigue'. Some scandals were given their own -*opoli* title. Examples included *Affittopoli* (cheap rents for politicians and their friends) and *Lattopoli* (the spectacular collapse of the Parmalat food conglomerate).

With increased foreign immigration the Lega became more and more racist, fanning the flames of anti-immigrant and anti-gypsy (and later Islamophobic) sentiment wherever it arose. A Lega militant-politician called Mario Borghezio specialised in the organisation of anti-immigrant marches and demonstrations. Some *Leghisti* formed themselves into self-styled police or vigilante groups, dressed in green, and organised so-called search parties – or 'ronde'. Lega militants, at various times, called for immigrants to be thrown out of planes or deported on trains, or rounded up and put in 'work camps', or hunted like animals, and for the castration of immigrants accused of rape. The Lega politician Roberto Calderoli later said of a black parliamentarian that 'I love animals, but when I see her, I can't help but think of an orangutan.'[20]

One of the effects of this anti-immigrant tendency, however, was to make the Lega into an increasingly *national* party (and even, at times, one with nationalist as opposed to regionalist sentiments). This was ironic, as the Lega's attempts to call for the division of Italy in the 1990s and 2000s had created a backlash that led to a reappraisal of national symbols on the left. The Italian flag – previously so problematic for many – changed its meaning. In opposition to the Lega, many on the left embraced a flag that had once been seen as a little distasteful.

The scandal that enveloped Bossi and his allies after 2012 led to a changing of the guard, with those close to Roberto Maroni taking over positions of power. The so-called 'magic circle' at the top of the Lega – which contained members of the Bossi family – was marginalised. In 2013 primaries were held for a leader of the movement, which saw a younger, more dynamic and aggressive personality – history graduate Matteo Salvini – elected with 82 per cent of the vote. Salvini modelled his party on Le Pen's Front National and made anti-immigrant, anti-Islam and anti-Traveller messages a priority. Of course, this type of propaganda has always been part of the Lega's strategy, but now it became central – alongside a strong appeal to Eurosceptics. Salvini was determined to make the Lega into a truly national party, and in the 2015 regional elections there were signs of growing support for the movement in traditionally red regions such as Emilia-Romagna, Tuscany and Umbria.

Mario Balotelli

A young Italian-born centre-forward made his debut for Inter Milan at the age of seventeen in 2007. He quickly became a celebrity, winning a series of titles in Italy and abroad. Mario Balotelli was born in Palermo, in Sicily, on 12 August 1990 but was brought up in the small town of Concesio, near Brescia in the north of Italy. Balotelli speaks Italian with a strong Brescian accent. His precocious footballing talent was spotted while he was still in middle school, and he played for a nearby team at Lumezzane at the age of fifteen, before signing professional terms with Inter Milan, one of Italy's biggest clubs, in 2006–7.

In the 2008–9 season Balotelli first caught the eye of football fans with two goals as Inter Milan beat Juventus in the Italian Cup, and he contributed to the championship victory that year, at the age of seventeen. Balotelli scored regularly for Italy's under-21 team. He was big and strong, with a powerful shot and right from the start he attracted a lot of attention. It is not surprising that Juventus fans jeered Balotelli during league matches in Turin. Inter Milan had always been rivals, and passions had been inflamed by the *Calciopoli* scandal of 2006. What was interesting, however, was the content of the abuse. It was not about football at all. This was one of the chants: *Non ci sono negri italiani. Balotelli sei un africano* ('There are no Italian negroes. Balotelli you are African'). Mario Balotelli is in fact Italian, and black. His biological parents are from Ghana, but they gave him up for adoption to an Italian family when he was just three.

Balotelli, despite being born and brought up in Italy, had to wait until he was eighteen to become an Italian citizen. Italy's discriminatory citizenship laws are out of step with much of the rest of Europe, and this meant that Balotelli was also in danger of losing all rights to being legally Italian if he left the country at any time. A day after his eighteenth birthday, a special ceremony was held to celebrate the acquisition of something that Balotelli felt was his right – a piece of paper which said he was officially Italian.

Many Italians hated (and hate) Balotelli. This is partly because at one time he played for Inter Milan, who were dominating the domestic game at the time. But the real reason is much more profound. Balotelli exposes all the contradictions of foreign immigration into Italy. Many Italians cannot accept Balotelli as one of them. He is an Other, black, African (used here as an insult, of course), inferior. And he has committed another crime. He is not humble. He does not bow and scrape, but seems – at times – almost to enjoy the notoriety he has received from fans and players alike.

The reaction to those chants at the Juventus game were illuminating. Many blamed Balotelli, arguing that his 'attitude' was provocative, and that he wasn't a 'real champion'. He didn't, it seems, know his place. The fans felt within their rights, therefore, to boo him, or at least they had some justification for doing so. Many denied that the chants were racist at all. After heavy criticism from Inter President Massimo Moratti, who said that he would have ordered the team to leave the pitch if he had been present at the match, the Italian football authorities decided to act, forcing Juventus to play their next match behind closed doors as a punishment. Juventus appealed against this punishment, and they had a point. Why had Juventus been singled out? Racist chants had always accompanied Mario, including the classic '*Balotelli. Negro di merda*'. Of course, we have been here before, both in Italy and in other countries. John Barnes was famously greeted with bananas during a derby match in Liverpool. But Italy is not just the Britain of twenty years ago. In Italy things were getting worse for a very simple reason: racism was being practised from above, encouraged by politicians, and above all those who held the reins of power.

When Balotelli scored a second, superb goal to knock Germany out of the 2012 European Championship semi-finals, the Italian newspaper *La Repubblica* wrote that the German keeper – Manuel Neuer – 'watched the ball go by like a peasant observing a lorry on the motorway'. Balotelli was briefly a national hero – his blackness conveniently forgotten for a short time. But when he performed poorly (alongside many others) in the 2014 World Cup, he was not forgiven. Instead, he became a convenient scapegoat. He didn't play for the national team at all between 2014 and January 2018. He was back to being black again.[21]

What the 'Balotelli case' reveals is the depth of hostility in Italy to what we might call a multi-cultural society. Immigrants are acceptable as long as they remain invisible. They are not supposed to be good at anything, or make money, or to be 'one of us'. Balotelli exposes the frightening contradictions of such a society. For this reason he inspires hatred, suspicion and fear. He is a vision of the future, and of a future (and a present) that many Italians find deeply troubling.

Pope Francis

Pope Benedict XVI's reign ended dramatically on 10 February 2013. A sharp journalist – Giovanna Chirri – who understood Latin suddenly realised that the Pope was doing something that was unheard of. She had picked out the word *'Renuntiare'* in his short statement. The Pope, she suddenly understood, was resigning. The last time that such a thing had happened had been 598 years ago. Pope Benedict said that 'both strength of mind and body are necessary' to hold such a post in the modern world, 'strength which in the last few months, has deteriorated in me to the extent that I have had to recognise my incapacity to adequately fulfil the ministry entrusted to me'. 'For this reason', he added, 'with full freedom I declare that I renounce the ministry of Bishop of Rome, Successor of Saint Peter, entrusted to me by the Cardinals on 19 April 2005, in such a way, that as from 28 February 2013, at 20:00 hours, the See of Rome, the See of Saint Peter, will be vacant and a Conclave to elect the new Supreme Pontiff will have to be convoked by those whose competence it is.'[22]

The world was in shock. Feverish speculation followed as to the real reasons for the resignation. Was the Pope terminally ill? Had he been involved in too many cover-ups linked to global sexual abuse scandals? Nobody really knew. He had not been a popular Pope. He was too cerebral, too private, too uncharismatic for a role that is now intimately linked to the media. The Church needed something different. In March 2013 they elected somebody who fitted the bill.

The reign of Pope Francis, which began in March 2013, has been a breath of fresh air for the Catholic world. He speaks directly to the people, and has made it his mission to reinforce the Church's role in coming to the aid of the global poor. 'The new pope, from the very choice of his name, made manifest ... preferential love of the poor, marginalised, excluded, unemployed, sick, disabled, "rejected", as well as the so-called "urban remnants".'[23] He has also attacked 'an economy that kills' and taken on aspects of consumer society. His popularity is immense, in stark contrast with that of his predecessor.

Pope Francis has often managed to surprise people, including those within the Church itself, with his pronouncements and trenchant positions. In June 2014, on a trip to Calabria, he made the following statement in front of an adoring crowd of some 250,000 people: 'The Church must say no to the 'Ndrangheta. Mafiosi are excommunicated.' The 'Ndrangheta was the Calabrian version of the Mafia, a vicious and deep-rooted criminal organisation that had managed to control vast areas of that southern region through violence and corruption over many decades. It was said that Church leaders were shocked by this phrase, which had not been in the Pope's original script.

The Church's relationship with organised crime in Italy had usually been one of co-existence, and sometimes of active support. There were occasionally cases of anti-Mafia priests, who often paid for their stance with their lives, but on the whole the Church and the Mafia (as well as the Camorra and the 'Ndrangheta) got along. The first Pope to even mention the Mafia was John Paul II in 1993. But Pope Francis's statement went much, much further. In theory, it expelled all *'ndranghetisti* (and, thus, logically, also all *mafiosi* and *camorristi*) from the Church altogether.[24]

Many leading *mafiosi* have always managed to argue that they were deeply religious, despite their criminal activities (which they often denied). What was to happen to them? And what about priests working with them in prison? In theory, excommunication was a tough deal. It meant no baptism, no confession, no religious marriage, no Catholic funeral. It meant, in short, that *mafiosi* were going to hell – all of them.[25] In practice, things were much more fuzzy. The translation into actual policy of the Pope's 'infallible' statements was a political and pragmatic issue. Time would tell as to whether the Church as an institution had really transformed its way of dealing with organised crime.

Yet a series of shocking revelations from within the Vatican show how difficult the Pope's task of reforming the Church has been. The *Vatileaks* affair, whereby secret documents and recordings were smuggled out to journalists by various people within the Vatican, reveal a Church hierarchy whose spending is out of control, and where bitter personal and political rivalries are being fought out through dossiers and backbiting. Money donated by the faithful and earmarked for 'the poor' was unaccounted for. Cardinals were revealed to be living a life of luxury. Attention focused on the impressive flat where a powerful figure called Cardinal Bertone lived. Expensive building work on the flat (the Cardinal said it comprised 300 square metres, others claimed it was more than double that size) appeared to have been paid for through money destined for a children's charity. A lovely terrace looked out onto Rome. Bertone later paid back 150,000 euros, although he said that the money had been used 'without his knowledge'.[26]

The Italian public were fascinated by these leaks, which were published in a series of best-selling books.[27] The Church's relationship with wealth seemed to be the opposite of that which the new Pope wanted to project. Pope Francis's attempts to wrest control of the Church's finances from an entrenched elite met with solid resistance. However, the Vatican reacted badly to the way information had been given to the press and journalists, and alleged leakers were put on trial through its own, strange, legal system.[28]

Pope Francis's revolution has not been easy, and the forces ranged against him are powerful. They know that they can bide their time, and wait for this Papacy to end. This is a fascinating struggle, which goes way beyond the geographical location of the Vatican in the heart of Rome. As one Vatican expert has written, 'The Catholic Church often mysteriously succeeds in electing the right pontiffs at epochal turning points. John XXIII arrived at the watershed of the thaw between the Western and Soviet blocks; Paul VI coincided with the planet-wide movement of decolonisation; John Paul II marked the taking down of the Iron Curtain. Francis has become pope at a time of global crisis. It isn't just third-world countries that are suffering from serious economic imbalance, poverty, marginalisation, corruption, violence, and the intolerable gap between the hyper-rich and swathes of society living close to the edge.'[29] Yet, anyone who knows about the Church would expect continuity to triumph over change. As the cliché goes, 'The Pope dies, you get another one.'

Life and Death

Catholic values still reach deep into Italian society. At certain times this has been revealed through the passionate debate and political controversy inspired by real-life stories. Eluana Englaro, from Lecco in the north of Italy, was just twenty-one when she was involved in a serious car accident, in 1992. She was left in what is often called a 'persistent vegetative state' and fed through a tube, looked after by nuns. Eluana had to be kept on her side as she was unable to take in her own saliva. Her father, Beppe Englaro, began a long and difficult legal battle (covering some eleven years) to obtain the right to suspend her 'treatment' and allow her to die. In July 2008 this whole issue suddenly became part of a national debate over questions of life and death and who could decide what in such situations. Beppe Englaro won his case in the Court of Appeal. The case divided Italy. The Church and many Catholic politicians defended Eluana's 'right to life', while secular Italy supported Beppe Englaro. A violent and emotional discussion ensued, which reached right up to the top tiers of the Italian state. Englaro was even accused of murdering his own daughter. At one point this led to an official judicial investigation.

In 2009 Silvio Berlusconi's government passed an unprecedented decree banning the suspension of food or drink for all patients. Berlusconi said at the time that Eluana was 'capable, hypothetically, of having a child in the future' and that she 'looked good'.[30] The Catholic politician Rocco Buttiglione stated that 'Eluana could even wake up, at any time'.[31] Sizeable counter-demonstrations backing Beppe Englaro and attacking this decree followed across Italy. President Napolitano refused to sign the 'emergency' measure. Much public debate centred on hypothetical questions around 'what Eluana would have wanted' while others argued that the case was above all an ethical and political one. Yet Berlusconi's government was not giving up. They opened the Senate for a special session to pass an identical law, but they were too late. The decision regarding Eluana was carried out as had been decided by the courts on 9 February 2009. She had been lying in a coma for seventeen years. Rome's neo-fascist mayor, Gianni Alemanno, announced that the Colosseum would be lit all night as a sign 'of mourning' and in protest for what he called 'a life that could and should have been saved'.[32] Berlusconi's decree law was withdrawn.

A partisan role was played in this story by politicians in the Lombard Regional Government, who did all they could to block Beppe Englaro in his attempts to allow his daughter to die with dignity. Englaro thus had to transport Eluana to Udine (in another region) because of the stance taken in Lombardy. In 2016 the Lombard Regional Government was ordered to pay the Englaro family compensation regarding their intervention in the case. The passions invoked by the Englaro story, and its emotional exploitation by politicians, was a strong indication of how divisions between secular and what many people saw as Catholic values still ran deep in Italy and cut across political boundaries between centre-left and the centre-right coalitions, both of which brought together Catholics and secular politicians.

A Floating Cemetery

Globalisation had a deep impact on Italy, given its central geopolitical position at the edge of and yet in the centre of Europe. Despite the problems for migrants and refugees in Italy, many still attempt the perilous journey towards her borders. Italy's geographical position at the borderland of the EU suddenly saw a small island find itself at the centre of a global crisis in terms of population movements on a vast scale.

Sometime during the night of Christmas Day in 1996, a vessel called the F174 went down off the Sicilian coast with the loss of some 300 lives – mostly of people from India, Pakistan and Sri Lanka. In the aftermath of this tragedy (which later became known as the Christmas Massacre) Sicilian fishermen began to catch body parts in their nets. They usually threw them back. Then an identity card turned up. It belonged to someone called Anapalgan Ganeshu. He had been seventeen years old, a Tamil from Sri Lanka. The press began to take an interest. Still, the authorities did nothing. The fisherman who had found the identity card took it to Rome, and gave it to an intrepid journalist from *La Repubblica*, Giovanni Maria Bellu, who then took matters into his own hands.

In 2001 Bellu hired a camera and a sort of mini-submarine, and began to look for the wreck. It wasn't that difficult. Soon he came across shocking evidence of a tragedy: bits of a boat, bones, skeletons still in their clothes, floating shoes. Later, a powerful artwork and play would be based on this catastrophe and the *omertà* around it.[33] At the time this was described as the greatest disaster to occur in the Mediterranean Sea since the Second World War. Unfortunately, this sad record would soon be beaten. By the second decade of the twenty-first century, such events were almost commonplace.[34]

Lampedusa, Italy and Europe: An Island of Dreams and Nightmares

In Gianfranco Rosi's powerful Oscar-nominated documentary *Fuocoammare* (*Fire at Sea*, 2016) there is a scene that remains in the memory well after the film is over. A boat is floating on the ocean. As the camera moves down into the lower reaches of the boat, it becomes clear that people have died here. Many people. Their bodies are piled up. A horrible silence accompanies the camera down in the hold. Yet this tragedy probably went largely unreported. Crossing towards Europe was a deadly risk that many were forced to take in the face of war, persecution and high levels of inequality. We will never know how many didn't (or won't) make it.

It is tiny in physical terms, but Lampedusa was perhaps the most important place in Italy in the late twentieth and early twenty-first century. This island lies some 230 kilometres from the Italian mainland, and has a resident population of just over 6,000 people. Electricity only arrived there in 1951, and the first telephone was installed in 1963. Five years later, an airport was built. It is a stunning place, rich in colours. This beautiful island is closer to Africa, and Malta, than it is to Italy itself. Just 167 kilometres away, across the sea, is the Tunisian coast. Libya is also relatively nearby – Tripoli is 355 kilometres away.

Up to the 1990s, Lampedusa had played very little role in any history teaching. Originally, in the nineteenth century, it had hosted a remote penal colony. The Allied invasion of Italy in 1943, which would eventually bring down Mussolini, began here (the island surrendered without a shot being fired), but the real war soon moved onto the Sicilian mainland. This time, however, things would be different. Lampedusa became not just a house-hold name, but an internationally famous place – a focus for polit-ical debate, controversy and catastrophe. Numerous politicians visited the island and local representatives tried to balance local and international needs.

Even the Pope turned up. In July 2013 he made an official visit to the island, and gave an impassioned statement. He took his cue from a newspaper headline: 'Immigrants Dead at Sea'. 'When I read this news,' he continued 'I couldn't think of anything else, like a painful stabbing to my heart ... and so I felt the need to come here today and pray ... as a gesture of solidarity but also to try to wake up our conscience so that what has happened should not happen again. *Please let us make sure this does not happen again* [my emphasis].'[35] Unfortunately, the Pope's powerful words could not prevent future tragedies.

The island had become a staging post for thousands of potential foreign migrants, refugees and asylum-seekers who were trying to make it to the European Union. The Mediterranean developed into a floating graveyard as countless people died in the attempt to sail across to Italy, while others managed to land at or were escorted into Lampedusa's port. This island thus turned into a touchstone for the way that the EU, Italy and the West as a whole managed and understood migration and globalisation – and how it reacted to 'others'.

'Lampedusa' entered the Italian political lexicon. The *'sbarchi'* or landings (a vaguely aggressive and problematic term) became a hot issue, with periods of 'emergency', disasters, and other moments when the whole crisis was nearly forgotten and became routine. Meanwhile, many on the island and elsewhere showed solidarity towards the migrants and their fate. Thus began the strange co-existence of this island as a place of arrival and departure with the processing of thousands of people who were usually described as potential migrants or refugees, and the continuing role of Lampedusa as a holiday destination. A local carpenter, Francesco Tuccio, started to collect pieces of wood from wrecked boats and make them into crosses, as a kind of tribute to those who hadn't made it across the sea. One of these crosses was later installed as a special exhibit in the British Museum. The wood was initially from pieces of a boat that failed to make it to the island in October 2013, with the deaths of 368 Somalians and Eritrean people. Over 150 people were saved in the same incident.

The details of these tragedies were often horrific. 'Many of the ... people who drowned never made it off the capsizing boat. Among the 108 people trapped inside the bow was an Eritrean woman, thought to be about twenty years old, who had given birth as she drowned. Her waters had broken in the water. Rescue divers found the dead infant, still attached by the umbilical cord, in her leggings.'[36]

Migration to Lampedusa had gone through a series of phases, with highs and lows, and different populations involved in the attempts to reach the island. These changes depended largely on the political and military context of their countries of departure – from Tunisia, to Morocco, to Libya and in other North African countries. The island was provided with new infrastructure – including a whole complex of buildings designed to host, hold and process migrants and asylum-seekers.[37]

What were the strategies adopted by Italy, and the European Union, in the face of these repeated arrivals of so-called 'boat people'? Lampedusa (and the sea around it) was to be a key focal point for the answer to this question. This was where Europe began, and ended. The migrants in boats and who made it to Lampedusa also experienced at first hand the effects of changing political circumstances in Italy (and the EU). There were shifts in policy in terms of the saving and escorting of boats to the shore (as dictated by the law of the sea and international law). And further changes were seen once people had reached shore. Were they refugees, or so-called 'economic migrants'? And if these categories were real ones, what was to be done with these people once they were placed in one category or another? Lampedusa and the seas around it were a place of dreams that often turned into nightmares.

Images of the 'sbarchi' ('the landings') were explosive. A kind of constant emergency was created, leading to fear and distrust but also to solidarity. Time and again the Italian media showed boats coming into port, packed with people, and reported certain selected 'human interest' stories linked to these arrivals (babies being born, deaths on board, violence). There was also a sense of 'disaster fatigue'. The stories were rarely human ones, but largely transmitted through faceless numbers.

Arrivals began to take place in line with a well-organised ritual, as Gianluca Gatta has described in his ethnographic research carried out on the island. 'As they arrive in the port, the migrants are brought off the boats one by one. They are counted and photographers take their first photos. On the port-side the migrants are placed in parallel lines with five people in each group, sitting on the ground. They are not allowed to move from this position.'[38] There are now chemical toilets near the port, but before 2005 'the migrants were taken to another part of the port, near to the arrival area, where they were allowed to urinate into the sea'.[39] The visual nature of this process, Gatta argues, 'led to a stereotypical representation of the arrival of the migrants, a series of images which created strong symbolic effects in terms of public discourse and ended up by representing the entire migratory phenomenon'.[40] Some have described this as 'the border spectacle'.[41]

Various types of police and military forces began to work around the 'landings', as well as humanitarian aid workers and coast guards. Sometimes these were national organisations, but often they were trans-national or international bodies. A whole series of 'interventions' thus co-existed at the same time, as did various levels of legality, frameworks, as well as fluid and changing borders. These organisations have changed over time, and usually for political reasons. Security questions interact with humanitarian activities. A lot of money was involved. Migrants attracted funding, and this, in turn, led to activities involving organised crime.[42] Migration was also big business. Meanwhile, the crossings and the unwritten tragedies continue almost daily. As Frances Stoner Saunders has written, 'In Lampedusa's cemetery, the many plaques that read "unidentified migrant" merely tell us that people have been dying in the Mediterranean for at least 25 years – more than twenty thousand of them, according to current estimates.'[43]

Lampedusa and Italian Politics

Lampedusa also became a stage upon which politicians could exhibit themselves. In 2009 the Interior Minister Roberto Maroni, a leading figure in the Lega Nord, claimed to have adopted a new policy – *'respingimenti'* – the 'turnings-back'. This policy, he said, would lead to the closure of the immigrant centre on the island. An agreement with Libya led to migrants found in the sea being taken, for a time, 'back' to that country (informally, and formally). Soon, however, under pressure from more arrivals, the centre on Lampedusa was reopened. Another 'policy' was adopted: Blame Europe (or the European Union). Politicians from both left and right argued that Europe had 'left Italy alone' to deal with the migration crisis. They looked for an EU-wide solution. Some, however, simply employed rhetoric.

Silvio Berlusconi appeared on the island in March 2011. As he tended to do, he arrived with pronouncements to make. He would be clearing out the immigrants, and quickly. 'Within 48 hours,' he promised, implausibly, 'this island will only be inhabited by *lampedusani.*[44] 'We have organised six boats,' he added, 'and we are trying to get a seventh.' More assurances were to follow. The island would be nominated for a Nobel Peace Prize, the islanders would get tax breaks, a golf club and a casino would be built. Berlusconi also said that he himself had bought a house there, that very morning, on the Internet. 'I will also become Lampedusan,' he said. Not surprisingly, very few of these promises were fulfilled. Journalists visited the villa purchased by Berlusconi in August 2012, and found it abandoned and in a state of disrepair.

Moreover, Lampedusa's importance was also due to its media presence – the spectacular nature of the migratory events linked to that place. The high visibility of the 'landings' there did not necessarily correspond with their importance in terms of migration to Italy. In fact, calculations showed that only one in ten, or so, of the migrants in Italy had come via sea, and even fewer by boats across the Mediterranean.

* * *

Italy's instability problem was exacerbated after the 2013 General Election. Once again, the Porcellum – designed in theory to produce stability – had failed to produce a working majority in both houses. The Senate was left without a clear majority for any of the coalitions or lists who had stood, leading to months of uncertainty as vain attempts were made to form a government. Finally, at the end of April 2013, a new broad coalition administration was formed with ministers from the centre-right and the centre-left, but without the support of the Five Star Movement. This was a kind of post-democratic Grand Coalition.

The Rise and Fall of Matteo Renzi

Matteo Renzi, born in 1975, was a child of Berlusconi's television output. Famously, he had appeared as a contestant on the popular programme *The Wheel of Fortune,* hosted by Mike Bongiorno. Renzi had won 48 million lire from the show, about £20,000 at the time. His political career had been spent in centre-left Catholic groupings and his rise to prominence had been swift. Appointed President of the Province of Florence in 2004, he became Mayor of Florence itself in 2009. When he was sworn in as Prime Minister at the age of thirty-nine in February 2014, he was the youngest person to hold that office in Italy's history. Renzi imitated Tony Blair, right down to his mannerisms when speaking. He also had few qualms about dining with Berlusconi at his villa, and governing with him after 2014. He was, perhaps, the first post-Berlusconi 'opposition' leader.

The ascent of Renzi was framed (by himself, and the media) as that of a populist and outsider, a seemingly obligatory role for new twenty-first-century politicians. But he was, despite protestations, a career politician. Renzi used his 'youth' as a political mobilising cry, and promised that he would 'demolish' those in charge of the Democratic Party. There wasn't much to demolish. The Partito Democratico (PD) was an empty husk, top heavy with leaders and bureaucrats, lacking in ideas and real activists, with no clear moral purpose or history behind it. Experts have also pointed to the ways in which Renzi had learnt from Berlusconi himself – his style, his personalisation of politics, his use of the media. However, Renzi has proved adept in his use of the Internet (like one of his other models, Barack Obama), something that Berlusconi never understood.

Renzi made his first bid for the leadership of the Partito Democratico in 2012. On that occasion, the primaries gave Pierluigi Bersani, a classic politician from the former Communist Party, a clear victory (although Renzi won over a million votes). Bersani was soon undone by his failure to deliver the Presidency of Italy to Romano Prodi in 2013. With Bersani gone, and alternative candidates barely credible, Renzi easily won a further primary in December 2013. Meanwhile, the Porcellum electoral law was in deep trouble. In the same month the Constitutional Court ruled that the law (which had been used twice for general elections) was unconstitutional. In theory, this meant that the entire current Parliament (and the previous one) was also illegitimate, but nobody pushed this delicate issue too far.

As Prime Minister, Renzi, in a 'grand alliance' with what remained of Berlusconi's alliance, steered through a small number of mild reforms, including a restricted form of gay marriage. He was also entrusted with forcing through yet further constitutional changes to the electoral system. These included the end of many of the powers attributed to the Upper House – the Senate. The Porcellum was replaced with something few saw as an improvement, but which Renzi dubbed the '*Italicum*' (he has a very good eye for marketing strategies, like Blair). The Italicum was even more complicated that the Porcellum, and designed to keep the major parties or coalitions in power. In its desperation to cling onto power, Italy's political class had tinkered with the electoral system in the 1990s and 2000s. With all of these reforms, the parties ignored the needs of the electorate. It was essentially about them – the members of the caste. Whatever the voters decided, the parties had to stay in power.

These reforms struggled through Parliament (the public were bored with the detail), but by the time they came to a referendum at the end of 2016 – required for major constitutional changes – Renzi's popularity had waned considerably. Unwisely, he had promised to resign if the referendum was lost. This arrogant statement galvanised opposition to him and the reforms at the same time, creating an unholy alliance that stretched from the Lega to the M5S across to the far left and internal opposition within the PD. A referendum concerning a complicated constitutional series of changes thus became, for many, a vote on Renzi and on the state of the economy. Very few Italians had seen any improvement in their lot in the twenty-first century. As Perry Anderson has pointed out, 'Since the introduction of the single currency, Italy has posted the worst economic record of any state in the Union: twenty years of virtually unbroken stagnation.'[45] December 2016 was a stunning defeat for Renzi, and he resigned soon afterwards. Nearly 60 per cent of Italians who voted in the referendum – some 19.5 million people – voted No. Ironically, the result also made it more difficult for any future government to pass reforms. But that didn't seem to matter to the Lega and the M5S, who both claimed victory. Now Italy was in limbo, and without a workable electoral law.

In October 2017, the major parties – but not the Five Star Movement or parts of the left – agreed on a new electoral system.

It was called – unofficially – the *Rosattellum* (named after the man behind the first text of the law, Ettore Rosato). Put simply, the law was a modified form of the *Mattarellum*, which had been used from elections from 1994–2006. The *Rosattellum* was another fiendishly complicated law, whose vagaries were of great interest only to psephologists and political scientists. In the lower house, 232 seats would be elected on a first-past-the-post system, while 386 would be assigned via proportional representation. Italian voters would be faced with one ballot paper in the voting booth but they would have *two* votes to cast: the first for a candidate, and the second for a party or coalition. They could, however, also choose to vote just once, and in that case their preference would count for both sides of the paper. Crucially, electors would not be allowed to opt for a candidate from one coalition and then a different grouping in the PR part of the ballot paper. Gender-equality clauses were included in the law for the first time.

Politically, the *Rosattelum* was clearly designed to keep the Five Star Movement from taking power at a national level, something that had seemed extremely likely after their stunning victories in Rome and Turin in 2016. Standing alone, without political allies, Grillo's movement was likely to lose out in many seats to rival coalitions, especially those on the centre-right. Incredibly (or perhaps not so incredibly) the likelihood was – once again – that nobody would win the election.[46] A fudged coalition seemed a probable outcome. Things had changed, but only so that they could remain the same, although the re-introduction of constituencies was seen as a positive move.

With the new electoral law finally in place, President Sergio Mattarella dissolved Parliament at the end of December 2017 and new national elections were fixed for 4 March 2018. The electoral campaign was marked by an episode of shocking racist violence. On 2 February 2018, in the market town of Macerata in central Italy, a 28-year old man with a shaved head went on the rampage with a gun. His name was Luca Traini, and he had stood as a candidate for the Lega in local elections in 2017 (votes won: 0). His target was black people – any black people he could find. Traini fired shots from his Alfa car in various locations, including at a group waiting at a bus stop, before giving himself up near the town's war memorial with a fascist salute, wrapped in an Italian flag. He has a far-right tattoo on his face. Six people were injured, and it was a miracle that nobody was killed. Traini also fired shots at the offices of the local Democratic Party. This racist attack was linked (in Traini's mind, and in the media) to the horrific murder of a young Italian woman, Pamela Mastropietro, whose dismembered body had been found near Macerata on the 31 January.

The political reaction to this event was surprising. Traini's bullets seemed, paradoxically, to strength the anti-immigrant tone of the centre-right coalition that had dominated media reports on the campaign right from the beginning. Matteo Salvini, the Lega leader, made a vague attack on 'criminality' but shifted the blame onto the left. 'It is obvious', Salvini argued, 'that uncontrolled immigration, an invasion like the one that has been organised and financed in recent years, will lead to social conflict.' Silvio Berlusconi quickly promised to send back '600,000 immigrants', if elected (although, by law, he couldn't have been elected). Roberto Saviano later wrote: 'The more I talk of migrants, the more I am accused of encouraging hatred of them. It's a kind of back-to-front logic: how is it possible, I wonder, that if I relate what is happening in Libya in the detention centres, if I speak of the mud-slinging machine against the NGOs who are operating in the Mediterranean, I manage the opposite of what I am trying to achieve?'[47]

73% of Italians went to the polls. As predicted, the new electoral system did not produce a clear majority for any coalition or party. Yet the winners were obvious. The Five Star Movement was easily the biggest political group, sweeping the south with over 32% of the vote nationwide. It did so well in Sicily that it ran out of candidates to elect. The other winner was Matteo Salvini of the Lega, who had run such an agile and aggressive anti-immigrant campaign across Italy. The losers were also easy to identity. Matteo Renzi's Democratic Party slipped under 20% of the vote, while the breakaway Free and Equal grouping made no impression at all. Ex-Prime Minister Massimo D'Alema won a mere 3.9% of the vote in his constituency. Silvio Berlusconi's 'party' had its worst ever showing, and for the first time the Lega was able to claim leadership of the centre-right. Many commentators quickly claimed that this was the real beginning of a *Third Republic*. However, alliances would still need to be formed. Which way would the Five Star Movement jump? To the right, and Salvini (with which they had much in common, politically); or to the centre-left, and the Democratic Party they had criticised so radically for so long? Or would these groupings split again into different parts? Perhaps there would be new elections, yet again? Whatever the outcome of these negotiations, the mass-party system of the post-war period was, by now, a distant memory. There was no trace of either the Christian Democrats or the Italian Communist Party. Italy was unrecognisable, politically, from the country that had emerged from the Cold War. Italy's long crisis was far from over as the nation prepared to celebrate the 70th anniversary of its anti-fascist Constitution.

Conclusion: Transformation and Crisis

'A journey around Italy lays bare the most mobile,
fluid and destructive society in Europe.'

Guido Piovene[1]

'Italy was ... a ... laboratory of political experiences.'

Eric Hobsbawm[2]

'No social form is ever willing to confess that it has
been superseded.'

Antonio Gramsci[3]

Since 1945, Italy has experienced momentous social, political and
cultural change. The peasantry has gone. By the 1980s and 1990s
it was joined in extinction by the class of factory workers and
an entire system of production – Fordism. These vanishings left
deep cultural, social and political gaps. Mass political parties –
which had patterned Italian life for most of the post-war period –
have also gone. Their support was largely based for much of that
period on the peasantry and the industrial working class. A once
flourishing trade union movement is in its death throes. Italy is
unrecognisable from the country that emerged from the war in
ruins in 1945, but it is also light years away from the optimism of
the boom years in the 1950s and 1960s.

Transformations of this dramatic importance have not been
managed by Italy's political class, who preferred to enrich themselves, holding onto power for as long as they possibly could. Italy

was a society that 'felt that it was not governed' and the effects were serious and long-term.[4] Apart from a brief and ephemeral boom in the 1980s, Italy's economy has flat-lined. Much of the post-war period, for Italy, has been lived in the shadow of a crisis. Looking back, if we take out two periods often seen as economic 'booms' – roughly 1955–65 (above all) and the 1980s (but certainly not the whole decade) – the talk has often been of an economic crisis, and this has usually been accompanied by claims of a political crisis and even of a 'crisis of the system'.

In the twenty-first century new generations of Italians – the post-baby boomers and millennials – enjoy less job security than their parents. Many left the country altogether to improve their qualifications, and find work. Following the financial crash of 2008, *La Crisi* ('The Crisis'), as Italians call it, has been long and deep, affecting all levels of society. There was little sign in 2017 that this long crisis was easing up. Will Italy ever emerge fully from '*La Crisi*'? This is a question that haunts the country – from Sicily to Milan, and across social groups.

If this book has a thread running through it, it is a sense of crisis and transformation in Italian history, and the ebb and flow of emergencies, where moments of deep crisis are broken up by periods of relative calm and even hope. Looking back, these periods of hope and boom seem concentrated and limited – the immediate post-war moment after 1945, the economic miracle, parts of the 1980s, *Tangentopoli*. Otherwise, it has been the sense of crisis and even decline that has held sway. Institutions themselves – above all the political system, but also the judiciary and the forces of law and order – have struggled to achieve high levels of legitimation amongst Italians. Despite the popularity of the constitution – a commonly agreed set of overarching rules – the system created by that constitution has remained deeply unpopular.

Around 1930 Antonio Gramsci wrote in prison that 'The crisis consists precisely in the fact that *the old are dying and the new cannot be born* [my emphasis]; in this interregnum a great variety of morbid symptoms appear.'[5] In Italy these 'morbid symptons' have included a long period under the sway of a business-personal 'party' whose actions were directed almost entirely towards the interests of one wealthy man. Since 2011, Italy has been governed by a series of unelected leaders and technical or 'emergency' governments, which constantly manipulated the electoral laws in order to cling on to power.

There seems very little prospect of an immediate resolution to this 'organic crisis'. Thomas Bates wrote in 1975 – writing about Gramsci – of 'a crisis ... in which people cease to believe the words of the national leaders and begin to abandon the traditional parties. The crisis may last a long time [and] in combatting the crisis, the intellectuals of the ruling class may resort to all sorts of mystification, blaming the failure of the state on an opposition party or on ethnic and racial minorities. This is a very dangerous moment in civic life, for ... if the progressive forces still fail to impose their own solution, the old ruling class may seek salvation in a "divine leader".[6] It is not clear, writing in 2017, whether this 'Caesar' has already appeared on the scene.

Italy today is unrecognisable from the country that emerged from the war in 1945. Physically, socially, culturally and economically, the country has been reinvented. A time traveller would struggle to understand what had happened in these short but tumultuous seventy years. In 1945 there were still sharecroppers and landed great estates, and in the 1950s and 1960s vast factories employed up to 50,000 workers. These social and economic structures are now part of history. Mass politics has come and gone. The Cold War has been fought and won. None of the political parties that oversaw the transition to democracy still exist. Immigration influences every area of the country, and generations of migrants have now grown up in Italy's cities and provincies. This is still Italy, but not as we once knew it. History helps us understand where this country came from, but also indicates where it might be going. Given the surprises and shocks of the last seventy years, Italy's future may not always be rosy, but it certainly won't prove uneventful.

Acknowledgements

This book is the result of more than two decades of teaching, talking and thinking about Italian history and politics in a variety of settings. As such, it is also the product of countless discussions with undergraduates, postgraduates, colleagues, friends and family, as well as complete strangers. I would like to thank the following for their help, advice or simply small acts of solidarity: Marina Arienti, Matthew Brown, Charles Burdett, Helen Castor, Phil Cooke, Rhiannon Daniels, John Dickie, Clare Fermont, Kate Foot, Lorenzo Foot, Matt Foot, Tom Foot, Ruth Glynn, Robert Gordon, Lawrence Grasty, Tristan Kay, Bob Lumley, Florian Mussgnug, Paolo Natale, Catherine O'Rawe, Simon Parker, Lucy Riall, Vanessa Roghi and Filippo Tantillo. Mike Jones provided superb advice at a crucial juncture. Michael Fishwick was (and is) an excellent editor at Bloomsbury. Richard Mason and Sarah Ruddick also carried out expert and invaluable editorial work on the text. My agent Georgina Capel never gave up hope that the book would finally appear, while Anita and William Metcalfe were always ready to help in an emergency.

Sarah Metcalfe provided love, sustenance and creativity.

In April 2011, Corinna was born, and I have enjoyed every second of her life so far. *The Archipelago* is dedicated to her.

Notes

PREFACE

1. John Agnew, 'The Myth of Backward Italy in Modern Europe', in B. Allen and M. Russo, eds., *Revisioning Italy: National Identity and Global Culture*, Minneapolis: University of Minnesota Press, 1997, p. 26.

INTRODUCTION

1. *The Reawakening*, New York: Simon and Schuster, 1965, p. 206.
2. From *Napoli milionaria* (1945) in *I capolavori di Eduardo*, Turin: Einaudi, 1973, p. 238. The phrase 'Ha da passa' 'a nuttata' has also has been translated as 'We must see the night through' in Eduardo De Filippo, *Four Plays*, London: Methuen Drama, 1992, p. 362.
3. Concetto Marchesi, *Scritti politici*, Rome: Riuniti, 1958, p. 145.
4. Primo Levi, *If This Is a Man*, in *If This Is a Man / The Truce*, London: Abacus, 1999, p. 15.
5. Pierre Chany, *Les Rendez-vous du cyclisme, ou Arriva Coppi*, Paris: La Table Ronde, 1960, pp. 11–12, and see also John Marks, 'Se faire naturaliser cycliste: The Tour and its Non-French Competitors', in Hugh Dauncey and Geoff Hare, eds., *The Tour de France 1903–2003: A Century of Sporting Structures*, Meanings and Values, London: Frank Cass, p. 218.
6. Harvey Sachs, *Toscanini*, London: Harper Collins, p. 288; Howard Taubman, *Toscanini*, London: Odhams Press, pp. 339–40.
7. Cited in Gustavo Marchesi, *Arturo Toscanini*, Turin: UTET, 1993, p. 213.

8. http://www.ilgiornale.it/news/e-colpo-bacchetta-toscanini-fece-rinascere-scala-916006.html https://pesaronotizie.com/2016/07/20/settantanni-dalla-riapertura-della-scala-con-due-grandi-pesa-resi-renata-tebaldi-e-cesare-esposito; Filippo Sacchi, *The Magic Baton: Toscanini's Life for Music*, Putman, London, 1957, p. 196. See also Harvey Sachs, who wrote of the same concert 'As Toscanini came on stage at precisely 9 p.m., the audience jumped to its feet, shouting, applauding, cheering the man who, to the Milanese public, was no longer *a* conductor, as he had been half a century earlier, nor even *the* conductor, as a quarter-century earlier, but who had become a living symbol of musical excellence, of personal integrity, and of that mixture of healthiness, severity and humanity which had given their country a Dante, a Michelangelo, a Verdi', in *Toscanini*, New York: Prima Publishing, 1995, p. 290.

9. *The Barrier Miner*, 14 May 1946.

10. Marchesi, *Arturo Toscanini*; Howard Taubman, *Toscanini*, London: Odhams Press Ltd., 1951.

11. Cited in Tag Gallagher, *The Adventures of Roberto Rossellini: His Life and Times*, Boston: Da Capo Press, 1998, p. 194. For *Paisà* see also ibid., pp. 180–227, and Peter Bondanella, *The Cinema of Federico Fellini*, Princeton: Princeton University Press, 1992; David Forgacs et al, eds., *Roberto Rossellini: Magician of the Real*, London: BFI, 2000, pp. 169–70; Giacomo Lichtner, *Fascism in Italian Cinema since 1945: The Politics and Aesthetics of Memory*, London and New York: Palgrave, 2013; Sam Rohdie, *Fellini Lexicon*, London: BFI, 2002, pp. 103–8; Christopher Wagstaff, *Italian Neorealist Cinema: An Aesthetic Approach*, Toronto: Toronto University Press, 2007; Stefania Parigi, ed., *Paisà. Analisi del film*, Venice: Marsilio, 2005.

12. The title of Rossellini's film works on a series of levels. It could be taken to mean, literally, a country, or a town, and it was also a term of address, something like 'buddy'. The title was often changed into *Paisan* for American and other English-speaking audiences, which signified more clearly a term like 'fellow countryman' or 'compatriot' – a study of an encounter between Italians and 'others' (one earlier title was *Seven from the US*); see Angelo Restivo, *The Cinema of Economic Miracles: Visuality and Modernization in the Italian Art Film*, Durham, NC: Duke University Press, p. 24. The title also connected to the landscape more generally. See for discussions and interpretations,

Giuliana Minghelli, *Landscape and Memory in Post-Fascist Italian Film: Cinema Year Zero*, London: Routledge, 2014, pp. 39–40, and Torunn Haaland, *Italian Neorealist Cinema*, Edinburgh: Edinburgh University Press, p. 104. Thanks to Catherine O'Rawe for her advice on this point.

13. Gallagher, *The Adventures of Roberto Rossellini*, p. 188.

14. Ibid., p. 194.

15. Brunetta cited in Lichtner, *Fascism in Italian Cinema*, p. 55.

16. Cited in Gallagher, *The Adventures of Roberto Rossellini*, p. 193.

17. Ibid., p. 194.

18. Ibid., p. 206.

19. Piero Calamandrei, 'Intervento all'Assemblea Costituente', 4 March 1947; http://temi.repubblica.it/micromega-online/resistenza-costituzione-e-identita-nazionale-una-storia-di-minoranze; Cited in Leonardo Paggi, 'Popolo dei Morti', in Sergio Luzzatto, ed., *Uomini e città della resistenza; Discorsi, scritti ed epigrafi*, Bari: Laterza, 2011.

20. It was not until 1957 – twelve years after his death – that Mussolini was finally 'laid to rest' at his birthplace, the small town of Predappio in Emilia, after a campaign led by the neo-fascist Movimento Sociale Italiano, and the chief grave-robber from 1946, Domenico Leccisi, with the support of mainstream journalists and the burgeoning popular magazine press. In the meantime Leccisi had become a Fascist MP and would later publish an autobiography entitled *Con Mussolini prima e dopo Piazzale Loreto – Così trafugammo la salma del Duce* [*With Mussolini before and after Piazzale Loreto – How we stole the Duce's body*], Rome: Settimo Sigillo-Europa Lib. Ed., 1991.

CHAPTER I

1. In Lidia Campagnano, '"Meglio ingenua che furba": la passione politica di Elvira Baracco', *Il Manifesto* (26 June 1986), cited in Maria Linda Odorosio et al., *Donna o cosa? Cronistoria dei movimenti femminili in Italia dal Risorgimento a oggi*, Turin: Edizioni Milvia, 1986, p. 167.

2. Only 1.45 per cent of Italians voted for the Action Party in June 1946.

3. Denis Mack Smith, *Italy and its Monarchy*, New Haven and London: Yale University Press, 1989, p. 327.

4. Cited in Aldo Ricci, *La Repubblica*, Bologna: Il Mulino, 2001, p. 176.

5. Ibid.; http://www.anpi.it/storia/286/porto-di-ortona-lapide (accessed 18 October 2017).

6. Palmiro Togliatti, 'Agli elettori', *L'Unità*, 2 June 1946.

7. Ibid.

8. F. Catalano, 'The Rebirth of the Party System, 1944–48', in S. Woolf, ed., *The Rebirth of Italy 1943–50*, London: Longman, 1972, p. 82.

9. Cited in Patrizia Gabrielli, *Il 1946, le donne, la repubblica*, Rome: Donzelli, 2009, p. 150.

10. Ibid., p. 168.

11. Ibid.

12. Percy Allum, 'The South and National Politics, 1945–50', in Woolf, ed., *The Rebirth of Italy*, p. 106.

13. Ricci, *La Repubblica*, p. 186. See also Allum, 'The South and National Politics', p. 108, and Stuart Woolf, 'The Rebirth of Italy, 1943–50', in Woolf, ed., *The Rebirth of Italy 1943–50*, p. 227. It is difficult to draw direct links between the votes for the parties and those for or against the monarchy, but it seems that most Christian Democratic voters also chose to reject the Republic. The historian Silvio Lanaro wrote that the Republican cause had won 'in a close vote', in *Storia dell'Italia repubblicana. L'economia, la politica, la cultura, la società dal dopoguerra agli anni '90*, Venice: Marsilio, 1997, p. 203.

14. Ricci, *La Repubblica*, p. 174.

15. https://fondazionenenni.wordpress.com/2015/12/16/le-parole-dautore-di-pietro-nenni-quarta-puntata (accessed 28 April 2017).

16. Benedetto Croce, *Taccuini di lavoro, 1946–1949*, Naples: Arte Tipografica, 1987, pp. 36, 41–2, 44, 50.

17. Cited in Catalano, 'The Rebirth of the Party System', p. 92.

18. Woolf, 'The Rebirth of Italy', in Woolf, ed., *The Rebirth of Italy*, p. 127.

19. Aurelio Lepre, *Storia della prima Repubblica. L'Italia dal 1943 al 1998*, Bologna: Il Mulino, 1999, p. 72.

20. Ricci, *La Repubblica*, p. 191. There are various versions of this event available, but no scholarly studies as far as I can ascertain. See also Maria Antonietta Macciocchi, *Letters from Inside the Italian Communist Party to Louis Althusser*, London: New Left Books, 1973, pp. 122–9. Macciocchi (p. 128) states that these events took place on 15 June.

21. Mack Smith, *Italy and its Monarchy*, p. 340.

22. Allum, 'The South and National Politics', p. 108.

23. Sergio Luzzato, *La mummia della Repubblica. Storia di Mazzini imbalsamato 1872–1946*, Milan: Rizzoli, 2001.

24. Massimiliano Boni, 'Gaetano Azzariti: dal Tribunale della razza alla Corte costituzionale', *Contemporanea*, 4, 2014, pp. 577–608, doi: 10.1409/78315, p. 595.

25. http://www.osservatorioantisemitismo.it/articoli/rimane-alla-corte-costituzionale-il-busto-del-presidente-del-tribunale-della-razza (accessed 15 January 2017).

26. G. Focardi cited in Boni, 'Gaetano Azzariti', p. 601.

27. See P. Nicoloso, 'I conti con il fascismo: Marcello Piacentini, "memorie" e invenzione del passato al processo di epurazione', *Rassegna di architettura e urbanistica*, 130–1, 2010, pp. 82–8. Cesare de Seta, 'Piacentini e la città fascista', in *Nuova informazione bibliografica*, 4, 2013, pp. 721–6, doi: 10.1448/75309.

28. http://binrome.com/featured/sapienza-in-restauro-laffresco-fascista-di-mario-sironi-epurato-da-piacentini (accessed 15 January 2017).

29. M. Battini, *The Missing Italian Nuremberg: Cultural Amnesia and Postwar Politics*, London: Palgrave, 2007.

30. Cited in Odorosio et al., *Donna o cosa?*, p. 169.

31. Ibid., p. 171.

32. Cited in Sandro Setta, 'Il qualunquismo', in G. Pasquino, ed., *La politica italiana. Dizionario critico 1945–95*, Bari: Laterza, 1995, p. 368.

33. Ibid., p. 365.

34. Mameli had written the words way back in 1847. This 1946 choice was 'provisional' and was only made definitive in 2006. Stefano Pivato, *La storia leggera. L'uso pubblico della storia nella canzone italiana*, Bologna: Il Mulino, 2002, pp. 7–17, 221–30.

35. Giuseppe Floridia, 'La costituzione', in Pasquino, ed., *La politica italiana*, p. 8.

36. See Perry Willson, *Women in Twentieth-Century Italy*, Houndmills: Macmillan, 2010, pp. 133–6, and Molly Tambor, *The Lost Wave: Women and Democracy in Post-War Italy*, Oxford: Oxford University Press, 2014.

37. Rossana Rossanda, *The Comrade from Milan*, London: Verso, 2010, p. 134.

38. James Edward Miller, *The United States and Italy, 1940–1950: The Politics and Diplomacy of Stabilization*, Chapel Hill and London: University of North Carolina Press, 1986, pp. 218–19.

39. Paul Ginsborg, *A History of Contemporary Italy: Society and Politics, 1943–1988*, London: Penguin, p. 115.

40. It is said that this slogan was invented by the writer and journalist Giovanni Guareschi, author of the popular *Don Camillo* books, set in Cold War Italy.

41. Santi Fedele, *Fronte popolare. La sinistra e le elezioni del 18 aprile 1948*, Milan: Bompiani, 1978. See also Massimo Caprara, *L'attentato a Togliatti. 14 Luglio 1948: il PCI tra insurrezione e programma democratico*, Venice: Marsilio, 1978, p. 220.

42. D. W. Ellwood, 'The 1948 Elections in Italy: A Cold War Propaganda Battle', *Historical Journal of Film, Radio and Television*, 13:1, 1993, p. 20.

43. For the results and a depiction of the election see Robert Ventresca, *From Fascism to Democracy: Culture and Politics in the Italian Election of 1948*, Toronto: University of Toronto Press, 2004, and John Foot, *Modern Italy*, London: Palgrave, 2014, pp. 204–5 and 235.

44. Cited in Rosario Forlenza, 'The Enemy Within: Catholic Anti-Communism in Cold War Italy', *Past and Present*, 235:1, 2017, p. 19.

45. Robert Ventresca, 'The Virgin and the Bear: Religion, Society and the Cold War in Italy', *Journal of Social History*, 37:2, 2003, p. 440.

46. *Excommunication of Communists, Decree of The Holy Office, Formulated by Pius XII, July 1, 1949*.

47. Carlo Ginzburg, *L'Unità*, 17 April 1988, p. 13, cited in D. Ellwood, 'The 1948 Elections in Italy: A Cold War Propaganda Battle', *Historical Journal of Film, Radio and Television*, 13:1, 1993, p. 23. For more details on these visions see Ventresca, 'The Virgin and the Bear'.

48. Forlenza, 'The Enemy Within', p. 20.

49. John Pollard, *Catholicism in Modern Italy: Religion, Society and Politics since 1861*, London: Routledge, 2008, p. 116.

50. *Appello di Gedda per le elezioni del 18 aprile 1948*.

51. See the account by President of Italy Francesco Cossiga, http://ricerca.repubblica.it/repubblica/archivio/repubblica/1992/01/14/armati-fino-ai-denti-io-non.html (accessed 17 June 2017).

52. Ventresca, *From Fascism to Democracy*, p. 234.

53. Rossanda, *The Comrade from Milan*, p. 114.

54. Lucio Magri, *The Tailor of Ulm: A History of Communism*, London: Verso, 2011, p. 91.

55. Ellwood, 'The 1948 Elections in Italy', p. 20.

56. Jussi Hanhimäki and Odd Arne Westad, *The Cold War: A History in Documents and Eyewitness Accounts*, Oxford: Oxford University Press, 2003, p. 134.
57. Silvio Pons, 'Stalin, Togliatti, and the Origins of the Cold War in Europe', *Journal of Cold War Studies*, 3:2, 2001, p. 23.
58. Cited in Vindice Lecis, *Ferrara 14 Luglio 1948*, Ferrara: 2Geditrice, p. 67. See also Walter Tobagi, *La rivoluzione impossibile. L'attentato a Togliatti, violenza politica e reazione popolare*, Milan: Il Saggiatore, 1978, p. 9.
59. Mario Isnenghi, *L'Italia in piazza. I luoghi della vita pubblica dal 1848 a oggi*, Milan: Arnoldo Mondadori, 1994, p. 431.
60. Giorgio Bocca, *Palmiro Togliatti*, Bari: Laterza, 1973, p. 512.
61. Andrea Grillo, *Livorno: una rivolta tra mito e memoria. 14 Luglio 1948. Lo sciopero generale per l'attentato a Togliatti*, Pisa: Biblioteca Franco Serantini, 1994.
62. Bocca, *Palmiro Togliatti*, p. 514.
63. Sandro Orlandini, *Luglio 1948. L'insurrezione proletaria nella provincia di Siena in risposta all'attentato a Togliatti*, Florence: Cooperative Editrice Universitaria, 1976, p. 91.
64. Romano Canosa, *Storia della criminalità in Italia dal 1946 a oggi*, Milan: Feltrinelli, 1995, p. 117.
65. Pietro Secchia, *Lo sciopero del 14 luglio*, Rome: CDS, 1948, p. 21.
66. Claudia Magnanini, *Ricostruzione e miracolo economico: dal sindacato unitario al sindacato di classe nella capitale dell'industria*, Milan: FrancoAngeli, 2006, p. 115.
67. Isnenghi, *L'Italia in piazza*, pp. 382–6.
68. Cited in Ventresca, *From Fascism to Democracy*, p. 262.
69. Percy Allum, 'Uniformity Undone: Aspects of Catholic Culture in Post-War Italy', in Zygmunt Baranski and Robert Lumley (eds.), *Culture and Conflict in Post-War Italy: Essays on Mass and Popular Culture*, Basingstoke: Macmillan, 1990, p. 85.
70. Mario Isnenghi, 'Microstorie di parrocchia', in Saveria Chemotti, ed., *Gli intellettuali in trincea. Politica nell'Italia del dopoguerra*, Padua: Cleup, 1977, p. 60.
71. Ibid., p. 64.
72. Allum, 'Uniformity Undone', p. 81.
73. Ibid., p. 82.
74. Giovanni Levi, 'Italy: Catholicism, Power, Democracy and the Failure of the Past', in Peter Furtado, ed., *Histories of Nations: How*

their Identities were Forged, London: Thames and Hudson, 2012, p. 266.

75. Pollard, *Catholicism in Modern Italy*, p. 109.
76. Ibid., p. 129.
77. M. G. Rossi, *Da Sturzo a De Gasperi. Profilo storico del cattolicesimo politico nel Novecento*, Rome: Editori Riuniti, 1985, p. 203.
78. Aldo Agosti, *Palmiro Togliatti: A Biography*, London: I. B. Tauris, 2008, p. 200.
79. Ibid., p. 200.
80. Bocca, *Palmiro Togliatti*, p. 586.
81. Comitato Centrale del Partito Comunista Italiano, *Per la morte di Stalin*, 1953.
82. David Kertzer, 'Political Rituals' in Luciano Cheles and Lucio Sponza, eds., *The Art of Persuasion: Political Communication in Italy from 1945 to the 1990s*, Manchester: Manchester University Press, 2001, p. 102.
83. Cited in Stephen Gundle, *I comunisti italiani tra Hollywood e Mosca. La sfida della cultura di massa*, Florence: Giunti, 1995, p. 186; see also Stephen Gundle, *Between Hollywood and Moscow: The Italian Communists and the Challenge of Mass Culture, 1943–1991*, Durham, NC: Duke University Press, 2000, p. 83.
84. Bocca, *Palmiro Togliatti*, p. 561.
85. http://www.senato.it/service/PDF/PDFServer/BGT/487877.pdf (accessed 18 October 2017).
86. Giuseppe Fiori, *Uomini-Ex. Lo strano destino di un gruppo di comunisti italiani*, Turin: Einaudi, 1993.
87. Roderigo Di Castiglia [a pseudonym used by Togliatti], 'I sei che sono falliti', *Rinascita*, 7:5, May 1950, pp. 242–3.
88. Aldo Cucchi, 'Letter of resignation fro the PCI', 25 January 1951; http://badigit.comune.bologna.it/mostre/magnacucchi/1.htm (accessed 18 October 2017).
89. For an example of the cult of personality around Togliatti see S. Scuderi, ed., *Vita di un italiano. Palmiro Togliatti*, Rome: Edizioni di cultura sociale, 1953.
90. Eric Hobsbawm, *The Italian Road to Socialism: An Interview by Eric Hobsbawm with Giorgio Napolitano of the Italian Communist Party*, London: The Journeyman Press, 1977.
91. Norman Kogan, *A Political History of Italy: The Postwar Years*, New York: Praeger, p. 88.

92. Cited in Bocca, *Palmiro Togliatti*, p. 425.

93. Pons, 'Stalin, Togliatti, and the Origins of the Cold War in Europe', p. 27; see also Elena Aga Rossi and Gaetano Quagliariello, eds., *L'altra faccia della luna: i rapporti tra PCI, PCF e Unione Sovietica*, Bologna: Il Mulino, 1997; Elena Aga Rossi and Victor Zaslavsky, *Togliatti e Stalin: il PCI e la politica estera staliniana negli archivi di Mosca*, Bologna: Il Mulino, 2007; Silvio Pons, *L'impossibile egemonia. L'Urss, il Pci e le origini della Guerra Fredda. 1943–48*, Rome: Carocci, 1999; Gianni Donno, *La Gladio rossa del PCI, 1945–1967*, Soveria Mannelli: Rubbettino, 2001.

94. *Statuto del Partito Comunista Italiano, XII Congresso del PCI – Bologna 8–15 febbraio 1969*, p. 3.

95. *Discorso del segretario del Pci Palmiro Togliatti pronunciato a Modena in piazza Sant'Agostino nel corso della cerimonia funebre delle vittime dell'eccidio del 9 gennaio alle Fonderie Riunite*, http://www.lavoro-politico.it/togliattidiscorsomodena.htm (accessed 17 January 2016).

96. Paul Ginsborg, 'Italian Political Culture in Historical Perspective', *Modern Italy*, 1:1, 1995, p. 11. This democratic role was also thanks to Togliatti's leadership. But his role during Stalin's purges, the Spanish Civil War and the Second World War (when he was in the Soviet Union, and Italy invaded the USSR) has always been shrouded in controversy.

97. Roberto Segatori, *I sindaci: storia e sociologia dell'amministrazione locale in Italia dall'unità a oggi*, Rome: Donzelli, 2003, p. 58.

98. David Kertzer, *Comrades and Christians: Religion and Political Struggle in Communist Italy*, Cambridge: Cambridge University Press, 1980, p. 157.

99. Davide Pero, 'The Left and the Construction of Immigrants in 1970s Italy', in Anna Cento Bull and Adalgisa Giorgio, eds., *Speaking Out and Silencing: Culture, Society and Politics in Italy in the 1970s*, Cambridge: Legenda, 2006, pp. 218 and 212–26.

100. John Foot, 'La normalità del 25 Aprile', *Internazionale*, 23 April 2015, http://www.internazionale.it/opinione/john-foot/2015/04/23/25-aprile-festa-liberazione (accessed 25 April 2015).

101. http://temi.repubblica.it/micromega-online/i-fatti-dungheria-e-il-dissenso-allinterno-del-pci-storia-del-manifesto-dei-101 (accessed 18 October 2017).

102. Adriano Guerra and Bruno Trentin, *Di Vittorio e l'ombra di Stalin. L'Ungheria, il PCI e l'autonomia del sindacato*, Rome: Ediesse, 1997, p. 138.

103. Ibid., p. 143.

104. Ibid., p. 154.

105. Maria Todaro-Faranda and Concetto Marchesi, eds., *Umanesimo e comunismo*, Rome: Riuniti, 1974, p. 114.

106. Rossanda, *The Comrade from Milan*, pp. 155–6.

107. Csaba Békés et al., eds., *The 1956 Hungarian Revolution: A History in Documents*, Budapest and New York: Central European University Press, 2002, p. 294.

108. Pietro Nenni (attrib.), 'La Spagna non c'entra', *Avanti!*, 13 November 1956.

109. See Ilaria Poerio, *A scuola di dissenso. Storie di resistenza al confino di polizia (1926–1943)*, Rome: Carocci, 2016.

110. http://www.treccani.it/enciclopedia/altiero-spinelli_ (Enciclopedia-Italiana)/ (accessed 16 January 2017).

111. Roberto Castaldi, 'Altiero Spinelli and European Federalism', in Ann Ward and Lee Ward, eds., *The Ashgate Research Companion to Federalism*, Aldershot: Ashgate, 2009, p. 328. When the whole EU project seemed under threat after the UK's Brexit vote in June 2016, Europe's leaders responded with a pilgrimage to Spinelli's grave on the former Italian prison island of Ventotene.

112. *European Parliament, Battling for the Union. Altiero Spinelli. 1979–86*, 23 May 1987. European Parliament, Luxembourg, 1987.

CHAPTER 2

1. Pier Paolo Pasolini, 'Fuori dal palazzo', *Corriere della Sera*, 1 August 1975.

2. Simonetta Fiori, 'L'Italia del boom spioni e bugie', *La Repubblica*, 10 January 1997.

3. Fausto Colombo, *Boom. Storia di quelli che non hanno fatto il '68*, Milan: Rizzoli, 2008, p. 14.

4. Emanuela Scarpellini, *Material Nation: A Consumer's History of Modern Italy*, Oxford: Oxford University Press, p. 181.

5. Ibid., p. 229.

6. Circolo Gianni Bosio and Alessandro Portelli, eds., *Il Borgo e la Borgata. I ragazzi di don Bosco e l'altra Roma del dopoguerra*, Rome: Donzelli, 2002, p. 38.

7. Giuseppe Virciglio, *Milocca al nord. Una comunità di immigrati siciliani ad Asti*, Milan: Franco Angeli, 1991, pp. 88–96.

8. John Foot, 'Migration and the "Miracle" at Milan: The Neighbourhoods of Baggio, Barona, Bovisa and Comasina in the 1950s and 1960s',

Journal of Historical Sociology, 10:2, June 1997, pp. 184–212, and *Milan since the Miracle: City, Culture, Identity*, Oxford: Berg, 2001.

9. Vittorio Vidotto, 'La nuova società', in Giovanni Sabbatucci and Vittorio Vidotto, eds., *Storia d'Italia, 6. L'Italia contemporanea*, Bari: Laterza, 1999, p. 19.

10. Agopik Manoukian, 'La famiglia dei contadini', in P. Melograni, ed., *La famiglia italiana dall'Ottocento a oggi*, Bari: Laterza, 1988, p. 47 (pp. 4–60).

11. Ibid.

12. Ibid., p. 58.

13. John Dickie, *Delizia! The Epic History of Italians and their Food*, London: Sceptre, 2007, pp. 1–7.

14. S. Oglethorpe, 'The End of Sharecropping in Central Italy after 1945: The Role of Mechanisation in the Changing Relationship between Peasant Families and Land', *Rural History*, 25:2, 2014, pp. 243–60.

15. Gianni Celati, *Visioni di case che crollano*, 2003.

16. C. Carboni, 'La Terza Italia', in P. Bevilacqua et al., *Lezioni sull'Italia repubblicana*, Rome: Donzelli, 1994, pp. 165–6, and Vidotto, 'La nuova società', pp. 24–5.

17. Beppe Fenoglio, *La Malora*, Turin: Einaudi, 1954.

18. E. Asquer, *Storia intima dei ceti medi: Una capitale e una periferia nell'Italia del miracolo economico*, Bari: Laterza, 2011.

19. Roberto Romano, http://www.treccani.it/enciclopedia/giovanni-borghi_(Dizionario-Biografico) (accessed 17 January 2017).

20. Goffredo Fofi, *L'immigrazione meridionale a Torino*, Turin: Nino Aragno Editore, 2009.

21. Scarpellini, *Material Nation*, p. 138.

22. Ibid.

23. In Antonio Calabrò, *Agnelli. Una Storia italiana*, Milan: Rizzoli, 2004, p. 65.

24. Lucetta Scaraffia, 'Essere uomo, essere donna', in Melograni, ed., *La famiglia italiana*, p. 248.

25. Enrico Deaglio, *Patria. 1978–2008*, Milan: Il Saggiatore, 2009, p. 11

26. Calabrò, *Agnelli. Una storia italiana*, p. 6.

27. Ibid., p. 111.

28. Ibid., p. 11.

29. G. Nevola, 'The Gianni Agnelli Funeral: A National Identification Rite', *Italian Politics*, volume 32, New York: Berghahn, 2017, pp. 184–99.

30. Luciano Bianciardi, *Il lavoro culturale* (1957), Milan: Feltrinelli, 1964, pp. 14–15.

31. Ercole Pizzuti in Alessandro Portelli, *Città di parole. Storia orale di una periferia romana*, Rome: Donzelli, 2007, p. 42.

32. Ibid., p. 51.

33. Dino Buzzati, 'Natura crudele', *Corriere della Sera*, 11 October 1963.

34. Maurizio Rebershack, *Il Grande Vajont*, Verona: Cierre Edizioni, 2016; Marco Paolini and Oliviero Ponte di Pino, *Quaderno del Vajont. Dagli Album al Teatro della Diga*, Turin: Einaudi, 1999. The TV play was called *Vajont 9 Ottobre '63. Orazione civile* by Marco Paolini and Gabriele Vacis, performed by Marco Paolini, 1997; Marco Paolini and Gabriele Vacis, *Il racconto del Vajont*, Milan: Garzanti, 1997 (second edition); Tina Merlin, *Sulla pelle viva. Come si costruisce una catastrofe. Il caso del Vajont*, Verona: Cierre Edizioni, 1997.

35. http://archiviopiolatorre.camera.it/img-repo/DOCU-MENTAZIONE/Assemblea_Regionale_Siciliana/V_Legislatura/Mozioni/1966_09_02.pdf (accessed 17 January 2017).

36. Richard Bosworth, *Italian Venice: A History*, New Haven and London: Yale University Press, 2014, p. 203.

37. P. Pavolini, 'I coreani di Milano', *Il Mondo*, 29 January 1963.

38. Cited in C. Di Biase, 'Due quartieri milanesi', in F. Della Peruta et al., eds., *Milano e il suo territorio*, Milan: Provincia di Milano, Silvana editoriale, 1985, p. 140.

39. Vittorio Gregotti, *Racconti di architettura*, Milan: Skira, 1998, p. 41.

40. E. Vaime, *Giorgio Gaber: cento storie che coinvolgono, Sipario*, 1972, now in M. Bonavia, ed., *Giorgio Gaber. Frammenti di un discorso*, Milan: Selene Edizioni, 2004; G. Gaber, 'Gaber-fluxus', in M. L. Straniero, *Il signor Gaber*, Milan: Gammalibri, 1979.

41. Gianni Borgna, *Storia della canzone italiana*, Bari: Laterza, 1985, p. 143.

42. See Stephen Gundle, 'Memory and Identity: Popular Culture', in Patrick McCarthy, ed., *Italy since 1945*, Oxford: Oxford University Press, 2000, pp. 186–90.

43. Gianni Borgna and Luca Serianni, eds., *La lingua cantata*, Rome: Garamond, 1994, p. 1.

44. Umberto Eco, 'Fenomenologia di Mike Bongiorno', in *Diario minimo*, Milan: Arnoldo Mondadori, 1963, p. 33.

45. 'Prefazione', in Gianni Borgna, *Storia della canzone italiana*, Bari: Laterza, 1985, p. v.

46. Adriano Bellotto, 'Gli italiani al video: uno nessuno tre milioni', *Avanti!*, 9 February 1963.

47. See the work of Emma Barron, *Mona Lisa Covergirl: Popularised High Culture in Italian Mass Culture 1950–1970*, unpublished PhD, Bologna and Sydney Universities, 2015, and 'Television Audience Enjoyment and the *Lascia o raddoppia?* Phenomenon', *Modern Italy*, 21:3, 2016, pp. 227–43.

48. Sergio Boccuccia in Portelli, *Città*, p. 132.

49. Cited in John Foot, *Milano dopo il miracolo. Biografia di una città*, Millan: Feltrinelli, 2003, p. 39.

50. Cited in Piero Melograni, *Dieci perché sulla Repubblica*, Ente per il diritto allo studio universitario dell'Università Cattolica, Milan, 2013, p. 104.

51. T. De Mauro, 'Lingua parlata e TV', in *Televisione e vita italiana*, Turin: ERI, 1968, pp. 245–94 (pp. 288–9).

52. At the time, 'concubinage' (living together outside of marriage) was against Italian law. This part of the Criminal Code was declared unconstitutional in 1969.

53. Aldo Capitini, *Battezzati non credenti*, Florence: Parenti, 1961, pp. 13–21.

54. http://ricerca.gelocal.it/iltirreno/archivio/iltirreno/1998/03/05/ZR101.html (accessed 20 January 2017).

55. Gianni Brera, *Coppi e il diavolo*, Milan: Rizzoli, 1981, p. 146.

56. *Corriere della Sera*, 18 November 1953.

57. Percy Allum, *Politics and Society in Post-War Naples*, Cambridge: Cambridge University Press, 1973; Turin: Einaudi, 1975, p. 19.

58. Ibid., p. 126.

59. Ibid., p. 154.

60. Ibid., p. 217.

61. See also the account of the Gava family in Macciocchi, *Letters from Inside the Italian Communist Party to Louis Althusser*, pp. 104–11.

62. Cited in Lichtner, *Fascism in Italian Cinema*, p. 57. Pier Paolo Pasolini, excerpts from 'Tears' from *Roman Poems* translated by Lawrence Ferlinghetti and Francesca Valente. Translation copyright © 1986 by City Lights Books. Reprinted with the permission of The Permissions Company, Inc., on behalf of City Lights Books, www.citylights.com.

63. Philip Cooke, 'The Italian State and the Resistance Legacy in the 1950s and 1960s', in *Culture, Censorship and the State in*

Twentieth-Century Italy, eds. Guido Bonsaver and Robert Gordon, Cambridge: Legenda, 2005, pp. 121–2 and passim.

64. http://www.centropertini.org/300660.htm (accessed 20 January 2017).

65. http://legislature.camera.it/_dati/leg03/lavori/stenografici/sed0313/sed0313.pdf (accessed 20 January 2017).

66. Cited in Piero Brunello, *Storia e canzoni in Italia: il Novecento*, Comune di Venezia-Assessorato Pubblica Istruzione-Itinerari Educativi, Venice, 2000, pp. 270–1.

67. Rossana Rossanda, *The Comrade from Milan*, London: Verso, 2010, p. 247.

68. Ibid.

69. Giorgio Bocca, *Palmiro Togliatti*, Bari: Laterza, 1973, pp. 1–2.

70. Massimo Cirri, *Un'altra parte del mondo*, Milan: Feltrinelli, 2016.

71. Giuliano Procacci, *Storia degli italiani*, Bari: Laterza, 1974, p. 554, cited in Paolo Spriano, *Sulla rivoluzione italiana. Socialisti e comunisti nella storia d'Italia*, Turin: Einaudi, 1978, p. 214.

72. Spriano, *Sulla rivoluzione italiana*, p. 215.

CHAPTER 3

1. Ugo Cerletti, 'La fossa dei serpenti', *Il Ponte*, V, 11, 1949, p. 1373.

2. L. Della Mea (ed.), *Manicomio 1914. Gentilissimo Signor Dottore, questa è la mia vita*, Milan: Mazzotta, 1978; see also Cristina Crippa, 'Storia di Adalgisa Conti', in Luigi Attenasio, *Fuori norma: La diversità come valore e sapere*, Rome: Armando, 2000, pp. 326–37.

3. Franco Pierini, 'Se il matto è un uomo', *L'Europeo*, 24 August 1967.

4. Nicola d'Amico, *Storia e storie della scuola italiana: dalle origini ai giorni nostri*, Milan: Zanichelli, 2010.

5. School of Barbiana, *Letter to a Teacher*, London: Penguin, 1970, p. 5.

6. Ibid, p. 69.

7. Don Milani (Scuola di Barbiana), *Lettera a una professoressa*, Florence: Libreria Editrice Fiorentina, 1967, trans. *Letter to a Teacher*, London: Penguin, 1970.

8. The letter, 'I preti e la guerra', was published in the Communist Party periodical *Rinascita*, 6 March 1965, and in pamphlet form with some other documents, *L'obbedienza non è più una virtù. Documenti del processo di Don Milani*, Florence: Libreria Editrice Fiorentina, 1965. http://www.liberliber.it/mediateca/libri/m/milani/l_obbedienza_non_e_piu_una_virtu/html/milani_d.htm (accessed 24 January 2017).

9. Mario Lodi, *Il paese sbagliato. Diario di un'esperienza didattica*, Turin: Einaudi, 1970, p. 16, and *C'è speranza se questo accade al Vho*, Turin: Einaudi, 1972.

10. Lodi, *Il paese sbagliato*, p. 19.

11. Ibid., p. 21.

12. Ibid., p. 23.

13. Elvio Fachinelli, et al., eds., *L'Erba voglio: pratica non autoritaria nella scuola*, Turin: Einaudi, 1971, p. 13.

14. Ibid., p. 33.

15. See also the highly successful set of films that began with Fausto Brizzi's *La notte prima degli esami* (2006).

16. On the Liceo Classico see Antonio La Penna, 'Il liceo classico', in Mario Isnenghi, ed., *I luoghi della memoria. Simboli e miti dell'Italia unita*, Bari: Laterza, 1996, pp. 197–213; Adolfo Scotto di Luzio, *Il liceo classico*, Bologna: Il Mulino, 2011. As with many other reforms from the 1960s and 1970s, the 'urgent' measures of 1969 were designed to be temporary – but in this case they stayed in place right up until the 1990s.

17. This was also possible thanks to the battle fought within the Constituent Assembly; see Molly Tambor, *The Lost Wave: Women and Democracy in Post-War Italy*, Oxford: Oxford University Press, 2014, pp. 141–68.

18. *L'Europeo*, 1974, p. 21, now in 'L'Italia degli anni Settanta', *L'Europeo*, 2, 2004, pp. 244 and 246.

19. Cited in Aurelio Lepre, *Storia della prima Repubblica: l'Italia dal 1943 al 2003*, Bologna: Il Mulino, 2006, p. 267. 'Gli italiani non sono più quelli', *Corriere della Sera*, 10 June 1974.

20. John Pollard, *Catholicism in Modern Italy: Religion, Society and Politics since 1861*, London: Routledge, 2008, p. 149.

21. Ibid., p. 150. Annual marriages in Italy fell from over 385,000 to 194,000 between 1970 and 2015, while separations and divorces rose steadily (to over 86,000 and 54,000 respectively by 2008). By 2010, 25 per cent of marriages in Italy were ending in divorce, despite the difficulties and costs involved in this process. In 2015 modifications were introduced to make divorce easier, and cheaper. A rush to divorce followed as many financial and legal obstacles were removed.

22. So, there were clear contradictions between and even within some of these clauses; Vincenzi Amato, 'La famiglia e il diritto', in P. Melograni, ed., *La famiglia italiana dall'Ottocento a oggi*, Bari: Laterza, 1988, pp. 667–9.

23. Ibid., p. 667.
24. Ibid., p. 671.
25. Ibid., p. 675.
26. Law 66, 9 February 1963, Giovanni Bianconi, 'Toghe con le gonne. La rivincita', *La Repubblica*, 27 January 2013.
27. http://timeforequality.org/dossier-la-giudice/donne-e-magistratura-in-italia (accessed 24 October 2017).
28. Iotti had also been part of the Constituent Assembly in 1946.
29. For the idea of the 'mass worker' see John Foot, 'Mass Cultures, Popular Cultures and the Working Class in Milan, 1950-1970', *Social History*, 24:2, May 1999, pp. 43–4; N. Balestrini and P. Moroni, *L'orda d'oro, 1968–1977. La grande ondata rivoluzionaria e creativa, politica ed esistenziale*, Milan: Feltrinelli, 2015; A. Negri, *Dall'operaio massa all'operaismo sociale. Intervista sull'operaismo*, Milan: Multhipla edizioni, 1979; R. Panzieri, *Lotte operaie nello sviluppo capitalistico*, Turin: Einaudi, 1976; M. Tronti, *Operai e capitale*, Turin: Einaudi, 1966.
30. Statistics from http://archivio.fiom.cgil.it/autunno69/autunno_caldo.htm (accessed 1 February 2017). The workers' statue was Law 20 May 1970, n. 300. For the 'hot autumn' see Roberto Franzosi, *The Puzzle of Strikes: Class and State Strategies in Postwar Italy*, Cambridge: Cambridge University Press, 1995.
31. Elio Petri, *La classe operaia va in paradiso*, 1971.
32. Eleanor Chiari, *Undoing Time: The Cultural Memory of an Italian Prison*, London: Peter Lang, 2012, p. 89.
33. G. Salierno and A. Ricci, *Il carcere in Italia. Inchiesta sui carcerati, i carcerieri e l'ideologia carceraria*, Turin: Einaudi: 1971, p. 440. See also in general Christian De Vito, *Camosci e girachiavi. Storia del carcere in Italia*, Bari: Laterza, 2009. See also G. Salierno, *Autobiografia di un picchiatore fascista*, Turin: Einaudi: 1976.
34. De Vito, *Camosci e girachiavi*; Monica Galfré, 'Se vuoi conoscere un paese visitane le prigioni', *Passato e Presente*, 80, 2010, pp. 153–64.
35. John Dickie, *Mafia Republic: Italy's Criminal Curse. Cosa Nostra, Camorra and 'Ndrangheta from 1946 to the Present*, London: Sceptre, pp. 324–5.
36. Ibid., p. 217.
37. Herbert Marcuse, *One Dimensional Man*, Boston: Beacon, 1964; R. D. Laing, *The Divided Self: An Existential Study in Sanity and Madness*, London: Penguin, 1961; Frantz Fanon, *The Wretched of the Earth*, New York: Grove Press, 1963.

38. 'Contro l'università' in *Quaderni Piacentini*, 33, 1968, now in Marco Boato et al., eds., *Contro l'università*, Milan: Mimesis, 2008, pp. 77–113. On Guido Viale see also Luisa Passerini, *Autoritratto di gruppo*, Florence: Giunti, 1968, pp. 115–21.

39. See my 'Looking back on Italy's "Long 1968": Public, Private and Divided Memories', in Ingo Cornils and Sarah Waters, eds., *Memories of 1968: International Perspectives*, Oxford: Peter Lang, 2011, pp. 126–7, and Alessandro Portelli, *The Battle of Valle Giulia: Oral History and the Art of Dialogue*, Madison, WI: University of Wisconsin Press, 1997.

40. Luigi Longo, 'Il movimento studentesco nella lotta anticapitalistica', *Rinascita*, 3 May 1968.

41. *Rinascita*, 7 June 1968, pp. 3–4. Amendola argued that Communists should struggle against capitalism *and* against the student movement.

42. Cited in Stuart Hilwig, 'Are you Calling me a Fascist? A Contribution to the Oral History of the 1968 Italian Student Rebellion', *Journal of Contemporary History*, 36:4, 2001, p. 590.

43. '25 aprile 1945–25 aprile 1962', *Quaderni Piacentini*, April 1962, also cited in Passerini, *Autoritratto di gruppo*, p. 48.

44. Sorbi was with a group of students. Years later he became an anti-abortion campaigner.

45. Alexander Vasudevan, *Metropolitan Preoccupations: The Spatial Politics of Squatting in Berlin*, Chichester: Wiley-Blackwell, 2015, p. 70.

46. 'The courage to choose to favour the poor and oppose the capitalist system', http://www.gazzettadiparma.it/news/parma/96049/Occupazione-del-Duomo-45-anni-dopo.html (accessed 24 October 2017).

47. Don Mazzi, cited in *Storia d'Italia: cronologia 1815–1990*, Novara: Istituto Geografico De Agostini, 1991, p. 657.

48. Gabriella Sobrino and Francesca Romana de'Angelis, *Storie del premio Viareggio*, Florence: Mauro Pagliai, 2008, pp. 84–5.

49. Edmondo Bruti Liberati, 'L'Associazione dei magistrati italiani', in Edmondo Bruti Liberati and Luca Palmara, eds., *Cento anni di Associazione Magistrati*, Assago: Editore Ipsoa, 2009, p. 18; http://www.associazionemagistrati.it/allegati/cento-anni-di-associazione-magistrati.pdf (accessed 24 October 2017).

50. 'Lettere dalle case chiuse', *Avanti!*, Milan and Rome, 1955.

51. http://www.enciclopediadelledonne.it/biografie/franca-viola (accessed 24 January 2017).

52. Damiano Damiani, *La moglie più bella* (*The Most Beautiful Wife*), 1970.

53. Niamh Cullen, 'The Case of Franca Viola: Debating Gender, Nation and Modernity in 1960s Italy', *Contemporary European History*, 25:1, 2016, pp. 97–115 (p. 114); Maria Pia di Bella, *Dire o tacere in Sicilia. Viaggio alle radici dell'omertà*, Rome: Armando editore, 2011, pp. 167–85.

54. Perry Willson, *Women in Twentieth-Century Italy*, London: Palgrave, 2010, p. 153.

55. Maud Bracke, *Women and the Reinvention of the Political: Feminism in Italy, 1968–1983*, London: Routledge, 2014, p. 67.

56. Ibid., p. 110.

57. Ibid., p. 5.

58. Ibid., p. 198.

59. Maria Linda Odorisio et al., eds., *Donna o cosa?: i movimenti femminili in Italia dal Risorgimento a oggi*, vol. 1, Turin: Edizioni Milvia, p. 189.

60. http://www.repubblica.it/cronaca/2016/10/20/news/medici_obiettori_ecco_i_dati_regione_per_regione–150182589 (24 October 2017).

61. Gabriele Ferluga, *Il processo Braibanti*, Turin: Silvio Zamorani editore, 2003, p. 49.

62. Ibid., p. 84.

63. Ibid., pp. 84–5.

64. The lawyer, Alfredo De Marsico, had been a Fascist Deputy in the 1920s and 1930s and member of the Fascist Grand Council. He derided Braibanti as someone with 'the air of a revolutionary thinker, while he does not have the force even to change a little ant colony', cited in Ferluga, *Il processo Braibanti*, p. 253.

65. Paolo Gambescia, *L'Unità*, 29 November 1969, cited in Ferluga, *Il processo Braibanti*, p. 255.

66. Alberto Moravia, Umberto Eco, Adolfo Gatti, Mario Gozzano, Cesare Luigi Musatti and Ginevra Bompiani, *Sotto il nome di plagio*, Milan: Bompiani, 1969, p. 13.

67. Ferluga, *Il processo Braibanti*, p. 247.

68. Percy Allum, *Politics and Society in Post-War Naples*, Cambridge, Cambridge University Press, 1973, p. 333.

69. Mario G. Rossi, *Da Sturzo a De Gasperi. Profilo storico dal cattolicesimo politico nel Novecento*, Rome: Riuniti, 1985, p. 199.

70. Giampaolo Pansa, *Bisaglia una carriera democristiana*, Milan: SugarCo, 1975, p. 89; http://www.treccani.it/enciclopedia/antonio-bisaglia_(Dizionario-Biografico) (accessed 24 January 2017).
71. Pansa, *Bisaglia una carriera democristiana*, p. 117.
72. Patrick McCarthy, *The Crisis of the Italian State: From the Origins of the Cold War to the Fall of Berlusconi and Beyond*, London: Macmillan, 1997, pp. 68–71.
73. McCarthy, *The Crisis of the Italian State*, p. 70.
74. Ferdinando Scianna, 'Parla Napoli: il nostro colera', *L'Europeo*, 1973, n. 39, now in 'L'Italia degli anni settanta', *L'Europeo*, 2, 2004, pp. 138–44.
75. For the way Naples is represented by the media and much more besides, see Nick Dines, *Tuff City: Urban Change and Contested Space in Central Naples*, New York: Berghahn, 2012, and 'Writing Rubbish about Naples: Urban Trash and the Post-Political Condition', in Christoph Lindner and Miriam Meissner, eds., *Global Garbage: Urban Imaginaries of Waste, Excess, and Abandonment*, London: Routledge, 2015, pp. 117–31; 'Bad News from an Aberrant City: A Critical Analysis of the British Press's Portrayal of Organised Crime and the Refuse Crisis in Naples', *Modern Italy*, 18:4, 2013, pp. 409–22.
76. Stella Cervasio, 'Il colera 40 anni dopo. I giorni della paura. Repubblica racconta attraverso le voci dei protagonisti la tragedia moderna di quell'agosto del 1973: il vibrione, l'epidemia, le vittime, la reazione della città', *La Repubblica*, 25 August 2013; http://napoli.repubblica.it/cronaca/2013/08/25/news/il_colera_40_anni_dopo_i_giorni_della_paura-65240129 (accessed 24 October 2017).
77. Laura Conti, *Visto da Seveso. L'evento straordinario e l'ordinaria amministrazione*, Milan: Feltrinelli, 1977; *Una lepre con la faccia di bambina*, Rome: Riuniti, 1978; Bruno Ziglioli, *La mina vagante. Il disastro di Seveso e la solidarietà nazionale*, Milan: Franco Angeli, 2010. See also the film by Gianni Serra, *Una lepre con la faccia di bambina* (1988).
78. Nullo Cantaroni, 'L'Italia è un paese cavia', *L'Europeo*, 32, 1976.
79. *L'Espresso*, XIII, 20, 14 May 1967.
80. Giangiacomo Feltrinelli, *Estate 1969. La minaccia incombente di una svolta radicale e autoritaria a destra, di un colpo di Stato all'italiana*, Milan: Feltrinelli, 2012 (1969), p. 5.

81. Introduction to Marco Nozza, *Il pistarolo. Da Piazza Fontana, trent'anni di storia raccontati da un grande cronista*, Milan: Il Saggiatore, 2011, p. 10.

82. Cited in Giorgio Boatti, *Piazza Fontana. 12 Dicembre 1969, il giorno dell'innocenza perduta*, Turin: Einaudi, 1999, pp. 7–8.

83. Ibid., p. 14.

84. For an alternative view of this case see Carlo Ginzburg, *The Judge and the Historian: Marginal Notes and a Late-Twentieth-Century Miscarriage of Justice*, London: Verso, 1999.

85. This led to a further set of trials, which got closer to the truth, but struggled to bring in definitive guilty verdicts. Once again, the sentence (a lengthy document) was more important, historically, than the judicial verdicts. See Marco Dondi, *L'eco del boato: Storia della strategia della tensione 1965–1974*, Bari: Laterza, 2016. The full sentence can be found here: http://www.archivioguerrapolitica.org/wp-content/uploads/2012/08/Sentenza-Ordinanza-Salvini-1998_1.pdf (accessed 25 January 2017).

86. Camillo Arcuri, *Colpo di stato. Storia vera di una inchiesta censurata. Il racconto del golpe Borghese, il caso Mattei e la morte di De Mauro*, Milan: BUR, 2007; Jack Greene and Alessandro Massignani, *Il principe nero. Junio Valerio Borghese e la X Mas*, Milan: Mondadori, 2008.

87. Cited in Luca Telese, *Cuori neri. Dal rogo di Primavalle alla morte di Ramelli. 21 delitti dimenticati degli anni di piombo*, Milan: Sperling and Kupfer, 2010, pp. 151–2.

88. His full name was Junio Valerio Scipione Ghezzo Marcantonio Maria dei principi Borghese.

89. It is also referred to as 'Tora-Tora' thanks to the code word used and the fact that the 'coup' was planned for the anniversary of Pearl Harbour.

90. 'Piano eversivo contro la repubblica, scoperto piano di estrema destra', *Paese Sera*, 17 March 1971. The Interior Minister Franco Restivo made a speech to Parliament the next day when he tried to play down the incident.

91. The next day's headline was 'Neofascist Conspiracy'.

92. Sentence, Corte d'Assise, 29 November 1984.

93. *Vogliamo i colonelli*, 1973.

94. See Tom Behan, *Dario Fo: Revolutionary Theatre*, pp. 51–8 and 143–5, and 'Allende, Berlinguer, Pinochet … and Dario Fo', in Cento Bull and Giorgio, eds., *Speaking Out and Silencing: Culture, Society and Politics in Italy in the 1970s*, Leeds: Italian Perspectives: 2006, pp. 161–71.

95. Giovanna Marini, 'We are by now in Reggio and the station/is full of people/tomorrow everything will be closed as a sign of mourning', from 'I treni per Reggio Calabria' (1973). The full lyrics can be sourced here: http://www.ossin.org/i-giorni-cantati/1656-i-treni-per-reggio-calabria (accessed 24 October 2017).

96. Guido Crainz, *Il paese mancato. Dal miracolo economico agli anni ottanta*, Rome: Donzelli, 2003, pp. 270–9.

97. See the scenes in the documentary film *12 Dicembre* (1972) by Giovanni Bonfanti and Pier Paolo Pasolini.

98. *L'Europeo*, 11 February 1971, cited in Fabio Cuzzola, *Reggio 1970. Storie e memorie della rivolta*, Rome: Donzelli, 2008, pp. 79–80.

99. Franco Pierini, cited in ibid., p. 41; *Il Giorno*, 29 July 1970.

100. The song was written by Giovanna Marini, 'I treni per Reggio Calabria'; the novel was Vincenzo Guerrazzi, *Nord e sud uniti nella lotta* (1974), Genoa: Frilli, 2003; the film was directed by Paolo Pietrangeli and Paolo Gambescia, *Bianco e Nero*, 1975, and was partly dedicated to the Reggio revolt.

101. For this, and an analysis of the entire revolt, see Luigi Ambrosi, *La rivolta di Reggio. Storia di territori, violenza e populismo nel 1970*, Soveria Mannelli: Rubettino, 2009, p. 186, and Cuzzola, *Reggio 1970*.

102. Carlo Feltrinelli, *Senior Service*, Milan: Feltrinelli, 2014.

103. Final guilty verdicts for a neo-fascist and another man linked to the country's secret services were confirmed by Italy's High Court in 2017.

104. London: Pluto Press, 1982.

105. For the history and politics of this plaque and the events surrounding the Lorusso killing, see Andrea Hajek, *Negotiating Memories of Protest in Western Europe: The Case of Italy*, New York: Palgrave, 2013.

106. In 1973, in the wake of the global slowdown linked to rises in oil prices, austerity came quickly. The government initially banned cars on Sundays, cinemas were closed, and TV schedules finished early.

107. R. Rossanda, 'Il discorso sulla Dc', *Il Manifesto*, 28 March 1978.

108. Alberto Franceschini, *Mara Renato e Io. Storia dei fondatori delle BR*, Milan: Mondadori, 1991, p. 63.

109. Ibid., p. 63.

110. Both quotes are from Phil Edwards, '*More Work, Less Pay': Rebellion and Repression in Italy, 1972–7*, Manchester: Manchester University Press, 2009, p. 64.

111. Marco Belpoliti, *La foto di Moro*, Rome: I sassi, nottetempo, 2008.

112. Miguel Gotor, *Aldo Moro: Lettere dalla prigionia*, Turin: Einaudi, 2008.

113. Comunicato dei familiari, 9 May 1978, cited in Leonardo Sciascia, *L'affaire Moro*, Milan: Adelphi, 2007, p. 158.

114. Ruth Glynn and Giancarlo Lombardi, eds., *Remembering Aldo Moro: The Cultural Legacy of the 1978 Kidnapping and Murder*, Leeds: Legenda, 2012; John Foot, *Italy's Divided Memory*, London: Palgrave, pp. 183–204.

115. Anna Cento Bull and Phil Cooke, *Ending Terrorism in Italy*, London: Routledge, 2013.

116. Giovanni Fasanella and Sabina Rossa, *Guido Rossa. Mio padre*, Milan: Rizzoli, 2006; Giancarlo Feliziano, *Colpirne uno per educarne cento: la storia di Guido Rossa*, Arezzo: Limina, 2004.

117. *Spingendo la notte più in là. Storia della mia famiglia e di altre vittime del terrorismo*, Milan: Mondadori, 2007, trans. as *Pushing Past the Night: Coming to Terms with Italy's Terrorist Past*, New York: Other Press, 2009.

118. Benedetta Tobagi, *Come mi batte forte il tuo cuore. Storia di mio padre*, Turin: Einaudi, 2010.

119. Ruth Glynn, 'The "turn to the victim" in Italian Culture: Victim-centred Narratives of the *anni di piombo'*, *Modern Italy*, 18:4, 2013, pp. 373–90.

120. Jeffrey McKenzie Bale cited in Greene and Massignani, *Il principe nero*, p. 207.

121. Giovanni Bianconi, *A mano armata. Vita violenta di Giusva Fioravanti terrorista neo-fascista quasi per caso*, Milan: Baldini & Castoldi, 1994, pp. 150, 152; http://archiviostorico.avvisopubblico.it/news/allegati/magistrati-vittime-di-terrorismo-schede_2011-05-05.pdf.

122. Bianconi, *A mano armata*, p. 233.

123. Ibid., p. 234.

124. Cited in Anna Lisa Tota, 'A Persistent Past: The Bologna Massacre, 1980–2000', in John Dickie, John Foot and Frank Snowden, eds., *Disastro! Disasters in Italy since 1860: Culture, Politics and Society*, New York: Palgrave, 2002, p. 282.

125. For Bus 37 see Tota, 'A Persistent Past', pp. 283–6, and Anna Lisa Tota, *La città ferita. Memoria e comunicazione pubblica*

della strage di Bologna, 2 Agosto 1980, Bologna: Il Mulino, 2003, pp. 87–91.

CHAPTER 4

1. Giuseppe Turani, 'I milanesi senza Milano', *La Repubblica*, 30 December 1988.
2. Gabriele Basilico, *Milano. Ritratti di fabbriche*, Milan: Sugarco, 1981.
3. Enrico Deaglio, *Patria. 1978–2008*, Milan: Il Saggiatore, 2009, pp. 639–42.
4. Interview with Eugenio Scalfari, *La Repubblica*, 28 July 1981.
5. Giulio Sapelli, *Cleptocrazia: Il meccanismo unico della corruzione tra economia e politica*, Milan: Feltrinelli, 1994.
6. Cited in Russell King et al., 'The Lure of London: A Comparative Study of Recent Graduate Migration from Germany, Italy and Latvia', University of Sussex, Sussex Centre for Migration Research, Working Paper no. 75, 2014, p. 21.
7. V. M. Caferra, 'La corruzione', in G. Pasquino, ed., *La politica italiana. Dizionario critico 1945–95*, Bari: Laterza, 1995, p. 413.
8. Italo Calvino, 'C'era un paese che reggeva sull'illecito', *La Repubblica*, 15 March 1980; Deaglio, *Patria*, pp. 87–8.
9. Mario Caciagli, 'The 18th DC Congress: From De Mita to Forlani and the Victory of "neodoroteism"', in Filippo Sabetti and Raimondo Catanzaro, *Italian Politics: A Review*, vol. 5, London and New York: Pinter Publishers, 1991, p. 10.
10. Caciagli, 'The 18th DC Congress', p. 21.
11. Patrick McCarthy, 'Italy: A New Language for a New Politics?', *Journal of Modern Italian Studies*, 2:3, 1997, p. 341.
12. Enrico Berlinguer, *Austerità, occasione per trasformare l'Italia*, Rome: Riuniti, 1977, cited in McCarthy, 'Italy', p. 341.
13. Phil Cooke and Gianluca Fantoni, '"We all miss you": Enrico Berlinguer in Post-Berlin Wall Italy', *20th Century Communism*, 11, 2016, p. 135.
14. Cooke and Fantoni, '"We all miss you"', p. 131.
15. Cited in Massimo Gamba, *Vermicino, L'Italia nel pozzo*, Segrate: Sperling and Kupfer Editori, 2007, p. 159.
16. Ibid., p. 222.
17. Ibid., p. 124.
18. http://www.ilfattoquotidiano.it/2012/06/11/alfredino-e-tutto-cambio/259947 (accessed 24 October 2017).

19. Reichlin and Padre Claudio Sorgi, cited in Gamba, *Vermicino, L'Italia nel pozzo*, pp. 164–5 and 212.

20. Walter Veltroni, *L'inizio del buio. Alfredino Rampi e Roberto Peci sotto l'occhio della tv*, Milan: Rizzoli, 2012, p. 169

21. Giuseppe Genna, *Dies Irae*, Milan: Mondadori, 2006.

22. See Anna Bisogno, *La tv invadente. il reality del dolore da Vermicino ad Avetrana*, Rome: Carocci, 2015. For Heysel see John Foot, *Calcio: A History of Italian Football*, London: HarperCollins, 2007, pp. 360–72, and Francesco Caremani, *Le verità sull'Heysel. Cronaca di una strage annunciata*, Ivrea: Bradipolibri, 2010.

23. Cited in Pollard, *Catholicism in Modern Italy*, p. 169.

24. Ibid., p 190.

25. Ibid., p. 171.

26. Bettino Craxi, 'La modernizzazione del Paese è un processo in cammino, un processo che io giudico irreversibile', Discorso alla Borsa di Milano, 1985.

27. Stephen Gundle, 'The Death (and Re-Birth) of the Hero: Charisma and Manufactured Charisma in Modern Italy', *Modern Italy*, 3:2, 1998, p. 184.

28. Guido Crainz, *Storia della Repubblica. L'Italia dalla Liberazione ad oggi*, Rome: Donzelli, 2016, p. 254.

29. Claudio Petruccioli, 'Hanno spinto Milano lontano dall'Europa', *L'Unità*, 30 March 1992.

30. Giulio Sapelli, 'The Italian Crises and Capitalism', *Modern Italy*, 1:1, 1995, p. 91.

31. Giulio Sapelli, *Cleptocrazia*, p. 121, cited in D. Della Porta, 'Political Parties and Corruption: Reflections on the Italian Case', *Modern Italy*, 1:1, 1995, p. 99.

32. Paul Ginsborg, 'Italian Political Culture in Historical Perspective', *Modern Italy*, 1:1, 1995, pp. 11–12.

33. Silvio Berlusconi, 'Il contratto di pubblicità per inserzione'.

34. Natalia Aspesi, Paolo Berlusconi, Gianni Brera, Graziano Cavallini, Marco Mascardi, Giorgio Medail, Enzo Siciliano, and Isa Vercelloni, *Milano 2, una città per vivere*, Milan: Edilnord centri residenziali, 1976.

35. Giorgio Bocca, *La Repubblica*, 11 March 1976.

36. In 2010 Massimo Ciancimino (son of the Christian Democratic politician and former Mayor of Palermo, Vito Ciancimino) told magistrates that the Mafia had put a lot of money into Milano 2 back in the 1970s. Ciancimino repeated this accusation at a trial

in 2016: http://espresso.repubblica.it/palazzo/2010/11/17/news/
milano-2-per-noi-fu-un-affare-1.26004.

37. See Dickie, *Mafia Republic*, pp. 180–2, 397–9; Federico Varese,
'Messages from the Mafia', *London Review of Books*, 27:1, 6
January 2005. David Lane, *Berlusconi's Shadow: Crime, Justice and
the Pursuit of Power*, London: Allen Lane, 2004.

38. Varese, 'Messages from the Mafia'.

39. Giuseppe Richeri, 'Hard Times for Public Service Broadcasting: The
RAI in the Age of Commercial Competition', in Robert Lumley
and Zygmunt Baranski, eds., *Culture and Conflict in Postwar
Italy: Essays on Mass and Popular Culture*, London: Palgrave, 1990,
p. 256.

40. In 2010 Marco DaMilano wrote that 'July 1990 was the first act
of berlusconism' http://espresso.repubblica.it/palazzo/2010/07/05/
news/vent-anni-di-leggi-ad-personam-1.22254 (accessed 31 January
2017). 'Il luglio 1990 rappresenta l'atto di nascita del berlusconismo.'

41. Stephen Gundle, 'Il sorriso di Berlusconi', *Altrochemestre*, 3, 1995,
pp. 14–17; 'How Berlusconi will be remembered: notoriety, collective memory and the mediatisation of posterity', *Modern Italy*, 20:1,
2015, pp. 91–109.

42. Scarpellini, *Material Nation*, p. 231.

43. Umberto Eco, 'A Guide to the Neo-Television of the 1980s', in
Lumley and Baranski, eds., *Culture and Conflict in Postwar Italy*,
pp. 245–55.

44. Ibid., p. 245.

45. Ibid.

46. Ibid., p. 246.

47. Franco Ferrarotti and Oliviero Beha, *All'ultimo stadio. Una repubblica fondata sul calcio*, Milan: Rusconi, 1983, p. 105.

48. For this scandal, see Oliviero Beha and Roberto Chiodi,
*Mundialgate. Dietro la vittoria italiana in Spagna una clamorosa
storia di corruzione*, Naples: Tullio Pironti, 1984, and Oliviero Beha
and Andrea di Caro, *Il calcio alla sbarra*, Milan: BUR, 2011. The
publisher Feltrinelli decided not to publish the book, and it later
came out with another publisher in Naples. See also Oliviero Beha,
*Trilogia della censura. Ieri come oggi: Mundialgate-Antenne rotte-
L'Italia non canta più*, Rome: Avagliano, 2005.

49. See John Foot, 'How Italian Football Creates Italians: The 1982
World Cup, the "Pertini Myth" and Italian National Identity', *The*

International Journal of the History of Sport, 33:3, pp. 341–5, and *Calcio*, pp. 468–73.

50. Luciano Curino, 'La lunga notte in tricolore', *La Stampa*, 13 July 1982.

51. Silvio Lanaro, *Storia dell'Italia repubblicana. Dalla fine della guerra agli anni novanta*, Venice: Marsilio, 1992, p. 419.

52. For example, in his first speech to Parliament on taking office in February 2014, thirty-nine-year-old Matteo Renzi said that 'On the 24 February 1990 ... Sandro Pertini died. I remember his attitude, which all of us remember, especially in the face of the problems of those terrible years, as well as in the better moments, as when the World Cup came back from Madrid.'

53. John Dickie, *Mafia Republic. Italy's Criminal Curse: Cosa Nostra, Camorra and 'Ndrangheta from 1946 to the Present*, London: Sceptre, 2013, pp. 249–50.

54. Joseph Farrell, *Understanding the Mafia*, Manchester: Manchester University Press, 1997, p. 17.

55. Ibid., p. 17.

56. Enrico Deaglio, *Raccolto rosso: la mafia, l'Italia e poi venne giù tutto*, Milan: Feltrinelli, 1993, p. 54.

57. Law 416bis stated that 'Mafia-type associations exist when those who are part of them use intimidatory force, associational links, codes of silence and forms of subjection to commit crimes, and to acquire in a direct or indirect way the control of economic activities, concessions and authorisations, public works and services contracts or in order to make profits, or achieve unfair advanatages for themselves or others.'

58. Deaglio, *Patria*, p. 224.

59. John Dickie, *Cosa Nostra: A History of the Sicilian Mafia*, London: Hodder & Stoughton, 2004, p. 402. See also pp. 391–403 and Dickie, *Mafia Republic*, pp. 345–56.

60. Stille, *Excellent Cadavers*, London: Random House, 2011.

61. From his film *Aprile* (1998). Moretti addresses these words to Massimo D'Alema, one of the leading figures in the Italian Communist Party and in its various configurations after 'la svolta'.

62. Lucio Magri, *The Tailor of Ulm: Communism in the Twentieth Century*, London: Verso, 2011, p. 369.

63. McCarthy, 'Italy', p. 351.

64. Although the Communist Party had been formed way back in 1921, thanks to a dramatic split from the Socialist Party in the coastal city of Livorno.

65. Svetlana Alexievich, *Second-Hand Time*, London: Fitzcarraldo, 2016, p. 162.

66. Nanni Moretti, *La Cosa*, 1990.

67. David Kertzer, 'Political Rituals', *The Art of Persuasion: Political Communication in Italy from 1945 to the 1990s*, Manchester: Manchester University Press, 2001, p. 100 (pp. 99–113).

68. This one was held in January–February 1991 in Rimini (almost exactly seventy years since the formation of the Communist Party in Livorno).

69. Cited in Magri, *The Tailor of Ulm*, p. 370.

70. Colin Crouch, *Post-Democracy*, Cambridge: Polity Press, p. 4.

71. Enrico Deaglio, 'Assomiglia a una gigantesco grappolo d'uva che si muove sul mare', *Patria*, p. 336.

72. Russell King and Nicola Mai, *Out of Albania: From Crisis Migration to Social Inclusion in Italy*, New York: Berghahn, 2008, pp. 1 and 101.

73. Later, Amelio would perform the same 'trick' for foreign migrants when he made explicit comparisons between new foreign migrations and recent, internal migrations, in his Golden Lion-winning film *Così Ridevano* (1998) set in Turin in the 1950s and 1960s.

74. Luigi Quaranta, 'E 20 mila disperati finirono prigionieri. Lo sbarco della Vlora venti anni fa', in *Corriere Del Mezzogiorno*, 5 August 2011.

75. Sergio Romano, 'Politica Adriatica Zero', *La Stampa*, 9 August 1991.

76. Indro Montanelli, 'Controcorrente', *Il Giornale*, 21 December 1985.

77. John Foot, *Milan since the Miracle: City, Culture and Identity*, Oxford: Berg, 2001, p. 105.

CHAPTER 5

1. Patrick McCarthy, *The Crisis of the Italian State: From the Origins of the Cold War to the Fall of Berlusconi and Beyond*, London: Macmillan, 1997, p. 7.

2. Antonio Di Pietro, cited in Guido Vergani, 'I mille giorni di Mani Pulite', *La Repubblica*, 7 December 1994.

3. Soon the *-opoli* part of the term became a kind of catch-all for subsequent scandals – much as Watergate and '-gate' have become

common in the English-speaking world; see John Foot, *Milan since the Miracle: City, Culture and Identity*, Oxford: Berg, 2001, pp. 164–78.

4. Perry Anderson, 'Land without Prejudice', *London Review of Books*, 24:6, 21 March 2002.

5. Fulvio Milone, 'Il forziere di Paperon de Poggiolini', *La Stampa*, 1 October 1993.

6. Guido Passalunga, 'Da Milano la Lega Lombarda punta al Parlamento di Roma', *La Repubblica*, 2 July 1985.

7. Cited in Gian Antonio Stella, *Tribù: foto di gruppo con cavaliere*, Milan: Mondadori, 2001, p. 34.

8. Sergio Romano, 'Carisma in cerca d'impiego', cited in *Tribù: foto di gruppo con cavaliere*, Milan: Mondadori, 2001, p. 37.

9. Luciano Cheles and Lucio Sponza, eds., *The Art of Persuasion: Political Communication in Italy from 1945 to the 1990s*, Manchester: Manchester University Press, 2001, p. 6.

10. Arturo Tosi, *Language and Society in a Changing Italy*, Bristol: Multilingual Matters, 2000, p. 113.

11. See Marco Belpoliti, *La canottiera di Bossi*, Milan: Guanda, 2012.

12. Maria Pia Pozzato, 'Fashion and Political Communication in the 1980s and 1990s', in Cheles and Sponza, eds., *The Art of Persuasion*, p. 295.

13. 'Se la sinistra vuole scontri, io ho 300mila uomini. I fucili sono sempre caldi', *Corriere della Sera*, 29 April 2008.

14. Luciano Cheles, 'Picture Battles in the Piazza: The Political Poster', in *The Art of Persuasion*, p. 161.

15. Carl Levy, 'Racism, Immigration and New Identities in Italy', in A. Mammone et al., eds., *Routledge Handbook of Contemporary Italy*, London: Routledge, p. 51.

16. Pier Paolo Giglioli, 'Ritual Degradation as Public Display: A Televised Corruption Trial', in Cheles and Sponza, eds., *The Art of Persuasion*, p. 307.

17. Pino Corrias, *Mani pulite*, 1997. Three parts are available on YouTube. This programme has never been released on DVD.

18. On one of Berlusconi's channels the art critic, politician and shock-jock broadcaster Vittorio Sgarbi (who became a TV personality around this time) defined the 'Clean Hands' magistrates as 'murderers'. Twenty-two years later his conviction for defamation was finally confirmed in the High Court.

19. http://legislature.camera.it/_dati/leg11/lavori/stenografici/steno-grafico/34744.pdf (accessed 27 October 2017).

20. Cited in Sergio Zavoli, *C'era una volta la prima repubblica: cinquant'anni della nostra vita*, Milan: Mondadori, 1991, p. 408.

21. Francesco Grignetti, 'Craxi con la scorta in TV', *La Stampa*, 1 May 1993.

22. Robert Lumley, 'The Last Laugh: Cuore and the Vicissitudes of Satire', in Cheles and Sponza, eds., *The Art of Persuasion*, pp. 233–57.

23. Alexander Stille, *Excellent Cadavers: The Mafia and the Death of the First Italian Republic*, London: Random House, 2011; John Dickie, *Cosa Nostra: A History of the Sicilian Mafia*, London: Hodder & Stoughton, 2004; Jane and Peter Schneider, *Reversible Destiny: Mafia, Antimafia, and the Struggle for Palermo*, Oakland: University of California Press, 2003.

24. Enrico Deaglio, *Patria. 1978–2008*, Milan: Il Saggiatore, 2009, p. 367.

25. But not always; see the analysis in Perry Anderson, 'The Italian Disaster', *London Review of Books*, 36:10, 22 May 2014.

26. John Dickie, 'Falcone and Borsellino: The Story of an Iconic Photo', *Modern Italy*, 17 February 2012, p. 251. See also Eleanor Canright Chiari, 'The Whisper with a Thousand Echoes: Tony Gentile's Photograph of Falcone and Borsellino', *Modern Italy*, 21 April 2016, pp. 441–52.

27. Cited in Dickie, 'Falcone and Borsellino', p. 255.

28. Chiari, 'The Whisper with a Thousand Echoes', pp. 441 and 443.

29. John Dickie, *Mafia Republic. Italy's Criminal Curse: Cosa Nostra, 'Ndrangheta and Camorra from 1946 to the Present*, London: Sceptre, 2013, p. 395.

30. Gianni Barbacetto, 'Cosa nostra presenta il conto', *Diario*, 26 July 2002.

31. Dickie, *Mafia Republic*, p. 368.

32. Fini had apologised on 'behalf of the Italians' for the anti-Semitic laws, in 2002. He then visited Israel in 2003 where he went further, calling the age of fascism 'an absolute evil' and the anti-Semitic laws 'a disgrace'. http://www.repubblica.it/online/politica/finisraele/integrale/integrale.html (accessed 27 October 2017); http://www.repubblica.it/2003/k/sezioni/politica/finisr/leggi/leggi.html (accessed 27 October 2017).

33. Berlusconi's influence over his core businesses during his time as a politician remained strong – even when he was elected Prime

Minister. And when he relinquished formal control, he maintained extremely close links with his media and sporting empire (or put his family in charge, or close friends). The literature on this issue is vast, but see, for example, David Lane, *Berlusconi's Shadow: Crime, Justice and the Pursuit of Power*, London: Penguin, 2005; Alexander Stille, *Sack of Rome: Media + Money + Celebrity = Power = Silvio Berlusconi*, London: Penguin, 2007; Giovanni Ruggeri, *Berlusconi. Gli affari del presidente*, Milan: Kaos, 1994. For the parallels between the political careers and personal lives of Donald Trump and Silvio Berlusconi see John Foot, 'We've seen Donald Trump before. His name was Silvio Berlusconi', *Guardian*, 20 October 2016.

34. The text of the speech is included in Silvio Berlusconi, *L'Italia che ho in mente. I discorsi 'a braccio' di Silvio Berlusconi*, Milan: Mondadori, 2000, pp. 289–92; Paul Ginsborg, *Silvio Berlusconi: Television, Power and Patrimony*, London: Verso, 2005, pp. 65–6. See also Guido Crainz, *Il paese reale. Dall'assassinio di Moro all'Italia di oggi*, Rome: Donzelli, pp. 308–9.

35. Marco Maraffi, 'Forza Italia', in G. Pasquino, ed., *La politica italiana. Dizionario critico 1945–95*, Bari: Laterza, 1995, p. 252.

36. Maraffi, 'Forza Italia', p. 253.

37. Deaglio, *Patria*, p. 425.

38. Donatella Della Porta and Alberto Vannucci (trans. Alex Wilson), 'Corruption and Anti-Corruption: The Political Defeat of "Clean Hands" in Italy', *West European Politics*, 30:4 (2007), pp. 830–53. In 2002 Paolo Berlusconi was convicted of crimes linked to a rubbish dump in a place called Cerro Maggiore.

39. A series of minor groupings followed, before the reformation of the Communist Party in 2009 – although none of these managed to gain more than a relative handful of votes.

40. *Corriere della Sera*, 22 November 1994.

41. http://www.archivioantimafia.org/sentenze2/andreotti/andreotti_accusa.pdf (accessed 8 February 2017).

42. Salvatore Lupo, *Andreotti, la mafia, la storia d'Italia*, Rome: Donzelli, 1996; Giuliano Ferrara and Lino Jannuzzi, *Il processo del secolo. Come e perché è stato assolto Andreotti*, Milan: Mondadori, 2000.

43. Richard Bosworth, *Italian Venice: A History*, New Haven and London: Yale University Press, 2014, pp. 231–3.

44. Cited in Alvise Fontanella, *Il ritorno della Serenissima. 1997. L'insorgenza indipendentista*, Venice: Editoria universitaria, 2005, p. 33.

45. The story appeared to have finished there. But more was to follow. In 2014, seventeen years after the incident in Venice, further arrests in the Veneto region picked up a number of men on suspicion of planned armed activity. One of the original Venetian assailants was among them, and another fake tank was involved. The men had planned, it seems, to occupy Piazza San Marco again. One of those arrested was Franco Rocchetta, who had been Junior Minister for Foreign affairs in the 1994 Berlusconi government. Trials began for some of these men in 2017 – who risked up to fifteen years in prison.

46. Cited in Gianni Barbacetto et al., *Mani pulite – la vera storia*, Rome: Riuniti, 2003, p. 678. See also 'The "Clean Hands" investigations do not seem to have led to the moral regeneration of Italian politics … Not only is the balance of action against corruption rather meagre, but profound divisions have emerged in the relationship between the judiciary and the "new" political class, with frequent attempts by the latter to restrict the autonomy of the former.' Della Porta and Vannucci, 'Corruption and Anti-Corruption', p. 831.

47. Cited in Marco Travaglio, *La scomparsa dei fatti. Si prega di abolire le notizie per non disturbare le opinioni*, Milan: Il saggiatore, 2010, p. 86.

48. She also wrote a book called *Forza Italia Addio!*, Florence: Loggia de' Lanzi, 1998.

49. Cited in Rosario Bentivegna and Alessandro Portelli, *Achtung Banditen: prima e dopo Via Rasella*, Milan: Mursia, 2004, p. 205.

50. A particularly important moment for this approach was represented by Claudio Pavone's path-breaking *Una guerra civile* (Turin: Bollati Boringhieri, 1991), translated as *A Civil War: A History of the Italian Resistance*, London, Verso, 2014. The international conference *In Memory* held at Arezzo in 1994 was another key moment and produced two important books, Giovanni Contini's *La memoria divisa*, Milan; Rizzoli, 1997, Leonardo Paggi et al., *Storia e memoria di un massacro ordinario*, Rome: manifestolibri, 1996, as well as providing the inspiration for Paolo Pezzino's fascinating research on another German massacre near Pisa, *Anatomia di un massacro. Controversia sopra una strage tedesca*, Bologna: Il Mulino, 2007. For all this see John Foot, *Italy's Divided Memory*, London: Palgrave, 2009.

51. Kappler, who was ill, died five months later, in his homeland. The political fallout from his escape was embarrassing, and Italy's Defence Minister resigned. It appeared as if the guards had left Kappler alone, but it is unclear whether this was due to orders from

above, or simply because of the date of the escape (in the middle of the summer holidays).

52. Alessandro Portelli, *The Order Has Been Carried Out: History, Memory and Meaning of a Nazi Massacre in Rome*, New York: Palgrave, 2003, p. 6.

53. Adriana Montezemolo, cited in Alessandro Portelli, *L'ordine è già stato eseguito. Roma, le Fosse Ardeatine, la memoria*, Rome: Donzelli, 1999, p. 352.

54. Ibid., p. 222.

55. All the material is now available online, https://archivio.camera.it/desecretazione-atti/commissione-parlamentare-inchiesta-sui-crimini-nazifascisti-leg-XIV/list (accessed 20 June 2017).

56. Filippo Focardi, 'La questione dei processi ai criminali di guerra tedeschi in Italia: fra punizione frenata, insabbiamento di Stato, giustizia tardiva (1943–2005)', *Storicamente*, 2:3, 2006, http://storicamente.org/focardi_shoa (accessed 27 October 2017); Marco De Paolis and Paolo Pezzino, *La difficile giustizia. I processi per crimini di guerra tedeschi in Italia (1943–2013)*, Rome: Viella, 2016; Robert Gordon, *The Holocaust in Italian Culture, 1944–2010*, Stanford: Stanford University Press, 2012.

57. http://www.ilgiornale.it/news/cronache/parla-lavvocato-dellex-ss-i-miei-18-anni-priebke-1068219.html (accessed 6 February 2017). Journalists later discovered where the cemetery was; http://espresso.repubblica.it/archivio/2015/07/09/news/nel-cimitero-segreto-di-priebke-1.220717 (accessed 27 October 2017).

58. http://www.treccani.it/enciclopedia/altiero-spinelli_(Enciclopedia-Italiana) (accessed 16 January 2017).

59. Alessandro Portelli, *Città di parole*, Rome: Donzelli, p. 199.

60. Mauro Valeri, *Che razza di tifo. Dieci anni di razzismo nel calcio italiano*, Rome: Donzelli, 2010.

61. Maurizio Ambrosini, 'Immigration in Italy': Between Economic Acceptance and Political Rejection', *International Migration & Integration*, 14, 2013, p. 175.

62. John Foot, 'The Creation of a Dangerous Place: San Salvario, Turin, 1990–1999', in R. King, ed., *The Mediterranean Passage: Migration and New Cultural Encounters in Southern Europe*, Liverpool: Liverpool University Press, pp. 206–30.

63. Don Ciotti, *Corriere della Sera*, 22 July 1997.

64. Meo Ponte, 'L'hanno fatto affogare. E ridevano', *La Repubblica*, 20 July 1997.

65. Cited in Ambrosini, 'Immigration in Italy', p. 176.

66. Alessandro Dal Lago, *Non-persone: L'esclusione dei migranti in una società globale*, Milan: Feltrinelli, 2004.

67. Cited in Ambrosini, 'Immigration in Italy', p. 191.

68. Maurizio Giannattasio, 'Bossi: abbiamo chiuso la moschea di Milano', *Corriere della Sera*, 5 July 2008.

69. http://www.corriere.it/Primo_Piano/Cronache/2006/09_Settembre/15/rabbia1.shtml (accessed 6 February 2017).

70. She died on 15 September 2006. In 2015 a two-part TV mini-series was made about her life.

71. Charles Burdett, *Italy, Islam and the Islamic World: Representations and Reflections, from 9/11 to the Arab Uprisings*, Oxford: Peter Lang, 2016, p. 31.

72. Oriana Fallaci, 'La rabbia e l'orgoglio', *Corriere della Sera*, 29 September 2001.

73. http://www.newyorker.com/magazine/2006/06/05/the-agitator (accessed 6 February 2017).

74. Umberto Eco, 'Le guerre sante: passione e ragione', *La Repubblica*, 5 October 2001.

75. Milan, as I write in 2017, still has no new mosque for an estimated 100,000 Muslims who live in and around the city.

76. John Pollard, *Catholicism in Modern Italy: Religion, Society and Politics Since 1861*, London: Routledge, 2008, p. 169.

77. http://www.ilsole24ore.com/art/mondo/2015-11-15/il-boom-musulmani-italia-passeranno-26percento-54percento-popolazione-entro-2030-131517.shtml?uuid=ACnOzbaB (accessed 7 February 2017).

78. Charles Burdett, 'Representations of the Islamic Community in Italy 2001–2011', *Journal of Romance Studies*, 13:1, 2013, p. 1.

79. Cited in Elahe Izadi, 'Pope Francis washes the feet of muslim migrants, says we are "children of the same God"', *Washington Post*, 25 March 2016.

80. Gabriele Turi, 'Una croce senza Cristo', *Passato e Presente*, 81, 2010, pp. 93–104.

81. See 'European Court of Human Rights rules crucifixes are allowed in state schools', *Guardian*, 18 March 2011; and religionclause.blogspot.co.uk/2011/03/European-courts-grand-chamber-upholds.html (accessed 3 January 2018).

82. Pierluigi Bersani, 'Strasburgo, no al crocifisso in aula. Il governo italiano presenta ricorso', *La Repubblica*, 3 November 2009.

83. Sergio Luzzatto, *Padre Pio: Miracles and Politics in a Secular Age*, New York: Metropolitan Books, Henry Holt, 2007, p. 1.

84. Paolo Conti, 'Un selfie con Padre Pio. Tutti in coda per il santo', *Corriere della Sera*, 4 February 2016.

CHAPTER 6

1. Indro Montanelli, cited in Alexander Stille, *The Sack of Rome: How a Beautiful European Country with a Fabled History and a Storied Culture Was Taken Over by a Man Named Silvio Berlusconi*, New York: Penguin, 2006, p. 258.

2. Cited in Maurizio Viroli, *The Liberty of Servants: Berlusconi's Italy*, Princeton: Princeton University Press, 2012, p. 31.

3. Ibid., p. 27.

4. Luca Ricolfi, *Tempo scaduto. Il 'Contratto con gli italiani' alla prova dei fatti*, Bologna: Il Mulino, 2006.

5. Here the figures are for the proportional part of the vote in the Lower House.

6. Stephen Gundle, 'How Berlusconi will be Remembered: Notoriety, Collective Memory and the Mediatisation of Posterity', *Modern Italy*, 20:1, 2015, pp. 91–109.

7. See the documentary directed by Francesca Comencini, *Carlo Giuliani. Ragazzo*, 2002.

8. http://www.radiopopolare.it/2016/07/g8-genova-i-racconti-di-quel-luglio-2001/ (visited 6.February 2017), https://www.amnesty.org/en/documents/eur30/012/2001/en (accessed 6 February 2017).

9. Viroli, *The Liberty of Servants*, p. xvii.

10. 'La legge è uguale per tutti' is a phrase often found in Italian courtrooms ('The law is equal for all').

11. Perry Anderson, 'The Italian Disaster', *London Review of Books*, 36:10, 22 May 2014.

12. Umberto Eco, *Turning Back the Clock: Hot Wars and Media Populism*, London: Random House, 2014, pp. 31–2.

13. Giovanni Sartori, *Il sultanato*, Rome: Laterza, 2009, p. 127.

14. Viroli, *The Liberty of Servants*, p. 12.

15. Ibid., p. 58.

16. See Sabina Guzzanti, *Draquila. L'Italia che trema*, 2010.

17. Paolo Ceri, 'Challenging from the Grass-Roots: The Girotondi and the No Global Movement', in Daniele Albertazzi et al., eds,

Resisting the Tide: Cultures of Opposition Under Berlusconi (2001–06), London and New York: Continuum, 2009, p. 89.

18. Stille, *The Sack of Rome*, p. 257.
19. Silvio Berlusconi, cited in ibid., p. 252.
20. Giovanna Orsina, *Berlusconism and Italy: A Historical Interpretation*, London and New York: Palgrave, 2014.
21. http://www.giurisprudenzapenale.com/2015/09/10/calciopoli-depositate-le-motivazioni-della-corte-di-cassazione-cass-pen-36350201 5 (accessed 27.10.2017).
22. Marco Materazzi, *Che cosa ho detto veramente a Zidane*, Milan: Mondadori, 2006.
23. 'Compravendita senatori, prescrizione per Berlusconi', *Il sole-24 ore*, 20 April 2017 (accessed 27 October 2017).
24. In May 2014, Marcello Dell'Utri, one of the key architects of Forza Italia and a central figure in the advertising sector, was given a definitive seven-year sentence for external links to the Mafia and sent to prison.
25. http://www.repubblica.it/2007/01/sezioni/politica/lettera-veronica/lettera-veronica/lettera-veronica.html (accessed 7 February 2017).
26. http://www.repubblica.it/2009/04/sezioni/politica/elezioni-2009-2/veronica-divorzio/veronica-divorzio.html (accessed 7 February 2017).
27. 'Letters', *London Review of Books*, 9 May 2002.
28. Piero Colaprico, *Le cene eleganti*, Milan: Feltrinelli, 2011.
29. See Fabio Serricchio, 'Italian Citizens and Europe: Explaining the Growth of Euroscepticism', *Bulletin of Italian Politics*, 4:1, 2012, pp. 115–34.
30. *Atlante. Gli anni di Berlusconi*, Rome: La Repubblica, 2011.
31. Pietro Castelli Gattinara and Caterina Froio, 'Opposition in the EU and Opposition to the EU: Soft and Hard Euroscepticism in Italy in the Time of Austerity', Institute of European Democrats, 2014, p. 6; https://www.iedonline.eu/download/2014/bratislava/IED-2014-Opposition-in-the-EU-and-opposition-to-the-EU-Pietro-Castelli-Gattinara-Caterina-Froio.pdf (accessed 16 January 2017).

CHAPTER 7

1. http://espresso.repubblica.it/attualita/2015/10/22/news/la-rara-fortuna-di-essere-un-professore-giovane-1.235654 (accessed 7 February 2017).

2. Russell King et al., 'The Lure of London: A Comparative Study of Recent Graduate Migration from Germany, Italy and Latvia', University of Sussex, Sussex Centre for Migration Research, Working Paper No. 75, p. 17. https://www.sussex.ac.uk/webteam/gateway/file.php?name=mwp75.pdf&site=252 (accessed 7 February 2017).

3. Cited in King et al., 'The Lure of London', p. 20.

4. Ibid., p. 21.

5. To quote King, they 'see themselves as a different "kind" of Italian – as having a different *mentalità* to those who stay behind in Italy. They self-identify as more adventurous, more keen to engage in a project of self-development, more critical of the culture of *raccomandazione* and nepotism, and thus as morally superior to those who simply stay at home with their parents and have an "easy life"', in ibid., 'The Lure of London', p. 23.

6. http://www.cafebabel.co.uk/society/article/influx-a-journey-into-the-pulse-of-italian-london.html (accessed 28 October 2017).

7. http://www.influxlondon.com (accessed 28 October 2017).

8. http://www.cafebabel.co.uk/society/article/influx-a-journey-into-the-pulse-of-italian-london.html (accessed 28 October 2017).

9. Giuseppe Scotto, 'From "emigrants" to "Italians": What is New in Italian Migration to London?', *Modern Italy*, 20:2, 2015, p. 153; http://researchonline.ljmu.ac.uk/3312/3/Modern%20Italy%20Scotto.pdf (accessed 28 October 2017).

10. Ibid., p. 159. 'The sense of a lack of meritocracy in Italy is something that results in a shared identity for members of this group.'

11. https://www.youtube.com/watch?v=4jdHN4edCqA (accessed 7 February 2017).

12. Grillo could count on 2.28 million Twitter followers by the beginning of 2017. Paolo Natale and Roberto Biorcio, *Politica a 5 stelle. Idee, storia e strategie del movimento di Grillo*, Milan: Feltrinelli, 2013.

13. Giuliano Santoro, *Un Grillo qualunque. Il Movimento 5 Stelle e il populismo digitale nella crisi dei partiti italiani*, Rome: Castelvecchi, 2013.

14. Ibid., p. 769; Sergio Rizzo and Gian Antonio Stella, *La Casta. Così i politici italiani sono diventati intoccabili*, Milan: Rizzoli, 2007.

15. http://www.gazzettadiparma.it/news/politica/383287/m5s-addio-nasce-effetto-parma-la-lettera-integrale.html (accessed 7 February 2017).

16. http://www.beppegrillo.it/listeciviche/liste/roma/codice_comportamento_M5SRoma.pdf (accessed 28 October 2017).

17. 'Da Roma ladrona a Padania ladrona', *La Stampa*, 4 April 2012, cited in G. Crainz, *Storia della repubblica*, Rome: Donzelli, 2016, p. 348.

18. 'Tesoriere sotto inchiesta, bufera nella Lega Vertice in via Bellerio, dimissioni in 45 minuti', *Il fatto quotidiano*, 3 April 3012.

19. http://www.corriere.it/politica/16_luglio_12/renzo-bossi-laurea-albania-b69af87c-48ea-11e6-ae06-0cc76a275352.shtml?refresh_ce-cp (accessed 28 October 2017).

20. http://www.repubblica.it/politica/2013/07/14/news/vedo_il_ministro_kyenge_e_penso_a_un_orango_e_polemica_per_la_frase_del_leghista_calderoli-62945682/ (accessed 27 October 2017).

21. See Luca Pisapia, 'Balotelli, the Thing', https://www.google.co.uk/?gfe_rd=cr&ei=H7ZHWcnqPNHv8AfhlYHIAg (accessed 20 June 2017).

22. The statement can be found here in various languages: http://w2.vatican.va/content/benedict-xvi/en/speeches/2013/february/documents/hf_ben-xvi_spe_20130211_declaratio.html (accessed 28 October 2017).

23. Juan Carlos Scannone, 'Pope Francis and the Theology of the People', *Theological Studies*, 77:1, 2016, p. 133.

24. See the documentary http://www.cbc.ca/passionateeye/episodes/the-pope-the-mafia (accessed 28 October 2017).

25. https://w2.vatican.va/content/francesco/it/homilies/2014/documents/papa-francesco_20140621_cassano-omelia.html (accessed 28 October 2017).

26. http:// espresso.repubblica.it/ archivio/ 2016/ 03/ 31/ news/ vaticanoinchiesta-attico-bertone-espresso-mostra-le-lettere- che-loinchiodano-1.256129 (accessed 28 October 2017).

27. Gianluigi Nuzzi, *Via Crucis*, Milan: Chiaralettere, 2015, and *Vaticano SPA*, Milan: Chiaralettere, 2015.

28. Two journalists were cleared by the Vatican court in 2016: http://www.corriere.it/cronache/16_luglio_07/vatileaks-assolti-giornalisti-nuzzi-fittipaldi-condannati-chaoqui-balda-211cb048-4457-11e6-a4dc-8aa8f57c2afd.shtml (accessed 7 February 2017).

29. Marco Politi, *Pope Francis Among the Wolves: The Inside Story of a Revolution*, New York: Columbia University Press, 2015, p. 110.

30. http://www.corriere.it/cronache/16_luglio_07/vatileaks-assolti-giornalisti-nuzzi-fittipaldi-condannati-chaoqui-balda-211cb048-4457-11e6-a4dc-8aa8f57c2afd.shtml (accessed 7 February 2017).

31. 'Eluana potrebbe anche svegliarsi, così, da un momento all'altro': http://www.repubblica.it/2008/07/sezioni/cronaca/eluana-eutanasia-2/camera-ok-conflitto/camera-ok-conflitto.html (accessed 7 February 2017). See Beppino Englaro and Elena Nave, *Eluana. La libertà e la vita*, Milan: Rizzoli, 2008.

32. 'una vita che poteva e doveva essere salvata': http://www.repubblica.it/2009/02/dirette/sezioni/cronaca/eluana/9feb/index.html?ref=kwhpt2 (accessed 7 February 2017).

33. Giovanni Maria Bellu, *I fantasmi di Portopalo: Natale 1996: la morte di 300 clandestini e il silenzio dell'Italia*, Milan: Mondadori, 2006; http://ricerca.repubblica.it/repubblica/archivio/repubblica/2003/10/22/chi-ha-paura-della-nave-fantasma-ecco.html (accessed 7 February 2017); http://www.teatrodellacooperativa.it/distribuzione/la-nave-fantasma (accessed 7 February 2017). The original article was published in Giovanni Maria Bellu, 'Nave fantasma, ecco le foto. Così morirono 283 clandestini', *La Repubblica*, 15 June 2001, and 'Abbiamo scoperto il più grande cimitero del Mediterraneo'.

34. Emma Jane Kirby, *The Optician of Lampedusa*, London: Allen Lane, 2016.

35. https://w2.vatican.va/content/francesco/it/homilies/2013/documents/papa-francesco_20130708_omelia-lampedusa.html (accessed 7 February 2017).

36. Frances Stoner Saunders, 'Where on Earth are You?', *London Review of Books*, 38:5, 2016.

37. *Centro per la ricezione e la reclusione dei migranti.*

38. Gianluca Gatta, 'Corpi di frontiera. Etnografia del trattamento dei migranti al loro arrivo a Lampedusa', *AM. Rivista della Società italiana di antropologia medica*, 33–4, 2012, p. 132.

39. Ibid., p. 132.

40. Ibid., p. 133.

41. Nicholas De Genova, 'The Legal Production of Mexican/Migrant "Illegality"', in *Latino Studies*, 2:2, 2004, pp. 160–85.

42. See, for example, the so-called Mafia Capitale scandal: http://www.ilfattoquotidiano.it/2014/12/02/mafia-capitale-buzzi-immigrati-si-fanno-soldi-droga/1245847 (accessed 17 February 2017).

43. Frances Stoner Saunders, 'Where on Earth are You?', *London Review of Books*, 38:5, 2016.
44. 'Lampedusa, il giorno di Berlusconi "L'isola libera in due-tre giorni"', *Corriere della Sera*, 30 March 2011; http://www.corriere.it/politica/11_marzo_30/berlusconi-lampedusa_3b538c30-5ac8-11e0-9f1f-2edbd1a49bbb.shtml#ryy4IZHyYXkp6bWj (accessed 7 February 2017).
45. Perry Anderson, 'The Italian Disaster', *London Review of Books*, 36:10, 22 May 2014.
46. For the Rosattellum see Paolo Natale, http://www.fondazionehume.it/politica/un-paese-elettorale-in-stallo (accessed 2.1.2018).
47. https://www.theguardian.com/commentisfree/2018/feb/11/fascism-is-back-in-italy-and-its-paralysing-politics, Roberto Saviano, 'Fascism is back in Italy and it's paralysing the political system', The Guardian, 11.2.2018.

CONCLUSION

1. Guido Piovene, *Viaggio in Italia*, Milan: Baldini and Castoldi Dalai, 2007, p. 872.
2. Eric Hobsbawm, 'Gramsci and Political Theory', *Marxism Today*, July 1977.
3. Antonio Gramsci, *The Modern Prince and Other Writings*, New York: International Publishers, 1968, p. 166.
4. Cited in Guido Crainz, *Il paese mancato. Dal miracolo economico agli anni Ottanta*, Rome: Donzelli, 2003, p. 437.
5. Antonio Gramsci, *Quaderni del carcere*, volume 1, *Quaderno 3* (Valentino Gerratana, ed.), Turin: Einaudi, p. 311; Quintin Hoare and Geoffrey Nowell-Smith, eds., *Selections from the Prison Notebooks*, New York: International Publishers, 1971, pp. 275–6.
6. Thomas Bates, 'Gramsci and the Theory of Hegemony', in James Martin, ed., *Antonio Gramsci: Critical Assessments of Leading Political Philosophers*. Volume II: *Marxism, Philosophy and Politics*, London and New York: Routledge, p. 258 (*Journal of the History of Ideas*, vol. 2, 1975, pp. 351–66).

Index

A Note on the Author

John Foot is Professor of Modern Italian History in the Department of Italian at the University of Bristol. His publications include *Milan Since the Miracle, Calcio, Italy's Divided Memory, Pedalare! Pedalare!, Modern Italy* and *The Man Who Closed the Asylums*. He spent twenty years in Milan in the 1980s and 1990s and now lives in Bristol.

A Note on the Type

The text of this book is set in Linotype Stempel Garamond, a version of Garamond adapted and first used by the Stempel foundry in 1924. It is one of several versions of Garamond based on the designs of Claude Garamond. It is thought that Garamond based his font on Bembo, cut in 1495 by Francesco Griffo in collaboration with the Italian printer Aldus Manutius. Garamond types were first used in books printed in Paris around 1532. Many of the present-day versions of this type are based on the Typi Academiae of Jean Jannon cut in Sedan in 1615.

Claude Garamond was born in Paris in 1480. He learned how to cut type from his father and by the age of fifteen he was able to fashion steel punches the size of a pica with great precision. At the age of sixty he was commissioned by King Francis I to design a Greek alphabet, and for this he was given the honourable title of royal type founder. He died in 1561.